D0449068

# THE FRAGMENTED NOVEL IN MEXICO

CAROL CLARK D'LUGO

THE UNIVERSITY OF TEXAS PRESS, AUSTIN

# THE

# FRAGMENTED

# NOVEL

# IN MEXICO

## THE POLITICS OF FORM

# THE TEXAS PAN AMERICAN SERIES

Copyright © 1997 by the University of Texas Press
All rights reserved
Printed in the United States of America
First edition, 1997

Requests for permission to reproduce material from this work should be sent to
Permissions, University of Texas Press, P.O. Box 7819, Austin, TX 78713-7819.

♾ The paper used in this publication meets the minimum requirements of American
National Standard for Information Sciences—Permanence of Paper for Printed Library
Materials, ANSI Z39.48-1984.

**Library of Congress Cataloging-in-Publication Data**
D'Lugo, Carol Clark, 1943–
    The fragmented novel in Mexico : the politics of form / by Carol Clark D'Lugo.
— 1st ed.
        p.      cm.
    Includes bibliographical references and index.
    ISBN 0-292-71587-0 (alk. paper). — ISBN 0-292-71588-9 (pbk.: alk. paper)
      1. Mexican fiction—20th century—History and criticism.   2. Narration (Rhetoric)
3. Politics and literature—Mexico.   4. Literature and society—Mexico.   I. Title.
PQ7203.D5     1997
863—dc20                                                              96-38728

For Popi, Michael, and Eve;
and in memory of Edith Stollery Clark

# CONTENTS

ix    Acknowledgments

xi    Introduction

1    Chapter 1: Fragmentation

19    Chapter 2: The Initiators

49    Chapter 3: Nationalist Literature

69    Chapter 4: Addressing the Reading and Writing Process

91    Chapter 5: Carlos Fuentes: Mexicanness and the Failed Revolution

123    Chapter 6: *Escritura*

163    Chapter 7: *La Onda*

187    Chapter 8: Writing from the Margins

227    Conclusion

233    Notes

253    Bibliography

269    Index

# ACKNOWLEDGMENTS

I would first like to thank the directors and staff of two libraries whose policies and collections made this effort possible. At Clark University's Goddard Library, under the able watch of University Librarian Susan Baughman, the Inter-Library Loan and Research Desk mainstays Mary Hartman, Ed McDermott, and Irene Walch offered constant support and remarkable patience, particularly when I would approach with yet another handful of pink and yellow slips. Sue Baughman's vision of what a library should be encourages all faculty to take full advantage of current technology. I thank also Laura Gutiérrez Witt, director of the Nettie Lee Benson Latin American Collection at the University of Texas at Austin, for her open-stacks policy and for the generous photocopying grant I was awarded. The library's massive collection and helpful staff made repeat visits inevitable.

Without the unwavering support and generous spirit of Theresa May, executive editor and assistant director of the University of Texas Press, this book could not have been completed. Theresa has the special skill of being able to offer encouragement without applying pressure, knowing precisely when to offer a kind word.

I will always be in the debt of José Amor y Vázquez, professor emeritus of Brown University, who directed my doctoral dissertation. Pepe initiated my fascination with fragmentation by randomly assigning Juan José Arreola's *La feria* (The Fair) as my first oral report in his graduate seminar on the Mexican novel. Thanks too to Geoffrey Ribbans and Inge Crossman for their useful suggestions as readers for the dissertation. A more recent mentor is John Brushwood, whom I met at a conference on Mexican literature. I enjoyed our conversations in Mexico City when we coincided in our book acquisitions. Both John and Carolyn Brushwood provided lively conversation and warm hospitality.

I am most fortunate to have received constant support from colleagues and friends. In particular, I must mention John Conron, who read early versions of dissertation chapters and helped me focus my thoughts as the vastness of the final project became clear. It would be impossible to mention everyone, but I would like to name María Acosta Cruz, Dorothy Escribano, Bill Ferguson, Nancy Ferguson, Ken Hughes, Marsha Kinder, Rose Masiello, Cathie Spingler, Michael Spingler, and Virginia Vaughan. Our department staff, Joanne Berg and Florence Resnick, have been more than generous with their emotional and technical support. I appreciate also conversations with the many fine students it has been my privilege to teach at Clark.

I have received grants from the Faculty Development Board and from the Higgins School for the Humanities at Clark University that have allowed me to continue my research in Mexico and to travel to the Benson Library. I would also like to acknowledge my gratitude to Alice Higgins and to the late Nettie Lee Benson for their support of the Humanities.

Finally, I wish to thank my friend, colleague, and husband, Marvin D'Lugo, for his unwavering support and understanding and for having established a model of excellence that I have attempted to emulate.

# INTRODUCTION

In his 1915 novel, *Los de abajo* (The Underdogs), long recognized as one of the most important works of the Mexican Revolution, Mariano Azuela employs a fragmented structure that complements his depiction of disorganized troops lacking a common cause or ideology. Toward the end of the century, in Rosamaría Roffiel's *Amora* (1989; Love), a lesbian novel that celebrates a woman's freedom to be whoever and whatever she wants, segmented pieces of prose serve to invoke the protagonist's doubly marginalized status as a lesbian and as a woman. That two such dissimilar works are linked through striking technical articulation is not so surprising, because one of the constants within narrative discourse in the Mexican novel of the twentieth century is fragmentation. At every seminal point of development, there are outstanding fragmented texts that epitomize the fundamental essence of each movement.

Mexican narrative is not the only national literature to exhibit fragmentation. No writer composes from within a vacuum, and at a minimum, many of the novelists discussed here have been influenced by authors from Western Europe and the United States, such as James Joyce, William Faulkner, and John Dos Passos. What is significant in Mexican letters is the writers' insistence on fragmentation as a literary technique throughout the century, both as a technical strategy within the aesthetic sphere and as a mode that, contextually or metaphorically, evokes the social and political realities of the country.

The most basic definition of a fragmented novel is a work that is broken into sections, with spaces or gaps that separate the pieces of prose. These spaces can be blank or filled with a variety of designs: asterisks, geometric figures, numbers, or, on occasion, vignettes. Other examples of textual fragmentation are experiments with spacing between words, the repeated use of sentence fragments, and the graphic depiction of disordered thoughts. One cannot reasonably ask *why* authors choose to fragment their novels. A more appropriate question is what is the *effect* of a novel's discourse as written that way, what are the implications for the reading process of textual segmentation?

All fiction is a construct, and, in marked contrast to more traditional fiction that maintains the narrative illusion in part through an apparently seamless narrative, these authors have elected to lay bare the building blocks of their "construction." In so doing, they invite readers to contemplate not only the artifice of fiction, but also the reading and writing process. The first consideration of fragmentation, then, is as a narrative strategy, one that will be shown to be effective in promoting a more active role for readers. A second focus results from the transition from the aesthetic to the social, from the textual to the contextual. It is difficult, if not impossible, for readers to respond meaningfully to Mexican fiction without contemplating the sociopolitical subtext, as illustrated by the epigraphs by Carlos Fuentes and Federico Patán that appear later in this book.

In the 1970s, much suggestive conjecture emerged within the rubric of reader-response criticism. Stanley Fish prompted abundant dialogue on the subject with his notion of "affective stylistics" (383–427), which focuses on the effect(s) of the text on readers through time. Norman Holland, generally considered to be the major proponent of the psychoanalytical approach during this period, dealt with subconscious responses to the written word. The phenomenological strategy, which places equal emphasis on the text and the reader in the production of meaning, was best described by Wolfgang Iser. Finally, Jonathan Culler explored the same problematic relationship among text-author-readers through a structuralist prism. These are but four of the most representative scholars and approaches of the time.[1]

No matter what the approach, there is an inherent subjectivity within reader-response criticism. Surely one's ideas about how readers respond to a text are rooted in one's experience in reading. In that sense, every critic's notion of the ideal reader is herself or himself. From a more objective viewpoint, the ideal reader is generally considered one whose experience of the novel most closely matches that of the author. In *The Act of Reading*, Iser refutes this possibility: "an ideal reader is a structural impossibility as far as literary communication is concerned. An ideal reader would have to have an identical code to that of the author; authors, however, generally recodify prevailing codes in their texts, and so the ideal reader would also have to share the intentions underlying this process. And if this were possible, communication would then be quite superfluous, for one only communicates that which is *not* already shared by sender and receiver" (28–29; emphasis in original).

It is impossible for readers to respond to a novel exactly as the author intended it. Even more, there could be, indeed have been, a number of distinct, yet equally competent responses to the same text. In the following analyses, it is necessary to keep in mind the distinction between the *product* of a response, that is, whatever meaning might be deduced by readers, and the *process* itself, the act of responding. I propose to demonstrate how discourse, that is, how the novel is written, is instrumental in determining the measure of potential response. As a technical strategy, fragmentation will be shown to evoke frequently a more participatory role for readers, denying a passive reading.

The distinction between active and passive readers or, as Vladimir Nabokov called them, major and minor readers (Bowers 2) refers to the degree of activity on the part of readers, not to the correctness of their response. The same distinction was suggested by Julio Cortázar's *lector cómplice*, the reader who becomes the author's accomplice, and his *lector hembra*, an unfortunate term for the reader who embodies all that is passive and supposedly feminine (453–454). Although I am not referring to specific individual responses, there are a few aspects of the notion of the production of meaning that are relevant to a discussion of active and passive reading responses. With the phenomenologists, I think that meaning is produced when the text and reader meet, that there is a role for each. The text provides the signifiers but does not have tight control over how they will be decoded as signifieds. Culler has provided an excellent description of this sense of limitation: "a series of signifiers whose signified is an empty but circumscribed space that can be filled in various ways" (19). By the same token, readers bring their own limits to the novelistic experience by virtue of their degree of literary competence. The possibilities are endless, and yet the notion of a circumscribed space holds true here as well. Different interpretations can be accepted if they are both plausible and justifiable when explained within the context of the established conventions of a genre (Culler 124).

After an initial chapter exploring basic concepts of fragmentation as modified by the Mexican context, the remaining seven chapters of *The Fragmented Novel in Mexico* will examine defining moments in the development of Mexican fiction and the role that fragmentation plays in each. Chapter 2 features the works of the early innovators, revolutionary in form and theme. I have selected Mariano Azuela's *Los de abajo* (1915) as representative of the novels of the Mexican Revolution. Included here also are novels of the Mexican vanguard, with particular emphasis on Gilberto Owen's *Novela como nube* (1928; Novel Like a Cloud) and Jaime Torres Bodet's *Proserpina rescatada* (1931; Proserpina Rescued). The chapter concludes by returning to Azuela, with his experimental trilogy, highlighted by *La luciérnaga* (1932; The Firefly). Chapter 3 examines Gregorio López y Fuentes's *El indio* (1935; The Indian) and Agustín Yáñez's *Al filo del agua* (1947; The Edge of the Storm), grouped as nationalist literature parallel in interesting ways to the muralist movement in the postrevolutionary period. Theirs is a theorized nationalism, however, for the realities of Mexican class segmentation remain firm after the failed revolution. In Chapter 4 I discuss texts that focus readers' attention on the process of reading and writing as examples of self-referential literature: Juan Rulfo's *Pedro Páramo* (1955) and Josefina Vicens's *El libro vacío* (1958; The Empty Book). Chapter 5 is distinct in that it is focused entirely on one author, Carlos Fuentes. The first two selections are pivotal: *La región más transparente* (1958; Where the Air Is Clear) and *La muerte de Artemio Cruz* (1962; The Death of Artemio Cruz). Both novels are crucial in their smashing of narrative norms and confirming of the locus of Mexico's atomization as the city. My final choice, *Agua quemada* (1981; Burnt Water), represents a return to the thematics established in the earlier two.

The 1960s in Mexico yield an ideological split between the tendency toward a more universalized, text-oriented practice dubbed *escritura* and a more social treatment of rebellious Mexican youth culture called the *Onda*. Chapter 6 details three canonical examples of *escritura*: Juan José Arreola's *La feria* (1963; The Fair), Salvador Elizondo's *Farabeuf* (1965), and José Emilio Pacheco's *Morirás lejos* (1967; You Will Die in a Distant Land). For Chapter 7's discussion of classical *Onda* fiction I have selected Gustavo Sainz's *Gazapo* (1965) and José Agustín's *De perfil* (1966; In Profile). I then append a later work, Héctor Manjarrez's *Lapsus* (1971) as an example of the maturing of *Onda* fiction. Chapter 8 has a split focus. The first half is devoted to gay and lesbian fiction: Luis Zapata's *El vampiro de la Colonia Roma* (1979; The Vampire of Colonia Roma) and *en jirones* (1985; in shreds), followed by Rosamaría Roffiel's *Amora* (1989). Ending the chapter is an examination of recent women's fiction that brings to the foreground the marginalized status of Mexican women and suggests ways of rereading Mexican history as a tool for renegotiating both national and personal identity. Featured here are Mónica de Neymet's *Las horas vivas* (1985; The Vibrant Hours), Carmen Boullosa's *Mejor desaparece* (1987; Better It Vanishes) and *Antes* (1989; Before), and María Luisa Puga's *La forma del silencio* (1987; The Form of Silence).

Although the range within conception and execution is wide, binding the varied treatments of fragmentation are notions of revolutionary activity promoting change, whether social or political, whether based within fiction (subverting traditional norms of narrativity), generational conflict, class conflict, or gender. In all of these novels, form complements content; discourse serves an essential function as reflector of theme and as a means of engaging readers with the text's thematics and with the text itself. Whether used metaphorically or as a vehicle for the manipulation of reader response, fragmentation is commonly paired with the following narrative strategies: disruption of conventional narrative norms; strategic placement of fragments; flaunted pluralisms that prohibit a tightly defined meaning; interpolated stories that emphasize the process of narration; narrators- and/or readers-in-the-text; discursive lures that promote a rereading and a consideration of the work as a unit; and intertextual references that expand the historical, aesthetic, or cultural reach of the novel. Thus as an aesthetic tool, as metaphor for sociopolitical realities, or, as will be shown to be a common occurrence, a combination of both, fragmentation has a profound impact on the reading experience.

The novels selected for analysis in *The Fragmented Novel in Mexico* break with traditional notions of narrativity in some way and invite, even demand, an active engagement from readers. There will be examples of texts that lay bare their pluralisms, inviting readers to ponder multiple responses; privilege portions of narrative by framing them; abruptly sever the narration, making readers aware of the writing process; address readers directly, whether seemingly sharing an intimacy or aggressively confronting them; provide readers-in-the-text who serve as models in dealing with convention-breaking narrative; and dramatize situations in which characters voice their view of the malaise of Mexican society or serve as models for ways of addressing the problems, specifically by questioning the status quo and by rereading the past from a nonphalocentric point of view.

Certain literary terms will be used throughout the analyses, and I want to make their meanings clear from the start. I distinguish *story*, as content, or the "what" of the narrative, from *discourse,* the "way" of the narrative, how the novel is presented or which technical strategies are employed, as used by Seymour Chatman. The term *diegesis* refers to story elements, and *diegetic* describes aspects of narrative rooted in story. *Interdiction* means the threatened or effected truncation of narrative, whether the graphic severing of a sentence or, in an echo of Miguel de Cervantes, a character's statement at a moment of suspense that he or she forgets the rest of the tale and cannot continue. The term thus reverts to the Latin meaning of a prohibition, in this sense, prohibiting narrative continuity.

All translations not otherwise credited are my own.

. . . las formas fragmentadas, elípticas de sombra y piedra de nuestra literatura contemporánea son todo menos gratuitas, derivativas o complejas por amor de la complejidad; son la reflexión fiel, casi diría fatal y absolutamente necesaria de la experiencia cultural . . .

[ . . . the fragmented, elliptical forms of shadow and stone from our contemporary literature are anything but gratuitous, derivative or complex due to an infatuation with complexity: they are the faithful reflection, I would almost say inexorable and absolutely necessary, of cultural experience . . . ]

—Carlos Fuentes, "Discurso inaugural"

Mexican fiction is quite aware of the shaky condition of its society; at the same time, it is quite aware of the need to reflect that shaky condition.

—Federico Patán, "Recent Mexican Fiction"

# THE FRAGMENTED NOVEL IN MEXICO

# CHAPTER 1

# FRAGMENTATION

Throughout the twentieth century, Mexican novelists have employed fragmentation in a blending of the sociopolitical with the aesthetic. The nation's fragmented social and political reality is consistently exposed in novels that dramatize a lack of cohesion, urban atomization, or disparities of class, race, and gender. Whether explicitly or implicitly, these narratives belie the notion of Mexico as a unified nation. Fragmented novels also serve to rupture the seamless narrative associated with the nineteenth-century literary canon. In both literary and cultural contexts, fragmentation stands out as a discursive device integral to the articulation of the process of change, challenging reified systems that have lulled people into passive roles. It is an agent of activism that positions readers to reflect critically on the status of the nation and to adopt a more participatory role within fiction.

The century begins with a fraudulent unity constructed by the dictator Porfirio Díaz. Although to outsiders the Díaz regime may have given the impression of Mexico as a controlled society undergoing massive productive growth in the form of industrialization and economic development, there remained a fixed class system that deeply divided the rich and the poor. Díaz's artificially forged cultural homogeneity masked a splintering of society rooted in economic disparity epitomized by *caciquismo:* "el nacionalismo porfirista fue marcadamente elitista y dejó afuera a la mayoría de la población" [the Porfirian idea of nationalism was markedly elitist and left out the majority of the population] (Granados Roldán 17). The Mexican oligarchy chose to ignore poverty: "que scan todo lo invisibles que se pueda los Intrusos (los pobres, los miserables), cuya sola presencia afea y calumnia a la única zona del país capaz de librarse del primitivismo" [let the Intruders (the poor, the wretched) be as invisible as possible, for their mere presence defaces and slanders the only area of the country capable of liberating itself from primitivism] (Monsiváis, "México: Ciudad del apocalipsis," 33). Although the Mexican Revolution effectively exploded Díaz's myth of a unified nation, because of a lack of cohesion among its participants, it fractured the populace even more.

According to Carlos Monsiváis, it was literature that served as an antidote to the Díaz regime's chosen blindness by describing the reality of the country, in particular the conditions in the capital city, in which, in addition to the mansions inhabited by the rich, there were whorehouses and massive sections of misery (Monsiváis, "México: Ciudad del apocalipsis," 33). As an example of this demythifying fiction, Monsiváis offers Federico Gamboa's *Santa* (1903), which focuses on the life of a prostitute. Subsequent Mexican literature of the twentieth century continued and expanded upon this challenge to official government attitudes that sought to portray the country as a modern state to the outside world while ignoring social realities at home. Novelists continually pointed to social, political, and economic marginalization, thus negating the idea of a modern Mexico having emerged from the revolution as a unified nation with a united collective history and revealing disturbing echoes within postrevolutionary governments of Porfirian strategies and themes that denied the fragmented status of the people.

Mexico is still a fragmented society, as so graphically demonstrated by the 1994 New Year's rebellion in Chiapas by the Ejército Zapatista de Liberación Nacional (Zapatista National Liberation Army), named for the one revolutionary leader truly committed to land reform, Emiliano Zapata,[1] and the June 28, 1995, massacre of workers near Aguas Blancas in the state of Guerrero, another area known for its poverty and violence. For, as demonstrated by current cultural analysts, the Mexican government persists in offering to the outside a mythified Mexico analogous to the mythic nation it attempts to present to its own citizens. Ironically, the state employs a fragmented vision in order to create a false unity, an action that, in turn, perpetuates the segmentation of society. As summarized by Claudio Lomnitz-Adler, "It [the state] prefers to invent that which it represents out of bits and pieces of images that are well known to all of us. This act of power stands in the way of the benefits of modernity (democracy) while it leaves the people vulnerable to its economic implications" (251).[2] The fact that the revolutionaries chose for their rebellion the first day of the implementation of the Tratado de Libre Comercio (TLC; NAFTA) repeats the polarization rooted in Mexican politicians' longstanding affair with foreign investment at the expense of Mexico's populace.

On an aesthetic plane and, in provocative ways, a parallel one, fragmentation serves as a graphic break with traditional narrative practice. Authors expose gaps on the page in such a way as to make the text announce itself as a nonwhole, thus rupturing the notion of a seamless, linear fiction. Mexican authors experimenting with innovative fiction, from Mariano Azuela's early trilogy (*La Malhora, El desquite,* and *La luciérnaga*) and the members of the Mexican vanguard movement through the more sophisticated writers of the 1960s *escritura* group and others who benefited from their audacious dissolution of fictional limits, joined an international community of experimental writers. These innovative artists challenged the sense of total control, the hegemony of the nineteenth-century author, and the codified traits that came to be considered the Novel, against which all novels were, by many still are, and by some always will be judged. As a consistent technical strategy throughout this period of change, fragmentation constitutes a rupturing that differentiates the new from the old.[3]

Thus fragmentation is an agent for change. In Mexico it fights the system on two fronts: as an antidote to government lies and deceptions and as a technique with which to break from canonical techniques. Binding the varied treatments in the novels selected for analysis in this study are notions of literary creation as a "revolutionary" activity: fostering innovation in narrative expression or challenging the state's hypocritical affirmations of wholeness. Whether the change promoted is artistic, social, or political, whether based within a rebellion against conventional literary practice, class conflict, generational division, sexual preference, or gender, discourse serves an essential function as reflector of theme and as a means of engaging readers in the text's thematics. At issue is the relationship among formal, discursive fragmentation (the literal breaking up of the narrative into pieces), its manipulative effect upon readers, and the array of social, political, and metanarrative references that fragmentation reflects as a symbolic representation. Although the relationship is there, it is not necessarily depicted in a straightforward manner. Readers are positioned into an active role not only to fill in the gaps so graphically exposed on the page, but also to contemplate implications for the narrative process and to carry fragmentation to deeper levels of interpretation.

## Aspects of Fragmentation

> The break, or rupture, demanded by fragmentary writing, implies a separation from traditional thought—the major defect of which was its tendency to be frozen into systems that give us the illusion of understanding and dominating existence. (Beitchman 61).

In order to better appreciate the relation between fragmentation as a sociopolitical phenomenon and segmentation as a literary strategy, it would be helpful to consider some of the implications of the tradition of fragmentation. Although a segmented discourse is frequently employed as a strategy with which to fracture the linearity of nineteenth-century narrative, the fact that a novel is fragmented is not an automatic indicator of an effort to break with conventional narrative practice. During the previous century, in fact, some eminently traditional novels manifested the technique. An especially fine example can be found among the works of the Spaniard Benito Pérez Galdós: *Fortunata y Jacinta* (1887). The novel consists of four parts divided into thirty-one chapters, with these units further segmented into 198 fragments. Yet Galdós's use of fragmentation does not disrupt the continuity of story.[4] In many instances, readers might well wonder why there is a break (a new fragment), as the end of the preceding segment leads immediately into the next within the same context, even within the same conversation.[5] Although it is not possible to reveal the author's intent in his use of fragmentation, a consideration of the text from the readers' point of view is highly suggestive. The segments in *Fortunata y Jacinta* serve to divide into more manageable sections what would otherwise have been unusually long chapters, some of them fifty pages or more. Galdós's use of fragmentation would seem to be a Cervantine strategy that aims at inducing readers to continue reading, and to do so under pleasurable conditions. Readers are simply more likely to continue reading when confronted by units easily completed rather than by what would appear to be a weighty chapter. Other techniques employed by Galdós support this notion as they, too, seem to urge readers on: ending a chapter at a climactic point; dropping a hint at the end of a chapter of something both imminent and provocative. The narrative urges readers on for their enjoyment of story.

Galdós's use of fragments does not change the novel's status as a linear text devoted to character development and descriptive passages in the service of story, faithful in following the lives of characters through changing circumstances to a denouement—in short, chiefly conventional in conception and execution.[6] Galdós's fragments also differ from those found in later convention-breaking texts in that they are fairly uniform in length. None stands out in any way or calls attention to itself as different. There is no reason for readers to focus on them as fragments, to be alert to segmentation as a discursive strategy.

Fragmentation that breaks with conventional practice can also be incorporated within standardized chapter divisions, although they frequently stand alone. One means of distinguishing a fragment from a chapter, although not sufficient as a solitary criterion, is length: fragments are generally much shorter than conventional chapters. Of more significance is the fact that novels that are divided into chapters tend to exhibit more or less equal portions. Although the length of chapters varies among novels, the proportionate length within one text is fairly uniform. Generally no one section stands out enough to divert readers' attention from story to discourse, for the means of construction must remain concealed in order to maintain the narrative illusion. Fragmentation employed as a reader-engaging strategy is more variable and does stand out, encouraging readers to focus on discourse. Within the novels in this study, fragments range in length from a couple of words to more than eighteen pages.

Length is not the only visual means of drawing readers' attention. In some cases, one is brought to focus on the unusual spacing on the page: fragments are generally clearly separated by a blank space or gap, which dramatizes the break with seamless narratives. Other methods of separation include numbers, symbols such as an asterisk at times presented in a geometric pattern, or, less frequently, a vignette. Spacing is also brought to the foreground when an author incorporates borrowings from other media into the narrative. Common examples of this strategy are representations from the graphic arts and newspapers. To this set of visual strategies can be added a variety of ways of calling readers' attention to the printed word. In Guillermo Cabrera Infante's *Tres tristes tigres* (1965; Three Trapped Tigers), for example, readers encounter the word "elevador" printed and spelled in such a way as to evoke an elevator's effect on one's equilibrium (143); an interpolated story about a shrinking man that is reflected in the printing of the words (209; the words take the form of an upside-down pyramid with the letter "o" as the apex); a fragment entitled "Algunas revelaciones" (259–263; Some Revelations), consisting of four blank pages; lists of names that exhibit the author's joy of puns and intercultural references

(267–269); a page with the term "blen" occupying the entire block of space normally devoted to novelistic prose (332); and a fragment consisting entirely of free verse (376–378). These strategies prompt readers to look attentively at the words themselves (or lack of them), to see words as entities rather than vehicles.

Thus it is possible to distinguish a number of characteristics common to convention-breaking fragmented novels in terms of form. Even more important, however, is the relationship of that segmented self-proclaiming form to content. On an aesthetic plane, the link between spatially separated form and content is one of self-referentiality: discourse is a dramatization of content. Fragmentation used as a rebellious strategy turned against nineteenth-century practice self-consciously calls attention to its status as a nonunit, a nonwhole. Thus its segmented condition reflects the incompleteness of story or the episodic narration common in these novels. The gaps in the text between fragments blatantly expose the ellipses in story and, even within the suggestion of a story, the breaking of linearity.

Most authors of fragmented texts do follow a basic notion of linearity in that the sections are generally read in the normal ordering sequence of first, second, and so on in a syntagmatic arrangement until the end of the novel. Certain writers, however, have further experimented with the ordering of the fragments, offering a choice of reading patterns or refusing any guidance whatsoever. Julio Cortázar's *Rayuela* (1963; Hopscotch) exemplifies the choice of readings: one is presented with a linear progression of "boxes" or the interpolation of expendable fragments (more boxes) that have been appended and are supposed to be inserted following a given numbered scheme.[7] A total absence of guidance is found in Marc Saporta's *Composition No. 1* (1962), composed of 150 unbound and unnumbered pages that readers are invited to shuffle as with a deck of cards. The resultant sequence determines the fate of the protagonist, known only as X.[8] Interestingly, readers are positioned to focus on their notions of linearity as they try to make sense out of the pages, using sequencing as an ordering device. Sharon Spencer reports: "The majority [of the pages] by far portray the completed 'actions' (thoughts, longings, fantasies, or conversations), but a few pages can be extracted according to their contents and rearranged into sequences representing phases of a single action conveyed on four, five, or six pages" (209).

Even when fragments are read in sequential order, traditional notions of linearity may be subverted. Although there are examples of fragments that merely reflect a minimal passage of time, the most commonly used strategy that effects a break in linearity is that of time jumps or lapses, ranging from hours or days to centuries, backward or forward. In many fragmented texts there appears to be a haphazard jumping among past, present, and future. In some, a stable present cannot be determined. Complementing temporal jumps, one finds spatial discontinuities, changes of scene with no apparent relationship recuperable through a story line. In addition, linearity is subverted through the frequent practice of using multiple points of view: a variety of characters speak out, not always on a common subject. It is not unusual to have one or more unidentified narrative voices among the speakers. Contiguity also allows experimentation with radical juxtapositions, for example, a strong contrast in tone or content.[9]

The result of these strategies is a lack of orientation for readers. Because the text refuses to define the relationship among its parts, readers must take it upon themselves to fill in the lacunae, to formulate the nexus among the segments, whether it be temporal, spatial, or thematic. Discourse produces disorientation; disorientation leads to action and awareness.

The end of the first fragment is a marker of readers' engagement. Although probably unaware of it, they approach the novel with notions of the conventions of story and continuity and therefore are likely frustrated when what was assumed to be the beginning of story is abruptly cut off. This is just one example of how consciousness of narrative conventions is awakened when they are violated. The lure of story is much more potent because of the threatened or effected denial of narrative continuity. Readers immediately question the text to discern the relationship between the first and second fragments. How is the second segment different? Is it a modified chapter division? Is there some connection through character or theme if either was established in the first unit? Does the second follow the first in a chronological sequence? If not, what is the new time frame, and how does it relate to what was initially presented? Multiple questions flash through readers' minds, for it is almost impossible to pass from the first segment to the second without interrogating the text. These are gaps that cannot be passed over or filled in unconsciously. They cannot be naturalized without some type of consciousness interference that alerts readers to the fact that they have had to respond actively to the text.

In order to illustrate the difference between a discursive gap that demands interrogation and the barely perceptible lacuna of conventional narrative, let us consider a hypothetical plot situation as potentially treated by each. The sample narrative action is very simple: the protagonist, Dr. X, leaves home on his way to the hospital. A traditional treatment might involve a description of his departure, perhaps including his going out the door and getting into his car. Most likely there would then be a small gap, with the description resuming when he reaches the hospital. There is no need to include a detailed account of the streets taken, turns made, or objects and people passed unless for some reason one of these is essential to story or plot development. The narrator omits expendable detail, giving only the information necessary to contribute to the narrative in a plot-pragmatic way,[10] thus tightening the text. Readers simply assume a journey by car to the hospital. There is no reason for readers to notice this gap.

The same situation in a text that exhibits fragmentation as a convention-breaking strategy could begin in a similar way: the initial segment might well detail the protagonist's departure, but would then break off with a blank space. The contiguous fragment would be almost anything *except* his arrival at the hospital. It might describe a circus act; record a conversation between two unidentified people, one of whom might be the protagonist; represent a scene between mother and child (Dr. X?) with an ever so slight suggestion of an Oedipal relationship. It is up to readers to consider a nexus between sections. Occasionally continuity is later recuperated by the text itself, but this is not necessarily so.

The initial questioning will subsequently be amplified with successive segments as readers continually try to relate contiguous parts. Eventually this effort will expand its focus to seek relationships *among* sections, as readers' attention departs from a linear, syntagmatic reading of the text to an overview. In this sense, the discursive arrangement of the fragments forces readers to consider the whole of the physical presence of the novel, which, in turn, can yield one or more visions of a totality. Since the fragmented structure refuses to yield story, meaning, even a simple relationship when read in a linear fashion, the parts should be rearranged in the readers' mind, not in an effort to find the "right" combination, but to experiment with different arrangements, to observe what meanings might arise or what effect is produced when noncontiguous segments are placed side by side or contemplated as a unit. Discourse promotes a consideration of the whole, which then prompts readers to search for unity, the implied unity in the text. It is at this point that readers are most susceptible to the author's textual clues. Codes will vary with each novel, but gradually a more general project of the text emerges as an energy that pushes readers toward the discovery of some type of narrative coherence.

In considering the notion of unification in fragmented novels that break with tradition, one should resist the thought that by rearranging the fragments readers can complete *the* novel that had been carefully concealed by the author. These novels usually manifest such plurality that they are never definitively completed, and this is their strength and vitality. They are forever alive in the minds of their readers, constantly changing, with different nuances from each reader, even from the same reader during a reconsideration. The result is not a whole with defined limits; it is a subjective, malleable whole, always capable of change.

The affinity these novels have with poetry is remarkable, as noted in the following comment by Octavio Paz: "En la dispersión de sus fragmentos . . . el poema ¿no es ese espacio vibrante sobre el cual se proyecta un puñado de signos como un ideograma que fuese un surtidor de significaciones? . . . fragmentos que se reagrupan y buscan constituir una figura, un núcleo de significados" [In the dispersion of its fragments, . . . isn't the poem that vibrant space upon which a fistful of signs is projected like an ideogram that was a fountain of significances? . . . fragments that regroup themselves and seek to constitute a figure, a nucleus of meanings] (*El arco y la lira*, 270). It is readers who maintain this vitality, questioning the text, filling in story in different ways, feeling exhilarated by the experience of working with the novel. And there is more. Readers are led to ponder the reading and writing processes, focus on their traditional assumptions regarding narrativity, be alert to their desire for story, and consider symbolic functions of discourse.

Rather than being a condensation, as a superficial consideration of discourse might assume, fragmentation actually results in an expansion beyond the limits of the text, the actual printed material. Fragments serve as a lure, as readers respond to discourse by actively supplying story elements and searching for a whole. In that process readers are not only rearranging and rethinking the text but also moving beyond the text to contemplate the story-making process itself, their personal relation to discourse as receivers of the fiction, and the implications of fragmentation as potential reflector of national issues. The whole of the tradition-fighting fragmented novel is infinitely greater than the sum of its parts, and the reason for this can be summed up by active reader response.

The analyses of the discursive aspects of Mexican novels that follow respond to the texts as they meet readers, considering what effect the narrative has upon them as written that way. Of utmost importance are the ways in which discourse draws attention to itself, leading to a consideration of how these novels work upon their readers and, in turn, are worked upon by readers. The starting point is fragmentation as a discursive strategy, which then expands to more symbolic or metaphoric functions of a segmented discourse.

One interpretation of the prevalence of fragmentation in twentieth-century fiction is that it serves symbolically as a representation of the world as we experience it. The control and unity associated with the world prior to World War I have crumbled. As Jay Graham argues, if the external world makes no rational sense, one is no longer able to impose order on experience, and art should reflect this status: "Art does and ought to imitate life, to re-present it; and if life is a chaotic fragmentation in which the connections have been severed and the images reduced to meaninglessness, art does and ought to imitate that life" (49). Other critics concur in the relation of fragmentation to the disintegration of abstract values, that "fragmentation reflects both the collapse of socio-religious order in the twentieth century and the psychoanalytic need to segment the psyche into various levels or personalities in order to better understand it" (Martin 121). Although John Akers makes the application more class and culture specific when he associates fragmentation with disillusioning reality, in this case the displacement and estrangement experienced by Chicano migrants (125), the notion of a chaotic external reality remains.

A second essential interpretation of fragmentation is that of a discourse that serves to destabilize the patriarchy, both in literary and more abstract, social terms: "literary fragmentation can be interpreted as a means of destabilizing both the patriarchal narrative that has helped to produce our current social values and the patriarchal ego that has produced the narrative" (Martin 121). Following the assumption that conventional novels are indelibly marked by white males, as are the notions of history and social order, Stephen-Paul Martin indicates the suitability of a segmented discourse for marginalized groups, specifically minorities, and links their use of this technique to the deconstruction of the white cultural system (122). Having noted that disenfranchised individuals are obviously able to express their frustration or rage and to expose racism and violence in the system within the norms of traditional fiction, Martin makes a case for the added benefits of a fragmented discourse. Citing the example of the African American author Clarence Major, Martin writes: "But Major's experimental structure allows him to approach the psyche on a more basic level, asking the reader to share with the narrator the confusions and transformations that occur when the masculine ego tries to free itself from the limitations of its own perspective" (122). Thus discourse is capable of magnifying and enriching the reading experience by creating in readers a replica of what the marginalized characters have experienced.

Other symbolic or metaphoric aspects of fragmentation have both positive and negative connotations, many of which relate in a sense to the dichotomy raised with regard to readership: active versus passive. Negative feelings of fragmentation are associated with yielding to external forces, a passive experience. A segmented discourse can be associated with a sense of personal failure or function as a reflector of mental illness.[11] People are "broken to pieces" in response to external circumstances such as the breaking off of a relationship or the death of someone close. Fragmentation dramatizes atomization, a product of today's impersonal society or overgrown metropoli, again in response to one's environment. It reflects a marginalized existence, in the negative examples imposed from without, as in the case of minorities, gays and lesbians, and women in general. For a number of these subgroups, fragmentation might announce the status of not feeling whole, connote a lack of sense of self or a lack of world vision, or reflect a feeling of not belonging or of being disconnected. As a personal inadequacy, this might take the form of a failure to cohere with other parts of a group or to connect with one's surroundings.

Used positively within the rubric of marginalization, fragmentation connotes a purposeful self-removal from a group. This could take the form of making a statement against a perceived evil, such as disassociating oneself from the Nazi movement, or distancing oneself from an older generation deemed hypocritical. The youth culture of the 1960s were largely self-marginalized. Its members chose to be different from their parents' generation and cultivated their own forms of expression. By choosing fragmentation, they found unity in a new sense of belonging within their peer group. In contrast to the marginalization described above, these are active decisions based on an involvement in or awareness of one's social and political milieu.

Finally, there is a symbolic sense of fragmentation that conflates with an apocalyptic vision. With the world out of control or the nation in apparent chaos, there comes a time when neither resolution nor redemption seems possible. Only total destruction can prepare for a new beginning. There are those who argue that Mexico is experiencing apocalyptic conditions (Monsiváis, "México: Ciudad del apocalipsis") and others who warn of another revolution at the end of the century to parallel the one at the beginning (Stavans), for as the fragmented literature of the twentieth century has demonstrated time and time again, the facade of a unified nation is a sham.

## The Mexican Context

The first truly modern Mexican author in the twentieth century, Mariano Azuela, embodies a break with the past, a challenge to reified systems on both a social and an aesthetic level. As revealed in his essays on literature, Azuela was an avid reader of nineteenth-century works rooted in realism and naturalism, and his early writings have strong traces of Western-European, particularly French, narrative techniques, in a sense reinventing European readership in Mexico in a type of literary colonization. Beginning with *Los de abajo* (1915), however, Azuela breaks with European style, turning instead to Mexican thematics and regional, colloquial language. Luis Leal observes: "Leyendo *Los de abajo* conocemos a México: sus hombres, su paisaje, sus problemas, sus aspiraciones, sus defectos. La novela toda revela el espíritu de inconformidad de su autor y sus deseos de ver un México en el cual reine un estado de mayor equidad y justicia social" [Reading *Los de abajo* we come to know Mexico: its men, its landscape, its problems, its aspirations, its defects. The entire novel reveals the nonconformist spirit of its author and his hopes of seeing a Mexico in which a state of better equity and social justice might reign] (*Mariano Azuela*, 49). Azuela's status as an advocate of reform is revealed also in his trilogy, in which he targets for change narrative form, as did members of the Mexican vanguard, the *estridentistas* and the *Contemporáneos*. In his three novels published between 1923 and 1932, Azuela employs experimental techniques and illogical sequencing of events that call readers' attention to a sense of difference as contrasted with his earlier literary models.

Fragmentation becomes a staple in both the novels of the revolution and vanguard fiction. Just as the revolutionary forces were fragmented, with separate groups in various regions of the country and equally if not more divided motivations for fighting, so the chroniclers of the upheaval offer but a partial view. Testimonial fiction was by force fragmentary, and many authors employed a segmented structure that dramatized their episodic narrations. As just one example, Nellie Campobello's *Cartucho: Relatos de la lucha en el norte de México* (1931; Cartucho: Stories of the Fight in the North of Mexico) in its first edition had three main sections containing thirty-three segments (seven, twenty-one, and five, respectively). Interestingly, the second edition, published in 1940, has additional fragments, for a total of fifty-six (seven, twenty-eight, and twenty-one). In her discussion of novels of the revolution, Margo Glantz comments that "narrative fragmentation reaches its highest point in *Cartucho*" ("The Novel of the Mexican Revolution," 99).

Vanguard experimentation in the 1920s and 1930s proposed an aesthetic revolution. Its rebelliousness is manifested in innovative techniques: breaking the control, the limiting regulations of nineteenth-century practice. The very poetic novels of Arqueles Vela, Gilberto Owen, and Xavier Villarrutia blur the distinctions of genres with their economy of expression and employment of rhetorical figures. The works are original to the point of appearing chaotic. For both *estridentistas* and *Contemporáneos*, fragmentation is a basic tool in demonstrating their rejection of codified norms in literature. At the same time, the authors sought to modernize Mexico by posing a more universalist style that contrasted with the parochialism of the novels of the revolution.

In sharp contrast to the vanguard experiments known for their privileging of style and lack of realism, Nationalist novels of the 1930s and 1940s are very much rooted in Mexican reality. Antonio Magaña-Esquivel groups them within the rubric of retrospective, autocritical novels of the revolution that seek to incorporate the masses within the national consciousness and thus to construct an integrated nation (Magaña-Esquivel xv). These novels that promote a true community, however, reveal an idealization that is not reflective of Mexican society of their time. The revolution did not bring together the fragmented populace.

A number of books written in the 1950s continue this fruitful blending of technical experimentation and national concerns. Juan Rulfo's *Pedro Páramo* and Josefina Vicens's *El libro vacío*, although clearly reflecting elements of the national psyche, explore technical variations with a recognizable accent on readership. Taking their narratives to new levels of interpretation, they engage readers in considerations of the processes of reading and writing. In addition, Carlos Fuentes's first novel, *La región más transparente*, is indicative of the second tier of novels of the revolution, the antihegemonic narrative that calls attention to the failures of the revolution and the continued, even augmented segmentation of society that result in a fragmented nation. Explicit in this first narrative and the later *La muerte de Artemio Cruz* are an exposé of the hypocrisy of Mexican "democracy" and a series of graphic segments and images of fragmentation that dramatize that unequal society.

Finally, there are the works written by and focused on marginalized groups, those who directly express their disconnectedness from the fraudulent whole. From the 1960s to the 1990s, the prime examples are the young writers of the *Onda*, the homosexual community (both gays and lesbians), and women. Of the three, only women's voices were to be heard before this period, among them some splendid writers such as Rosario Castellanos. It is just that too few of them were able to penetrate the male-dominated world of publishing. In the more liberated period opened by *Onda* authors and sociopolitical events of the 1960s, however, women have the opportunity to move to the center. All three groups make ample use of a first-person narration that literally gives voice to the disenfranchised and of a fragmented structure that graphically dramatizes their disconnectedness, whether socially imposed or self-chosen.

Within this brief overview, certain dichotomies emerge as constant tensions throughout the century. They may be summarized as follows: national versus international, national versus individual, and tradition versus modernization. In each grouping, fragmentation is associated with both discourse and diegesis. As a formal literary technique it falls under the international, linking Mexican authors with artists from Europe and the United States such as André Gide, James Joyce, William Faulkner, and John Dos Passos. Despite Azuela's experiments with foreign techniques, the fundamental body of his work is squarely Mexican. The *estridentistas* and *Contemporáneos*, however, followed European artists in breaking with narrative norms and blurring the boundaries of genres, only to be criticized for their neglect of national issues at a time when the country was in need of redefinition. It is Agustín Yáñez who achieves a blending of experimental form and national issues in *Al filo del agua*, but subsequent writers demonstrate that the tension remains. There are those who retain that sense of fusion, such as Juan Rulfo, Carlos Fuentes, and Juan José Arreola, and others, like Salvador Elizondo, who appear to universalize works such as *Farabeuf* to the point of stripping them of all that could be marked Mexican. From the *Onda* and beyond, however, when fragmentation becomes almost a standard in technique, Mexican thematics predominate.

In the second half of the century there is a steady presence, as in the onslaught of an invading disease, of the intruding culture from the north. In *La región más transparente*, Fuentes begins by satirizing international influences from both Europe and the United States with his depictions of phony aristocrats and the idle rich. The abundance of English and French phrases that punctuate the conversations of the upper class are testimony to the invasion. Reflecting a different sense of intrusion, he introduces characters such as Federico Robles and, later, Artemio Cruz, ruthless in their absorption of "gringo" capitalist practices. The 1960s' adolescent culture in Mexico was clearly influenced by the music, language, and dress of the United States.[12] *Onda* literature is replete with words hispanized from the English, such as "grogui" (252; groggy)[13] or "maic jamers" (286; Mike Hammers) and with characters fully familiar with their neighbor's consumer goods: they prefer "párliament" (235; Parliament cigarettes), wear "vaqueros lee" (235; Lee jeans), and make references to "rémington" and "twinky wónder" (206). Fragmentation graphically captures the sense of being caught between cultures, as one of a number of dividing influences, of not experiencing a solid uninational core.

Within the notion that Mexico is a spurious unity, the tension between the national and the individual appears inevitable. As an obvious example, the indigenous population has never been integrated completely into Mexican society, but race is just one measure of separation within the system. In the novels selected for analysis there are depictions of isolation based on class, gender, age, and sexual preference as well. Even in novels that portray a range of social classes, such as *La región más transparente*, the solitude of the individual is dramatized. Although some representations of marginalization are self-imposed (the youths in the 1960s for example), the fact that the distinct majority of disenfranchised groups retain that status is due to forces from without. This is particularly clear in the fictions appearing in recent years by gays, lesbians, and other women writers.

Aspects of fragmentation within the conflict between tradition and modernization break down into two main subgroups: the focus on the city as site of the modern (Mexico City's growth into a megalopolis) and the splitting of the country into two or more Mexicos. From Mariano Azuela to María Luisa Puga, novelists have characterized the turmoil associated with the atomizing urban center. Among the novels selected for analysis, *La luciérnaga, La región más transparente, La muerte de Artemio Cruz, Gazapo, De perfil, El Vampiro de la Colonia Roma, Amora, Las horas vivas,* and *La forma del silencio* treat one or more aspects of poverty, violence, prostitution, illness, corruption, unscrupulousness, and atomization associated with the Federal District. Steven Cassedy has argued that any urban milieu is synonymous with modernity, instability, and fragmentation: "the choice of an urban setting—*any* urban setting—in post-Enlightenment literature is a certain sign of fragmentation or of withdrawn meaning. The city in general, with its spatially concentrated diversity, allows for the relatively close temporal juxtaposition of disparate elements, and thus establishes a base of experience— thoroughly 'modern'—which is naturally unstable" (Cassedy 44).

The immense growth of Mexico City from the 1940s to the present must also be considered as a factor in a fragmented populace. Ledda Arguedas takes this notion even further, seeing the city as an agent of fragmentation and dispersal (57). The population exploded from 1.76 million in 1940 to 18.5 million in 1988 (Monsiváis, "México: Ciudad del apocalipsis," 34), and by 1992 the number had grown to over 21 million.[14] The immediate comparison that comes to mind is that of Los Angeles, which from 1850 to 1930 expanded from a town of 1,610 to a city of 1.2 million and a metropolitan district of 2.3 million (Fogelson 1). Significantly, these cities have certain characteristics in common that contribute to fragmentation: residential dispersal, business decentralization, and reliance on the automobile (Fogelson 185).

Monsiváis concludes that "la ciudad ha crecido hasta perder la conciencia de límites" [the city has grown to the point of losing awareness of limits] ("México: Ciudad del apocalipsis," 31). In a sense, then, the city's exploding populace forms a parallel with fragmentation's role as a literary technique that ruptures the limits of fictional norms. Monsiváis adds the following statistics: 22 percent of the country's population lives in the Federal District (34), and 74.4 percent of the city's population is under thirty years of age (42). Mexico City has become a megalopolis or a chain of cities (Monsiváis, "México: Ciudad del apocalipsis," 42) in which all classes experience a degree of fragmentation. There are examples of isolating living spaces for the full spectrum: many poor live in the *"ciudades perdidas"* (lost cities), the middle class escape to the suburbs such as Satélite where all their needs are met, thus avoiding contact with undesirable elements, and the very rich build houses in Pedregal or Lomas de Chapultepec surrounded by high walls for their protection. As Elena Poniatowska has said, "nos hacemos la vida en cuadritos" [we live our lives in little squares] (*¡Ay vida, no me mereces!*, 171).

The city's enormity and its inhabitants' sense of alienation have produced an identification more with the colonia in which one lives than with the Federal District. Divided in a manner similar to Paris's arrondissements, Mexico City has colonias that have developed personalities and associations known to all. Azuela's early linking of a fiction with a particular colonia, the concentration on Tepito in *La luciérnaga*, will become a standard as the city continues to expand. For example, *Onda* writers feature colonia Narvarte, Armando Ramírez has a series of books grounded in the subculture of Tepito, and Luis Zapata situates a gay protagonist first in Roma and then in Cuauhtémoc, two colonias he presents as being known for their concentration of homosexuals. The size of the city precludes a complete treatment, as argued by Héctor Manjarrez: "ya no es posible hacer una novela sobre la ciudad de México en su totalidad; o sea, ya no se puede hacer otra *Región más transparente*" [it is no longer possible to write a novel about Mexico City in its entirety; that is, one can no longer write another *La región más transparente*] (Teichmann, 209–210).

Monsiváis detects the notion of two Mexicos at the level of the city, stating that for the poor there is one city that all construct personally from their home and work space, and then there is "la otra ciudad, la del anonimato sin excepciones" [the other city, the one of anonymity without exception] ("México: Ciudad del apocalipsis," 37). The notion of a split Mexico, however, is more frequently applied to the nation. The commonplace is that from Mexico City north is what is known as industrialized Mexico, and the rest of the country has been left behind. For Mexico, modernization is synonymous with industrialization, and that means foreign investment. In the twentieth century this particular aspect of the tension between the traditional and the modern has taken the form of a cyclic pattern that highlights the disparities within Mexican culture: the struggle for financial gain, for the attainment of first-world status, and for acceptance as a modern nation at the expense of the marginalized, the oppressed, and the forgotten.

In repeated fashion, successive administrations have attempted to present a united nation to the outside and to deny the fragmented status of its people. The century began under Porfirio Díaz and his illusory modern state. Yet those who moved into positions of power after the revolution, most notably the financiers who took advantage of postrevolutionary opportunities, wound up repeating the patterns of the previous regime. Fuentes captures this cyclical rhythm most effectively in *La región más transparente*. It would seem that the revolution merely created a new oligarchy and enabled the entrenchment of a middle class. The importance of the

1968 Olympics for the Mexican government was that again it would have the opportunity to present itself to the world as a modern state. There were, however, workers and students who challenged the idea of a "unified" nation and struggled for their own recognition and expression. The rapidity with which the government resorted to violence and the intensity of the confrontation with student protesters at the Plaza de Tlatelolco suggest the need to quell disturbances before the influx of foreigners began. In the 1990s the government's push to join the United States and Canada in NAFTA represents yet another echo of the Díaz regime's myopic view of the nation. The Salinas administration was adamant in its desire to be a modern financial partner yet persisted in ignoring its own failure to effect social change in the areas of the country that lack the most basic living essentials. With the cyclical emphasis on foreign investment, trade, and first-world status, it was too easy to forget those without plumbing and electricity.

Finally, there are certain events that punctuate the century in dramatization of a crumbling of whatever unity might have been: the 1913 assassination of Francisco Madero, the first president after the revolution and one of the few who upheld democratic ideals; the student massacre at Tlatelolco in 1968; and the 1985 earthquake that so shattered the Federal District. With these three events, one feels the collapse of the revolution and its idealism, of the falsified unity of the nation, and even of the concrete fabric of the city.

# CHAPTER 2

# THE INITIATORS

Fragmentation joins form and content at the beginning of the century in the novels of the Mexican Revolution. Techniques of segmentation are suggestively reflective of the thematics of the ten-year conflict: disparity among social classes, contrasting ideological positions, and a lack of coordination or cohesiveness among the revolutionaries. A fragmented society is thus dramatized by means of a fragmented text. One cannot, of course, assume authorial intent in this linking of form and content, but the insistent employment of fragmented structures in novels that depict a splintered society does suggest an underlying conceptual nexus.[1]

Some of the writers who recorded episodes of the Mexican Revolution were more chroniclers than novelists, their focus more historical than literary. For these authors, a fragmented structure might have seemed appropriate to their purpose, that of reporting occurrences, rather than a weaving of characters, images, description, and action intrinsic to the narrativization of history. Even Mariano Azuela's *Los de abajo* (1915) first appeared in installments in *El Paso del Norte*, the fragmentation of the events it portrays suggested by the original subtitle, "Cuadros y escenas de la revolución actual" (Portal 74; Pictures and Scenes of the Current Revolution). The early use of fragmentation thus constitutes a discourse analogous to the documentary newsreel, but also with deep roots in Mexico's cultural history as a personalized chronicle in the style of Bernal Díaz de Castillo.

Although Azuela is linked with the discursive origins of the wide use of fragmentation in Mexican chronicles of the revolution, that is, *historical* texts, one must also recognize his *literary* interests as manifested not only in *Los de abajo*, but also in his more technically experimental *La luciérnaga* (1932). Azuela's early employment of fragmentation as metaphor evolves into an innovative artistic articulation of atomized existence in the latter work. Thus, his contributions as a novelist in part demonstrate the richness achieved by an aesthetic rendering of historical material, making way for subsequent fragmented novels rooted in sociopolitical issues, but fashioned as art, such as Gregorio López y Fuentes's *El indio* (1935) and Agustín Yáñez's *Al filo del agua* (1947). In addition, Azuela's more innovative trilogy, *La Malhora, El desquite,* and *La luciérnaga,* positions him as precursor of writers grouped within the rubric of the Mexican vanguard, the *estridentistas* and the *Contemporáneos,* who in the 1920s and 1930s broke with conventional manners of expression in order to experiment with the possibilities of an expanded notion of fiction.

The novels selected for examination in this chapter, Azuela's *Los de abajo* and *La luciérnaga* and the vanguard novels *El Café de Nadie, Novela como nube, Dama de corazones,* and *Proserpina rescatada,* although varied in degree of innovation or technical experimentation, all contain the use of fragmentation as complement to the text's thematics. In some, such as *Los de abajo,* the segmentation is more metaphoric than discursive in use, but in others, for example *Proserpina rescatada* and *La luciérnaga,* fragmentation is clearly a reader-oriented strategy calling for active involvement with the text. All of the works echo their fragmentation thematically as novels of collision. *Los de abajo* epitomizes the novel of the Mexican Revolution, evoking not only the national upheaval itself, but also the splintering among reformers resulting in disillusionment. In *La luciérnaga,* Azuela emphasizes the clash between urban and provincial life while at the same time overtly breaking with conventional narrative techniques. Here the author literalizes the collisions depicted, as the novel begins with a traffic accident. The authors of the vanguard flaunt their clash with conventional norms of narration by offering iconoclastic texts that appear closer to poetry than to fiction. Along with Azuela's trilogy, these experimental novels constitute the first demonstrable collision with nineteenth-century practice in Mexican letters.

## Mariano Azuela, *Los de abajo* (The Underdogs)

Despite the fact that it took some nine years to receive appropriate critical response, Mariano Azuela's *Los de abajo* (1915) has since been acknowledged as *the* novel of the Mexican Revolution. Clearly, Azuela captures in his brief work a combination of the initial idealism associated with the revolt, the gradual disillusionment stemming from its multiple failures, and the brutal realities experienced by those who, like the author, participated in its uncontrollable momentum. Looking beyond the sociopolitical realm, critics have praised *Los de abajo* as "revolutionary" in terms of the development of the genre. Marta Portal cites Azuela's use of popular expressions and the appropriateness of speech to social class (63), and Luis Leal argues that Azuela breaks with European tradition to forge a genuinely American novel "admirablemente adoptada al tema" [admirably adopted to his theme] (*Mariano Azuela*, 48).

Although praising *Los de abajo* in terms of vision, content, and language, critics have been less generous in their appreciation of *how* the novel is assembled. Essentially, their discomfort centers on the apparent lack of an ordering mechanism for the episodes, constituting a structural flaw.[2] Contributing further to the perception of disconnectedness is the text's fragmentation; although consisting of three major parts, the novel in its revised form is broken into a total of forty-two pieces.[3] Despite a sense of choppiness in the linear development of the novel, however, there are indications that Azuela's modified text reflects a consciousness of form as well as of content.

As Seymour Menton describes the tripartite structure of *Los de abajo*, each section corresponds to a distinct period within the development of the revolution (1004–1005). The lengthiest part is the first (twenty-one fragments), in which Azuela inscribes the idealist notion of *anticaciquismo*. Readers are introduced to the protagonist, Demetrio Macías, and his reasons for beginning his association with the revolt, subsequently contrasted with the intellectualized notions of Luis Cervantes and Alberto Solís. Part 2 (fourteen fragments) reflects both the political maneuvering contributing to the fragmentation of the revolutionary forces and the barbarism inherent in revolutionaries' fighting without a clear cause, seeking pleasure in looting as well as killing for sport. The last part is brief (seven fragments) in its depiction of failure, as Demetrio and his remaining men return to the sierra where he had achieved his initial success only to be stricken down now in an inversion of the earlier episode.

Albeit incapsulated, this description of the novel reveals two basic structural components of *Los de abajo*: the geometric reduction inherent in the number of fragments and the circularity evoked from beginning to end. Significantly, each in its own way is evocative of the novel's message regarding the Mexican Revolution and is thus used metaphorically to reiterate Azuela's conception, suggesting a coherence within development and execution. By methodically reducing the number of fragments (twenty-one, fourteen, seven), Azuela evokes the increasing pace of the revolution, with its correlative sense of veering out of control, by using a form that approximates its velocity. One feels the inevitability of the conclusion, as Demetrio is incapable of withstanding the force of continued violence. When asked by his wife why he keeps on fighting, he voices what has become a famous phrase: "Mira esta piedra cómo ya no se para . . ." [Look at that stone; how it keeps on going] (137).[4] If one were to continue the geometric regression, the next figure would be zero, an apt symbol of Demetrio's death.

The novel's circularity, which can be perceived on multiple levels, has been readily noted (Portal 60; Leal, *Mariano Azuela,* 124).[5] In addition to returning to the same mountain region for the final battle, Demetrio and his men trace a circle from the south to the north and back again in the course of their nearly two-year association with the revolution (1913–1915). Furthermore, having left his wife and child in the initial segment of Part 1, Demetrio is reunited with them in the penultimate fragment of the novel. Leal likens the circularity to the repeated image of a *bola* as metaphor for the revolution (*Mariano Azuela,* 124), which supports the notion of Azuela's use of discourse to reinforce the novel's thematics.[6] The resultant image is Sisyphean, expressing the disillusionment and frustration of a failed revolution.

Other than these ordering systems, Azuela does not flaunt the fragmentation discursively; he does not address readers in an overt fashion either through jarring temporal jumps or disorienting contiguity. The occasional interior gaps within fragments in general connote the passage of time, most frequently from one day to the next. The most significant example of the employment of spacing privileges the use of the metaphor *bola:* at the very end of Part 2, immediately after a break on the page, General Natera exhorts: "¡Cierto como hay Dios, compañero; sigue la bola! ¡Ahora Villa contra Carranza!" [As sure as there's a God in heaven . . . this mess hasn't blown over yet. Now it's Villa fighting Carranza!] (122).

Despite the intellectualized voicing of the ideological base of revolutionary activity (Cervantes, Solís, and, later, Valderrama) and the integration of discourse with the novel's thematics, it would seem that Azuela's preponderant emphasis is on story. There is clearly more action than description in the narrative; the short paragraphs, many consisting of one or two sentences, emphasize the rapidity of movement. Azuela allows deeds, more than words, to mark Luis Cervantes's slide from spokesman for the cause to a man consumed by greed.[7]

It would seem that Azuela recognizes the power of story to convey a message, but one must also be aware of the author's focus on *how* to tell that story. A revealing indicator of Azuela's concern is the insistent dramatization of the storytelling act: the inclusion of at least nine examples of or references to the narrative process in the text of *Los de abajo*. In many cases, readers are not privy to the actual story, but almost all of the examples have the potential to prompt some reflection on methods of narration or the value of narrativization. Fortunata's tale of the abduction of her daughter bores her listeners because of her excessive detail (33). Venancio fares somewhat better with his recounting of sections of *El judío errante*, although his interested public is limited to Luis Cervantes (36). Fictionalized accounts of actual exploits receive such a positive reaction that they become the preferred version. When Solís narrativizes Demetrio's achievements, the latter enjoys the story so much that he not only repeats it but begins to believe it (63–64). Similarly, the actual deeds performed by Villa and his men pale against their recounting: "Pero los hechos vistos y vividos no valían nada. Había que oír la narración de sus proezas portentosas" [The bare facts, the mere citing of observation and experience meant nothing. But the real story . . . was quite different] (68). The contagion of narrations is apparent when Margarito's brief summarization of a killing instigates a series of imitations, each beginning with the words "yo maté" [I killed] (77–78).[8]

One of the most significant interior narrations is Demetrio's story of what led him to his present circumstances. Readers are prepared for a tale at the end of the preceding segment (Part 2, fragment 12), as Demetrio sets the scene by asking for a couple of beers and having Cervantes sit near him: "Siéntese, curro, siéntese, para contarle" [Sit down here, . . . I'll tell you] (41). His story, however, turns out to be awkwardly told, its brevity (two paragraphs) counteracted by a series of run-on sentences frequently joined by the conjunction "and" (41–42). It is further flawed by historical inaccuracy, as Demetrio reveals his inattention to detail or ignorance of fact: "Usté ha de saber del chisme ese de México, donde mataron al señor Madero y a otro, a un tal Félix o Felipe Díaz, ¡qué sé yo!" [You must have heard something about that story in Mexico City—about the killing of Madero and some other fellow, Félix or Felipe Díaz, or something—I don't know] (43).[9]

Although reduced in scale, Demetrio's narration can be viewed as an interpolated contrastive discourse in opposition to what Azuela appears to seek in the full text. Macías's formless fluidity and uncertainty regarding factual information stand in contrast to *Los de abajo*'s focus on action, forward momentum, and careful precision regarding historical material. Furthermore, the combination of a fragmented structure and the emphasis on a limited perspective of events as dramatized by an individual's personalized account of historical occurrences constitutes what may be seen as a critique of the chronicle style of telling. A number of the novels of the revolution are both fragmented and sharply limited in perspective. Of course, no single work is capable of capturing the enormity of the event nor its complexity as evidenced by the multiple factions and ideologies. By placing such emphasis on the act of telling in *Los de abajo*, however, Azuela produces a self-referential text that acknowledges its limitations while at the same time faulting those who are ignorant of or oblivious to their incomplete vision of the whole.

Implicit in the bringing to the foreground of the storytelling process is an awareness of audience reception. As staged in *Los de abajo*, those who listen to the fragments of oral history are enthralled by what they hear. The discrete portions of revolutionary activity narrated within the text are received as tales of adventure, provoking great enthusiasm as forms of entertainment. The chroniclers' limited vision, however, is carried over to the listeners' response, for the public dramatized in Azuela's novel displays, in turn, a fragmented consciousness of the revolution, its causes, and its ramifications. This is, finally, the source of their inevitable failure: they are unable to grasp the whole. Although engaged with history in the form of fragmentary events, these characters lack the imagination to move beyond the unit to relate the parts in a consideration of larger issues.

This is exactly what Azuela's readers must do. It is perhaps toward this end that Azuela includes representatives of a higher level of consciousness in Cervantes and Solís, who point the way toward a more complete understanding. The readers of *Los de abajo* have a privileged position, that of being able to see beyond the single occurrence and to assemble the various segments of narrative, carrying the process one step further in an overall view of the author's projected meaning. For Azuela's storytelling would appear to have a clearly defined objective: to convey to readers his disillusionment with the revolution (Leal, *Mariano Azuela*, 20). As such, he attains a coherence between story and discourse from within a finite perspective; both style and content are subordinated to an overall message. It is not surprising, then, that there is not much experimentation in narrative form in *Los de abajo*.

Much more technically innovative is a trilogy of novels composed in the 1920s: *La Malhora* (1923), *El desquite* (1925), and *La luciérnaga* (1932, but composed around 1926).[10] Evidently, Azuela's decision to modify his style involved a combination of pragmatism and cynicism. He lamented the lack of response to his earlier works (Ramos 8–10)[11] and turned to current developments in narrative in an effort to attract critical attention: "cansado de ser autor sólo conocido en mi casa, tomé la resolución valiente de dar una campanada, escribiendo con técnica moderna y de la última hora. Estudié con detenimiento esa técnica que consiste nada menos que en el truco ahora bien conocido de retorcer palabras y frases, oscurecer conceptos y expresiones, para obtener el efecto de la novedad" [Tired of being an author known only in my own home, I resolved valiently to join the cutting edge, writing with the latest literary techniques. I studied carefully that technique that consists basically of the now well-known trick of twisting words and phrases, obscuring concepts and expressions, in order to obtain the effect of being new] (Azuela, "El novelista y su ambiente," 1113).

Azuela writes his experimental trilogy in part right before and in part overlapping the early years of the Mexican vanguard. Even though not all of the vanguard novels have spatial breaks, their thematics and imagery are rooted in fragmentation and they are important in the development of the Mexican novel, particularly for their rebellion against traditional norms. Therefore, I will pause to give grounding information on this movement generally assigned to the 1920s and 1930s and consisting of two main groups, the *estridentistas* and the *Contemporáneos*.[12] The former were more inclined toward including within their technical experimentation social issues integral to Mexican experience, clearly aligned with Azuela's leanings in *La luciérnaga*. This might seem paradoxical to some, as the *estridentistas* were, at the same time, considered to be more radical in their technical innovations. This is an early example, however, that interest in literary innovation need not be incompatible with nationalistic concerns. Nevertheless, the vanguard novels stand apart from Azuela's work in that they are clearly less involved with national issues, so much so that at the time much criticism was leveled against these innovators as being elitist, hermetic, even retrograde in the apparent return of some to art for art's sake.[13] Particular targets were the *Contemporáneos*, more universal in outlook, focusing on the process of literary creation in their effort to open Mexican letters to a new universalism through exposure to the innovative techniques then currently in practice in Western Europe, particularly France, and the United States (M. H. Forster, *Los contemporáneos 1920–1932*, 22).

Critics argued that writers should instead focus their attention on a redefinition of the nation as it emerged from its civil conflict. As the name implies, writers associated with the vanguard movement, no matter what their particular affiliation, sought to break with the conventions of traditional narrative expression in both content and form. Although the authors were known more for their poetry, many of Mexico's vanguardists did turn to novels: the *estridentista* Arqueles Vela (*El Café de Nadie*, 1926); and the *Contemporáneos* Gilberto Owen (*La llama fría*, 1925; *Novela como nube*, 1928), Xavier Villaurrutia (*Dama de corazones*, 1928), and Jaime Torres Bodet (*Margarita de niebla*, 1927; *La educación sentimental*, 1929; *Proserpina rescatada*, 1931; and *Estrella de día*, 1933, among others).[14]

In *Idle Fictions*, Gustavo Pérez Firmat presents a well-documented discussion of vanguard novels of Spain and of Mexico's *Contemporáneos* with regard to their general characteristics, their reception at the time of publication, their relationship with traditional novelistic forms, and the implications for the reading experience. As he reasons, in very basic terms, "the new novel emerges precisely from a systematic opposition to the conventions of the old" (30). Because of their "newness," their flaunting of difference, vanguard novels quickly came to be called by a series of alternative terms or modifications on the word "novel," for they were deemed too radical to fit within the codified definition. The texts were referred to as "new novels," "poematic novels" "narrations," "minority novels," "essayistic novels," and "pre-novels" (Pérez Firmat 19–25, 57). Although the aspects singled out by critics, whether for praise or for censure, varied, and not every work contained all of the traits, one can assemble a listing of the predominant characteristics: poetic prose with a particular tendency toward abundant metaphors, an obtrusive author-narrator, the privileging of style over plot and character, lack of realism, absence of lifelike characters, first-person narration, and brevity.[15] Designated artistic influences were mainly from the French: Marcel Proust and Jean Giraudoux (21). Significantly, Vicky Unruh emphasizes how these novels display their own artifice (83) and notes their impact on readers, which is supported by the manifestos that accompanied the majority of the Latin American vanguard movements in an attempt to construct new, active readers (Unruh 41).

Specifically describing the Latin American vanguardist movement, Merlin H. Forster and K. David Jackson also comment on the basic notion of the novels' having broken with tradition in that they "maintained an iconoclastic stance against logic and reason, expressing a pervasive sense of alienation from accepted social and literary values" (5). It is within this aspect that one finds reference to fragmentation, as Forster and Jackson argue that, in vanguard fiction, "the accepted link within observable reality and artistic creation is severed completely in the twentieth century, with all freedom given to the creator. Individual works can be geometric or abstract . . . violently destructive, or fragmented in keeping with a disordered subconscious flow" (5). Fragmentation as a more faithful reflector of one's naturally occurring illogical thoughts is an important aspect of vanguard fiction, but even more fundamental is the text's laying bare its break with traditional notions of linearity and controlled unity.

Focusing completely on Mexican prose fiction of the period, Edna Aguirre Rehbein characterizes vanguardist novels as demonstrating experimentation in three primary areas: "the introduction in narrative prose of poetic and metaphorical language; the fragmentation of time, space, phrase and page; and the role of the author, narrator, and character" (320). Common to many of the Mexican novels are an elusiveness of character,[16] a barely perceptible plot, self-referential commentary, a fluid prose containing ample poetic tropes, references to Western European artists, both literary and visual, and a brevity more akin to poetry that to the massive tomes one associates with the nineteenth-century realist tradition. Significantly, there were those, including the Spanish writer Azorín, who referred to the vanguard novels as "fragments" in acknowledgement of this briefness (Pérez Firmat 10, 35), and others who rebuked the volumes for their fragmentariness (Pérez Firmat 36). The employment of fragmentation within discourse, it should be stated, is only at times graphically displayed, most consistently in the novels of Jaime Torres Bodet, in which, in the original editions, segments are separated by a space containing an asterisk.[17] In other works, the fragmentation is temporal, spatial, or reflective of thought processes, without a visual cue. In this more abstract consideration, Unruh joins the aesthetic and ontological by noting the frequent inscription of the artist within vanguard novels. She argues that these authors, responding to the collision of their artistic legacy with the chaotic world surrounding them "seek to piece together their own elusive and fragmented identities" (123).

It is important to note that properties of fragmentation found in these early novels—as dramatization of disordered thought, as vehicle for temporal and spatial jumps, and as graphic display that calls readers' attention to the printed page and thus to discourse and lack of conventional linearity—will carry into the next decades as writers continue to experiment and to challenge codified concepts of narrative tradition. The vanguard novelists truly lead the way for more sophisticated treatments that follow from authors such as Juan Rulfo, Salvador Elizondo, and José Emilio Pacheco, to name but a few.

### Arqueles Vela, *El Café de Nadie* (No One's Cafe)

Recognized as the only *estridentista* to dedicate himself to prose, Arqueles Vela is best known for his three short novels grouped under the title *El Café de Nadie: Novelas* (1926): *El Café de Nadie, Un crimen provisional,* and *La señorita Etcétera.*[18] All three are extremely brief and broken into segments that average two pages in length.[19] As summarized by Luis Mario Schneider, Vela's style, the epitome of *estridentista* prose, reflects an intellectualization of the emotions and the free association of lyrical images (*El estridentismo,* 29). To this one should add a proclivity for paragraphs composed of but one or two sentences, as if they were, in fact, lines from a poem, and a clear departure from traditional notions of character development and plot. The deviation from the norm was considered so notable that, when *La señorita Etcétera* first appeared in 1922, the editor included a comment about the author's iconoclastic style: "despojado de todos los lugares comunes literarios" [despoiled of all literary commonplaces] (Schneider, *El estridentismo,* 85).

The café of the title is a reference to the Café Europa in Mexico City, later called El Café de Nadie by the artists associated with the *estridentista* movement and site of the first exposition of their work (Schneider, *El estridentismo,* 18). Its protagonist would seem to be a prostitute named Mabelina, although she is not introduced until the third segment out of a total of ten. Instead, references to the café open and close the novel, giving prominence to ambience over character. Two regular patrons of the café also appear at the beginning and the end, but they hardly constitute a force in the novel, as they are obstinate in their anonymity, serving more as background than as participants. The majority of the fragments focus on Mabelina, her visits to the café with various escorts, dialogues with two of the men, and a poignant final section that provides insight into her inner being. These brief glimpses are more like vignettes than portions of a developed story line, for there is no sustained plot and little to promote interchange among segments. The third-person narration offers scant information about

Mabelina's personal situation, which finds a parallel in the lack of orienting details regarding the location of the café. No street or even city is named, and when Mabelina gives instructions to a taxi driver, they consist only of directionals; no street names are provided (224).

Part of the café's attraction is that it affords privacy: "Es encantador. Nunca hay nadie. Nadie lo espía a uno, ni lo molesta" [It's enchanting. There is never anyone there. No one spies on you or bothers you] (224). This sense of anonymity, however, can be carried to extremes, as seen in the central character. Despite the rather trivial problems initially presented, such as her not being able to sit in the booth she prefers in the café, readers discover that Mabelina suffers a true identity crisis. Having been with so many men has left her bereft of a core, as she feels herself to be a different woman with each companion: "Después de ser todas las mujeres ya no era nadie" [After being all women now she was no one] (231). Mabelina is a marginalized being who cannot seem to connect meaningfully with those around her. In this sense, the fragmented structure, which allows a glimpse but not a true understanding of her character, seems most appropriate. The angst introduced is internal and does not relate to the urban surroundings unless that bridge is made by readers. Mabelina may depart the café at the end of the novel as the dawn breaks over the city, but one senses that there is little hope for her, that her fragmented existence will endure.

## Gilberto Owen, *Novela como nube* (Novel Like a Cloud)

Gilberto Owen's *Novela como nube* (1928) is aptly named, for both form and content are elusive when approached from within a traditional framework. As Florence Olivier argues, the title "anuncia el desvanecimiento de la novela" [announces the fading of the novel] (294). Owen suggests rather than details a series of relationships experienced or pursued by the protagonist, Ernesto (no last name is provided), with a number of women who appear at times to be interchangeable from his point of view. Having been told that Ernesto has suffered a number of misogynist crises (16, 27), however, readers should be somewhat prepared for his confusion among Eva, Ofelia, and Elena, one or more of whom are reduced generically to Eva the Second or the Third, indicating not necessarily a dynasty or succession, but more likely an insignificance in status or a lack of individualizing traits.

*Novela como nube* is divided into two parts, each containing thirteen numbered and titled segments, ranging from two to six very small pages in the first edition. Merlin H. Forster refers to the segments as "chapters" only within quotation marks and adds a more provocative reference to "átomos narrativos" [narrative atoms] (*Los contemporáneos*, 114). The two main parts also have titles, Ixión en la tierra (Ixion on land) and Ixión en el Olimpo (Ixion on Olympus), that signal the novel's rather loose correspondence to the myth of Ixion. As summarized by Rehbein, Jupiter saves Ixion and provides a place for him to live, only to have Ixion fall in love with Jupiter's wife, Juno. In response, Jupiter castigates both by condemning Ixion to Hades and turning Juno into a cloud (187–188). Although there are correlations between the novel and the myth, there are clear differences as well. Beyond the ephemeral evocations of Ernesto's musings and his confusions about the women he is with, little concrete action can be discerned. At the end of Part 1, Ernesto is apparently shot by the enraged companion of a woman he has confused with one of his Evas, here called Eva the Second. Readers' lack of certainty about the occurrence is echoed by Ernesto, as he resolves to check the following day's newspaper in order to ascertain if "los otros" (the others) understood what has transpired (44). Subsequently, for his recuperation he goes to the house of Uncle Enrique, who is apparently married to Elena, the woman previously and, it seems, still the object of Ernesto's desire. None of this is clearly stated. Even the exact familial relationship with Enrique is cloudy, leading critics to disagree as to whether he is Elena's uncle (Rehbein 188) or Ernesto's (Rivera-Rodas 116). Despite the confusions, one can find parallelism with the Ixion myth in that Enrique offers his house for Ernesto's convalescence but then is betrayed when Ernesto tries to arrange a meeting with Elena in order to have her for himself. There is no need for Jupiter's vengeance, however, for Ernesto, in his bumbling and inherent capacity for confusing one female for another, mistakenly establishes a rendezvous not with Elena but with her verbose and intelligent (two attributes he clearly does not esteem) sister, Rosa Amalia. His punishment, his confinement in Hell—marriage to the sister—is of his own doing.

With such an emphasis on enigmatic suggestion and evocation rather than description and clearly depicted action, it seems somewhat ironic that the first section of the novel bears the heading "Sumario de novela" (novel's summary), evoking notions of more conventional fiction. When one considers the content and form of the initial segment, however, it becomes apparent that it is indeed an indicator of what is to come, a precursor, in a way, of Agustín Yáñez's "Acto Preparatorio" (Overture) in *Al filo del agua*. The first sentence of Owen's work is incomplete, a nominal phrase, a fragment. As well, it lacks context in terms of referent or situation: "Sus hermosas corbatas, culpables de sus horribles compañías" [His (or her or their) beautiful ties, guilty of his (or her or their) horrible companies] (7). The androgynous pronoun refuses to orient readers. References to Ernesto, to his uncle, and to a friend are not particularly useful in clarifying the situation (7–8). There are, however, other people mentioned, names that should alert readers to the influences that will be present in the development of this prose: [André] Gide and [Pablo] Picasso (8), both instrumental in breaking with perceived antiquated patterns of expression. In addition, Owen presents immediate references to poetry, announcing from the very beginning a position of privilege, the blending of prose and verse that will be explored in *Novela como nube*. Indeed, the author's poetic sense of language and rhythm permeate the text, with ample examples of metaphors, similes, nominal phrases, and alliteration.

Owen's use of fragmentation is more internal than graphic. That is to say, he does not separate the prose within subsections or lay bare spaces on the page, other than between titled segments. One finds, however, multiple levels of fragmentation within the novel, ranging from fragmented images, particularly of the female body; temporal and spatial jumps; fragmented sentences as signifiers of jumbled thoughts; and the isolation of certain segments as if they were vignettes.

Early in the novel, Owen presents a description of the female body with a decidedly cubist influence. Leading with a reference to a "rostro descompuesto" [a broken face] (13), he then details a being with a nose below the mouth and two pair of eyes where the ears are normally found. The forehead occupies inordinate space in the face of this woman who is described as "despedazada" and "fragmentaria" [broken into pieces and fragmented] (14). Within discourse, the fluidity of Owen's poetic prose is counteracted by the segmentation into twenty-six pieces, with one section broken down further into nine portions, each with its own title (section 22, 76–83). This same division makes it possible to set off certain descriptive passages as if they were vignettes to be appreciated visually, such as the portrait of Pachuca, where Ernesto convalesces (section 19, 66–69). Here Owen has not concerned himself with integrating the piece into the fuller narrative; it is as if he simply wanted readers to enjoy the descriptive powers of words.

A fundamental function of the internal fragmentation in *Novela como nube* is that of dramatizing the disorder of the protagonist's thoughts. Rehbein remarks on the effect of stream-of-consciousness techniques, with their lack of logic, stating that they augment the fragmentation of the narrative (200). There are numerous examples of disconnectedness, changes in time and place, fluctuation within focus, and textual ambiguities, all of which provide an engaging counterpoint to traditional notions of linearity, narrative coherence, and the illusion of a more rational reality. One of the more striking examples of discontinuity in time is section 5, which recounts aspects of Ernesto's convalescence. The title, "espejo hacia atrás" [mirror toward the past](15), could well alert readers to a retrospective, yet the occurrence that justifies this so-called backward glance will not take place until the end of Part 1, eight sections later. This would thus be more aptly termed "mirror toward the future," but in Owen's fictional universe, notions of time, also, are to be set against narrative norms.

The emphasis on broken images, interrupted thoughts, and fragmented discourse do not preclude markers of unity. As one suggestion that these twenty-six segments do, in fact, constitute a whole, Owen makes use of a basic technique that will be employed quite consistently in later fragmented works by a variety of authors: reiteration of language. Sections 5 and 6 are joined by the repetition of the words "los cinco sentidos" [the five senses] (19, 20). In another example, the first line of section 8 responds to the last sentence of section 7, a strategy that Juan José Arreola will later refine in *La feria:* [7] "Le interesaba el amor. [8] Bueno, el amor, precisamente, no" [He was interested in love. / Well, not exactly love] (25).

As a revolutionary within narrative practice, however, Owen appears well aware that the ultimate unifiers of his segmented text are the readers. Having presented them with a nonconformist text, he introduces an authorial voice almost halfway into Part 2 that self-referentially comments on the text's deviations from conventional practice, particularly with reference to character development and plot (65). Even more importantly, however, "some words from the author," as the title of the segment designates them, call attention both to the status of a nonunit and to the role readers must play if they are to take full advantage of the experience of reading *Novela como nube:* "Me anticipo al más justo reproche, para decir que he querido así mi historia, vestida de arlequín, hecha toda de pedacitos de prosa de color y clase diferentes. Sólo el hilo de la atención de los numerables lectores pueden unirlos entre sí" [I enter here, in anticipation of the most justified reproach, to say that I want my story this way, dressed like a harlequin, all made from little pieces of prose of different colors and classes. Only the thread of attention of its few readers can unite them] (64). Subsequently, this first-person authorial voice makes fairly frequent intrusions, commenting on the relevance of the material presented (71–72) or remarking on the suitability of a person or thing as an object for a writer to consider (73). Owen thus creates a metanarrative commentary (Rivera-Rodas 120) that invites readers to focus on the process of narration, an aspect that will be further explored by subsequent writers such as Juan Rulfo and Josefina Vicens.

The acknowledgment of readers is such that the authorial voice addresses them directly. Significantly, the term of address is *caballeros,* an exclusionary word that precludes women. Moreover, the word has its roots in Spain, Mexico's colonizer from which independence was won, but that now is one of the countries whose literary figures provide inspiration for the Mexican vanguard movement. Further evidence of Owen's nod to Spain is the use of the *vosotros* command form when referring to his readers (65, 71, 77). The exclusion of women and the employment of foreign terminology, although not unique to Owen, contribute to a sense of elitism, which was part of the criticism directed against the *Contemporáneos.* Nevertheless, Owen's textualization of readership can be seen as significant in that it demonstrates a recognition of reception, a cultural context, that indicates that this is not a completely hermetic fiction. In fact, Owen appears conscious of the degree of difficulty readers will have with this narrative that flaunts its differences from conventional practice. They cannot engage in the passivity evidenced by Ernesto's need to consult the paper to have an external confirmation of his own reality. Ernesto makes a very negative example of a reader-in-the-text, as he even lacks a grasp of traditional fiction. When he bungles a situation, he is chastised by the authorial voice: "Parece que no has leído novelas francesas, Ernesto" [It appears that you haven't read any French novels, Ernesto] (87).

In counterpoint to Ernesto's ineptitude, Owen supplies a positive example of a suggested reading process in the section entitled "Some Words from the Author." Immediately after detailing some of the ways in which this text deviates from established norms, the authorial voice urges readers not to give up on this iconoclastic fiction and reports what he terms an extraordinary experience: "He estado, de noche, repasando un álbum de dibujos. Por el aire corría el tren de Cuernavaca, en esa perspectiva absurda que se enseña . . . en las escuelas de pintura al aire libre. Y cuando lo miraba más y más intensamente, llegó hasta mi cuarto, aguda y larga, la sirena de un tren verdadero. A mí me sucedió esta cosa extraordinaria" [At night I was looking through a book of drawings. In the air one could hear the Cuernavaca train, in that absurd perspective that is taught . . . in the outdoor painting classes. And when I looked at it more and more intensely, there came to my room, sharp and long, the whistle of a real train. This extraordinary thing happened to me] (65).

Although Owen presents a model from a different medium, the suggestion here is that one must involve oneself deeply within the literary experience, so much so that one actually lives the event or truly feels the ambience. Words have the same evocative powers as images, but there must be an engaged reader or viewer in order to achieve the fullest pleasure. As Picasso challenged notions of perspective, Owen asks for more freedom in expression. Owen's prose is poetic and very visual, given to the creation of images rather than to plot elements. He demands from his readers thought and perception, both integral to the reading experience occasioned by this new narrative. As another of his metanarrative comments would indicate, he realizes that the attributes of his craft, his lyrical novel, could be easily overlooked: "Son las cosas demasiado diáfanas las que no se ven, aire, cristal, poesía" [It is the things that are too diaphanous that are not seen: air, crystal, poetry] (43).

## Xavier Villaurrutia, *Dama de corazones* (Queen of Hearts)

Xavier Villaurrutia completed only one work in prose, *Dama de corazones* (1928), a very short piece of fewer than fifty pages. The novel is divided into eight main sections marked by an enlarged capital letter, all but two of which are further segmented by a blank space, for a total of fifteen pieces. As in Owen's *Novela como nube*, the fragmentation at times serves to dramatize illogical shifts in thought patterns, as suggested by the author's comments on what he had hoped to achieve: "an interior monologue in which I followed the consciousness of a character during a precise real time and during a psychic time conditioned by the conscious reflections, by the emotions and by the real or invented dreams of the protagonist" (Dauster 40). Once again, the plot elements are minimal. Julio, a Mexican exchange student in the United States, returns home for a visit with his aunt, Madame Girard, and two cousins, Susana and Aurora. At first confused as to the identities of the young women, he quickly finds symmetrical inversions in their physical and personal qualities, which make Susana like the spring and Aurora like the winter (13–15). Their inverted status is reflected in the image used as title for the work, the queen of hearts from a deck of cards. Attracted to them both but with clear leanings toward Susana, Julio engages in a series of mental wanderings that incorporate musings about the cousins' likes and dislikes, the concept of character, travel, literature, and death, including an imagined sequence of his own demise and funeral. It is Madame Girard who dies, however, prompting Julio's departure.

Villaurrutia shares Owen's penchant for the blending of genre. Indeed, Frank Dauster argues that "a number of lyrical passages . . . are virtually poetry arranged in prose form" (40). Especially suggestive of poetic arrangement are the sections consisting of a series of short paragraphs, ranging in length from one to four lines, that evoke a grouping of verses rather than narrative text, such as the pages devoted to comparing Susana and Aurora (13–15). Significantly, within the content, Villaurrutia includes one attribute that the women have in common: their writing consists of extremely long paragraphs. Readers' attention is called to the contrast between the content referring to writing and the way that content is displayed. They are invited to consider the process of narration. In counterpoint to these brief segments, elsewhere there are long paragraphs of fluid prose, perhaps in echo of the cousins' style, with very poetic rhythm and imagery. In a number of cases, one finds repetition at the beginning of sentences within the paragraphs, suggesting anaphora (24, 30). With such an emphasis on poetic qualities, there emerges a second function for the spacing among fragments: they acquire the status of the break between strophes in a poem.

Villaurrutia eschews conventional notions of plot, character development, and narrative coherence. Although he refrains from the authorial intrusion of the metanarrative commentary seen in *Novela como nube*, he includes numerous references in the text to both the inadequacy of nineteenth-century fiction (31) and his character's thoughts about the new literature: "las frases de novela moderna que jugábamos a inventar con un arte próximo al vicio, con un arte perfecto" [the sentences of the modern novel that we played at inventing with an art near to vice, with a perfect art] (30). Villaurrutia's commitment to a new art is reflected in the four illustrations he drew for the first edition that clearly evoke the influence of Picasso. The painter is, in fact, one of the artists mentioned in the text, the only one whose name is printed in capital letters, thus standing out on the page (27). Of the four drawings, three are images of fragmented bodies. The first is that of a man with fountain pen in hand, but whose hands are detached from the rest of his body. It appears before the epigraph by Jean Cocteau and evokes the status of author. The second segmented body is that suggesting the image of a queen of hearts, but a figure that is doubly truncated (between pages 20 and 21). Instead of having the women share the same body, as indicated within the text in Julio's fantasy (15), here the women's bodies, only partially in view, are slashed by a rigid line that cuts off the rest of their torso. Furthermore, they are already segmented, with the heads detached from the neck as if beheaded, and segments of limbs superimposed on what can be seen of the upper body. One hand partially covers the face in each of the inverted images, and the lips are completely removed from the face, appearing to the side of the upper head. The large $Q$ as seen on a playing card is appropriately placed, standing in contrast to the rest of the drawing by conforming to convention. Finally there is a segmented figure (between pages 30 and 31) whose face is apparently masculine, but whose naked body refuses to reveal gender, as sexual parts are either covered or turned around. Again, the head is severed, and the limbs are in pieces.

In *Dama de corazones,* Villaurrutia is more concerned with images and the ontology of character than with traditional character development. The plot is so minimal as to be deemed nonexistent, as noted by one contemporary critic (Pérez Firmat 57). According to Dauster, Villaurrutia was dissatisfied with his experiment in the genre and abandoned prose writing to return to poetry. Alberto Ruy Sánchez, however, praises the work for its poetic prose and its capturing of the semidream state in the style of Marcel Proust (84).

### Jaime Torres Bodet, *Proserpina rescatada* (Proserpina Rescued)

Analogous to Owen and Villaurrutia's novels, Jaime Torres Bodet's works are known for their poetic prose and experimentation with aspects of narrative technique. In addition, Merlin H. Forster offers a summary of characteristics associated with the author's fiction: fragmented plots, first-person narrator, time jumps or reversals, flashbacks, the free association of ideas, and the use of a framing device to establish the present, thus providing unification, and to enable an extension of the time portrayed ("La obra novelística," 68–69). All of these traits apply to *Proserpina rescatada* (1931), and most have a clear association with fragmentation.

As with Torres Bodet's other novels, *Proserpina rescatada* is clearly fragmented, its four parts broken down internally to constitute a total of twenty-eight segments. Although the segmenting of the text allows for temporal changes, the jumps are not as radical as those presented by Azuela in *La luciérnaga*. Instead, after establishing a present, Torres Bodet employs the fragments as a tool with which to dramatize the wandering of the human mind in the process of memory. The novel is centered on a doctor, Delfino Castro Valdés, and his relationship with the title character, Proserpina Jiménez, also known as Dolores Jiménez, a fellow student during medical school and, until they determine that marriage between two doctors would be futile, his lover. In the novel's present, as narrated by Delfino, Proserpina phones unexpectedly, asking him to come over immediately. After many years of separation, this contact prompts Delfino to recall, in an unsystematic, illogical way appropriate to the process of memory, aspects of his relationship with his former classmate. Proserpina's duality as evidenced by her two names is but a small part of her inscrutable character. She is a woman who passes from being a bright medical student to a medium who acts as conduit for the departed.[20] Although the fragmentariness of her being is stressed in notions of duality, which aligns with her mythological name (M. H. Forster, *Los contemporáneos*, 49), there are other suggestions of multiple selves, as reflected in her being the voice for innumerable souls. After an extended period of nostalgic recall involving numerous changes in time and place, Delfino arrives only to find Proserpina close to a diabetic coma. Acquiescing to her pleading, Delfino injects Proserpina with a medication that will hasten her death.

Torres Bodet's use of poetic language and tropes in *Proserpina rescatada* is ample to the point of excess. In addition to easily recognized examples of personification, synesthesia, simile, and metaphor, one finds abundant approximations of anaphora that provide a flowing rhythm to the prose.[21] Some take the form of a series of prepositional or noun phrases, which, when combined with the other numerous examples, can become overwhelming. Indeed, at the time of publication one critic complained of the ubiquitous commas occasioned by this practice (Solana 19).

The author succeeds admirably, however, in his integration of fragmentation at various levels of the text. Readers learn to envision Proserpina as a segmented being, almost a split personality, a being halved. This image is reinforced first by his description of her lying in bed when the lighting appears to cut her body in two and then by her own words in the very next sentence: "he vivido segmentándome" [I have lived segmenting myself] (242). Proserpina is not alone, moreover, for the narrator describes another woman acquaintance as a composite of fragments of other women's bodies and manners (213). It is on a more transcendent plane, however, that Torres Bodet extends the reach of fragmentation in the novel. Fernando Burgos argues that *Proserpina rescatada*'s segmentation joins temporal fragmentation with that of the wandering, haphazard patterns associated with memory (146). He further advances a correlation between the multiple levels of the text and that of the protagonist's personality (147). Even more importantly, Burgos observes the rupture of a totality into fragments as related to the sociopolitical ambience of Mexico in that period, exposing a discontinuity symptomatic of a society in continual transformation, as well as the discontinuity inherent in the authors' breaking with narrative tradition (140–141). María José Bustos Fernández concurs with the former more abstract, social/ontological manifestation of fragmentation, arguing that the central modern conflict addressed in the novel is precisely fragmentation as a way of being (27).

Significantly, Torres Bodet also provides a mischievous early example of a narrator-in-the-text whose initial discourse is fragmented. The speaker is a spirit who communicates through Proserpina: "Insertaba, entre los párrafos de lo que decía, espesos silencios de alumno que no sabe la clase" [He inserted, between the paragraphs of what he was saying, thick silences of a student who doesn't know the lesson] (228). Silences punctuate the spirit's discourse just as fragments occasion pause in the novel. Again, given the extremes within poetic language and style, these breaks may be likened to that between strophes in a poem. Torres Bodet's playful posture, however, appears further on, when the spirit is invited to proffer a character description of Proserpina. Attentive readers would be hard put to ignore the implicit contrast between this experimental fiction and traditional offerings as they read that the spirit is berated for delivering a feeble character description of the enigmatic protagonist; the spirit's name is "Dostoiewski."

The status of this fiction as modern literature standing in contrast with works by more traditional authors is reflected in various references to art and artists. Early in the novel Delfino likens himself to a perfect sentence: "Soy, como una frase perfecta, una sucesión de sílabas que nadie podría cambiar de orden" [I am, like a perfect sentence, a succession of syllables whose order no one could change] (160). Also, as with other vanguard novelists, the author names contemporary innovators within the world of art, in this case Picasso, Stravinsky, and Reverdy (197).

Even more importantly, however, Torres Bodet demonstrates an awareness beyond the fiction itself: a sensitivity to reader reception. In the first example, one feels that he is teasing his readers. After receiving the initial telephone call, Delfino plays a recording of Proserpina's voice that she had given him as a form of introduction shortly after they met. In it, she remarks on her interest in insects, especially flies. This would seem appropriate for a medical student, yet her description soon extends to torturing them and exulting in her deeds. Despite its brevity, the passage quickly builds tension as Proserpina explains how she outgrew her fascination with flies and adds: "Así fue como principié a torturar a mi madre" [that's how I began to torture my mother] (172). At that moment of heightened expectation, there is an interruption in the form of a spatial break and the narrator's words beginning the next fragment stating that the record has stopped. Readers' anticipation is then fueled by a reference to infantile sadism, quickly followed by the resumption of the record on its second side. The author is not through with his game, however. Prosperina begins with a background study of her parents, followed by a generalized overview of her plans, nothing specific. Then the moment arrives: "Un día . . . cuando mi madre se disponía a rezar el rosario . . ." [One day . . . when my mother was preparing to recite the rosary . . . ] (174). At this point the record breaks, denying readers the desired particulars. Delfino has already stated that he has heard the record before (170), but he does nothing to relieve readers' frustration. Instead he exacerbates the situation by acting as a reader-in-the-text who is *not* privy to the information: "Desenlace imprevisto. El disco se ha roto en el minuto en que las confesiones de Proserpina empezaban a interesarme" [An unforeseen denouement. The record has broken at the moment Proserpina's confessions were beginning to interest me] (174). The second suspension is both more final and more forceful than the first.

Thus Torres Bodet acknowledges his readers in the form of building expectations only to deny fulfillment, a technique later used to advantage by Agustín Yáñez in *Al filo del agua*. In recompense for this teasing, perhaps, he includes also a positive indication of how to respond to this modern fiction, with particular reference to its fragmentation. Toward the end of the novel and at the beginning of a fragment, in a placement that emphasizes its importance, the narrator states: "No consigo ya unir todos los fragmentos, todas las páginas sueltas del libro desencuadernado, del almanaque en desorden que esparce sobre mi memoria los recuerdos de nuestra vida de Nueva York" [I cannot yet unite all the fragments, all the loose pages of the disassembled book, of the almanac in disorder that scatters in my memory the recollections of our life in New York] (232). The glimpses of Proserpina and the life that they shared, whether as lovers or as friends, is indeed scattered throughout the fragments of the novel. Since Delfino cannot achieve a sense of unification, then readers are the ones to attempt such a task, by means of a more active participation in the narrative process.

By most counts, the *estridentista* movement declines in the late 1920s and the *Contemporáneos* advance only into the early 1930s. According to Pérez Firmat, the genre was agonizing almost from the moment of birth (21), at least in part because of the persistent caustic criticism attacking the authors for not being able to write real novels, for being too intellectual, even for being effeminate.[22] In Mexico, however, one must add the loss of political patronage as a contributing factor for the dissolution of both groups. Each had been sustained partially by its members' having been granted bureaucratic positions and when its advocate left was hard-pressed to continue (M. H. Forster, *Los contemporáneos*, 18–22). Although the temporal span of the movements was brief, one should not underestimate the contribution made by these authors to Mexican letters. They were among the first to challenge the status quo, in a rebellion analogous to the revolution. Their literary activity opened the discussion of universalism versus nationalism, focused attention on the potential yet to be realized within the genre, and wrenched the reading public from complacency and passivity. Although their deviation from the norm largely took the form of poetic style and narrative ambiguity, their experimentation with fragmentation clearly paved the way for more sophisticated treatments to follow.

### Mariano Azuela, The Trilogy

Although *Proserpina rescatada* includes elements grounded in daily life in Mexico City, it is Mariano Azuela who succeeds in infusing his novels with the truly gritty reality of the subculture buried within the urban milieu. As such, he forms a stronger link than any of the vanguard authors with subsequent writers like Agustín Yáñez who focus on national issues. *La Malhora* (1923) suggests, rather than describes in full, episodes from the life of a young prostitute in the Federal District, Altagracia. After a somewhat lengthy establishing section in which readers are introduced to the protagonist, her circumstances, and the main characters influencing her, the text turns to three brief segments resembling those of a picaresque novel in sequencing and content. La Malhora (Altagracia's nickname) serves as a maid to a series of unusual characters: a patently crazy medical surgeon, who sees her as the reincarnation of his dog, Lenin; the pious Gutiérrez women, who teach her the healing qualities of religion; and an aged Porfirista soldier. In the fifth and final section, Altagracia returns to her origins in Tepito, where she confronts la Tapatía and Marcelo, the two most responsible for her miserable existence, including her dishonor and the death of her father. Having learned from her experiences, however, she pulls out a rosary instead of a knife, even though she had sworn revenge, and the novel ends on a note, albeit ambiguous, of forgiveness.[23]

Although sharing a sense of circularity with *Los de abajo*, the discursive aspects of *La Malhora* are considerably more experimental. Leal cites as innovative technical aspects of the novel the use of fragmentation, abrupt changes in focus, time jumps, a lack of logic in the plot development, flashbacks, interruption of scenes, and the denial of complete character description (*Mariano Azuela*, 126). Elsewhere, he refers to the author's impressionist style (*Mariano Azuela*, 114). Raymundo Ramos comments on the importance of interior monologue and adds to discursive innovation "el contraste de tiempos rápidos y tiempos lentos" [the contrast of rapid and slow pacing] (13).[24] Significantly, the experimental techniques cited by both critics are largely rooted in fragmentation.

The most important consequence of Azuela's stylistic choices in *La Malhora* is that readers must interrogate the text in order to orient themselves. Thus Azuela begins to emphasize greater reader engagement and, by implication, the act of reading. At the end of the first lengthy segment, for example, in a very enigmatic episode in which it is suggested, not stated, that Altagracia is left for dead, an unidentified person comes to her aid. The next segment, "La reencarnación de Lenín" (The Reincarnation of Lenin), constitutes a radical change in narration in that an unidentified voice rambles on in the first person. Readers must assemble clues in order to make coherent the unstable prose. Subsequently one learns that the new narrator is a forty-five-year-old doctor who has spent time in an asylum. Then, as he speaks of his wife, he reveals that she has taken it upon herself to rescue fallen women, the most recent of whom is Altagracia.

Azuela's choice of a fragmented structure blends well with his decision to vary his prose style and narration. While consisting of five major parts, each bearing a title as in a more traditional chapter division, the novel exhibits as well interior fragmentation in the form of gaps on the page. Moving beyond the use of spaces to connote the passage of time as seen in *Los de abajo*, Azuela's employment of a segmented discourse now marks a more disjointed narrative. Changes in time, space, pace, and narration are common.

*El desquite* (1925; Revenge) has been the least favorably received critically of the trilogy. Although acknowledging its innovative, choppy, fragmented technique, Leal faults the extraneous bullfight scenes and the weak denouement (*Mariano Azuela*, 56). Discursively, Azuela continues with the experimental use of fragmentation, as the very short novel (thirty pages in the Fondo de Cultura Económica edition) is broken into thirteen sections, each with a title. It is *La luciérnaga* (Firefly), however, that reflects his mastery of the technique.

With *La luciérnaga*, Azuela perfects his use of experimental strategies, especially interior monologue (occasionally interior dialogue) and fragmentation of action. His manipulation of a segmented structure is so advanced, in fact, that it can be seen as a precursor of the complex fragmented texts of Mexican novels of the 1960s. The novel focuses on Dionisio Bermejillo, his family, and the circumstances that cause his ruination economically and spiritually. After fighting with his brother, José María, over their inheritance and plans for the future, Dionisio departs with his wife, Conchita, and their children for Mexico City, where he hopes to succeed in business. From the very start, however, Dionisio is involved in one scam after another, whether perpetrated by a hotel manager or by his supposed friends and *paisanos*. As his money dwindles, Dionisio succumbs to both alcohol and marijuana. The catalyst for his even more rapid descent comes in the form of an accident, when Dionisio slams his vehicle into a streetcar, killing four and maiming many others. As his alcoholism progresses, Dionisio's economic circumstances naturally decline, culminating in the family's being forced to the miserable Tepito district. His daughter, María Cristina, assimilates all too well into the sordid atmosphere and is finally killed during an orgy involving government officials. Despite an influx of capital from his brother's death and relative success from a *pulquería*, Dionisio finds that money cannot resolve life's problems. His son, Sebastián, dies of consumption, a loss that drives Conchita and the two remaining children back to Cieneguilla, their provincial home. Dionisio sinks even lower, to the point that even his old cronies will not offer him a job. When one *paisano*, Chirino, finally proposes a deal, it sours, and Dionisio contemplates deserting him by taking a trip to Cieneguilla to seek Conchita. As he departs from a cab at the station, Dionisio meets Chirino, who evidently attacks him. Upon reading about the incident in a newspaper, Conchita, the faithful, dutiful wife, the *luciérnaga* of the title, returns to Mexico City, where she and Dionisio are reunited as he leaves the hospital.[25]

Although this summary of *La luciérnaga*'s plot appears straightforward, its presentation in the novel is decidedly disjunctive. Azuela divides the text into five chapters, four of which contain internal divisions marked by roman numerals. Many of these sections are further segmented by gaps on the page, producing a fragmented structure. Some of the breaks in the narrative signal changes in point of view, others signify a lapse of time, but the essential effect of Azuela's fragmentation is related to time jumps or the illogical, nonsequential ordering of events. Even within the fragments, there are numerous instances of a radical change of content and/or discourse.

Chapter 1 begins with the accident involving the streetcar. There is no orientation as to characters, time, or circumstance; only two pages later do readers learn that Dionisio is the man who walked away from the scene and not until the very end of the chapter is it revealed that he, and not his regular driver, was, in fact, the guilty party. Between the initial carnage and the revelation of its actual cause, Azuela presents a jumble of times and actions: Dionisio's resumption of drinking after the accident; the brothers' dialogue regarding Dionisio's initial proposal to go to Mexico City and José María's disapproval of his schemes; the circumstances of the inheritance; a newspaper report on the crash; a neighbor's intercession as Dionisio prepares to attack Conchita and the children with a razor; a friend's desire to go into business with Dionisio when the family first arrived in the city; that friend's mistress and her questionable behavior, which leads Conchita to spurn their hospitality; two unfortunate business deals with *paisanos*; men from the Ford agency who come to repossess Dionisio's vehicle; a dinner the first night in Mexico City; the purchase of a Buick and its demise eight months later; and the newspaper report regarding the death of his driver. Essentially the chapter centers on the accident and the circumstances leading to that point, as can be seen even from the illogical sequencing of events, but the arrangement of the pieces of narrative prompts readers to engage with the text in an attempt to render a coherent ordering.

The second chapter is short enough to constitute a fragment itself and is the only major textual division not to have interior segmentation. In a span of some three pages, Azuela evokes Dionisio's thoughts of suicide, José María's evident guilt regarding his brother's family's impoverished circumstances, and María Cristina's sudden wealth, which marks her assimilation into Mexico City's vice-ridden atmosphere. In a sense, the changes in point of view prepare readers for Chapter 3, which is told from José María's perspective. In a very well elaborated sequence, Azuela uses interior monologue and interior dialogue, as well as a third-person narration reminiscent of nineteenth-century omniscience at its best to capture José María's guilt and self-deception with regard to money. Nicknamed "don Chema Miserias" (Don Joey Misery), Dionisio's brother is a master at "dialéctica interior" [interior logic] (114) in rationalizing his avarice, but Azuela makes certain that others are shown to share the greed, especially the clergy, in the person of padre Romero.

Chapter 4 reverts to the style established in Chapter 1, although the sequencing is more linear. The main developments include Dionisio's going into a *pulquería* business, his attempts to confess his responsibility regarding the accident, Sebastián's illness, and Conchita's departure subsequent to her son's death. In the final chapter, three of the four major subsections are related from Conchita's point of view. During the year she and the children spend in Cieneguilla, she comes to realize her strength, a fortitude she needs upon hearing of Dionisio's injury and deciding to return to the hated atmosphere of Mexico City. The other segment relates the probable circumstances resulting in Dionisio's final confrontation with Chirino.

Although Azuela spoke with some cynicism of the deliberate obfuscations associated with the modern novel, it is clear from his successful handling of innovative narrative strategies in *La luciérnaga* that he had understood both the effectiveness of experimentation with regard to the expression of character and thematics and the relationship between unconventional discourse and reader reception.[26] In a type of literary journal, "El novelista y su ambiente [II]" (The Novelist and His Milieu), Azuela reflects on innovation's effect on readers:

> no todo consiste en tergiversar palabras y vocablos, oscurecer conceptos y enmarañar cosas, sucesos y personas, como se compone un rompecabezas. Al primer intento, en efecto, el lector desprevenido se desconcierta en absoluto desde las primeras páginas del libro: gentes, cosas y sucesos se le ofrecen en forma tan enrevesada que se sentirá tentado a desecharla desde luego como producción de un cerebro

anormal, beodo, mariguano o loco. Pero si se toma el trabajo de meditar, de detenerse en los pasajes más oscuros, de estudiarlo todo de cerca y con acuciosa mirada, experimentará análoga impresión al del melómano escuchando por primera vez una obra que sólo después de repetidas audiciones permite descubrir la belleza de sus temas. (1121)

[not everything consists of twisting words, obscuring concepts, and mixing things, events, and people, as one composes a puzzle. On the first try, in fact, the unprepared reader becomes totally disconcerted from the first pages of the book: people, things, and events are thrown at him in a form so complex that he will feel tempted to dismiss it as the product of an abnormal mind, a drunk, a drug addict, or a madman. But if he takes the time to think, to pause over the most obscure parts, he will experience an analogous impression to that of the music fanatic listening for the first time to a work that only after repeated playings allows the beauty of its themes to be discovered.]

These words promoting a thoughtful reading with particular emphasis on initial confusion could well be directed specifically at *La luciérnaga*, for its beginning sequence is of utmost importance, especially regarding reader reception. By starting with the accident, Azuela denies readers grounding information about traditional notions of narrative: time, characters, and motivation. Dionisio's disorientation upon contemplating the wreckage could well dramatize a reader's response. Even more significantly, Azuela's grotesque imagery of broken steel, body parts, and the streetcar turned upside-down constitutes a diegetic representation that parallels his literary conception: *La luciérnaga* reflects normative literature turned on its head, its conventional sequencing smashed into pieces.

In its privileged positioning, the accident scene heralds a different kind of narrative, one that requires readers to think, to contemplate its difference, to decipher its systems. In fact, in an earlier version of the text, the accident scene appears to have been even more elusive. According to Francisco Monterde, who saw the now lost original form, Azuela began the novel with "una serie de bruscas imágenes, con las que sugería el choque" [a series of brusque images, with which he suggested the crash] (*Azuela: Obras completas I*, xvi). As if to ensure that readers would have no illusions regarding the unconventionality of the subsequent narrative, Azuela quickly continues with a surreal vision. In the cathedral on the Zócalo[27] where Dionisio has gone for refuge, statues come to life, winking and sticking out their tongues at him (78). Although in a sense naturalized as the perception of a man under the influence of both marijuana and post-trauma stress, the moving statues also serve to reiterate Azuela's metaphorical declaration of literary experimentation and aggressive confrontation of readers.

Pairing certain elements of more traditional narration with his innovative techniques, Azuela employs a third-person omniscient narration among the interior monologues, interior dialogues, and instances of dialogue lacking orienting commentary. As Leal describes it, "técnicamente" [technically], Teodomiro is the narrator (*Mariano Azuela*, 60). Leal's qualifier is due to the fact that Teodomiro's identity as narrator is mentioned only once. In the third subsection of Chapter 1, the narration suddenly changes to first-person for one brief paragraph, in which the speaker refers to his two-year service "de juez menor" (as a minor judge) in Cieneguilla (94). Two pages later, Dionisio mentions the very same wording with reference to Teodomiro, adding that the judge was ungrateful for a kindness of theirs. A defensive response, enclosed within parentheses, would appear to be the narrating judge's aside. Yet the use of Teodomiro as narrator is inconsistent. He surfaces nowhere else, which is particularly strange because later in the novel he misses another opportunity to exonerate himself when Dionisio relates a story focused on the judge's stinginess (136).

The third-person narration is used very effectively, however, to strengthen Azuela's social and political criticisms. There are strong critiques aimed at the administration of Plutarco Elías Calles with its disregard for the welfare of the people. Doctors and the clergy fare poorly as well: the former may be good at diagnosis but cannot cure (the specialist Dionisio hopes to consult regarding Sebastián's illness has died of that very disease), and the latter are consistently shown to be concerned primarily for themselves and material gain. Finally, Azuela directs his attack on the city— Mexico City, specifically Tepito. In contrast to the embodiment of the country, Cieneguilla, which, as the ending would suggest, provides Conchita with the values and strength necessary to ultimately save her husband, Mexico City is depicted as dirty, immoral, and cancerous. Those who assimilate to its ambience are doomed to prostitution, larceny, or abject poverty. If the government hasn't completely ruined your economic circumstances, your neighbor will; as José María tells Dionisio: "Hazte ladrón o métete al Gobierno, que es lo mismo" [Be a thief or join the government, it's all the same] (139). From the haven of Cieneguilla, Conchita sums up her experience in Mexico: "Con el terror retrospectivo del México de las diarias engañifas, de las iniquidades, de las inquietudes y de las desconfianzas perpetuas" [with the retrospective terror of the Mexico City of daily deceptions, inequities, concerns, and perpetual uncertainties] (158). The city is referred to as "México bandido" [thieving Mexico] (99) and as "Babilonia" [Babylon] (118). The last segments of the novel are particularly graphic in their description of the filthy conditions, with dead dogs and cats lying for weeks in the gutter because no one pays any attention. This vision of Mexico is of the poor and the corrupt; "los de arriba" [those on top] (137) and "los de abajo" (those on bottom, the underdogs) are evidently equally contaminated.

The consistent message of atomization, of both the characters and the city itself, relieved only at the very end by Conchita's faithfulness, is suggested from the start. Once again, the crucial accident scene serves as metaphor for the fragmented existence to be portrayed in the following pages. Thus the wreckage symbolizes at once the breaking with traditional narrative order and the splintered urban existence. The horrorific imaging of the streetcar as a beast—"Patas arriba, la bestia muerta, salpicada de masa encefálica y cabellos ensangrentados, dejaba oír los débiles gemidos de los que no se acababan de morir adentro de sus entrañas abiertas y entre sus tripas retorcidas" [Upside down, the dead beast, like a sauce of encephalitic mass and bloodied hair, gave up the feeble cries of those who had not yet died inside its open guts and among its twisted intestines] (77)—is echoed later in the text as Conchita reflects on Mexico City with its "entrañas de infierno" [hellish guts] (161).

Azuela's rhetorical devices pair well with his use of fragmentation, both discursive and metaphoric. The extensive employment of interior monologue and interior dialogue, while allowing direct communication with readers, also accentuates a lack of interchange with the character's family and acquaintances. It is as if both Dionisio and José María have retreated into themselves in refuge. Similarly, the frequent instances of nominal phrases, fragments of sentences, reiterate Azuela's conceptualization of an atomized existence. A particularly effective description both captures Dionisio's somnambulist state with a dizzying flow of images and reproduces in microcosm the illogical ordering of the text's pieces:

> Entonces volvió la espalda a su mujer Conchita, y se precipitó en
> un aeroplano de lana, pesos, pesos, pesos, cervezas, aritmética, las

barbas de chivo del antipático don Alberto, los ojos de lechuza de Teodomiro, la negación apendicular del chato Padilla y camiones, tranvías, fragmentos de calles y edificios iluminados, chile pasilla, porcelanas y cabezas bellísimas reproducidas al infinito en un mar de manteles, servilletas y blancos delantales, en los grandes espejos del restorán que se viene abajo de luces, cristalería, voces y meseras. (97)

[Then he turned his back on his wife Conchita, and threw himself into a whirl of money, pesos, pesos, pesos, beer, math, nasty don Alberto's goatee, Teodomiro's owl eyes, pugnosed Padilla's refusal, buses, trolleys, fragments of streets and lighted buildings, pasilla chili, china, and beautiful heads reproduced to infinity in a sea of tablecloths, napkins, and white aprons, in the great mirrors of the restaurant that's falling down amidst lights, crystal, voices, and waitresses.]

In *La luciérnaga*, fragmentation relates both to narrative experimentation and to thematics, particularly as focused on Mexico City, constituting one of the earliest visions of Mexico City as a fragmented metropolis. Thus the urban center is at the root of both literary advancement and an atomized existence, a development that will continue in the work of later generations after Carlos Fuentes reestablishes the theme in *La región más transparente* (1958). Azuela's status as premier Mexican novelist of the beginning of the twentieth century is secured on two fronts. With *Los de abajo*, he steers Mexican letters toward national themes and language, moving away from European influence. Paradoxically, his narrative innovation in the "hermetic" trilogy (Monterde, "La etapa de hermetismo") helps to open the Mexican novel to international currents. As summarized by Eliud Martínez, Azuela's experimentation with psychological analysis, hallucinatory visions, and critical depictions of Mexico City also enriches national literature, as it constitutes an artistic prefiguring of subsequent landmark texts such as Agustín Yáñez's *Al filo del agua* (1947), Juan Rulfo's *Pedro Páramo* (1955), and Carlos Fuentes's *La muerte de Artemio Cruz* (1962) and *Cambio de piel* (1967) (E. Martínez, 94). Of equal importance is Azuela's refinement of the strategic use of fragmentation with an increasing awareness of the consequent reader reception. Mariano Azuela begins a trajectory of experimental fragmentation that will continue to evolve throughout the century, calling for a full range of reader participation.

# CHAPTER 3

# NATIONALIST LITERATURE

A side from the vanguard's experimental fiction, the postrevolutionary period is largely one of national introspection. Although descriptive novels of the revolution continued, many novelists looked inward to Mexican customs and conditions.[1] Some writers, such as Rosa de Castaño (*La gaviota verde*, 1935; *Rancho estradeño*, 1936), limited their focus to regionalist customs, but as Brushwood points out, a self-examination of provincial customs can easily metamorphose into social protest (*Mexico in Its Novel*, 215). Predominant among the novels of protest were a critique of the society that the revolution had produced and an attempt to bring to the center those groups marginalized from the social order, thus highlighting the problems of the workers, the poor, and the Indians. Gregorio López y Fuentes's *Huasteca* (1939) focuses on the exploitation of oil workers, and José Guadalupe de Anda's *Juan del riel* (1943) chronicles the railroad workers' fight for improved conditions. Magdalena Mondragón (*Yo como pobre*, 1944) and Jesús R. Guerrero (*Los olvidados*, 1944) were among the authors who strove to "communicate the actual conditions of the elements that were still not really incorporated into the social pattern of the nation" (Brushwood, *Mexico in Its Novel*, 230), in this case the basest of the poor. Novels dealing with the plight of the Indians included Mauricio Magdaleno's *El resplendor* (1937) and Miguel Ángel Menéndez's *Nayar* (1941), but the work that has stood out within this category is clearly López y Fuentes's *El indio* (1935), winner of Mexico's first Premio Nacional de Literatura (National Prize for Literature).[2]

López y Fuentes's social consciousness was not limited to concern for indigenous groups. In addition to writing on workers' issues, for example, he composed *Acomodaticio* (1943), a satiric novel targeting political opportunism, a theme he had introduced in his earlier *¡Mi general!* (1934). One reason for *El indio*'s prominence in Mexican letters is precisely its embodiment of aspects of nationalist concerns, specifically the necessity of integration of fragmented groups into the national fabric. As voiced by the *maestro*, the mouthpiece within the novel for López y Fuentes's ideas, what was needed was an effort to regain the trust of the Indians by treating them as human beings and as Mexican citizens. As Antonio Magaña-Esquivel argues, the characters of *El indio* constitute a type of common denominator of a national consciousness (xv). Although clearly of artistic merit, the novel appears more concerned with social message than with an artistic presentation, which, as Brushwood contends, was fairly typical of the period: "art was considered subordinate to message" (*Mexico in Its Novel*, 11).

An exception to this statement is the second novel to be considered in this chapter, Agustín Yáñez's *Al filo del agua* (1947). Profoundly Mexican in thematics, the novel depicts life in rural Jalisco during the period immediately before the revolution. Magaña-Esquivel groups both *Al filo del agua* and *El indio* in his third category of novels of the revolution: those that take a retrospective look, a self-critical examination of the war and its consequences (xv). Yáñez's criticism can be considered somewhat subtle, but harsh. Writing with the analytic advantage of more than twenty-five years since the end of the revolution, he allows his readers to feel the absence of change, the persistence of circumstances in the 1940s that were to have been altered by the upheaval (Brushwood, *Mexico in Its Novel*, 8). Like López y Fuentes, Yáñez favors the collective over the individual; instead of standing out, his characters tend to cohere as a kind of composite protagonist (Sommers, *After the Storm*, 39). The two authors also share a borrowing from another medium, which strengthens their presentation by enhancing artistic possibilities: López y Fuentes turns to a visual emphasis akin to the muralists such as Diego Rivera, and Yáñez brings in a multitude of voices in a choral effect.[3] Each in his own way explores innovative ways of conveying the nation's story.

Yáñez, however, goes much further than his contemporaries in combining the social and the artistic. He opens himself to prevailing international intellectual currents and technical strategies, adapting them to his Mexican thematics. His deft use of psychological penetration, particularly interior monologue, has long been recognized. What needs exploring, however, is his addressing of readership and his manipulation of story elements as part of the artistic project.

## Gregorio López y Fuentes, *El indio* (The Indian)[4]

Just as Azuela appropriated the chronicle and from it shaped a novel, Gregorio López y Fuentes adapts into narrative the 1920s policy of disseminating the mythologies of the nation via muralism. Significantly, fragmentation is instrumental in the execution of this adaptation. Although rightly known more for its contribution to *indigenista* literature, *El indio* also reflects an innovative use of a segmented structure as complement to the text's thematics. As employed by López y Fuentes, fragmentation aids in emphasizing the folkloric aspects of the narrative by framing the scenes as if in tableau.

*El indio* traces in linear fashion the story of a tribe of Mexican Indians on both a personal and a more abstract, social level. The personal focuses most consistently on two men and a woman involved in a love triangle and the complications that result for their respective families. This conflict loosely binds the text's segments as the one continuing narrative element carried through to the end of the novel. The fact that no names are given for these characters nor for any others (they are referred to by occupation, race, or physical attributes) contributes to the emphasizing of a more distanced view of the status of native Mexicans in relation to their oppressors. In this way, the thematics of injustice and suffering predominate, as López y Fuentes is able to open the span of the novel to centuries of submission and generations of persecution.

Within the time frame of *El indio,* which is not specified but measured by events, every association between the *naturales* and the *blancos* (the natives and the whites) brings disaster. Whether through rape, torture, deceit, religious instruction, or direct armed confrontation, the whites and frequently the mestizos are clearly the empowered groups. The Indians yield time and again, facing yet another disaster at the novel's end, their leader having been politicized by the white man's systems: "Como todos los suyos, sólo saben que la *gente de razón* quiere atacarlos; que en la sierra y en el valle, los odios, en jaurías, se enseñan los dientes; y que el líder goza de buena situación en la ciudad" [Like the rest of their people, all they know is that the *gente de razon* [sic] want to attack them. That hatreds snarl in packs in the valley and the sierra. And that, in the city, the leader is well taken care of] (123).[5]

López y Fuentes divides the novel into three major parts, which contain, respectively, five, nine, and seven chapters.[6] All but five chapters are further segmented, with the divisions marked, in the illustrated second edition (Botas 1937), with a triangle of asterisks and, in the Colección Suma Veracruzana edition, by two parallel, horizontal lines of four dots flanked by hyphens. Many of the breaks are similar to those in *Los de abajo*, signaling a change in focus or a time lapse. There are two, however, that stand out for their discursive use. The first precedes a flashback: the concluding chapter of Part 2, "Otra víctima" (Another Victim),[7] begins with a brief two-paragraph description of a group searching for a native messenger assumed drowned. The contiguous fragment details the circumstances leading to the man's being lost in the swollen river and then moves ahead to the discovery of the body. The other break is employed diegetically: when the families of those involved in the love triangle bring their dispute to the village elders, the *huehues*, there is a gap between the presentation of the grievance and the *huehues*' judgment. Thus the break represents the elders' time for thought.

By far, however, the most significant effect of fragmentation in *El indio* is that of framing the folkloric scenes so crucial to the narrative. By being segmented from the rest of the text, the descriptions of native practices and daily life take on an extra dimension, attaining an almost visual status akin to the murals so popular in the 1920s. It is not surprising that the British edition of *El indio* (1937) included illustrations by the famed muralist Diego Rivera (Pasquel xi). Among the indigenous customs portrayed are meal preparations, agricultural methods, fishing, fiestas with the special *volador* (in which men swing upside down, hanging from ropes attached to a very tall pole), a system of justice as dictated by the elders of the tribe, and the beliefs and practices of witchcraft.[8] Contributing to the accent on visual interpretation or the tableau effect is the marked silence within the text. In contrast to the prevalence of dialogue in *Los de abajo*, *El indio* consists almost entirely of description and indirect discourse as related by a third-person narrator. When the youngest of the three intruding white men gives chase to a native woman, only a brief unintelligible murmur on his part breaks the silent scene until her cries signal the rape. Similarly, the priest's enforced pilgrimage designed to ward off further epidemics is accented by silence:

> El sacerdote que les había ordenado acudir en peregrinación . . . para dar gracias a la milagrosa imagen, se acercó a la tribu e imperativo, mediante presiones bruscas en los hombros, los hizo arrodillarse.

Cuando terminó la misa y la nave se fue vaciando de creyentes, el mismo sacerdote condujo a la tribu hasta el altar donde se hallaba el santo. Todos, arrodillados, dieron gracias por la salud concedida, pero las bocas no se movían: eran los ojos los que imploraban. (108)

[The priest who had ordered them to make this thanksgiving pilgrimage to the fiesta of the saint saw them standing and peremptorily, pushing on their shoulders, made them kneel.

When the mass was over and the nave was being emptied of worshipers, the same priest took the tribe to the altar of the miraculous saint. They gave thanks on their knees for the health granted them, but their lips did not move: they implored with their eyes.]

Although there are a series of interpolated stories within the narrative, they serve to contribute to the effect of *costumbrismo* rather than to focus on the process of narration. Thus, as opposed to Azuela's apparent concern with how best to tell his story, here López y Fuentes centers his text on the imaging of indigenous lore. The stories function as an aid to interpret or resolve a problem confronting the characters or as a reinforcement of tribal beliefs. Examples of such tales include the lovesick princess who dies from pining because she is forced to marry another man, thus constituting an interior duplication of the woman in the love triangle (71–72); the man who rents a snake to clear his land of pests but is bitten himself because he chooses to ignore the prohibition against alcohol when working with the serpent (75–76); the contrary wife who, when drowned, is found upstream because she has always gone against the current (88–89); and the drafted native who refuses to return to the tribe even after his father saves for a year to purchase his freedom from the military (111–112).

The two main focuses of *El indio*, indigenous customs and oppression from the white man, stand in opposition in treatment and tone. The peaceful native practices contrast forcefully with the deceit and violence associated with the persecutors. By using a fragmented discourse, López y Fuentes is able to make that contrast even more pronounced through juxtaposing the two in contiguous segments. One of the best examples comes early in the text, in the second chapter, entitled "Mestizaje." The first two fragments are almost timeless in their description of early-morning activities in preparation for the workers' departure, followed by the planting techniques themselves. The next segment begins with the aforementioned rape.

*El indio* thus reflects fragmentation integrated with thematics. The text's segmented status serves both to isolate pictorial descriptions of the Indians' long-standing customs and to emphasize the contrast between their peaceful practices and those imposed by the white aggressors. Although the latter function implies an effect on readers, it is Agustín Yáñez's *Al filo del agua* that makes clear fragmentation's usefulness as a strategy both instrumental in the manipulation of reader response and fundamental as a vehicle of narrative expression.

## Agustín Yáñez, *Al filo del agua*
## (The Edge of the Storm)

*Al filo del agua* (1947) is generally considered to be one of the first examples of more complex, experimental narrative in Mexican fiction. In support of this notion, numerous critics have made specific reference to Yáñez's use of interior monologue, among a variety of technical innovations, and to the possible influence of Joyce, Faulkner, Huxley, and Dos Pasos.[9] Indeed, Yáñez succeeds in refining Azuela's contributions by employing current technical strategies, notably psychological penetration and fragmentation, yet maintaining a steady focus on Mexican characters and ambience. Of even more importance, however, is Yáñez's significant advance in the addressing of readership in Mexican fiction, for his use of fragmentation suggests concern for the storytelling process, awareness of reader conditioning, and desire to shape reader response.

Thus, *Al filo del agua* is an initiating force for not only modern narrativity but also modern readership in Mexican letters. Although showing himself to be a masterful innovator of narrative form, Yáñez does not effect a complete break with traditional practices, but uses a combination of techniques that act together to shape active readers, making them aware of their grounding in more traditional storytelling methods and leading them to consider the process of narrativization and their relationship to it. Although innovative qualities predominate, *Al filo del agua* is really an intermediate step between conventional and modern narratives: a fragmented discourse confined within a traditional chapter division; a discourse capable of effecting a repositioning of readers paired with an authorial presence reminiscent of the comforting, omniscient narrator who guides readers' response to the novel. To understand Yáñez's accomplishment, one needs to focus on how fragmentation relates to the kind of reading the novel proposes and to the type of readership Yáñez constructs. Essential to this approach are (1) the notion of storytelling in the novel, (2) the series of textual moves Yáñez employs that disrupt narrative conventions, (3) guidelines supplied for readers that induce them to render this a coherent text, (4) the dramatization of both a narrator- and a reader-in-the-text, and (5) the implications of this reconstituted reader/reading and its potential effect on the definition of the readers' role.

The text of *Al filo del agua* consists of an "Acto preparatorio" (Overture)[10] followed by sixteen chapters. Within the chapters, however, are 136 fragments, the shortest of which is just over one line (10;6),[11] the longest approximately seventeen pages (4;4). With each new fragment there is a change in focus, yielding multiple perspectives, although throughout this perspectivism an omniscient narrator provides commentary. Despite the segmentation of discourse, there are no radical time jumps: the chronology is basically linear, confined between March 1909 and 1910 (Dellapiane 183). Fighting this linearity on a microlevel is a supplement to the structural fragmentation in the form of an extensive use of sentence fragments (phrases of one word, two words; subjects with no verb; verbs with no subject), which appears to reinforce Yáñez's technique of providing parts, not a whole. Yet in contrast to the sentence fragments and short sentences, there are passages that provide a flowing movement in the form of very long paragraphs, usually describing a character's intimate, intense feelings (15;1/15;6). It would seem that the text contains a dual energy: one that exerts a repeated stop-and-go rhythm, another that pushes forward with an uncontrollable momentum.[12]

Such changes of pace can be disconcerting at times for readers. The vivid contrast is difficult to ignore; readers are made conscious of the effectiveness of the two styles, the poetic qualities of each. Thus their attention is called to the novel's discourse. The emphasizing of the artifice of telling is made even more potent, however, when one considers the most accessible and, paradoxically, the most elusive element in *Al filo del agua:* the notion of story. Most critics are in agreement that the first four or five chapters serve as an introduction to characters and that the "plot" begins around Chapter 5 or 6 . . . or 8.[13] It is interesting that there is some disagreement as to which chapter actually initiates "story." In fact, there is no one complete story in this text; there are multiple story units, some of which intersect, others that do not. Most importantly, the units cannot be combined to form a single, unifying plot line.

Chapter 1, "Aquella noche" (That Night), establishes the relative parity of the townspeople in reference to their individual stories. In four sections readers are introduced to four people: don Timoteo Limón, Leonardo Tovar, Mercedes Toledo, and Micaela. None of the four stands out as being of exceptional importance in relation to the others; no one's story has more relevance to the novel or to readers. This same chapter gives an intimation of the importance of readers in relation to the novel. Theirs is a privileged position, for they are the only ones capable of knowing that there is a collectivity involved as the characters suffer in the night, feeling alone in their agony.

Although centered around specific characters, the next four chapters, through their fragmentation, reveal information about other townspeople. Although focusing on don Dionisio, Chapter 2 also serves to introduce Padre Reyes and to enter the minds and reveal the thoughts of the men and women as they suffer through their spiritual exercises. Similarly, chapter three moves beyond the presentation of don Dionisio's nieces to reveal additional characteristics of the priest. This multiplicity of story elements without a unifying thread is further emphasized in Chapter 3 with the inclusion of newspaper reports from *El País*, reports that are really stories, two of the many interpolated tales within the narrative.

Normally one might expect the title of a novel to be of aid in illuminating its primary focus. As interpreted by the author in a preface, *Al filo del agua* would seem to indicate that this is a novel of the Mexican Revolution: "es una expresión campesina que significa el momento de iniciarse la lluvia, y—en sentido figurado, muy común—la inminencia o el principio de un suceso" [(it) is a farmer's phrase for the beginning of the rainy season and is often used figuratively to mean the imminence or beginning of an event] (2). Yet in a novel that describes events taking place during the years 1909 and 1910, clearly the period immediately preceding the revolution, this event seems to have a secondary role to the passions and repressed desires of the many characters. The impending "storm," namely the Mexican Revolution, is given very little description, nor is it immediately clear that what is presented is in any way causative or symptomatic of the uprising.

Since there is no established, strong story line to carry the many ministories within the text, readers might more productively move from a futile search for conventional story to an examination of *how* stories are treated in the novel. The focus then falls on Lucas Macías, the grand storyteller and chronicler of the town. Lucas would seem to have a story for everything; current events remind him of past occurrences that he relates in narrative form.

The inclusion of eight stories narrated by Lucas makes him a model of a storyteller-in-the-text and, as well, establishes a revealing identification of conventional storytelling with a traditional narrator. Upon analyzing the way he tells his tales and pondering the reaction of his listeners, however, one questions the efficacy of his methods. Lucas is, in effect, a more fully shaped dramatization of the type of chronicler Azuela critiques in *Los de abajo*. By emphasizing the negative characteristics associated with an extremely personalized accounting, limited in perspective and closed to audience participation, Yáñez leads readers to consider the process of storytelling itself.

If given a free reign and a patient audience, Lucas would never stop. His is a rambling, conversational style, replete with run-on sentences and associative digressions. For the most part, his listeners are tolerant of his loquacity and listen eagerly to his anecdotal historical narratives. Occasionally, however, a member of his public becomes frustrated, as in Chapter 16 (16;2). After a seemingly endless introduction, represented in one extremely long paragraph emphasizing its excess, a listener breaks in: "Bueno, bueno, ¿y qué te contó don Alfredo?" [Well, what did Don Alfredo have to say to you?] (322). Lucas's general strategy is to ignore such interruptions and to continue his narrative.

Apparently recognizing the effect of this type of storytelling on the listener/reader, the narrator mercifully interrupts a few stories that threaten to bore both the public listening to Lucas and the readers of *Al filo del agua*. Although showing compassion for readers, he most abruptly silences Lucas in the middle of a sentence: "Yo no acabaría nunca de contarles las desgracias que ha traído agosto. Familias hay—ustedes lo saben muy bien—que no pasa un año sin que se les muera algún deudo, en agosto, y a veces más . . ." [I could go on forever telling you of the disasters which have happened in August. There are families, as you very well know, where someone dies every August, and sometimes more than one] (256). Readers may be thankful that the threat contained in the first line of this passage is not carried out. But the narrator must intervene, because if there were no interdicting force to stop Lucas's narrative, he would continue until his listeners and Yáñez's readers were exhausted.

Through Lucas, Yáñez has depicted an important stage of his reconstruction of the act of reading: an overexposure of the traditional norm, narrativity without the balance of a limiting form. He makes readers feel the effect of a narrative voice lacking the controlling mechanisms of pacing, the knowledge of what to reveal and when. Essential to this undoing of tradition is the depiction of the listeners' (readers') frustration.

Upon considering the eight segments in which Lucas tells his stories, one realizes that Lucas's interpolated narratives stand in opposition to the full body of *Al filo del agua* in terms of discourse. As for content, they are treating similar material: occurrences within the ambience of a small Mexican town. It is the contrast of *how* they tell their stories that focuses readers' attention on the storytelling process. Yáñez appears to be moving his readers toward a desire for change by pitting himself and his narration against the force of tradition embodied in Lucas.

In contrast to Lucas's long-winded narrative, Yáñez uses structural and sentence fragmentation and, in general, keeps his paragraphs short. In Lucas's narration there is no dialogue; the only point of view is his own. Yáñez makes extensive use of dialogue and interior monologue, opening his narrative through the use of multiple perspective and attaining more objectivity by letting the characters' thoughts and words speak for themselves. Psychological penetration, so characteristic of Yáñez's novel, is not used at all by Lucas; instead, he narrates only events or action. Lucas emerges as a model of an egocentric storyteller who has very little concern for his listeners. Here the pleasure of story is reserved for the narrator.

Through Lucas's negative example, Yáñez brings to the foreground the centrality of the storytelling process in *Al filo del agua*. The interpolated tales encourage readers to discern by opposition more powerful and engaging ways of telling and their resultant involvement with the text. The discourse of *Al filo del agua* works toward achieving a shift in readers' expectations and consciousness by challenging conventions of narrativity. Yáñez demonstrates through his narrative that the passive experience of listening to Lucas's stories is no longer adequate.

Integral to the achievement of reader involvement are the techniques employed by Yáñez that foster an awareness in readers of their assimilated desire for story. From this point of view, the most important strategy to consider is interdiction, the threatened or effected truncation of story. Given that there is very little cohesive plot in the novel, that the segments constituting a continuing tale are few, the most important stories quantitatively would be those of Damián and Micaela, Victoria and Gabriel, and Luis Gonzaga. The tale of Damián and Micaela and Luis's story are dispersed within the fragmented structure of the novel, but that is not the full extent of Yáñez's manipulation of his readers' desires. Playfully, he whets his readers' appetite for story and then makes use of two basic techniques of narrative interdiction: the delay of story by the insertion of digressions and the apparent suspension of storytelling, which leads readers to fear that the narrator has no intention of resuming the tale.

The teasing, playful quality of these techniques is best illustrated by the story of Damián and Micaela. Elaine Haddad and José Rojas Garcidueñas have acknowledged readers' readiness for the episode because of their having recognized portents (Haddad 526; Rojas Garcidueñas 156). To understand Yáñez's manipulation of his readers, however, one must analyze in detail his discursive ploys: how he integrates fragmentation (discourse) and suggestions of an exciting tale (story) to promote readers' consciousness of the narrative process.

The first allusion to what will be later called "La desgracia de Damián" (The Downfall of Damián Limón) in the title of Chapter 13 occurs as early as Chapter 8 (8;10):

> Los planes de Micaela, infaustamente, horriblemente, habían de acabar como los de la lechera que llevaba el cántaro al mercado.
>
> Nefasto día ese dos de mayo en cuya noche Micaela Rodríguez inició relaciones formales con Damián Limón. ¡Desgraciada noche! (174)
>
> [Alas! Micaela's plans, like those of the milkmaid carrying milk to market, ended in disaster.
>
> It was an unlucky day, that May 2, when Micaela Rodríguez set out in earnest to subjugate Damián Limón. A disastrous night!]

Then the matter is totally dropped until Chapter 11 (11;1), which is centered around Padre Islas. Almost as an afterthought, at the very end of a fragment describing the excessive rigidity of the town's spiritual director, the narrator adds, "Luego vino el desastrado caso de Damián y Micaela, que robusteció la temorosa autoridad del Padre Islas" [Then came the dreadful affair of Damián and Micaela, which strengthened Father Islas' authority] (221). In the contiguous segment, the narrator pursues his train of thought, consequently raising readers' expectations. He ends with the following revelation:

> "No puedes esperar más que una muerte violenta, que llene de terror a las gentes"—le dijo una y muchas veces.

Y el pronóstico se cumplió al pie de la letra, por la obcecación de la infeliz. (221)

["You can expect no less than a violent death, which will fill the people with terror."
The Chaplain's warnings were fulfilled to the syllable.]

Now there can be no doubt about readers' interest. They know that there is going to be a violent death and, although it might be lamentable in moral terms, one must acknowledge an attraction to this element of story. Taking advantage of readers' desires, the narrator immediately moves away from the story, adding a teasing gesture: he employs a reference to Damián and Micaela as the point of departure for a section devoted to some of the Hijas de María who also get into trouble by ignoring Padre Islas's advice (11;3). The first words of the fragment are "El caso de Damián y Micaela" (The case of Damián and Micaela),[14] but the subject treated does nothing to illuminate the "event." Subsequently, although Damián and Micaela appear in various fragments, there are no references to the anticipated violence until Chapter 13, the title of which would suggest that readers' desire for story will be satisfied: "La desgracia de Damián." The readers' literary fulfillment, however, will not be reached so easily; there are obstacles ahead.

One readily accepts the narrator's starting with a chorus effect in the first fragment, anonymous voices spreading rumors about the possibility of a forthcoming marriage between Micaela and Damián's father, for this marker of pluralism has been a constant in the novel. The second fragment seems to set the stage by describing the month of August as one of death and misfortune. Appetites are definitely whetted by the end of the third section, in which the narrator warns ominously:

[Micaela] No contaba con el aviso de San Pascual.
　No contaba con el destino. (253)

[She failed to reckon with San Pascual's warning.
　She failed to reckon with fate.]

At this moment of heightened anticipation, there is an interdiction. The intruder interrupting the narrative is, of course, Lucas Macías, who has an unrelated story to tell. Frustration on the readers' part is very likely, as Lucas's digression postpones the desired story of love and violence. Just as probable, however, is the readers' consciousness of their desire for story and of Yáñez's ironic technique of delaying the anticipated tale precisely through the strategy of interpolating another story.

At the end of this section is the above-cited passage in which Lucas is cut off in midsentence. Yáñez's compassion, one hopes, might extend to allowing closure. But the playfulness continues. In the fifth fragment there is a prediction of Micaela's ruin—another warning, another tease. In the sixth Yáñez injects a further postponement, as the narration moves back in time to follow don Timoteo's actions.

The culmination is reached as the narrator skirts around "lo pasado" (what happened), managing to tell his readers nothing, consequently frustrating them even more. There are references to "el momento supremo" [the supreme moment] (261), "La víspera de los hechos" [the night before the deeds] (261), and "cuando éste [Damián] hizo lo que hizo" [when this one (Damián) did what he did] (262). Upon reading the words "la difunta" [the dead woman] (263),[15] readers realize that they have moved beyond the deed in time and still do not know what happened. The delay of story reaches an absurd point when in fragment 8 Damián is in jail after having been beaten by the townspeople for "what he had done." Upon reading the interrogator's question, "¿Por qué has hecho esto?" [Why did you do it?] (263), readers are likely to reach a point of total frustration, as everyone seems to talk around the event without naming it or supplying the desired details.

The final revelation of story is anticlimactic. First the bare facts are presented in a chorus effect from children who glean their information from the adult's gossip. The children reduce the story to a provocative minimum: "'Mató a su padre.' 'Mató a una mujer.' 'Por poco mata al Santo del pueblo.' 'Es un monstruo'" ["He killed his father!" "He killed a woman!" "He nearly killed the village saint!" "He's a monster!"] (264). Appearing sensitive to his readers' reactions yet insistent in his teasing playfulness, Yáñez gives voice to readers' frustration and desire for detail in a self-conscious statement: "Predomina en muchas bocas la pregunta: '¿Cómo fue lo de Padre Islas?'" [Many voices asked the question, "How did Father Islas come into it?"] (264–265).

In answer to the question within the text and to the readers, a partial description is given by a few eyewitnesses, a method very appropriate to *Al filo del agua*, for the readers' knowledge of the story is also partial or fragmented and never reaches completion. In fact, the recounting of "lo de

Damián y Micaela" becomes an interior duplication of the novel, a product of several voices presented in fragmented discourse. A tertiary duplication lies within the eyewitness account, in which Prudencia's emotions prohibit a continuous narrative, leaving her sentences jumbled and segmented. Carrying the fragmentation to the minutest possible level, Yáñez introduces a fourth manifestation in the narrator's description of Prudencia's words, itself a sentence fragment: "Frases inconexas, lagunas de llanto, fugas de respiración, improperios" [Disjointed phrases, interrupted by sobs, sighs, maledictions] (268). In their frustration, readers may begin to perceive a vertiginous quality to the duplication in the sense that the awaited details of story would seem to be delayed by a character's jumbled narration of that same tale. Tension mounts as one realizes that the narrator and, by extension, Yáñez will not provide details. Readers never receive the full story of Damián and Micaela.

Thus Yáñez insists on reader participation by refusing to tell the full tale. Some may well envy the priest who, in the function of his office, is audience to everyone's story and, specifically in this instance, evidently receives more information than readers: "a gritos iban contándole cientos de bocas lo acaecido" [Hundreds of voices shouted out accounts of what had happened] (267). But Yáñez's message to his readers is that if their desire is so great, then it is they who must actively participate and fill in the missing details to form a cohesive narrative. Because he has denied both a continuous and a complete story, it is not just a matter of combining the pieces of the puzzle, but also the process of shaping or creating the missing pieces.

In this manner, Yáñez leads his readers to the discovery of the function of form. Even more importantly, he makes them resent structure imposed arbitrarily by others, thus moving them to intuit the need to assume a more active, participatory role in order to shape the meaning potential in the information provided.

The story of Damián and Micaela reveals a ludic element in the way that the narrator suggests a tale and then suddenly moves away from it, in a type of point-counterpoint in constant movement toward and away from the notion of story. Significantly, this is not an isolated technique reserved for "lo de Damián y Micaela," but can be analyzed as an integrative strategy in Al filo del agua,[16] one that illuminates both Yáñez's approach to narrative and his attitude toward his readers. Yáñez's use of a fragmented structure is perfectly paired with this contrapuntal movement, since upon finishing a fragment, one leaves a character's mini-story to focus on another's. There

is no seamless narrative in the novel. Repeatedly, Yáñez follows a story fragment to a climactic point and then abruptly switches to a completely different focus frequently combined with a change of style and pacing. Sudden changes occur not only between chapters but also between fragments
within chapters. The frequency of the shifts suggests a narrative pattern
that in turn illuminates Yáñez's manipulation of his readers: leading them
toward climax, then pulling away, forcing them into an awareness of their
desire for story.

Understanding this technique helps readers appreciate the positioning
of what to date has been an enigmatic chapter: "Victoria y Gabriel" (Victoria and Gabriel). Haddad has summarized the critics' generally negative
reactions to this chapter, describing it as "an unexpected interlude which
disconcerts and displeases because of its melodramatic overtones" (525).
Rojas Garcidueñas contributes to an unfavorable response, criticizing "Victoria y Gabriel" precisely because of its "cambio de ritmo" [change of
rhythm] (155). On the other hand, John Brushwood views the same chapter as a key element of a symmetrical structure in *Al filo del agua*, arguing
that it serves as a preamble to the second part of the novel, paralleling the
"Acto preparatorio" in function and poetic style ("La arquitectura," 101–
102),[17] and Floyd Merrell maintains that this chapter and the previous
one, "Canicas" (Marbles), are central to Yáñez's depiction of the dialectical
struggle between the sacred and the profane (54). Upon examining the
mixed comments on "Victoria y Gabriel," one finds elements in each that
have relevance to this discussion on narrative strategy: changes of pace;
something that disconcerts; a special placement outside of the narrative
progression because of its seeming inconsistency with previous chapters;
and the poetic quality that is comprehended in a change of style.

In order to probe the seeming intrusion of "Victoria y Gabriel," one
must first examine the end of the previous segment. Chapter 8, "Canicas,"
is approximately the center of the novel, a critical point to be sure, since
Yáñez has stated that during the composition of the work he was uncertain
at that juncture as to the narrative's development and the future of his
characters (Haddad 525). Accepting Yáñez's uncertainty, one still feels led
toward the end of the chapter in the direction of the revolution. The pace
quickens; the fragments are shorter, as are the sentences. Expectations
reach an extremely high point upon reading the final fragment (8;12),
which, in its wording, reveals a significant parallel with the contrapuntal
pacing: "Las canicas van rodando a su final destino, lentas o rápidas, con-

tenidas en algún cruce de caminos, indecisas, luego violentamente precipi-tadas. Como en los juegos de feria, en tablas policromas, con rutas acotadas por clavos. Va rodando la bola" [The marbles were rolling towards their final destiny, some slowly, some swiftly. Some of them hesitated at a cross-slot, and then were pushed violently forward. Just like the games at the Fair, played on painted boards, where the paths are marked out by nails. The ball was rolling! Things were on the move!] (176).[18] In the previous sections there have been references both to "lo de Damián y Micaela" and to political developments. The phrase "Va rodando la bola" could refer to either the personal or social violence deemed imminent. One cannot be sure, even though "la bola" is an accepted metaphor of the Mexican Revolution and thus would seem to prepare readers for an explosion within the political realm.[19] It clearly does not prepare them for what follows: a romantic, poetic, slowly paced examination of an unusual relationship between the town's youthful bell ringer and the sensual widow.

Once again Yáñez has manipulated his readers. This poetic chapter, at the same time that it is a startling change of pace capable of producing frustration, is entirely consistent within the established structural move-ment of the narrative. Upon positioning readers in their expectations, Yáñez then dislodges them yet another time from their assumed placement as pas-sive receiver of story. The cumulative effect of such interdictions encourages readers to question the relationship among author-text-reader. It is obvious that Yáñez has rejected a continuous narrative. His choice of a fragmented structure and his playful refusal to reach any closure are indications of a desire to modify the reader's role. He does not want a passive reader.

Yáñez appears also to recognize and assume the responsibility of edu-cating his public in their new, more active roles as modern readers. An early indication of his inviting reader participation comes in a preface: "Quienes prefieran, pueden intitular este libro *En un lugar del Arzobispado, El antiguo régimen,* o de cualquier modo semejante. Sus páginas no tienen argumento previo; se trata de vidas—*canicas* las llama uno de los protagonistas—que ruedan, que son dejadas rodar en estrecho límite de tiempo y espacio, en un lugar del Arzobispado, cuyo nombre no importa recordar" [Those who wish to do so may call the book *In a Village of the Archdiocese, The Old Order,* or something of the sort. Its pages tell no preconceived story; it deals with lives—"marbles," one of the characters calls them—which roll around, which are allowed to roll round in a narrow stretch of time and space, in a village, any village, of the Archdiocese of Guadalajara].[20] Yáñez indicates that nothing is fixed; readers are free to make of these pieces of life what they will. The suggestion is that readers have the freedom to participate in the creative process by joining the fragments in accordance with their desires, filling in the gaps and searching for the unity evoked within the segments.

As an innovative writer, however, Yáñez appears not entirely convinced that his employment of fragmentation and forms of interdiction are sufficient to stimulate full participation from his readers. In an effort to guide the public, he repeatedly enters the text by means of the narrator. Eduardo Romano has recognized Yáñez's intrusions to correct possible misconceptions, to give his opinion, and to ask rhetorical questions (68–70).[21] Romano concludes that the effect of Yáñez's entrances is that it is finally the author's perspective that predominates despite the apparent objectivity of the fragmented perspectivism (68). Although it is true that Yáñez's intrusions shape his readers' interpretation of events to a certain extent, it is not necessary to conclude that he is pushing his point of view. Instead, one might consider this activity as the mark of an author who wants to make sure that readers comprehend the connections and take advantage of the textual clues he has left. There are so many gaps to be filled creatively that readers will still have an active role to play.

Occasionally, from the point of view of a modern reader, Yáñez's intrusions seem annoying, his guidelines too obvious, as when he reminds readers of something they should know already if they have been reasonably attentive: "(Ignora María que unos oídos de mujer, los oídos de la forastera funesta, sí escucharon la voz de amor en las campanas de Gabriel)" [María did not know that the ears of a woman, the ears of the fatal foreigner, had heard the voice of love in Gabriel's ringing] (313). In fact, Yáñez's intrusions counter the very effect he appears to be seeking. By employing strategies that help shape readers' responses, Yáñez actually denies them a full participatory experience. One faults him for overstating the obvious at times and yet must remain mindful that Yáñez's audience in 1947 might have seemed to him not yet experienced enough to respond fully to the strategies introduced in *Al filo del agua* without some narrative guidelines.

Much more successful are his cues to readers that are contained, if not concealed, within the text and do not surface as intrusions. There are, for example, multiple impetuses toward a unification of the novel within the text's thematics and emphasized images.[22] Yáñez presents textual stimuli to lead readers in their perception from the fragments in *Al filo del agua* to a more comprehensive view that fills the gaps, unites the fragments, and completes the novel.

With a recognized emphasis on constructing readership, it is significant that Lucas Macías again emerges at the end of the novel, this time as a positive role model for unification. Within the perspective of unity, Lucas stands out as a temporal unifier. He is the town chronicler; it is he who keeps track of births and deaths and narrates any description of the town's history. Thus Lucas is the link between the present and the past. But his unifying effect extends even into the future, as he is considered a seer by many. Lucas has a second opportunity, however, to serve as a role model, one that is much more important in terms of a reader's response to the novel as a *whole*. It is Lucas, and Lucas alone, who puts together the pieces of information that have reached the town regarding the revolutionary activity (16;31). All the others are passive, either still submerged in their incommunicative state or not alert enough to bother to look. Lucas does not simply consider the individual pieces but moves beyond them to read a potential whole: revolution. The readers of *Al filo del agua* must imitate Lucas's energy and intelligence in order to transform the fragments of the novel into a whole.[23]

Within the text, Lucas is identified as a spectator of life: "Cronista fiel, carece de historia personal: en la vida sólo ha sido espectador y notario de acontecimientos ajenos" [A faithful chronicler, he has no personal history; all his life he has been merely the observer and recorder of things that have happened to other people] (125). Lucas's lack of history makes of him a type of Everyman and, although one hesitates to use the term Everyreader, it is clear that Lucas speaks directly to the literary experience and aids readers in focusing on their roles. Although the description of Lucas as a spectator of life would seem to reflect a passive reading experience, certain of Lucas's statements lead one to suspect that he has much in common with an active reader. In fact, the inclusion of both types of characteristics suggests that it is never too late to change, that passive readers can become active, exactly what must happen in order to comprehend this new type of novel.

In the course of his "historical" narrations, Lucas frequently describes things he has never seen and is a strong defender of his use of imagination: "Con la imaginación basta y sobra; para mí que es mejor imaginar que ver" [I've got imagination, haven't I? Lots of it. I'd rather imagine than see some things] (126). Just as Lucas uses his imagination to describe things he has never seen, so readers must be creative in filling in the gaps left by the fragmentation in *Al filo del agua*. Transferred to a literary experience, Lucas's statement that it is better to imagine than to see suggests that co-creation is far more pleasurable than passively receiving the author's description or the narrator's version of a continuous story. Despite the momentary frustrations produced by fragmentation and interdictions to story, the final experience is much more fulfilling when readers have accepted an active role. Yáñez is clearly calling for a more participatory action on the part of readers.

In *Al filo del agua* active readers not only fill in the gaps to story but also generate an overview by being mentally active, inspired by the suggestions of life offered in fragmented form. Moreover, on a more significant level, readers enlarge their focus from the notion of story to narrative discourse as they contemplate the multiple examples of storytelling within the novel. More than a cumulative story to be constructed from many smaller stories, *Al filo del agua* would appear to be a self-conscious story of how (not) to tell a story and how (not) to read one.

Is it a story of the Mexican Revolution? The answer is both yes and no. The personal emphasis on the individual characters and their "stories" would appear to stand in opposition to a social or political consideration of the Mexican Revolution, which is given very little space in the novel. Yet part of the role of active readers is to discern Yáñez's statement about the revolution based on what is *not* said in the novel, only suggested. Yáñez leaves no doubt about his insistence on readers' accepting a more active role. The final touch is achieved as the "story" fails to draw to a close even on the last page, "ending" instead with suspension points. There is simply no closure for the readers of *Al filo del agua*; if that is what they want, they must supply it themselves.

Through his denial of a complete, continuous narrative, Yáñez has given readers no choice but to participate in the novel or to remain unfulfilled. At the same time, his use of contrapuntal pacing combined with a fragmented discourse leads readers to direct their attention to the narrative process, a focus that will be continued and expanded in the following decade by Juan Rulfo and Josefina Vicens. Finally, by including a storyteller-in-the-text and a reader-in-the-text, each embodied by Lucas Macías, Yáñez brings to the foreground both ways of writing *and* ways of reading. In effect,

Yáñez profiles modern, active readers, as *Al filo del agua* presents them with a new freedom: they connect, consider, and reconsider. Mexican readership truly "comes of age" (Langford) with *Al filo del agua*, for Yáñez's fragmented discourse has awakened readers to the adjustments they must make in order to advance, with him, into the modern narrative.

# CHAPTER 4

# ADDRESSING THE READING AND WRITING PROCESS

Yáñez's more sophisticated blending of national themes and discursive innovation, combined with an awareness of readership, are expanded upon in the 1950s by two powerful novels, Juan Rulfo's *Pedro Páramo* (1955) and Josefina Vicens's *El libro vacío* (1958). Rulfo's targeting of readers is part of a manipulative strategy that seeks to liberate them within and by means of the process of reading. Vicens privileges the process of writing but also includes ample references to her protagonist as a reader. The authors' treatments are quite different: although both focus on the processes associated with the narrative experience, Vicens's text is much more accessible to the average reader. In addition, Rulfo's novel, although subtle in terms of how it develops a reader-in-the-text, is at the same time more revolutionary in the way it breaks with traditional narrative structure. The artistry reflected in Rulfo's novel has deservedly placed *Pedro Páramo* among the classics in Mexican literature. Although lesser known, Vicens's *El libro vacío* also merits recognition as a text that focuses on the creative process from both a writer's and a reader's point of view. Both writers maintain a profound Mexicanness in ambience without excessive detail of place or character, Rulfo evoking the ruthless power of the *cacique* in rural Mexico and Vicens capturing the atomizing effect of the urban milieu.[1] Their artful use of suggestion rather than elaborate description makes way for readers' involvement in the narrative process.[2]

Rulfo has provided insight into the fragmented quality of his only novel in an interview with Joseph Sommers: "Quise cerrar los capítulos de una manera total" [I tried to close down chapters definitively] ("Los muertos no tienen ni tiempo ni espacio," 19). And indeed he has. Rulfo not only abandons novelistic structure based on chapter divisions but also effectively challenges such traditional notions as narrative linearity, defined time and space, character description, and a stable narrative voice. *Pedro Páramo* conclusively situates the Mexican novel within contemporary innovative narrative and augments the readers' role as a product of its exquisitely constructed confusion. Rulfo achieves a shift in the readers' manner of approaching narrative by means of a sophisticated text that is at once a modern novel with universal value and a regionalistic work that makes manifest the author's love for his native Jalisco and the language of its inhabitants.

Like Yáñez, Rulfo chooses a fragmented novel to effect the liberation of his readers' dependency on story. In formal terms, the two novels have much in common: a great reliance on dialogue and interior monologue, segments that represent different characters' points of view, and no tangible story line of the traditional mold. The most noticeable differences between the works cluster around the notions of time and authorial presence in the text. In contrast to *Al filo del agua*'s basically linear temporality, *Pedro Páramo* makes numerous time jumps. Indeed, often the temporal reference is so nebulous that it is extremely difficult for readers to orient themselves, a fact that leads one critic to state that Rulfo has done away with time (Langford 94). Also, possibly uncertain that his readers would comprehend their role from his manipulation of them through discourse, Yáñez guides them, making the text, through his intrusions, perform a didactic function. Whereas Yáñez's intrusions counteract the liberating effect of his extensive use of dialogue and interior monologue, techniques that should allow a more direct involvement between characters and readers, Rulfo's narration clearly reflects the author's refusal of the conventional power awarded his position. Rulfo relies almost entirely on dialogue and interior monologue, weaving them into a confusing fabric through his use of fragmentation. *Pedro Páramo* effects a repositioning of readers without an authorial presence.

## Juan Rulfo, *Pedro Páramo*

In *Pedro Páramo* (1955),[3] Rulfo presents an allegory of reading within the text, exemplified by a fictional character, Juan Preciado, who serves as surrogate for readers. Rulfo's strategy is to bond readers to their fictional counterpart as a means of repositioning them in their relation to the text and eliciting from them a liberated, active response to a similarly emancipated discourse. *Pedro Páramo* is a novel released from the constraints of traditional narrative practices into the status of a writerly text (Barthes 4). Of even greater importance is the fact that the reading of this novel can be translated into a process of liberation for readers, as they are dislodged from their conventional conditioning to a passive experience.

Although much has been written about the formal innovations of Rulfo's narrative, one needs to understand the context in which these techniques operate, the context supplied by readers. Instead of asking why the author uses certain narrative strategies, one should question what happens when he does. Thus the focus falls on the effects caused by Rulfo's carefully constructed narrative: the joining of the act of reading with the allegory of reading, resulting in a repositioning of readers.

There are no passages of didactic prose to orient readers to a new active role, as there will be later with Julio Cortázar's use of "Morelliana" in *Rayuela* (1963). This is Rulfo's way of engaging readers, forcing them to work with the text itself. Indeed, part of Rulfo's achievement is that he alters the act of reading from within the structure of assumed narrative conventions. His desire to liberate readers has infiltrated the novel, but without the mark of the author; it has become the project of the text.

To illustrate this process, two fundamental aspects of the reading of *Pedro Páramo* need to be explored: the stages through which readers move as they respond to the syntagmatic arrangement of fragments and the discovery of the project of the text as the readers' emancipation from traditional fictional norms. An examination of how the author has constructed this segmented, confusing novel reveals how Rulfo creates, through textual strategies, a dependency between readers and Juan Preciado and then, by subverting this bondage, forces readers into an acceptance of discourse itself as the impulse toward a complete literary experience. In order to comprehend fully Rulfo's manipulative finesse, one must be led by the manner of the telling and by the reader response that the sequencing of segments generates.

In its revised edition *Pedro Páramo* consists of seventy fragments ranging in length from three lines (segment 65) to eight or nine pages (fragments 31 and 41).[4] Other than fragmentation, there is no further formal structural division of the parts within the text, although most critics are in general agreement that there is an implicit two-part structure marked by readers' awareness of Juan Preciado's death in segment 37.[5] Such an arrangement would divide the novel into two approximately equal parts based on the number of fragments: Part 1: 1–36; Part 2: 37–70.

Part 1 is centered around Juan Preciado's search for his father, a feared and hated *cacique* whose ruthless actions in obtaining land through cunning or force reflect the basic inequalities and sense of injustice that led to the revolution. The section includes his encounter with deceased residents of Comala, where his father Pedro Páramo lived, interspersed with the words of Juan's mother, Dolores; scenes from Pedro's childhood as well as illustrative episodes from his more recent past; and the funeral of Miguel Páramo, Pedro's son. Part 2 focuses more directly on Pedro Páramo, presenting various episodes from his past, but also includes dialogues among other characters, some again with reference to Miguel Páramo's death. The novel ends with two revelations: Comala dies because, upset by the festive activity after Susana's death, Pedro folds his arms, literally and figuratively, and lets the town waste away; and Pedro has died at the hands of his illegitimate son, Abundio.

Although to someone unfamiliar with the novel these two deaths might seem to indicate an end to story in the traditional sense, readers have known these facts from the start. As early as the end of fragment two, some five pages into the novel, one reads in a dialogue between two men known only as a son of Pedro Páramo and a muleteer who claims a similar relationship:

> —No, yo preguntaba por el pueblo [Comala], que se ve tan solo, como si estuviera abandonado. Parece que no lo habitara nadie.
> —No es que lo parezca. Así es. Aquí no vive nadie.
> —¿Y Pedro Páramo?
> —Pedro Páramo murió hace muchos años. (12)

> ["No, I was asking about the town, which looks so lonely, as if it were abandoned. It seems like nobody lives there."
> "It's not that it looks like it. That's the way it is. Nobody lives here."
> "And Pedro Páramo?"
> "Pedro Páramo died many years ago."]

Considering this knowledge, one can hardly view the novel's end as a denouement in a conventional sense. As Joseph Sommers points out, Rulfo denies his readers the pleasure of suspense regarding the outcome of the work: "Death as a narrative vantage point heightens the sense of inexorability. The fate of those whose lives are recalled is viewed from a perspective which reduces the importance of anecdote and conflict, since climax and resolution are cut off in advance" (*After the Storm*, 74).

Yet *Pedro Páramo* begins with every appearance of being a traditional novel. Readers are brought into the fiction by a first-person narrator who, although unidentified, feeds the readers' narrative assumptions by seeming to direct his tale to them. Readers are further nestled into a passive role by the narrator's invocation to story: "Vine a Comala porque me dijeron que acá vivía mi padre, un tal Pedro Páramo. Mi madre me lo dijo" [I came to Comala because they told me that my father lived here, a guy named Pedro Páramo. My mother told me about it] (7). Just as the narrator has awakened in them an interest in his father's story, so readers expect to be told a double tale: that of Pedro Páramo, since he has been identified before the narrator and his name serves as the title of the novel, and that of a son's search for his father, which offers a mythic dimension to the story (Colina, "Susana San Juan," 19–21; Ortega, "La novela de Juan Rulfo," 76–87). Readers begin to identify with the narrator, later revealed to be Juan Preciado, and with his search for the story of Pedro Páramo.

As in all fragmented texts, the first gap in the narrative makes readers search instinctively for the nexus between the first and second segments. There is an isolating frame to the first section, however, as it begins and ends with the same phrase: "vine a Comala" (I came to Comala). The short paragraph at the start of fragment two provides little help in breaking this closure and relating the contiguous section, for it is a general statement about the hot August breeze. There then follows a confusing change in discourse, as the text goes from regular type to italics, enclosing the italicized words within quotation marks. Someone is speaking, but who? After a brief conversation between two unidentified people (one can be naturalized as the narrator asking about Comala), readers again encounter the italicized commentary, but this time there is a strong indication that it represents the words of the narrator's mother.

Subsequently the text returns to the dialogue regarding Comala; the voices remain unidentified, but readers feel secure in the assumption that one is the narrator, as the latter affirms that he is going to Comala to see his father. The other voice is obstinate in its anonymity: "oí que me preguntaban [I heard that they were asking me] (8); "dijo él" [he said] (8). The text's refusal to identify the nature of this voice becomes quite blatant: "volví a oír la voz del que iba allí a mi lado" [I again heard the voice of the person at my side] (9). Only retrospectively will readers grasp the text's conditioning them to experience voice without name, without body.

The narrator does not fare any better, as his interlocutor says to him: "Sea usted quien sea, se alegrará de verlo" [Whoever you are, he will be happy to see you] (9). Within the second fragment, however, readers do learn the profession of the unidentified companion, a muleteer, and quickly add to that information the stated fact that he, too, is a son of Pedro Páramo. The immediately contiguous traditional death image, crows passing above, is difficult to interpret in a first reading and perhaps remains unnoticed by many readers. By the time they learn of Pedro Páramo's death at the hands of Abundio, it is quite possible that readers have forgotten that the latter is the muleteer from the beginning of the novel (Leal, "La estructura de Pedro Páramo," 52).

The second fragment draws to a close in more confusion. First there is a sudden shift from the past tense to the present (11), leading readers to believe that there might be a temporal present in the narrative of which they have been unaware. Yet the very next paragraph remains in the present tense, although apparently it refers to the same situation previously narrated in the past. There are no further clues, for the remaining dialogue is not linked temporally. There seems to be no distinction between past and present.

In the first paragraph of fragment 3, one again notes ambiguous references to time: "Era la hora en que todos los niños juegan en las calles de todos los pueblos, llenando con sus gritos la tarde. Cuando aún las paredes negras reflejan la luz amarilla del sol" [It was the time when all the children play in the streets of all the towns, filling the afternoon with their shouts. When the black walls still reflect the yellow light of the sun] (12). This nonspecificity is reinforced three paragraphs later as the narrator states, "Fui andando por la calle real en esa hora" [I went walking on the main street at that hour] (12).

After the text repeats its refusal to identify the muleteer, referring to him as *aquel fulano* [that guy] (12), readers are confronted with more confusion. The narrator reports the sighting of a woman who disappears and then reappears. Again, this description of her can make little sense as of a first reading: "Me di cuenta que su voz estaba hecha de hebras humanas, que su boca tenía dientes y una lengua que se trababa y destrababa al hablar, y que sus ojos eran como todos los ojos de la gente que vive sobre la tierra" [I realized that her voice was made of human thread, that her mouth had teeth and a tongue that moved upon speaking, and that her eyes were like the eyes of everyone who lives on earth] (13). It is only retrospectively, as readers gradually come to the realization that most of the people with whom the (still unidentified)[6] narrator has contact are dead, that they can appreciate the need to comment that a particular woman looks like a living human being.

At the end of fragment 3, the sense of confusion merges with a feeling of unreality, as the narrator knocks at a door that apparently does not exist, for his hand makes contact only with air. Once again, there is a voice with no name, a woman's voice asking him to enter. Fragment 4, a flashback to the narrator's departure from the muleteer, sheds light on the woman's identity (doña Eduviges) and also reveals the name of the muleteer (Abundio). Segment 5 is joined to fragment three by the repetition of the words "Pase usted" (Come in), spoken by doña Eduviges. This technique, the reiteration of dialogue and images, will prove useful to readers as they move through the text with respect to the orientation and identification of fragments and speakers. Perhaps the best-known example of this strategy is the joining of segments 12 and 18 by the words "Más te vale" (So much the better for you).

Despite the uncertainties—the lack or postponement of identification, the sense of unreality—readers can piece together a bit of coherence from fragments 1 through 5, as they all involve a somewhat linear treatment of the narrator's journey to Comala in search of his father's story. Readers are no longer bothered by the italicized comments by Juan's mother, since they have become an accepted part of the discourse and therefore have been naturalized within the reading experience.

With fragment 6, however, any sense the most diligent reader might have constructed is shattered. Suddenly, the narration changes from first to third person, and the content apparently has nothing to do with the previous segments. After a very poetic opening paragraph describing natural elements after a rain storm, there follows an abrupt change: "¿Qué tanto haces en el excusado, muchacho?" [Why are you taking so long in the bathroom, young man?] (18). After a brief exchange between mother and son, there are three paragraphs, enclosed within quotations, directed to Susana San Juan. Luis Leal rightly concludes that these are the child Pedro's thoughts, although the wording is decidedly not juvenile (*Pedro Páramo*, 22, nn. 3, 4). Then, once again comes a jolting interdiction to the thoughts:

"Tus labios estaban mojados como si los hubiera besado el rocío."
—Te he dicho que te salgas del excusado, muchacho. (18)

["Your lips were wet, as if kissed by the dew."
"I told you to get out of the bathroom, young man."]

And so the text will continue to display interdictions among fragments and within fragments, sweeping among Juan's encounters, Pedro's childhood, reminiscences of other characters, some identified, others not. Occasionally, a few consecutive fragments will reveal linear coherence: Fulgor's participation in the wedding arrangements between Pedro and Juan's mother, Dolores; Juan's strange encounter with Donis and his sister/wife. But the text never returns to *one* narrative line, continuing instead with an intentionally jumbled and disturbing series of pieces of story.

Consequently, readers may react in various ways. They attempt to (re)order the fragments, trying to make them come closer to their preconceived notions of narrativity. They search for textual signifiers: images or scraps of dialogue that serve to join at least some of the fragments and, in some instances, to identify the speaker. Finally, they cling to Juan Preciado's first-person narration as the only apparently stable story line within the narrative. His is the one fragmented, disjunctive, and yet basically continuous story that readers can discern.

In essence, Juan Preciado becomes the embodiment of the reader-in-the-text. Readers have already identified with his search for his father and have assumed Juan's curiosity as their own; collectively readers are, with Juan, active seekers of story. The identification becomes even closer when, as surrogate reader, Juan reacts in wonder as he realizes that the majority of those he meets are dead; he voices the readers' sense of bewilderment combined with curiosity as he tries to decipher the strange ambience. Juan gradually accepts the fact that he is conversing with *almas en pena* (lost souls) just as readers begin to naturalize that very strange aspect of the narrative. Readers move with Juan through the stage in which he queries, "¿Está usted viva, Damiana?" [Are you alive, Damiana?] (56) to the inverted "¿No están ustedes muertos?" [Aren't you dead?] (61) asked of the incestuous couple.

This sense of comfort through identification with Juan Preciado, however, is a snare. Rulfo positions his readers into a tenuous feeling of security only to dislodge them quite forceably, about halfway through the novel, at the beginning of what is generally called Part 2. There it is revealed that

Juan Preciado is dead and shares a tomb with Dorotea. Although they had come to accept the fact that a majority of the characters in *Pedro Páramo* were deceased, readers most likely had not suspected that the narrator might also be dead. His being dead violates specific notions of traditional narrativity. With this realization, readers experience a definite, violent loss of innocence as to their relationship with the text. And one is likely to view this as a calculated move on Rulfo's part upon comprehension of the full impact of Juan's relationship with Dorotea: his story was not directed to readers at all, but to the woman who shares his tomb. Readers have been repositioned from their status as receivers of story; they have been decentered.

Curiously, there is a paragraph very early in the novel that not only prefigures this sense of abandonment but also leads to a notion of subsequent freedom. If Juan Preciado is a surrogate reader-in-the-text, a reevaluation of the passage seems most significant: "Yo creía que aquella mujer estaba loca. Luego ya no creí nada. Me sentí en un mundo lejano y me dejé arrastrar. Mi cuerpo, que parecía aflojarse, se doblaba ante todo, había soltado sus amarras y cualquiera podía jugar con él como si fuera de trapo" [I thought that that woman was crazy. Then I didn't think anything. I felt that I was in a far-away world, and I let myself be pulled in. My body, which seemed to fall limp, bent before any obstacle. It had left its moorings and anyone could play with it as if it were a rag] (17). The location of these words further strengthens their importance, for they come at the end of the fifth fragment, immediately before the text loses what little coherence it had built in terms of Juan Preciado's journey. Although it is doubtful that readers are ready at this point to experience the parallel literary release, this is precisely the reaction that must take place in order to appreciate fully Rulfo's text.

If the readers' liberation from the confines of traditional fictional norms has not been achieved by the halfway mark, surely it must take place there, as it is impossible for them to continue beyond this fragment from within a conventional framework. Manuel Durán argues that fragment 37 necessitates a reinterpretation of all the preceding material (*Tríptico mexicano*, 49, n. 10). If one examines a particular passage from this section, the discourse's insistence upon a reevaluation, a rereading, becomes clear:

> [Dorotea] Mejor no hubieras salido de tu tierra. ¿Qué viniste a hacer aquí?

[Juan] Ya te lo dije en un principio. Vine a buscar a Pedro Páramo, que según parece fue mi padre. Me trajo la ilusión. (77)

[(Dorotea) It would have been better if you had not left home. Why did you come here?
(Juan) I already told you at the beginning. I came to look for Pedro Páramo, who apparently was my father. An illusion brought me here.]

Juan's words are most significant. Indeed he did tell Dorotea his motives earlier, at the *beginning* of the novel ("en un principio"). The reference is quite literal. In addition, the word *ilusión* is a direct connector with the first fragment, as one notes upon a rereading: "Hasta que ahora pronto comencé a llenarme de sueños, a darle vuelo a las ilusiones" [And then I began to fill myself with dreams, to let the illusions fly] (7). In retrospect, it is easy to trace a relationship from Juan's projected illusions about his father to the readers' illusions of story that, having been set loose at the beginning of the novel, are so effectively destroyed in fragment 37. Juan Preciado's words support his self-referential function as a reader-in-the-text paralleling the activities of the novel's implied reader.

The bonding between the readers and Juan has been broken. Thus it should come as no surprise that Juan's presence in the second half of *Pedro Páramo* is greatly diminished. His job is done; he can rest now. Dislodged from their conventional status as receivers of story, readers look to the text itself. Discourse alone is now sufficient to induce readers to reread, to reevaluate, and to flow with the text. The rereading promoted by Nabokov and Barthes as the activity of an active, involved reader is demanded in *Pedro Páramo* through the agency of manipulative discursive strategies.

Such an impulse to reread based on discourse alone can be found at the end of the novel, where one discerns more than one connector with the beginning. The more commonly cited circularity is the presence of Abundio, as the assassin of Pedro Páramo at the end and as Juan Preciado's guide at the beginning (Leal, "La estructura," 52; O'Neill, "*Pedro Páramo*," 311). There is also the powerful image of hands. Pedro's hands as he is dying— "Sintió que su mano izquierda, al querer levantarse, caía muerta sobre sus rodillas" [he felt that his left hand, upon trying to rise, fell dead on his knees] (157)—acquire special importance when they are reinforced within half a page by "Quiso levantar su mano para aclarar la imagen; pero sus piernas la retuvieron como si fuera de piedra. Quiso levantar la otra mano y fue cayendo despacio, de lado, hasta quedar apoyada en el suelo como una muleta deteniendo su hombro deshuesado" [He tried to lift his hand to make the image clearer, but his legs held it as if it were made of stone. He tried to lift the other hand and it fell slowly to the side until it found itself propped on the floor like a crutch holding up his boneless shoulder] (158). By giving so much attention to the image, Rulfo symbolically joins Pedro's hands with those of Dolores Preciado in the first fragment: "y de tanto decírselo se lo seguí diciendo aun después que a mis manos les costó trabajo zafarse de sus manos muertas" [and because of telling it to her so many times, I kept on telling her even after I had difficulty disengaging my hands from her dead hands] (7). These exceptionally forceful inducements to reread are reinforced by numerous instances within the text of isolated statements of ambiguous references that are clarified only in later fragments. Samuel O'Neill comments on this strategy, rightly concluding that one effect of this technique is to keep readers involved ("*Pedro Páramo*," 311–312).[7] But let us not overlook the fact that the attention factor also works in reverse: the later revelations force readers into a reconsideration of what was already read.

Readers move forward and backward, reevaluating whole sections and individual references to characters. Much of this activity can occur during a first reading, as readers work with the text to discern patterns and connections. The text's insistence upon a rereading, however, helps fulfill the potential for an even richer literary experience. Illustrating this phenomenon is an evocative image in *Pedro Páramo*: the last words of the text that, by virtue of their location, are imbued with extra significance: "Se apoyó en los brazos de Damiana Cisneros e hizo intento de caminar. Después de unos cuantos pasos cayó, suplicando por dentro; pero sin decir una sola palabra. Dio un golpe seco contra la tierra y se fue desmoronando como si fuera un *montón de piedras*" [He leaned on Damiana Cisneros's arms and tried to walk. After a few steps he fell, pleading from within, but without uttering a single word. He dropped hard against the ground and began to crumble as if he were a *mountain of stones*] (159, emphasis added). Certain possibilities of interpretation regarding this image could be made without a rereading. Julio Ortega has noted the semantic linkage of Pedro with *piedra* [stone] ("La novela de Juan Rulfo," 85). One might then read the final paragraph as the ultimate blending of the man, Pedro Páramo, and the land, Comala. Even without the symbolism of the name, such an interpretation would have been possible, but the decomposition of *Pedro* into a heap of *piedras* after falling to the earth makes this reading even more forceful. In addition, this particular image is a remarkable reflection of the novel's discourse: *un mon-tón de piedras* can be conceptualized as a whole made up of individual parts, at once a symbol of unity and of fragmentation, thus capturing not only the composition of the text but its implied reading as well.

The force of this image, in turn, makes one more sensitive to nuances and new significances of other imagery upon a reconsideration of the novel. Most noticeable, perhaps, are the images that reproduce the wording of the last phrase (94, 101–102, 111). In addition to references to fragmentation and unity that are linked through exact words, there are also abundant instances of images that call attention only to a fragmented status: "Su sombra descorrida hacia el techo, larga, desdoblada. Y las vigas del techo la devolvían en pedazos, despedazada" [His shadow drawn toward the ceiling, long, bent. And the ceiling's beams returned it in pieces, all broken up] (22). This is one of the more obvious examples of imagery that reflects a whole breaking into parts, all seeming to make manifest the segmented, trun-cated, or fragmented whole that is *Pedro Páramo.*[8]

With such a self-conscious emphasis on the status of fragmentation, a logical, active response is for readers to question the concept of unity in the novel. Significantly, almost every scholar writing on Rulfo's text offers a version of unity in *Pedro Páramo.* Thematic unifiers have been suggested by a number of critics. George Ronald Freeman's extensive work, *Paradise and Fall in Rulfo's 'Pedro Páramo,'* reveals unity through the notion of a fall from grace (4/2).[9] Other thematic unifiers are offered by Carlos Fuentes (nature) ("*Pedro Páramo,*" 58), Julio Ortega (the mythic search) ("La novela de Juan Rulfo," 83), and Ricardo Estrada (death) (124). Enrique Pupo-Walker joins theme and structure in his argument that "antithesis" is a unifier that be-lies the appearance of a series of isolated nuclei. Among Pupo-Walker's examples are the contrastive elements life and death, the water motif and dry land, Comala in Juan's eyes and his mother's idealized version, and the characters' slow-paced monologues and their turbulent emotional state (123–127). Luis Leal ties the notion of unity to the reader's role through his identification of an association of character with motif. According to Leal, readers gradually make a connection between the world of Pedro Pá-ramo and the appearance of water as a recurring image ("La estructura," 49–50). In this sense, the use of a motif unifies in a double way, through pure repetition and as an aid for the identification of voice, which serves to unify specific passages. Analogously, Susana San Juan is paired with light, Dolores with the wind, Miguel with falling stars, and Pedro's father with gray sky. In addition to the repetition of motifs, Leal points to the retelling of certain episodes in both parts of the novel (the death of Miguel Páramo) and unity through character (Abundio's roles at the beginning and the end) ("La estructura," 51–52). Interestingly, other critics have supported the notion of unity through character, although their choice of character is different. Freeman and José de la Colina see Pedro Páramo as unifier, and Colina even finds an echo of discourse in his interpretation that the other characters are fragments of Pedro (Freeman, *Paradise and Fall*, 1/27; Colina, "Notas sobre Juan Rulfo," 54). Mariana Frenk cites Comala as the protagonist, hence unifier, of the novel (37), which would find support in Rulfo's own statement, "Hay que notar que algunos críticos toman como personaje central a Pedro Páramo. En realidad es el pueblo" [It should be noted that some critics see Pedro Páramo as the central character. Actually, it is the town] (Sommers, "Los muertos," 19). Finally, both Pupo-Walker and Leal mention the text's poetic tone as a unifying element (Pupo-Walker, 133; Leal, "La estructura," 54).

Such a variety of response when speaking of unity attests to the outstanding qualities of *Pedro Páramo*. Rulfo's text is a very carefully constructed pluralistic novel that demands a response from all readers. The fact that critics have supplied so many visions of unity reinforces the notion of an active response to an enigmatic text and demonstrates that *Pedro Páramo* is a *unified* fragmented novel. Rulfo appears to have had a firm vision of the whole when writing this novel and has managed to convey a sense of that vision with artistry, without constraining readers. Rulfo succeeds in freeing his public from their assumed narrative conventions by means of a complicated discourse that, without blatant, exterior guidelines, maneuvers readers through the stages of (1) traditional assumptions, (2) attempts at coherence, (3) shock of dislodgement, and (4) adjustment to a liberated status through reassessment, rereading, and a free-flowing enjoyment. He has staged a literary revolution before our eyes.[10] Rulfo honors his readers by presenting them with a pluralistic text that engages and liberates—a paradox perhaps, but when associated with the reading experience of *Pedro Páramo*, it enables one to intuit a meaning for a simple and sweet complexity.

## Josefina Vicens, *El libro vacío* (The Empty Book)

In contrast to Rulfo's constructed disorder, Josefina Vicens's use of fragmentation is more thematic than discursive. The consistent employment of self-referential comments on writing, combined with the presence of a number of stories on a microlevel rather than a sustained tale in a more conventional vein, however, contributes to an analogous shifting of readers' focus from the notion of story itself to a consideration of the *process* involved in the articulation of experience (narrativization) and, on a more subtle level, the act of reading. Vicens's narrator/writer emphasizes for readers the difference between *El libro vacío* and traditional norms by making reference to both conventional narrative practice and the ways in which his efforts fail to conform.

Technically, the text is divided into twenty-nine sections (some might say chapters), ranging from a minimum of two paragraphs (79)[11] to a maximum of nineteen pages (139–157). The irregularity of length favors the designation of sections or fragments rather than the more traditional term chapters. Although unnumbered, the units stand clearly apart, as each starts on a right-hand page. Internal fragmentation is limited to three instances (166, 209, 227), when the narrator states that he cannot continue with the previous train of thought. In these cases, the break is presented as a blank space.

*El libro vacío* is not so much a fragmented text that flaunts its status as a nonwhole as it is a novel about fragmentation in the sense of marginalization either self-imposed or as a consequence of social conditions. While one might have hoped for a female protagonist from a female author, Vicens's narrator is male, fifty-six-year-old José García, an office worker who is married and has two children.[12] *El libro vacío* chronicles José's attempt to write and, paradoxically, to break with his obsession for writing. His plan is to keep two notebooks; in one he will feel free to experiment and in the other he will record only the best, the most polished sections from the first. Consequently, the second notebook remains untouched, hence the title of Vicens's narrative.[13] At the novel's end, José is still searching for that elusive first sentence.

What José does write, however, is very revealing of himself, his familial relationships, his roles as defined by Mexico's patriarchal society and interpreted in a self-analytic way, and, most importantly, the practice of writing.[14] From the start, José establishes the tenets of his writing code and then proceeds to break with them, especially with the notions that he would not write about himself (179) nor use a first-person narration (28). Instead, readers receive a picture of a man isolated from his family, in part literally, as he hides away in a separate room in order to pursue his literary vocation, and in part figuratively, as revealed by his inner thoughts concerning the lack of communication among family members. Unable to express his feelings to his wife or children, he writes retrospectively what he might have said or what he would like to have communicated. Significantly, the characteristics described here are clear dramatizations of the traits outlined in Octavio Paz's *El laberinto de la soledad* (1950; The Labyrinth of Solitude), which advanced a view of the soul of Mexico. Both Vicens and Carlos Fuentes, who published his first novel, *La región más transparente,* in the same year that *El libro vacío* was published, present male characters rooted in aspects of Mexican culture as presented by Paz.

José's relationships, not only with his family but with his colleagues as well, are governed by society's codified roles. As Paz describes, Mexican males are not allowed to be too intimate or to reveal their true feelings. They must at all times be aware of their presence as perceived by others. José considers from an early age what it means to be a man, and frequently readers are privy to a male's consciousness regarding machismo. The concept of male and female roles is omnipresent, whether in relation to the younger generation, as in the problems relating to the younger José's infatuation with a waitress, or pertaining to the narrator's relationship with his wife, who remains nameless throughout, known only by her function in José's life: *mi mujer* (my wife; more literally, my woman). More than once, as characters respond to their circumstances, it is made clear that they are following a prescribed pattern of behavior, even voicing the lack of choice regarding their response: "no podía hacer otra cosa" [there was nothing else that I could do] (143),[15] or a variation thereof (137).

José's words reveal his sense of marginalization on multiple levels. His work at the office is boring, and he has few colleagues whom he can truly call friends. Of the two workers about whom José writes extensively, one's embezzlement case provokes more of an opportunity to write creatively than any sense of sympathy, and the other's main function is to advise him, from a fixed masculine point of view, about an extramarital affair. Even when José enters into a relationship with a mistress, his focus is on himself, for his stated interest is to find out what kind of woman would select *him* as a potential lover. José's sense of himself, finally, is that of a mediocre human being, one of the group he calls "nosotros" [we] as opposed to "ellos" [they] (168), both terms defined by class standing, with *nosotros* representing the lower working class. Yet, despite the collectivity implied in the first-person plural, there is no indication of a true sense of belonging on José's part. The emphasis is on exclusion.

José's feelings of isolation are manifested in the recurring theme of solitude that lies at the core of Paz's analysis. José's attitude is that man is all alone in the world, in birth and in death, and this notion of man would seem to be of gender rather than species: "pensaba en los hombres y en su gran soledad. Pensaba que llegamos al mundo solos, terriblemente solos . . . el hombre nace solo. Y que igual que nace, permanece y muere solo" [I would think of man and his great solitude. I'd think that we come into the world alone, terribly alone . . . man is born alone. And just as he is born, so does he remain and die alone] (103). Feeling marginalized from his family and colleagues, José turns to a solitary pursuit, writing.

It is precisely José's obsession with creative expression that provides the focus on the process of writing. Yet even the creative process causes more anxiety than pleasure for him. He is dissatisfied with the majority of his efforts and frequently laments his inability to capture exactly what he wants in an image or a description. As he expresses frustration concerning his failures, he draws to the readers' attention more traditional character-istics of narrative that then stand in contrast with the book they are read-ing. Foremost among his disappointments are his efforts in physical descrip-tion of characters, plot, and environment (30–32), which reinforce the perception of his initial project as a conventional narrative: "Mi propósito, al principio, era escribir una novela. Crear personajes, ponerles nombre y edad, antepasados, profesión, aficiones. Conectarlos, trenzarlos, hacer de-pender a unos de otros y lograr de cada uno un ejemplar vigoroso y atrac-tivo o repugnante o temible" [My goal in the beginning was to write a novel, to create characters, to give them names and ages, ancestors, profes-sions, and interests; to interconnect them, weave them, make them depend on each other, and make of each one a vigorous and attractive or perhaps a repugnant or fearsome example] (30). José's lament brings to mind an-other example of contrastive discourse, that of Alain Robbe-Grillet in his examination of character in the *nouveau roman* within his collection of theo-retical essays, *For a New Novel*. For Robbe-Grillet, the notion of character as described by José is entombed in the nineteenth-century past, as indicated in this wry description:

> A character—everyone knows what the word means. It is not a ba-
> nal *he*, anonymous and transparent, the simple subject of the action
> expressed by the verb. A character must have a proper name, two if
> possible: a surname and a given name. He must have parents, a he-
> redity. He must have a profession. If he has possessions as well, so

much the better. Finally, he must possess a "character," a face which reflects it, a past which has molded that face and that character. His character dictates his actions, makes him react to each event in a determined fashion. His character permits the reader to judge him, to love him, to hate him. It is thanks to his character that he will one day bequeath his name to a human type, which was waiting, it would seem, for the consecration of this baptism. (27; quotations and emphasis in the original)

Having abandoned the idea of writing a "novel" inscribed within conventional norms, José turns to more of a journal in which he records both recent and childhood experiences and sensations punctuated at all times by his reactions-*cum*-analysis of *how* he has written them more than of actual content. Apparently, nothing satisfies him; there is nothing suitable for that second notebook. He laments that he cannot capture the essence of his grandmother or the metaphysical thoughts provoked by the late afternoon, yet it is just when he describes his failures that he succeeds in doing precisely what he feels incapable of achieving. At these moments, there is a fluidity in the prose expressed graphically in the form of elongated paragraphs.[16]

There is a consistent self-consciousness about José's writing, a metanarrative commentary that addresses various issues pertinent to the process of writing, leading John Brushwood to describe *El libro vacío* as the first clearly self-referential novel in Mexican literature (*La novela mexicana*, 51). Although some of José's thoughts may seem frivolous, as does his temporary impulse to write an escapist book designed to entertain, "un relato ameno" [a pleasant story] (173), other comments go right to the core of an author's considerations. At one point he claims to write what he feels (88), while later he laments that feelings, when transcribed into literary language, lose their strength and authenticity (109). More than once there are reflections on the immense difference between written words and everyday speech (107, 109), with repeated reference to the deformation inherent in the process of narrativization (167). It is, finally, the simple words that prevail, both in José's conscious consideration of the process of writing and in the fragments that constitute *El libro vacío*: "mis palabras sencillas, que expresan mis verdades y mi vida, sencillas también" [(my) simple words that express my truths and my life, which is also very simple] (107).

A good example of the successful focus on the commonplace or quotidian elements of life and narrative is José's version of his colleague's embezzlement case. Although at first enthusiastic about the prospect of writing an account of his fellow worker's plight, José never realizes a descriptive treatment of the full circumstances and trial. Instead, his narrative is centered on two simple objects, a red handkerchief and a gift watch, both of which bring to the foreground the humanity and pathos of the characters and their circumstances (161–170).

José's feelings as expressed in his journal are similarly focused on the simple, everyday occurrences of his life. A remarkable sensitivity is revealed at times in the narrator's thoughts regarding his children. One must bear in mind, however, that this is a female writer's enunciation of male consciousness, which may well bring readers to consider the possibility of gendered discourse. Of particular interest is a woman writer's interpretation of both a male's sense of machismo and a husband's thoughts regarding marital roles. José's journal contains numerous passages that are provocative with regard to one's understanding of the male psyche. Feeling that his wife cannot possibly understand his need to write, he makes readers privy to words he would like to say to her in explanation of his source of irritation toward her: "Te trato mal porque me molesta tu equilibrio, porque no puedo tolerar tu sencillez. Te trato mal porque detesto a las gentes que no son enemigas de sí mismas" [I treat you badly because your composure bothers me, because I can't tolerate your simplicity. I treat you badly because I detest people who aren't their own enemies] (22). When he has been particularly unfair to her, he observes: "Como de costumbre no contestó, no se defendió" [As usual, she didn't reply and she didn't stick up for herself] (73). At one point, some strange force seems to take over, and he in a sense observes himself acting out masculine behavior as codified by society's notion of machismo (121–125).

Yet despite, or perhaps because of, José's recorded attitudes and feelings, one senses the presence of a strong female in the unnamed wife, which allows Vicens to belie Paz's generalized view of passive females. As José struggles with his writing and with his narcissistic analyses, it is she who manages the household budget on his meager salary, she who handles all practical matters. Although she very likely is aware of his affair, she says nothing, which upsets José, since if he had the opportunity to fight with her, it might ease his conscience somewhat (143).

It is precisely José's affair with Lupe Robles that enables Vicens to reveal the childishness of his behavior. Since she is using a first-person narrator, and José's self-awareness is not such that he could consciously recognize his puerile comportment, Vicens employs reiteration of language that, when noticed by readers, reveals her message. Specific elements of José's affair at age fifty-one parallel those of an earlier sexual encounter when he was fourteen. As a youth, José maintained a masochistic relationship with an older woman. Despite their physical pleasure at night, she would coldly reject him toward morning, forcing him to leave. Although clearly angered by this treatment, José continued to return while at the same time threatening to leave her forever (93–96). Although circumstances differ, José's later involvement reflects the same inability to break the relationship combined with the very specific wording, "le juraba que iba a dejarla para siempre" [I'd swear to her that I'd leave her forever] (145). Thus language both joins the two episodes and suggests meaning beyond the actual phrases, encouraging readers to find other parallels.

Despite the fact that Vicens's use of fragmentation is not as demanding as that employed by Rulfo in the sense that her readers are not disoriented by the lack of coherence from a syntagmatic reading, it seems likely that she is aware of potential response because of the textual clues she leaves. On a rather superficial level, one notes José's addressing of his journal to a plural audience by his use of a *ustedes* command, "créanme" [believe me] (9, 49) or "Perdonen" [Forgive me] (12). He also voices his concern regarding the need to capture the readers' attention from the very first page of his diary: "Al principio uno no sabe cómo hacer para atrapar a los lectores desde la primera palabra. A los lectores o a uno mismo" [In the beginning, you don't know how to snare the reader with the first word, to snare the reader or to snare yourself] (19). There are other impetuses, however, in the form of discursive devices, that push readers into a consideration of the whole. The most frequent technique used to join the various segments is the repetition of specific words or a reference to previous content. Language can connect occurrences separated both spatially within the text and temporally, as in the example of José's affairs. In another instance, a special phrase from his writing apparently instigates a subsequent action: "este primer peldaño del que ya no puedo pasar" [on the bottom rung of the ladder, where I'm trapped] (118), written in a self-analytic moment, is later repeated as he confronts his boss: "un hombre no puede quedarse siempre en el primer peldaño" [a man can't stay on the bottom rung of the ladder forever] (125). A similar joining of segments is produced when a section provides a postscript to a story started in the previous fragment (139).

Readers are encouraged to look for a joining of segments, a cohesiveness to the fragments, a notion put into words as a part of José's journal:

> Si alguien desglosara mi cuaderno y me pidiera que ratificara aisladamente sus páginas, me negaría. No obstante, sí lo haría en su conjunto porque de todos modos, deshilvanado, torpe y hasta contradictorio muchas veces, contiene mis ideas, mis acontecimientos, mis emociones. Puede no interesar a los demás, pero a mí, en su totalidad, me expresa. En cambio, desmembrado, no sólo no me expresa, sino que me desvirtúa y me traiciona, porque cada una de mis verdades deja de serlo si se la priva de su relación con las otras. (191–192)

> [If someone were to edit my notebook and ask me to endorse certain pages, I'd say no. Nevertheless, I would endorse the notebook as a whole because, even though it's sketchy, clumsy, and sometimes even contradictory, it contains my ideas, my emotions, my life's events. Maybe it doesn't interest anybody, but it expresses me in my totality. On the other hand, when it's dismembered, it not only doesn't express me but slanders and betrays me, because each of my truths is no longer a truth if it's deprived of its relationship to the others.]

Analogously, each section of *El libro vacío* must be considered in relation to the other parts. It is only by becoming involved with the totality of the segments that readers conceptualize the stories contained within. For, although there is not a story in the traditional sense, no linear treatment of a coherent narrative, the fragments of José's life and thoughts do yield stories on two levels. The first is a cultural autobiography constituted by memories, in mixed temporal ordering, from José's childhood through his most recent circumstances, with emphasis on his familial relationships and atomized existence.[17] The second is a story about writing, one that moves beyond José's obsession, his need to compose, to focus on the process (story) of writing itself.

Despite the duality in terms of focus, there is a coherence governing the text, once again given voice in José's journal. Acting as his own reader, José consciously adopts the task of discerning the linkage inherent in his writings: "A menos que mi protagonista sea el pensamiento, con toda su ilimitada y espléndida libertad, no veo la forma de hilvanar algo de todo esto" [Unless my character becomes thought itself, in all of its splendid, unbounded liberty, I can't see any way to stitch something together from all of this] (179). It is precisely the thought process that unites both levels, as José's writings produce a blending of the two. Because of his marginalized status, he dedicates himself to writing, which in turn is a solitary endeavor, since, as he states, he cannot share his notebooks with anyone, neither family nor friends. Yet writing is a form of communication, and one must then presume a recipient of these words. Once again, José seems to function as his own reader, as evidenced by his statement toward the end of the text: "Yo escribo y yo me leo, únicamente yo, pero al hacerlo me siento desdoblado, acompañado. Cuando incurro en contradicciones soy mi interlocutor y oigo sorprendido las respuestas que surgen de mi profundidad más íntima" [I write and read myself what I've written. I'm alone when I do it, but I feel accompanied, split in two. When I'm guilty of inconsistency, I begin a dialogue with myself and, with great surprise, I listen to the answer that emerges from my most hidden depths] (193).

Thus José serves a double function: he is at once a narrator and a reader-in-the-text, which dramatizes on a literary level his feeling of having multiple beings within his body. He speaks of having two *yos* (Is) and even considers giving them names, just as he has numbered his notebooks (38). Even more importantly, José's dual role transcends the text to implicate readers in the literary process as they consider the functions of writing (José as narrator) and reading (José as reader). Readers must emulate José in his capacity of reader as he analyzes what he has written, in terms of both content and discourse, and, ultimately, relate the parts to the whole. José recognizes that there can be meaning in nothingness: "Está vacío, lo sé muy bien, no dice nada. Pero yo sé, yo únicamente, que ese vacío está lleno de mí mismo" [It's empty; I know full well it says nothing. But I, and only I, know that this void is full of myself] (198). Readers of *El libro vacío* also come to understand that, in a novel that fails to conform with normative literary practices and in which almost nothing happens, there is much to consider on both a human and a literary plane.

Both Rulfo and Vicens contribute toward raising the level of readership in Mexican fiction. By letting discourse alone effect responses, without guidelines or an authorial presence, they show respect for their readers by inviting them to participate at a more sophisticated plane. At the same time, they manage to retain a focus on Mexican culture, thus not sacrificing a concern for the national as they develop their artistry. In doing so, they lead the way for writers of the 1960s, both those who, like Carlos Fuentes and Juan José Arreola, blend the universal and the national in form and content and those who press in their novels for a truly cerebral engagement of readers but in doing so largely move away from Mexican issues, such as Salvador Elizondo and José Emilio Pacheco.

# CHAPTER 5

# CARLOS FUENTES: MEXICANNESS AND THE FAILED REVOLUTION

¡Qué chasco, amigo mío, si los que venimos a ofrecer todo nuestro entusiasmo, nuestra misma vida por derribar a un miserable asesino, resultásemos los obreros de un enorme pedestal donde pudieran levantarse cien o doscientos mil monstruos de la misma especie! . . . ¡Pueblo sin ideales, pueblo de tiranos! . . . ¡Lástima de sangre!

[What a colossal failure we would make of it, friend, if we, who offer our enthusiasm and lives to crush a wretched tyrant, became the builders of a monstrous edifice holding one hundred or two hundred thousand monsters of exactly the same sort. People without ideals! A tyrant folk! Vain bloodshed!]

—Mariano Azuela, *Los de abajo*

Three years after Rulfo's *Pedro Páramo* and in the same year as Vicens's *El libro vacío*, Carlos Fuentes published his first novel, *La región más transparente* (1958), a veritable explosion of fragments. Fuentes looked outward to the United States and Europe for experimental literary techniques but turned them inward for a depiction of Mexico and the Mexican psyche played out against the center of the nation, Mexico City. This work firmly institutes a new wave of novels of the revolution, those that explicitly focus on its consequences rather than depicting its battles (Fernández Retamar 123), and changes the locus of those novels from the countryside to the city. In Mexican letters, only Azuela's *La luciérnaga* had treated the urban ambience with such intensity. The expanding metropolis, however, was ripe for literary scrutiny, and Fuentes's text would be followed shortly by Yáñez's *Ojerosa y pintada* (1959).[1] In *La región* Fuentes combines the indigenous past with the postrevolutionary 1950s, the latter shown to be analogous in structure and ideology to the prerevolutionary Díaz empire, only now with an entrenched middle class. The novel expands to encompass the extremes within Mexican social classes, the effect or lack thereof of the revolution on all the characters, and a troublesome dramatization-*cum*-warning regarding the current situation of the country.

*La muerte de Artemio Cruz* (1962) repeats certain themes of *La región*, particularly the atomization of the individual, the rise of a new oligarchy in Mexico, and the failure of the Mexican Revolution, but does so by focusing on one individual rather than encompassing the massive social fabric addressed in the earlier volume. In this novel Fuentes succeeds in integrating at multiple levels the notion of fragmentation: in imagery, in graphic display within the text, in the individual, and in the nation. Having established his place in Mexican letters with a formidable literary output, in 1981 Fuentes evidently felt the need to return to his focus on disparities of class and failed revolutionary principles in *Agua quemada*, ostensibly a series of short stories but in reality a fundamentally cohesive depiction of the nation that promotes in readers a return to Azuela's initial critique of the revolution and thus a reconsideration of its failures as echoed in the social and political realities of the present. In aspects of thematics and technique, *Agua quemada* can be viewed as a companion piece to *La región más transparente*.

As his career extends from the late 1950s to the present, it is obvious that Fuentes's works could be included in various chapters of this study. I have elected to place him at the gateway of the 1960s explosion in narrative experimentation known in Mexico and elsewhere in Latin America as the "Boom." The novels under consideration here are three of his best. All are rooted in a presentation of fragmentation that constitutes the complete coordination of form and content and the fusion of the national and the international: experimental discourse that reflects the atomization of the individual, particularly within the urban milieu, and the discrepancies of social classes inherent within the Mexican nation.

### *La región más transparente* (Where the Air Is Clear)

In *La región más transparente* (1958), Fuentes offers a chronicle of Mexico City in the 1950s but with deep roots extending through the revolution and the Díaz hegemony to the nation's indigenous past. By means of his ambitious reach, which accommodates not only all social classes but also a timeless spiritual Indian presence, Fuentes subordinates character to place, resulting in what he has termed a biography of Mexico City (Reeve 55). Instead of mere surface description, Fuentes gives depth to his novel, utilizing his characters' circumstances and life choices both to probe the national psyche and to dramatize his concerns about the products of greed and apathy in the aftermath of the revolution. Fundamental to the construction of this thematic are the notions of fragmentation and cyclic return, change and stasis, which serve to link characters, to conflate time, and to unify segments of a most complex segmented presentation.

Fuentes employs fragmentation on both a discursive and metaphoric level, multiplying images of atomized individuals, isolationist class parameters, and segmented prose to such an extent that it appears that fragmentation is the fundamental characteristic of the social as well as spiritual condition of Mexico City. As early as the 1950s,[2] the city is perceived to be on the verge of or already engaged in a period of uncontrollable growth, depicted at the start of the narrative as "la ciudad extendiéndose cada vez más como una tiña irrespetuosa" [the city forever spreading like a creeping blot] (24).[3] Fuentes speaks of four million inhabitants of Mexico City in the novel, but that population had already mushroomed to over five million by the time it was published (Reeve 35).

La región más transparente is a massive text consisting of three main parts that are divided into a combination of lengthy pieces, which give the appearance of a traditional notion of chapters, and smaller, italicized segments, for a total of thirty-eight. All of the chapter-length sections are further subdivided into fragments. The shortest segment is a single line of dialogue (58),[4] and the longest, Ixca Cienfuego's final words, extends to over fifteen pages. Within some fragments there is additional segmentation, in which italicized wording alternates with the regular text.

A major function of the fragmentation is to allow for a focused consideration of a vast number of characters. Their numbers are such that later editions include a separate catalog of characters that indicates the range of people encompassed: the de Ovanda family; the Zamaconas; the Polas; a group that embodies the bourgeoisie; the socialites; the foreigners; the intellectuals; the representatives of the lower class; the revolutionaries; and the so-called guardians, Ixca Cienfuegos and his mother Teódula Moctezuma, clearly representative of Mexico's indigenous population. Paradoxically, while serving to include such an array of city dwellers, the fragmentation at the same time dramatizes their separation. Even at four million inhabitants, the Federal District fosters atomization: "Cuatro millones se alineaban, sin tocarse las manos, cada uno rígido al lado de los otros" [Four million were standing in line without touching hands, each stiff beside his neighbor] (241).

Emphasizing separation, the discursive fragmentation also evokes the metaphoric aspects of enforced segmentation based on social class. Although the novel will chronicle some movement between classes, firm boundaries define social positioning and there remains an abyss between the rich and the poor, both before the revolution and afterward. That sense of distance is captured by Federico Robles, a character who manages to climb from a peon status to that of a financier. From his new elevated position, he looks with disdain at those who remain below: "Robles gustaba de inclinarse, imperturbable, desde la ventana, y saborear el pulgueo sin molestias de los pelados, de todas las hebras de la ciudad que pasaban inconscientes del rascacielos y de Federico Robles. Dos mundos, nubes y estiércol" [Robles liked to lean out his window and smell the flea circus hopping below without being bitten by all the necessary nobodies and all the nonentity weavers of life who passed oblivious to skyscrapers and to Federico Robles. Two worlds: clouds and excrement] (64). In his summation of the inexorable distance between social classes, Lanin Gyurko uses the term *gap*, which echoes the novel's fragmented structure: "The gap between the lower and the upper classes, between indigenous Mexico and the cosmopolitan Mexico slavishly pursuing foreign standards of elegance, culture, and materialism, remains unbridgeable" ("Abortive Idealism," 294). Beyond social classes, there is a more encompassing notion of a segmented existence, one with a feeling of almost cosmic proportions. It is voiced by Manuel Zamacona, early identified as an intellectual, one who is capable of thinking and of questioning the status quo. Clearly expanding the sense of disconnectedness to the nation, Zamacona writes: "No sentirnos parte de ningún engranaje racional, susceptibles de alimentarlo y permitir que nos alimente" [We do not feel ourselves part of any rational system we can feed or be fed by] (67).

Fuentes's embrace of such a vast representation of classes and types combined with his incorporation of numerous time periods within a fragmented structure have prompted analogies between his novel and the frescoes of Diego Rivera.[5] Just as Rivera's murals were instrumental in the movement to define the nation in the period immediately following the revolution, so Fuentes's treatment expands readers' focus beyond the individuals depicted: first to the city, then to all of Mexico. Due to the lack of dominance of any one character, there is no protagonist in the novel. Instead, it can be considered a study of a city or, given its technical strategies, a collage of a city, as termed by Conrado Zuluaga (83). Manuel Durán offers Mexico City as the protagonist (Review, 78) yet gives emphasis to Ixca Cienfuegos as the center of the novel, the one who links the myriad characters and urban places depicted (Review, 80).

Indeed, Ixca does serve as a unifier, for he touches the lives or penetrates the soul of all of the characters. With some minor personages, he may be merely passing by as they briefly hold the focus of the narration, his contact limited to a casual observance of a group of youths, for example. With others, he engages in conversation in such a way as to invade their inner being, forcing revelations of a most personal nature or, even without conversation, penetrating their thoughts. He appears to have some supernatural power against which there is no defense, coupled with a superior wisdom marked by his ubiquitous smile. Characters simply open up to him, even when they seem cognizant of his force and try to resist revealing their private thoughts, as in the case of Rodrigo Pola. Ixca's powers are such that he can be viewed as an omniscient-narrator-in-the-text, an unusual occurrence in narrative practice.[6]

Of the other characters, two stand out both for their relative prominence in the novel and for their symbolic function in the text's thematics: Federico Robles and Rodrigo Pola. Although they have little personal contact with each other, they are inextricably paired throughout, to the point that they constitute a reciprocal inversion: as Robles's empire collapses, Pola's fortunes improve. Fuentes's orchestration of the men's changing fortune forms a second inversion: economic improvement results in spiritual impoverishment and vice versa.[7] Robles's bankruptcy leads to his marrying Hortensia and returning to his roots, having regained a sense of self, while Pola's riches are gained through self-debasement, as he abandons poetry for commercial film scripts. Significantly, the key elements of their changes are located together in the novel: gossip regarding the bankruptcy adjoins a section showing Pola in animated discussion with studio producers, and Pola climbs into his new Jaguar as a paperboy shouts the news of Robles's ruin. Contiguous also are the indications that Cienfuegos was instrumental in both changes of fortune. At the end of one fragment he offers to introduce Pola to the producers, and at the beginning of the next, Robles indicates that he has followed Ixca's advice in his financial dealings, which will lead to his downfall.

Although the other characters are of varying importance, relationships exist among them too, forming part of the unification of the novel. In counterpart to the fragmentation, readers begin to discern a Galdosian network of contacts among classes and generations. Moving beyond the common link with Ixca Cienfuegos, they learn, among the many intertwining threads, that Robles's parents were peons on an estate owned by don Ignacio de Ovando; Robles is the father of Manuel Zamacona; Mercedes Zamacona's brother is the army official who shot Gervasio Pola, Rodrigo's father, during the revolution; numerous representatives of the lower class work for the bourgeoisie in a service capacity; and Rodrigo Pola marries Pimpinela de Ovando, having finally given up his love for Norma Larragoiti, Robles's first wife. In a further joining of characters, four people die on the same night: Jorge Morales, Manuel Zamacona, the wetback Gabriel, and Norma.

This linkage among characters is paralleled by the nexus among fragments. Segments are linked by specific actions (Bobó's party), by characters (the fragment depicting the death of Gervasio Pola is followed by a segment that begins with a reference to his son), by image (a reference to Carlos IV of Spain closes Part 1, and the image of El Caballito, an equestrian statue of the monarch, begins Part 2), and by date (the four deaths on Independence Day join the segment on Feliciano Sánchez, who died on the same day, although in a different year). Furthermore, as the fragmentation fosters a focus on so many characters, readers at times receive information from one character that contrasts or complements that given earlier by another. Such is the case with Rosenda Pola's comments about her son's spying on her and Ixca's suspicion that Rodrigo was trying to commit suicide. As a final example of unification at the level of character, all depicted are touched in some way by the notion of money and by the invasive, devouring atmosphere of the city. As one character remarks, "en la capital, hay que andar abusando, o nos comen el mandado" [in the capital, you had to keep on your toes. If you don't, *mano*, you've had it] (36).

Just as discursive fragmentation moves beyond the text to metaphoric applications, so too does the notion of unification. On a personal level, Federico Robles feels a sense of wholeness when he is with Hortensia. His status as a unifier, moreover, takes on greater importance when, toward the end, he is said to have taken on himself the sadness and desolation of all Mexicans (391–392). It is Manuel Zamacona, however, who fully expands the notion of unification to encompass the nation. Disillusioned with the failed revolution, Manuel writes in the same essay that suggested the atomization of the nation the following recipe for real change in Mexico, rooted in unification: "Valor-poder-responsabilidad son la gran unidad, la que nos liga a unos con otros, con la naturaleza y con Dios" [Value-Power-Responsibility are the great unity, that which ties us together, with nature and with God] (73–74).[8] Later, in a conversation with Robles, he calls for "Una verdadera integración de los miembros dispersos del ser de este país" [A true integration of the scattered members of what this country is] (282). In a statement that reflects back on the novel's structure, in which multiple focuses are necessary in order to capture a sense of the reality of Mexico City, Zamacona argues that there is never a single truth, but two, three, an infinity of truths, and that to be guided by a single one is tantamount to lying (282).

Complementary to this stress on an extended unity now pointing to the nation are the accumulation of inherently Mexican characteristics emerging from the characters' actions and traits that reflect Paz's analysis in *El laberinto de la soledad* that purported to reveal the core of Mexico and Mexicanness. *La región más transparente* offers numerous dramatizations of Paz's pivotal points, many of which contribute to a sense of isolation, of a segmented existence. Among them are an emphasis on the Mexicans' wearing of masks to hide their real identity (162, 242, 244);[9] the need to keep up one's defenses, to keep oneself closed off from the Other (163, 181); men who are violators and closed unto themselves and women who are violated, open, and torn (69, 145);[10] women who are seen as either saints or whores (176); the commonplace of an unknown father (68); implicit or explicit admiration for the *chingón*, the violator (121); machismo exhibited by husbands to wives (350–352); the acknowledgment of words that need to be communicated yet are never spoken (162); and the sense that the only time that Mexicans really come together and open themselves to others is in the fiesta (408). The last example is particularly interesting as depicted in the novel, for it relates to the prevailing theme of the atomization of the individual. After the fiesta of Independence Day, one reads: "La ciudad se había descascarado" [The city had broken into pieces] (408).[11] After a brief moment of togetherness, Mexicans return to their segmented existence.

Fundamental to Paz's analysis of the essential Mexican being is the pervasiveness of the past in the present, with particular emphasis on the legacy of the Aztecs and the sense of national violation at the hands of the Spaniards. The representatives of the indigenous past in *La región,*

Teódula Moctezuma and her son Ixca Cienfuegos, embody that presence in the Mexico of the 1950s. Teódula is purer in her adherence to the old traditions, maintaining the bodies of her deceased husband and children under the floor of her dwelling. She appears to have powers even greater than Ixca's, for he comments on her control over his life. It is Teódula who demands a sacrifice to ensure the sun's reappearance and travels to the Robles mansion as it burns with Norma inside. Although mingling more with the infidels, to the point of having a passionate affair with Norma, Ixca is clearly rooted in his past, as revealed by his constant association with the sun.[12] A less frequent but no less significant link is established between Ixca and blood, reinforcing the sun imagery as having a correlation with sacrifice. The lovemaking between Ixca and Norma is marked by violence: bites and nail-scratching draw blood (313). In their first encounter, Ixca is likened to a flame, evoking both heat and the sun (312). A more momentous scene takes place in the Zócalo, center of the old Tenochtitlán, where the presence of the ancient civilizations is so strong (and where the Templo Mayor would be uncovered some twenty years later).[13] Jorge Morales bites Ixca's hand, producing blood. Ixca then bites his own hand in the same place, augmenting the wound. As blood fills his mouth, Ixca moves from the notion of sacrifice to a vision of healing that involves imagery of fragmentation and unification as he wishes for a different night: "Una noche en que se puedan recoger los fragmentos de la luna, todos los fragmentos rotos del origen, y volver a tocarlos íntegros" [a night when pieces of the moon may be gathered up, all the broken fragments of origin, and can be put back together again] (253).

It would seem that, despite the association with violence and sacrifice (or, perhaps, because of it, from within an indigenous mindset), Ixca has the potential to be an agent of healing. This restoration apparently involves a blending of the past and the present, which resonates in his desire to unite the pieces into a whole. It must be seen as significant that Ixca also embodies a *mestizo* being, the blending of the ancient civilization with the Hispanic conquerors. His name is part Nahuatl (Faris 19; Ixca means "to roast") and part Spanish (Cienfuegos translates into "one hundred fires"). Both names relate to fire with a facile transition to sacrifice, and Aida Elsa Ramírez Mattei points out further harmony inherent in the name: "Ixca es el símbolo de México, con la dualidad indígena y española expresada en su nombre. . . . Es un nombre que recuerda el mestizaje de contrarios que buscan armonía en un nuevo ser" [Ixca is the symbol of Mexico, with the duality of the indigenous and the Spanish expressed in his name. . . . It is a name that recalls the blending of opposites that searches for harmony in a new being] (97). Ixca is a unifier: he begins and ends the novel; he brings the indigenous past to the atomized present; he touches the lives of all the other characters; he emcompasses all of Mexico City;[14] he yearns for a truly integrated society, much as Manuel Zamacona had desired. At the end of the novel, he dissolves into fog and is depicted as having become the city: "Cienfuegos era, en sus ojos de águila pétrea y serpiente de aire, la ciudad" [he became, in his stone-eagle, air-serpent eyes, the city itself] (453).[15] He then closes the novel with a discourse, called by some a prose poem, that Leal maintains "recapitulates the history of Mexico City from its foundation to the present" ("History and Myth," 8).

Ixca's emphasis on unity connotes a positive conflation of beings and customs and thus offers an optimistic outlook. This is countered, however, by a second tier of unification within the novel, that of circularity. The Aztecs followed a calendar of fifty-two-year cycles and firmly believed in the notion of return, of recycling the past. Thus *La región más transparente* discursively blends fragmentation and cycles, the former strongly associated with the present status of alienation and atomization and the latter related to not only the remote indigenous past but also the more recent *porfiriato*.

The most obvious example of circularity in the novel is in the repetition of words. The text begins and ends with Ixca's voice combined with a focus on the city, but the repetition that stands out is the specific duplication of three sentences at the end of the first and last fragments: "Aquí nos tocó. Qué le vamos a hacer. En la región más transparente del aire" [Here we bide. What are we going to do about it. Where the air is clear] (21, 470).[16] There are, however, many other levels of cycles within the novel that illustrate Fuentes's emphasis on change and stasis. One of the most devastating aspects of cyclical occurrences in this presentation of postrevolutionary Mexico falls within the rubric of cycles of abuse in the name of progress, cycles of foreign investment, cycles of oligarchies. Robles, the revolutionary-turned-financier, is repeatedly likened to Porfirio Díaz. Early in the novel, upon gazing at his reflection in the tinted windows of his office, even he notes the resemblance: "Se había blanqueado, igual que el General Díaz" [Pale he had become, like General Díaz] (32). Although Robles interprets the similarity as positive, the mark of a distinguished individual, readers will soon be able to relate the whiteness as a stamp of artifice, for Robles has denied his Indian roots and embraced the economic pragmatism of financial dealings with the United States. Should any doubt remain, this is confirmed later in the novel when Robles is shaving. The description reads, "piel oscura bajo máscara blanca" [the dark face beneath the white mask of lather] (385). Ostensibly a reference to shaving cream, the image connotes much more. In an interesting inversion of the Mexican use of the word "coco" (coconut) for someone deemed brown on the outside and white on the inside, here Fuentes indicates that Robles's core is brown. Ixca's penetrating vision also finds parallels in word and dress between Robles and Díaz (122). Furthermore, Robles's attitudes echo those of the dictator, as Zamacona accuses him: "Esto equivaldría a decirle al pueblo de México: 'Estás bien como estás. No es necesario que pienses o hables. Nosotros sabemos lo que te conviene. Quédate allí.' Pero, ¿no es esto lo mismo que pensaba Porfirio Díaz?" [Which is the same as saying to the Mexican masses, You're quite well off as you are. Don't think, don't speak. We know what's best for you. Just lie quiet. Isn't that precisely what Porfirio Díaz said?] (284–285).

Porfirio Díaz may be gone, but there are plenty of men like Robles to form a new oligarchy. As Mario Castro Arenas has argued, the one-man dictatorship of Díaz is replaced by a political party's dictatorship, the businessman substitutes for the *latifundista,* and the Frenchified oligarchy is replaced by a Yankified oligarchy (45–46). More men may participate in the power base at the top, the focus may have changed from the country to the city, and appropriated poses and masks may have transferred from Europe to the United States, but the cycle continues. Ironically, this is reaffirmed within the novel by Pimpinela de Ovando, who recalls her family's earlier participation in the iterative pattern: "igual que la aristocracia porfiriana vio con horror la entrada a México de los Villas y los Zapatas, ella y las viejas familias vieron entrar a Díaz y a los suyos el siglo pasado" [just as the Porfirian aristocracy were horror-struck when Villa and Zapata marched into Mexico City, so she (Pimpinela's grandmother) and the old families were horror-struck when Díaz marched in a century ago] (165–166). Recognizing the continuation of corruption and exploitation first under Díaz and then under Robles and his kind, Lanin Gyurko adds the next name to the list: Roberto Régules, the man instrumental in Robles's downfall ("Abortive Idealism," 295–296).

The constancy of cycles helps to illuminate the emphasis on change and stasis in the novel. Movement between classes is shown to be possible, although those who attain a higher status generally do so at the expense of others and at a loss of self. Norma and Federico make their way into the upper class but in the process deny their roots. Norma's behavior is particularly heinous when she allows her mother to be mistaken for her servant. She has attained wealth but not class. Descendants of the de Ovando family and other representatives of the old rich in Mexico may retain their class, but only in the sense of refinement, for they have lost their holdings. Pimpinela, however, having dropped in economic status, uses her pedigree to reverse her fortune again by marrying Rodrigo Pola, who, in turn, has tossed principles aside in his personal ascent to riches. Beyond these individual cases, there is the establishment of a stable middle class, labeled in the text as the only product of the revolution (120).

This movement, both up and down the economic ladder, does not negate the fundamental stasis within Mexican society that was well established before the revolution and continues to this day: the vast gap between the rich and the poor. Upon observing some beggars waiting for handouts at the Robles mansion, the intellectual Zamacona considers the poor: "Manuel los imaginó, idénticos, en todas las épocas, en todas las vidas. Como un río subterráneo, indiferente y oscuro, que corría por debajo de cualquier cambio o idea" [He thought of them as identical in all epochs, all ages. Like a subterranean river, indifferent and dark, flowing far below idea or change] (275). Mexico remains a fragmented nation. Although the players may be different, the extremes of poverty and wealth remain constant; a true blending of citizens has not been achieved.

Thus the notion of returning to the past has both positive and negative implications. Following Ixca's model, one must learn to integrate the past into the present in order to attain a sense of wholeness. The fragmentation of the present and the atomization of the individual, however, are incompatible with that vision. They would tend to support the more pessimistic outlook inherent in the text's recycling of abusive powermongers. *La región más transparente* dramatizes the fruits of the revolution's failure to address social disparity, and the prognosis for the future is grim if the cycles continue. Gyurko states that "the Mexican Revolution is evoked by Fuentes as only a brief, exhilarating moment of national unity and national transcendence followed by a relapse into alienation, oppression, and greed" ("Abortive Idealism," 294). At least one critic, Conrado Zuluaga, criticizes Fuentes for his negativism, arguing that the circularity of Ixca's words constitutes a closed novel that offers no possibility of resolution (84). According to Zuluaga, in *La región* one either sells oneself in order to succeed or resigns oneself to the sociopolitical realities of postrevolutionary Mexico (89, 93). At the same time, however, Zuluaga recognizes that Fuentes lets readers reach their own conclusions (82). At the end of the novel, none of the characters is in a position to work for change in Mexico. Pola and Régules are reaching for economic supremacy; Robles saves himself by marrying Hortensia and returning to the land, but his new understanding benefits no one else; and the one man who voices opinions similar to Ixca's and levels criticism against the failed revolution, Manuel Zamacona, loses his life in senseless violence. Stopping the cycle is something that must be achieved beyond the text, and Mexican readers are thus in a sense invited to recognize themselves in one of the many characters and to analyze the consequences of their position. There is, however, a danger inherent in couching a call of alarm for the soul of a nation within a prose style that is difficult for all but the most cultured reader (Ramírez Mattei 82). Zuluaga argues that, by engaging in an excess of technical experimentation, Fuentes effectively closes off communication with a majority of Mexicans (93). One should not, however, minimize the importance of Fuentes's achievement: the alarm has been sounded. Unfortunately, it will not be heeded. A basic reference to the Plaza de Tlatelolco within the text (390) will immediately signal for subsequent readers a cycle of violence evocative of Aztec sacrifice a mere ten years after the publication of the novel: the student masacre of 1968. And the cycles continue. In 1993, while Carlos Salinas de Gortari campaigned for the Tratado de Libre Comercio (TLC; NAFTA), the Indians of Chiapas were sorely limited in economic possibilities to selling firewood, charcoal, and trinkets, growing corn, or begging. According to the government, NAFTA was the ticket to first-world status, but the call for progress and industry, linked with a foreign presence in Mexico and divorced from a consideration of all the citizenry, echoed Díaz's actions once more.

## *La muerte de Artemio Cruz*
## (The Death of Artemio Cruz)

In *La muerte de Artemio Cruz* (1962) Fuentes again uses fragmentation in both discursive and metaphoric practice. Discursively, the text engages readers in active participation and dramatizes the atomization of the individual within Mexican society. Fuentes joins Yáñez and Rulfo in combining form and content by means of a segmented structure. Furthermore, he integrates fragmentation at various levels within the text, including thematics, language, and imagery. Although using literary techniques common in the United States and Europe, he situates his story of a dying industrialist in a fundamentally Mexican setting, one that parallels structure in its fragmented existence. By so doing, Fuentes equates his protagonist with the nation, inviting readers to consider the similarities between the two and the dangers inherent in that sameness. *La muerte de Artemio Cruz* provides a critical examination of Mexican social, political, and economic circumstances with a particularly negative assessment of the Revolution of 1910.

Fuentes breaks his text into thirty-eight fragments, thirteen each of sections beginning with the pronouns *yo* (I) and *tú* (the familiar you) and twelve that start with *él* (he). In the *yo* sections, Artemio is in his wife's house in the elegant district of Lomas, as opposed to the residence he shares with his mistress. It will be the last day of his life, and he knows he is dying. Focusing primarily on his physical state, he is acutely aware of body parts and processes. Artemio shuns his immediate circumstances, remarking disparagingly about incompetent doctors and about his wife, Catalina, and daughter, Teresa, who, he believes, seek only information about his will. His preferred audience is his aide, Padilla, who brings tape recordings of recent business dealings for Artemio to savor. This subjective narration is characterized by the repetition of key phrases and images and by the use of sentence fragments separated by suspension points. The *yo* portion is narrated in the present tense.

In the segments beginning with *tú*, an accusatory voice speaks to Artemio, as if in an oneiric state. The voice has been interpreted as Artemio's alter ego, as his subconscience, even as the voice of the Mexican people, as suggested by Fuentes himself ("Diálogo," 225). Others are of the opinion, however, that this voice represents a facet of Artemio Cruz and thus is a self-critical discourse, one that provides some distance from the *yo* narration. Although the majority of the fragments consist of one long paragraph, the style is very poetic.[17] A sense of flow is produced by the use of run-on sentences and sentence fragments, joined by ample examples of poetic devices such as synesthesia, alliteration, and, in particular, anaphora. The *tú* narration speaks in the future tense even though it refers to actions in the past.

The twelve fragments that commence with *él* carry also a specific date, one for every month except March, with December represented twice. It is here that readers receive more objective, concrete information in third-person-omniscient narration regarding Artemio's life. The dates are by no means chronological, instead reflecting what might be seen as the haphazard arrangement appropriate to a character's dwelling on incidents as they come to mind.[18] One learns details of Artemio's relationships with Regina, a woman he raped then came to love; Catalina, who was given to him by her father, don Gamaliel, as a means of preserving the family's holdings; Lorenzo, Artemio's only son, who died in a sacrificial role in the Spanish Civil War; and others who witnessed or participated in Artemio's movement from youthful idealism to Machiavellian pragmatism. These sections emphasize the past tense.

The uneven tripartite structure can be read as an introductory section of two segments, in the way of a prefatory segment or establishing sequence, followed by twelve complete cycles of *él/tú/yo* (Dixon 95). Most critics, however, interpret the structure as twelve full cycles of *yo/tú/él* with a thirteenth truncated by Artemio's death (Hammerly 209, Lower 19). There are reasons to support each point of view, which seems appropriate in a novel replete with perspectivism as dramatized by the three narrative voices proferring different views of Artemio Cruz.

The initial segment in the first-person, does, in fact, serve as an establishing sequence. If readers are informed only by conventional narrative, however, it yields more confusion than comprehension. Names are scattered within the prose with no narrative commentary to identify the people, to provide description or orientation. Yet the segment serves as preparation in a more conceptual way in that multiple aspects of discourse are sown here. Lanin Gyurko remarks that the fragmentation within language echoes the "disintegration of Cruz's physical self and the shattering of his spiritual self" ("*La muerte de Artemio Cruz* and *Citizen Kane*," 82). In addition, there are important images of both fragmentation and unity that will relate not only to the novel's structure but also to the readers' role and the text's thematics.

As the novel commences, fragmentation is clearly the empowered image. On the very first page, Artemio sees himself reflected in the uneven reflective quadrangles in his daughter's purse, thus segmenting his face, and he identifies himself with the distorted likeness: "Soy esto. Soy esto. Soy este viejo con las facciones partidas por los cuadros desiguales del vidrio" [That's what I am. That's what I am. That old man whose features are fragmented by the uneven squares of glass] (9).[19] The emphasis on a broken or decomposed physical presence not only calls attention to Artemio's debilitated state but also, even more suggestively, provokes an image of a decentered, demoralized being. Furthermore, Artemio continues his self-examination in the reflection by contemplating pieces of his face, one by one. Again, the emphasis is on dismemberment or fragmentation, as each feature is isolated through naming, repeated two or three times, with many related to old age in some way before Artemio passes to the next. Significantly, a brief mention shortly afterward of a unified body ("cuerpo unido," 10), a healthier image, is rapidly corrected to the distorted, broken view, which will be perceived subsequently as a more accurate reflector of Cruz's and Mexico's reality. Later in the novel, the image of a sponge will reinforce this double focus on fragmentation and unity, analogous to the *montón de piedras* in *Pedro Páramo*, which served as a simulacrum for the novel: "Dicen que las células de la esponja no están unidas por nada y sin embargo la esponja está unida" [They say the cells in a sponge are not linked but nevertheless the sponge is one] (88). Once again, a fragmented image is presented as a unified entity, prompting readers to work to make coherent this segmented text.

Language, in particular, plays an important role in the establishing sequence. As Artemio begins to try to remember the recent past, he says, "si *pienso* en lo que *hice* ayer no *pensaré* más en lo que está pasando" [If I think about what I did yesterday, I'll stop thinking about what's happening to me now] (12, emphasis added). What appears to be an innocuous phrase, easily naturalized within diegesis, is, in fact, a presentation of the three verb tenses and, by extension, perspectives, that will be featured in segmented fashion as the narration splits into its tripartite structure (Gyurko, "Structure and Theme," 38).

Before the textual separation, the voices are united, and they will reunite at the end of the narrative. During the course of the novel, however, the emphasis is on fragmentation at almost every conceivable level: among characters, among social classes, in the Mexican Revolution of 1910, in the city, in the nation, and within the text's discourse. On a personal level, there is a clear distance between Artemio and Catalina. Not only do they maintain separate bedrooms (26), but Artemio has a second residence for himself and his mistress, a *casa chica* [little house] (31), as referred to among the Mexican middle and upper classes. Since the beginning of their marriage, Catalina has striven vigorously to sustain a separation between body and soul: although she yields sexually to Artemio, mentally she nurtures rancor in response to her suspicions about the circumstances of her brother Gonzalo's death. Artemio also fosters isolation among men, as noted even in his twenties during the Mexican Revolution when he remains aloof, separated from his men (171). As death nears, that sense of fragmentation is literalized, as Artemio experiences the disintegration of self both spiritually and physically: "estoy separado . . . muero . . . me separo" [I'm apart . . . I'm dying . . . I'm parting] (270).

Among characters there is also a fundamental lack of communication, a trait inherently Mexican as noted in Paz's study and depicted on a smaller scale in *La región más transparente.* Paz speaks of the hermeticism of the Mexican people, particularly the males, how they close themselves off, fearing an open exchange would diminish them in the eyes of an interlocutor. Following codified practice, Artemio relies on learned social behavior: "Pero él no se atrevía a preguntar, a hablar. Confiaba en que los hechos acabarían por imponerse; la costumbre, la fatalidad, la necesidad también" [But he did not have the courage to ask, to speak. He was sure the facts would eventually take control: habit, fatality, need also] (102). A good example of this lack of communication is a confrontation between Artemio and Catalina. There *are* words that could break the silence between them, making her forget the past and be willing to start anew with her husband. Artemio, however, cannot bring himself to speak them. He can only think the words, in a silent discourse to which readers are privy, enabling his audience to grasp the foolishness of the Mexican perversion of stoicism (114). Interestingly, when Artemio opts for silence, the omniscient narrator comments, "No se atrevía" [He didn't dare] (114),[20] the repetition of the verb appearing to undermine the association between machismo and the act of closing oneself off from others.

The fragmentation associated with the Mexican Revolution is rooted in the disparity among social classes, the inequalities that spawned the revolt and the imbalance that remains. Beyond that, one should recall the inability of the revolutionaries to cohere as a unit, resulting in split ideologies and forces. Fuentes captures this sense of division on various levels. During the revolution, the combatants are atomized, without feelings (185). Of even more significance, however, is the disintegration of troops, an early marker of a failed cause. At one point Colonel Zagal describes Villa's outfit: "La División está desintegrada. Se ha fraccionado en bandas que se perderán por las montañas" [The Northern Division has collapsed. It's broken down into small bands that will get lost in the mountains] (184). Another reference emphasizes the anonymity of the conflict: "ambos bandos de la guerra de facciones fusilaban inmediatamente a los oficiales del grupo contrario" [both bands of the war of factions were immediately shooting the officials of the opposing side] (176).[21] The disputing groups need not be identified, as the lack of cohesion among the fighters obviates the need for such precision. Since Fuentes repeats the notion of a *guerra de facciones* at least twice more (194, 195), such an emphasis should not be overlooked. The fact that it appears four times within twenty pages is a marker, not of excess, but of consequence. Significantly, it is the same word, *facciones*, that Fuentes uses to describe Artemio's fragmented state at the beginning of the novel (9), thus strengthening the association between Artemio and the revolution. Finally, readers come to these words, as spoken by a participant: "Nos hemos dejado dividir" [We've let ourselves be divided] (194). Taken literally, this can describe the disbanding of troops. It is much more ominous, however, when applied to the ideological underpinnings of the revolution, as it suggests, even as the event is taking place, the disintegration of the motivating idealism that will result in the subsequent corruption and self-promotion epitomized by Artemio Cruz.

The accusatory tone of the *tú* narrative voice appropriates the notion of disintegration and applies it geographically and ontologically to encompass the nation. Among a list of items that Artemio, as a member of the new oligarchy generated by the failings of the revolution, will bequeath to the Mexican people is "sus fraccionamientos elegantes" [their elegant subdivisions] (277), which establishes the city as one marker of fragmentation among social classes. The differences among the people, however, extend beyond economics, leading to a vision of the nation parallel to the double focus on segmentation and unity: "¿Recordarás el país? Lo recordarás y no es uno; son mil países con un solo nombre" [Will you remember the country? You will remember it, but it isn't only one country. It's a thousand countries with a single name] (274).

This sense of fragmentation finds a further correlation within the novel's discourse. In addition to the tripartite structure resulting in thirty-eight segments, there are abundant examples of sentence fragments, many of which are separated by suspension points or dashes to accent their division. Fuentes also employs a barrage of simultaneous conversations and segments of conversations, exposing readers to fragments of dialogue. In the former (86–88), despite the brevity or truncated nature of the phrases, the content is easily grasped. Key words evoke a fuller ambience; gaps are filled because readers are all too familiar with the cultural and political roots suggested by even the briefest of references. In the example cited, snatches of conversation concern archetypal Mexican business practices involving control, abuse, corruption, and blackmail. Specific examples are unnecessary, as all Mexican dealings are evidently the same. A well-known illustration of the employment of fragments of conversation is in the section describing the party held at Artemio's home in Coyoacán. As the dancing couples pass by, Artemio is exposed to a rapid succession of truncated phrases (260), which is then recuperated and expanded upon as if in a symphony (263–266). In this case, the words relate to the travels, business dealings, and social activities of the new oligarchy. Once again, a fuller description or more concrete context need not be presented, as these fragments are fully capable of evoking a whole view of Mexican society and the pervasiveness of these characteristics within it for those familiar with Mexican culture.

The process involved in filling the gaps in the multiple and fragmented conversations reflects, on a microscopic level, the role readers are invited to play throughout the novel. As they expand upon the information suggested by the truncated phrases, they envision *a* whole rather than *the* whole. Analogously, readers need to work within and among the fragments and with the different perspectives as presented by the three narrative voices in order to form an opinion about the protagonist and his cultural and political milieu.

The repetition of language is a fundamental aspect of discourse that serves as an indicator of the movement between and among fragments, thus encouraging similar activity from readers. Reiterated words and phrases function as links between segments, in particular between those introduced by *tú* and *él*.[22] At times the wording is exact, as in the example of Catalina's words: "Me dejé ir" [I let myself go] (92, 93) when she succumbs to Artemio's physical attraction. In other instances, key words or simple variations of verb tenses call attention to the sameness: "apartarás las cortinas" followed by "El apartó las cortinas" [You will open the curtains / He opened the curtains] (147). The best-known example of repeated phrasing is the enigmatic "Esa mañana lo esperaba con alegría. Cruzamos el río a caballo" [That morning I waited for him with pleasure. We crossed the river on horseback] (12). In its initial presentation it is most cryptic, functioning, as Lanin Gyurko argues, in a fashion similar to that of the word "Rosebud" in Orson Welles's *Citizen Kane* (1941) ("*La muerte de Artemio Cruz* and *Citizen Kane*," 69). In the film, however, Welles dramatizes the motivating force to pursue the significance behind the mysterious utterance, as a surrogate spectator-in-the-text suggests that discerning the word's meaning might provide an insight into the life of the newspaper magnate.[23] In Fuentes's novel, there is but a brief response to the first utterance, in the words of Artemio's wife, Catalina. Hers is a passive reaction, as she simply dismisses that which she does not comprehend: "¿Qué dices? No hables. No te canses. No te entiendo" [What's that? Don't try to talk. Don't wear yourself out. I don't understand what you're saying] (12). Surely at this early point readers do not understand either, but Fuentes provokes a more active response from them by means of systematic repetition of the phrases. Their appearance in the $yo$ fragments is so consistent that readers soon come to expect them, thus naturalizing this aspect of the narrative to the point that a mere fragment will suffice (141, 143, 221, 222, 307). Readers' curiosity upon confronting these baffling sentences prompts them to assume the responsibility of determining why the words are so important. Significantly, their frequency increases as the narrative approaches the section devoted to Lorenzo, Artemio's only son and the inspiration for the phrasing.

Textual movement toward the unification of the novel that prompts readers' action also takes place in a more subtle fashion in the intrusion of one established narrative discourse into another.[24] During the reading process, the three voices, each with a distinctive style, have attained their own identity and personality, as readers become well acquainted with each. Having authenticated the autonomy of the narrations, however, Fuentes then begins a process of intratextual references. The first instance is barely noticeable: the $tú$ voice invades the $él$ narration, albeit briefly, barely a line in the prose: "No te duermas, estate listo" [Don't go to sleep, stay alert] (180). The words can be readily naturalized because Artemio is, in effect, speaking to himself. Other enunciations in this section, however, are not as clearly self-addressed but instead comment on the situation or ponder the future. A more significant example is the invasion of the narrative technique associated with the $tú$ segments into a $yo$ section, as the style switches to the fluid form without periods or capital letters that one has come to associate with the accusatory voice. The rigid parameters of the tripartite structure are beginning to crack. This intermingling of the three discourses increases as the novel progresses. Initially separated, the units seem to be pushing toward unification, just as the various facets of Artemio Cruz, as dramatized by the three narrative voices, converge in death.

Perhaps the most startling example of intratextuality is when the enigmatic reference to crossing the river on horseback, naturalized as a signature phrase from the *yo* segments, suddenly appears in the more objective *él* narrative in fragmented form or as a variant in the third-person singular. It surfaces not once but five times within two pages, as if to make sure readers were alerted to this trespassing (267–268). The defensive structure has fissures; control is no longer viable. Furthermore, the point of weakness originates in Artemio's relationship with his son, Lorenzo. There would seem to be an instinctive movement toward the joining of discourses, toward unification, paralleling what is happening to Artemio as he approaches death. Whether Artemio does this purposefully or not, whether the joining represents a conscious intent to comprehend his total self or the involuntary meshing that could occur before death, the various perspectives of his life are being brought together. Fuentes dramatizes through discourse the process in which readers must engage in order to reconcile the diverse positions presented in the novel.

In a sense, then, Artemio Cruz, as an agent or as a subject of unification, emerges as a type of reader-in-the-text. In opposition to Catalina, who has rejected what seemed incomprehensible to her, Artemio, the self-isolated macho, the conniving, deceiving industrialist who for so long has enforced a separation from family and acquaintances, opens himself in the most profound way to the reconciliation of the facets of his being. In order to comprehend the full implications of this transformation, it is useful to return to the essential characteristics of Mexicanness as described by Paz, which form a context for understanding the breakthrough in Artemio's behavior. Paz depicts Mexicans as hermetic, closed off from one another, living in essential solitude, all of which can be applied to Artemio.[25] What men dread most is the shame of opening themselves to others, particularly to another male. This too is captured in the novel after Artemio has a political discussion with his fellow prisoner, Gonzalo Bernal: "Y la rabia era contra sí mismo, porque él se había dejado llevar a la confidencia y a la plática, se había abierto a un hombre que no merecía confianza" [His rage was directed against himself, because he had allowed himself to drift into intimacy and talk, he had opened himself to a man who did not deserve that kind of confidence] (197).[26] Finally, there is Paz's emphasis on the verb *chingar*, which can carry a variety of meanings but has an underlying base common to all uses: "la pluralidad de significaciones no impide que la idea de agresión—en todos sus grados, desde el simple de incomodar, picar, zaherir, hasta el de violar, desgarrar y matar—se presente siempre como significado último. El verbo denota violencia, salir de sí mismo y penetrar por la fuerza en otro" [the ultimate meaning always contains the idea of aggression, whether it is the simple act of molesting, pricking or censuring, or the violent act of wounding or killing. The verb denotes violence, an emergence from oneself to penetrate another by force] (Paz, *El laberinto,* 69).[27] As recognized by a number of critics, Artemio is a literalization of the *hijo de la chingada,* the son of a violated woman,[28] as he was conceived in rape (Gyurko, "Structure and Theme," 35; Meyer-Minneman,"*La muerte,*" 91). He is thus doubly marked, as *all* Mexicans are *hijos de la chingada* in Paz's description of the nation and its inhabitants in terms of violators and victims, *conquistadores* and vanquished. Fuentes echoes this dichotomy in a character's words, dividing the world between *chingones* and *pendejos* [motherfuckers and assholes] (129), followed shortly by the famous *tú* section based entirely on the verb and its multiple applications (143–147). As it is about to spill into excess, the list is introduced by the words "resumen de la historia: santo y seña de México: tu palabra" [summary of history: Mexico's password: your word] (144).

Thus Fuentes establishes Artemio Cruz as the embodiment of Mexico and Mexicans. At first this might seem improbable, when one considers the protagonist's elevated status. It is difficult to see how one man could stand for such a divided community. Yet, as Gyurko points out, Artemio represents a fusion of characteristics common to the Mexican people: "the diverse, contradictory aspects of the Mexican national character are compressed into the personality of but one man, who appears as both Spanish *conquistador* and as Aztec god, as Revolutionary idealist and as exploitative *latifundista*" ("Structure and Theme," 30).[29] His initial idealism cedes to cynicism and self-aggrandizement. Within his personal life he experiences the full range of economic conditions that illustrate the extreme gap between the rich and the poor in Porfirian Mexico and in the period following the revolution. One senses in Artemio Cruz both the solitude of the Mexican people and the failure of the Mexican Revolution.

Fuentes verbalizes the feeling of disillusionment with the revolution at various points in the text. In an encapsulated version of the rapid fall of idealistic reforms, the revolutionaries begin by making changes in the territories they conquer (imposing a limited work schedule, distributing land to the peasants) only to fear the potential danger of armed workers and to conclude that it is prudent to postpone major social reform until the revolution is victorious (70). Gonzalo Bernal, clearly disabused of his earlier notions of justice, reminds Artemio of the beginning of the revolution, "[c]uando esto se hacía no para elevar a un hombre, sino a todos" [when we weren't doing this to raise up one man but to raise up all men] (194).

There can be no doubt about Fuentes's having continued a basic theme introduced by Mariano Azuela in *Los de abajo*. In case one needs prompting in order to make the connection, Fuentes makes explicit reference to elements of Azuela's work within the text of *La muerte de Artemio Cruz*. There are brief phrases that could trigger a connection between the two novels for alert readers: "los de arriba" and "los de abajo" [the ones on top and the ones at the bottom] (120) and "el peligro de este paseo por el cañón" [the danger of this march through the canyon (a reference to the site of both Macías's first victory and his final defeat)] (173). Of more significance is the remark made in a *tú* section that Artemio will throw a *pedruzco* (boulder; Azuela uses the word *piedra*, stone): "lo arrojarás por la pendiente para que alcance un minuto de vida propia, veloz, enérgica" [you will toss it down the hill so that for a minute it will possess a swift, energetic life of its own] (311). This is a direct link with that famous image of *Los de abajo* when Demetrio tosses a stone into the canyon, frequently interpreted as having to do with the momentum of the revolution. One last parallel is curious in that it represents an inversion of the order established in the earlier work. In a well-known circularity of *Los de abajo*, Demetrio and his men travel from the south to the north and back. As presented by Fuentes, the direction is reversed, but the negative message is the same: "¿Qué se andan creyendo? ¿Que vamos victoriosos hacia el sur, como antes? Pues no. Vamos derrotados, hacia el norte, de donde salimos" [What do you think, that we're on our way south, winning all the way, like before? Well, we aren't. We're lost and we're heading north, back where we came from] (177).

Fuentes's variant of Azuela's symbolism is but one of many examples of circularities or cycles to be found in *La muerte de Artemio Cruz*, just as there had been in *La región más transparente*. The most obvious are the twelve tripartite cycles serving as structural foundation of the novel. In addition, references to both the revolution and to the nation are couched in cyclical terms. As Artemio thinks about aligning himself with the most probable candidate for president, one reads: "Hoy debía hacerlo porque mañana, fatalmente, los ultrajados de hoy lo ultrajarían a él" [He had to do it because, inevitably, the guys who got screwed today would end up screwing him tomorrow] (137). The same notion is expressed by don Gamaliel,

Catalina's father, with a more encompassing view of the nation reminiscent of Azuela's prediction used as epigraph for this chapter: "desventurado país que a cada generación tiene que destruir a los antiguos poseedores y sustituirlos por nuevos amos, tan rapaces y ambiciosos como los anteriores" [unfortunate land that has to destroy its old possessors with each new generation and put in their place new owners just as rapacious and ambitious as the old ones] (50).

Historical discourse, then, repeats itself as well, and, judging by the tone of the characters' comments, this would appear not to bode well for Mexico.[30] Once again Fuentes depicts the nation locked into a cycle of aggressions and deceptions, simulating a ritual not unlike that of the indigenous populations. Fuentes expands on this analogy in structural terms in the dates presented as significant moments in the protagonist's life. Excluding the days marking his birth and his death, the full time span separating the other dates is one of fifty-two years, a most critical number in Mexican Indian religious rites and time measurement.[31] In addition, Klaus Meyer-Minnemann points out that Fuentes's novel is published fifty-two years after the onset of the Mexican Revolution ("La muerte," 94). Although the latter example could well be coincidence, there is compelling reason to consider the relationship among this novel, the revolution, and the notion of repetition through time.

At first glance, focusing on inexorable cyclic patterns in Mexican history provides impetus to respond with pessimism and disillusion. Projecting toward the future, Donald Shaw speaks of "circular destiny" (142) and voices doubt with respect to the lasting value of sacrifices such as those made by Lorenzo Cruz and Gonzalo Bernal. Meyer-Minnemann, on the other hand, interprets the bringing to the foreground of cyclical history as a crucial warning that, without significant effort to break the cycle, another revolution could well occur ("La muerte," 95). In a more positive light, Gyurko would seem to welcome the possibility of another war "that will ultimately attain the goals of unity and of social justice for which the Revolution of 1910 was fought" ("Structure and Theme," 39).

Although condemning the failures of the Revolution of 1910, Fuentes also suggests a positive note at the end of the novel. Artemio, whose initial image was that of a man in fragments, as reflected in his daughter's purse, is seen reconciling the facets of his being. The three narrative tenses, having begun in unity, now resume their closeness: "Tiene una razón tu cuerpo . . . Tiene una razón tu vida . . . Eres, serás, fuiste el universo encarnado" [Your body has a reason for being. . . . Your life has a reason for being. . . . You are, you will be, you were, the universe incarnate] (313). The final segments of the three narrative voices are substantially reduced, fitting on a mere three pages. Near death, the voices conflate to oneness. In its entirety, the *yo* segment states: "Yo no sé . . . no sé . . . si él soy yo . . . si tú fue él . . . si yo soy los tres . . . Tú . . . te traigo dentro de mí y vas a morir conmigo . . . Dios . . . El . . . lo traje adentro y va a morir conmigo . . . los tres . . . que hablaron . . . Yo . . . lo traeré adentro y morirá conmigo . . . sólo [*sic*]" [I don't know . . . I don't know . . . if I am he . . . if you were he . . . if I am the three . . . You . . . I carry you inside me and you are going to die with me . . . God . . . He . . . I carried him inside and he is going to die with me . . . the three of us . . . who spoke . . . I . . . will carry him inside and he will die with me . . . alone . . . ] (315). This one section contains the three subject pronouns and the three verb tenses, as they come together in the final moments of his life.

It is only at the instant of death that Artemio is capable of using the first-person plural as seen in the final words of the text: "los tres . . . moriremos . . . Tú . . . mueres . . . has muerto . . . moriré" [all three . . . We shall die . . . You . . . are dying . . . have died . . . I shall die] (316). Until now, the extremely limited usage of a first-person plural conjugation was confined to Artemio's nostalgic thoughts about his deceased son in "cruzamos el río" (Gyurko, "Structure and Theme," 31). In contrast, the insistent employment of singular voices emphasized Artemio's solitude, again reflecting Paz's conception.

Gyurko finds irony in the fact that Artemio is able to achieve a unity of selves only at the moment of death ("Self, Double, and Mask," 364). If one accepts the equation of the protagonist and the nation, however, a different interpretation emerges. The first of five epigraphs of the novel reads "La préméditation de la mort est préméditation de liberté" (Montaigne; The premeditation of death is the premeditation of liberty). If death releases Artemio from his spiritual incarceration and is therefore a positive force, then readers should move beyond the text to consider the novel's potential message regarding the nation. It is well known that Fuentes was critical of the Mexican Revolution and favored the ideological principles and practices of its Cuban counterpart.[32] Indeed, Fuentes indicates that a portion of the text was written in Havana (316). It is quite possible, then, that Fuentes's emphasis on unity toward the end of the novel is a reflection of a Marxist idealized unity that *should be* the product of a successful revolution, as suggested in the text: "El niño, la tierra, el universo: en los tres, algún día, no habrá ni luz, ni calor, ni vida . . . Habrá sólo la unidad total, olvidada, sin nombre y sin hombre que la nombre: fundidos espacio y tiempo, materia y energía . . . Y todas las cosas tendrán el mismo nombre" [The boy, the earth, the universe: in those three, someday there will be no light, no heat, no life . . . There will be only total, forgotten oneness, nameless, without a man to give it a name: space and time, matter and energy all fused into one . . . And all things will have the same name] (313).

In a sense, the narration achieves what the Mexican Revolution did not. In the present of the novel, the revolution has failed, and the country is fragmented, as is the protagonist. Invoking unification can therefore be seen as a call for the bringing together of classes, of races, of all the diverse parts of the Mexican community. By linking the destiny of Artemio Cruz with the destiny of the nation within the ritualistic fifty-two-year cycle, Fuentes reiterates in a forceful way a statement, if not a warning, that he first articulated in *La región más transparente* about the need to break the pattern of cyclic abuse and powermongering. Although Artemio Cruz had done nothing to alter the cycle, perhaps *La muerte de Artemio Cruz* could.

### *Agua quemada* (Burnt Water) [33]

Nearly twenty years after *Artemio Cruz*, Fuentes returns to the concept of Mexico City as the fragmented protagonist of a national, cultural narrative. In the intervening years, he has employed fragmentation and featured the urban milieu in a variety of ways, but it is with this eccentric novel that gives the appearance of being a group of short stories that he reverts to the thematics and techniques that launched his literary career. The ominous implication of this return is that his call for action has not been heeded and that the conditions decried in the earlier novels remain.

Fuentes has commented on the sameness in the works, referring to *Agua quemada* as "una obra compañera de *La región más transparente*, . . . una especie de elegía" [a companion piece to *Where the Air Is Clear*, . . . a type of elegy] (S. Fuentes 92). Indeed, one of the later novel's two epigraphs is from Alfonso Reyes's "Palinodia del polvo": "¿Es ésta la región más transparente del aire? ¿Qué habéis hecho entonces, de mi alto valle metafísico?" [Is this where the air is clear? What have you done, then, with my lofty metaphysical valley?] (7). The second epigraph, taken from Octavio Paz's

"Vuelta," reveals the source of the title as rooted in Mexico's origins. In tandem, these selections reflect a historical trajectory of Mexico past and present. As readers work with the four narrations, they are once again engaged and prodded to move beyond individual characters to consider a most complex narrative of a city. *La región más transparente* and *Agua quemada* constitute a consideration and a reconsideration of that city and all that the sameness or lack of change implies with respect to the status of the nation.

In order to understand the prominence of Mexico City in *Agua quemada*, let us first examine briefly the external shape of the text. The first section, "El día de las madres" (Mother's Day), details the relationship among three generations of Mexican men: General Vicente Vergara, an active figure in the Mexican Revolution, now well past his prime, a man who clings to the memory of better days when men knew how to be men; his son, Agustín, clearly a disappointment to him for having squandered the family's money despite having converted the fertile fields from *jitomates* to *amapolas* (from tomatoes to poppies), living off drug money; and Plutarco, the first-person narrator, named after a former president of Mexico whom the general calls "el jefe máximo de la revolución" [the Maximum Leader of the Revolution] (17).[34] Plutarco forges a much stronger relationship with his grandfather than with his father, expressing his admiration for the revolutionary times and figures. Yet it is Plutarco who finally links the generations, as one notes from the final image of the three men in the cemetery with their hands entwined.

The second part, "Estos fueron los palacios" (These Were Palaces), is a beautiful story of the relationship between a crippled boy, Luisito, and his friend, Manuelita, an old woman considered eccentric at best, more probably mad, by their common neighbors in an old mansion in the very center of Mexico City, once grand, now housing the poor as well as assorted businesses.

Section three, "Las mañanitas" (The Mandarin), focuses on Federico Silva, an upper-middle-class landlord, who seems to lack direction, even identity. He is a man who tries to stage his death just as he had staged his life, the latter with imitations in clothing and gesture of Maurice Chevalier, Anthony Eden, Cole Porter, and F. Scott Fitzgerald. For his death, he instructs his servant to have playing Schubert's "Unfinished Symphony" when the body is discovered and, next to the corpse, an open copy of Dickens's *The Mystery of Edwin Drood* (85). Yet his game of an unfinished, unfinished symphony and an unfinished, unfinished novel, despite its amusing redundancy, is for naught, as his life is cut short by some of the street hoodlums whose territory includes his area in Colonia Juárez. He is displaced by a new generation of Mexicans.

The final portion, "El hijo de Andrés Aparicio" (The Son of Andrés Aparicio), traces the development, or, perhaps better stated, the degeneration of Bernabé Aparicio. The son of an idealist who tried to bring justice to the state of Guerrero,[35] Bernabé sells his soul to the very man who broke his father's spirit. From his impoverished childhood, during which he cleaned windshields to make a little money, Bernabé learns to claw his way to the top, to flatter the powerful, and to kill.

Although on the surface these could appear to be a series of four disconnected stories, throughout the work there are indications of an interior cohesiveness that generate a rethinking of the material and a consideration of the whole. Readers responding to the novel's dynamics are rewarded with a reading of cohesion analogous to that of *La región más transparente* and *La muerte de Artemio Cruz*. In an echo of Fuentes's first novel, the clearest unifiers of the four sections are the interrelationships among characters: eccentric Manuelita, more comfortable with dogs than with people, was formerly a servant to the Vergaras and a nurse for Plutarco; among the houses sustaining Federico Silva is the old mansion on La Moneda street in which Manuelita and Luisito live; in childhood, Bernabé was friends with Luisito, and Bernabé's brothers work at a garage owned by Agustín Vergara; Bernabé's maternal grandfather was head groom to General Vergara.

Also easily noticed are the repeated specific references to places in Mexico City. The novel begins in Pedregal, an upper-class area south of the central area that, in the case of the Vergaras, represents the old rich (something the general makes clear).[36] Section two moves to the historical center, around the Zócalo, the cathedral, and the Merced market. With Federico Silva, the place-names are again very familiar: Insurgentes, Chapultepec, and Génova among others in Colonia Juárez. Finally, in "El hijo de Andrés Aparicio," one comes full circle, back to Pedregal, only this time with a newer generation of those with political influence.

Characters and place-names are, however, only the beginning. Active readers are likely to become conditioned by these readily seen unifiers, stimulated to probe other levels and to challenge the text to yield other unities. It is in this way that the fluidity of the work, the processes of narration, begin to show their patterns. Tellingly, all of these signifiers of unity are prepared from the very start: on the title page, *Agua quemada* is qualified as a "cuarteto narrativo" (a narrative quartet), a blending of poetry and prose.

Within the novel are a number of progressions that readers can discern through a syntagmatic consideration. The most apparent is a series of drawings taken from the front cover.[37] The full sketch shows two men dressed in typical garb of the revolution, a bathtub, and what appears to be a boot sticking out at an odd angle and spilling out of the frame of the picture, as do a portion of the tub and one man's sombrero. Then, preceding each section of the *cuarteto* is a more penetrating view of the top left quadrant of the cover picture. Since the first segment shows a full quarter of the sketch, one could assume that succeeding fragments might present the other three in turn. Instead, Fuentes focuses more intently, as the image paradoxically is at once magnified and diminished; the bigger the image, the less that fits on the page. By the time readers reach the final section, the picture is almost a blur, yet they recognize it because they have been guided by the text. What would have been a blur becomes decipherable. Furthermore, it must be seen as significant that, instead of staying on the surface, which showing the four quadrants would have done, Fuentes has chosen to probe deeper, adding dimension to his examination. The object that is magnified is a man's head, connoting thought. One moves deeper and deeper into the Mexican consciousness.

A second progression can be found in the method of narration of the four segments, this time achieving an apparent distancing. "El día de las madres" is narrated in the first person; Plutarco is speaking directly. "Estos fueron los palacios" moves to a third-person omniscient narrator. "Las mañanitas" continues in third-person but is broken into four fragments. "El hijo de Andrés Aparicio" continues the progression, exploding into sixteen sections, each bearing a title, as if they could be considered separate essays, separate entities. Paralleling the distancing in narration is a progression to be found in the declining use of dialogue. There is a mixture of dialogue, description, and thoughts in the first three sections in varying degrees, but tending toward more description, more fluidity in the prose. The fourth segment makes its difference known quite clearly. In addition to its fragmented status, "El hijo de Andrés Aparicio" quickly establishes another pattern: each portion appears as an essay, a literal block of narrative ending with a line or two of dialogue. Section eleven, which consists of all dialogue, breaks the existing pattern (thus reinforcing the rule that has been violated and making readers aware of it), and then the text returns to the naturalized norm. The block essays are full of thoughts, of memories, of streams of words that seem to rush forward on their own momentum, moving into an interior consciousness that parallels the intensity of the fourth image discussed above.

Finally, let us consider the titles of the last part of the *cuarteto* that serve as a history in miniature of the city itself. One moves from the origins, "El lugar" (The Place), "El padre" (The Father), and "La madre" (The Mother) to a vision of Mexico City today. It is here that readers likely respond to the impetus to consider the city, thus leading to further reflections on the already read. Fuentes signals that jump with the following passage describing "El lugar": "Que este lugar no tuvo nombre porque era algo así como todo lo que fue la ciudad grande, aquí estaba lo peor de la ciudad y puede que lo mejor también, . . . y por eso no pudo tener un nombre especial" [That this place had no name because it was like the huge sprawling city itself, that here they had everything that was bad about the city but maybe the best too . . . and that's why it couldn't have a name of its own] (98). Through it all, there is Mexico at its best and at its worst; "El lugar" as a microcosm of Mexico City, Mexico City as a microcosm of the country itself, although it seems strange to consider Mexico City a microcosm of anything, given its vastness.

All signs lead to Mexico. It is, however, a Mexico that can unite spatially but still maintains its own fragmented status, demonstrating that the twenty-three years separating *Agua quemada* from *La región más transparente* have seen little to change fundamental inequalities. The characters are clearly separated by social class; even the links among them have their roots in class related positions: servants, landlords, grooms, and masters. The place-names mentioned immediately connote economic position: Pedregal, the Zona Rosa (the Pink Zone, now a major tourist area), and the run-down mansions of the Centro, which happens to be the closest in roots to the old Mexico, the grand city that was, evoked by the title *agua quemada*.

Many characters voice their criticism of present-day Mexico. Within Plutarco's meditations one reads: "Qué lastimoso intento de castidad urbana en una capital como la nuestra, despierte, abuelito, mírela de noche, México, ciudad voluntariamente cancerosa, hambrienta de extensión anárquica, pintaviolines de toda intención de estilo, ciudad que confunde la democracia con la posesión, pero también el igualitarismo con la vulgaridad" [What a pitiful attempt at urban chastity in a capital like ours, wake up,

Grandfather, look at it by night, Mexico City, voluntarily a cancerous city, hungry for uncontrolled expansion, a hodgepodge of styles, a city that confuses democracy with possessions, and egalitarianism with vulgarity] (37). Federico Silva makes the historical contrast more blatant, as he laments the loss of the early morning smells that he associates with the old lake bed (71). Federico complains bitterly about the grotesque cement structures that surround his building: "Le daba vergüenza que un país de iglesias y pirámides edificadas para la eternidad acabara conformándose con una ciudad de cartón, caliche y caca" [He felt ashamed that a country of churches and pyramids built for eternity should end up contenting itself with a city of shanties, shoddiness, and shit] (72–73).

One is presented with a Mexico full of corruption and drugs, in which the purity of the past has given way to the commercialism of the present, as the *jitomates* gave way to the *amapolas*. It is a land whose upper-class citizens wear Eisenhower jackets (12) and Jantzen bathing suits (26); Plutarco drives a Thunderbird (12), his father a Lincoln Continental (26). Plutarco's ride around the *periférico* (the expressway that circles the city) makes him a witness to the intruding northern neighbor's influence. Readers follow a wave of commercial impressions as rapid as the ride: Santa Claus, Coca Cola, and Donald Duck blend with beer and vacuum cleaner ads, and these, in turn, mesh with visions of traffic cops and bribery. One keeps returning to inequalities, to the rich and the poor, to the disparity that spawned the revolution and the disparity that remains: *los de arriba y los de abajo* (those on top and the underdogs).

The wording, of course, reverts once more to Azuela's novel of the revolution with its expression of disillusion and inequality and an analogous circular route from the south to the north and back. Even more significantly, Fuentes highlights the sameness through image and language, both focused on the term "bola" as metaphor for the revolution. At the beginning of *Agua quemada*, as General Vergara shares his memories of the revolution, he relates the history of Pancho Villa: "Entonces Villa fue a buscarlos uno por uno, a convencerlos de que había que seguir en la bola" [Villa went and searched them out, one by one, to convince them they had to keep fighting] (15). Shortly afterward, speaking of Cárdenas, he adds, "Las viejas haciendas no producían. Los campesinos las habían quemado antes de irse a la bola" [The haciendas, the old agricultural estates, weren't producing. The peasants had burned them down before going off to fight] (21). The imagery in Spanish is exact and unmistakable, especially when one notes its relationship with the end of "El hijo de Andrés Aparicio." On the final pages of the fourth section, el Güero gives Bernabé a gun for self-defense, "y le dijo que no se preocupara, el Jefe tenía razón, no había manera de controlarlos una vez que empezaban a rodar, *mira esa piedra como ya no se para* [and (he) told him not to worry, the Chief was right, there was no way to stop them once they got rolling, *look at that rock, how it keeps rolling*] (138, emphasis in the original). The final words of this passage, in italics so as to draw them to readers' attention, are the very words used by Azuela (137).

*Agua quemada* is a novel of Mexico, of the revolution, and of the disillusionment regarding the revolution's aftermath. The agents to unify the segments, the characters, and the images are, of course, its readers, as Fuentes mentions in his interview with Sylvia Fuentes. Speaking of Cervantes's *Don Quijote* and of his own *Terra nostra*, he calls for active readers: "hay un desafío de co-creación con el lector . . . yo quiero tener la compañía de esos co-creadores, de esos co-autores, y que les cueste" [there is a challenge of co-creation with the reader . . . I want to have the company of those co-creators, of those co-authors, and may it make them work hard] (102).

For Fuentes, however, the need for unification achieves a more universal plane, one linked with the focus of his work, Mexico: "el origen antiguo de México nace del desmembramiento, de la ruptura de la realidad, en este caso una madre totalmente desmembrada por sus hijos, sus pedazos lanzados al universo, al cosmos, al vacío, y de ahí la obligación humana de reconstruir el origen, de reconstruir la unidad" [the ancient origen of Mexico is born from the dismemberment, from the rupturing of reality, in this case a mother totally dismembered by her children, the pieces of her body thrown to the universe, to the cosmos, to the emptiness of space, and from there the human obligation to reconstruct the origin, to reconstruct the unity] (S. Fuentes 83).

The novel is fragmented, as is the city, as are the characters. This notion is graphically expressed in that series of pictures preceding the four sections of the novel. With each magnification, what began as a representational depiction is more and more segmented, finally resulting in a collection of blotches and spots, reminding one, to a certain extent, of a painting by Georges Seurat. It is a lesson in pointillism or divisionism, the latter evidently the term preferred by the artist (Janson 506). Standing very close to such a painting, one sees the dots, thus observing the technique but not appreciating the whole. A more distanced view is required in order to capture the full impact. Similarly, readers must achieve a distance from the four stories that constitute *Agua quemada* in order to appreciate this new novel of the revolution. With this work, readers become historians, voyagers, decipherers, and unifiers. They read the past as they read the text, along with Plutarco and his reading of memories. History, memory, and unification are crucial to *Agua quemada*, to Carlos Fuentes, and to all who are concerned with breaking the cycles detailed in *La región más transparente* and *La muerte de Artemio Cruz*, which this novel of the 1980s indicates have yet to be stopped.

Fuentes's two early volumes would prove to be instrumental in shaping subsequent Mexican fiction. Their immediate impact can be felt in the novels of the 1960s in the two main currents of Mexican fiction: *escritura*, or novels that privilege form and the theme of writing, and *la Onda*, novels associated with the younger generation, both of which will be discussed in the following chapters. Fuentes himself would publish in 1967 *Cambio de piel* (A Change of Skin), a novel that comes under the rubric of *escritura*. Both groups would continue the practice of fragmented fiction and experimental strategies now firmly established by Fuentes's having so completely integrated international techniques into Mexican thematics. *Escritura* writers such as Salvador Elizondo, Juan José Arreola, and José Emilio Pacheco would expand upon narrative experimentation that breaks with tradition in ways much more sophisticated than those used by the vanguard writers, at least in part because of the trajectories within prose and readership established by Rulfo, Vicens, and Fuentes. José Agustín and Gustavo Sainz, initiators of the *Onda*, would benefit in particular from a combination of discursive and story elements in *La región más transparente* that mark a sense of new freedom within narrative, such as the inclusion of language typical of the lower classes; untranslated foreign languages; a cynical view of the children of the bourgeoisie; a homosexual character, Gus; and a reference, albeit brief, to student demonstrations.

# CHAPTER 6

# *E* S C R I T U R A

The 1960s was a decade of extraordinary creative productivity in Mexico and elsewhere in Latin America, a period known in literary circles as the "Boom." International recognition came not only to Juan Rulfo and Carlos Fuentes, but also to Juan José Arreola, Rosario Castellanos, and Octavio Paz. Although important Mexican novels of the 1960s are extremely varied in both form and content, there is general consensus that there emerge two fundamental groups whose denomination reflects a major focus of the artists' works: those whose novels are refinements of the narrative tradition devoted to the process of writing, as had been observed from Azuela through Fuentes, who fall under the heading *escritura* (writing); and those who seek to capture in their narrative an irreverent social attitude directed against the bourgeoisie, "*la Onda*" (Leal, "Nuevos novelistas mexicanos," 92). Each movement in its own way adapts universal currents, whether in literary or social practice. The *escritura* novelists join an international group of authors whose interests lean toward universal themes and nontraditional narrative forms.[1] Although not with the same intensity, members of *la Onda* echo their counterparts in Europe and the United States in expressing the restlessness and sociopolitical dissatisfaction that culminate in 1968 in Mexico (Tlatelolco) as they do in France and the United States.

Although there has been general recognition of these distinct tendencies, establishing clear definitions that would preclude overlapping of both distinguishing characteristics and authors has not been easy. Margo Glantz, who addressed the issue of differentiating the two as early as 1971, cites as a fundamental concern of the *escritura* writers an essential preoccupation with language and with structure (*Repeticiones*, 106). She aligns these authors with the practitioners of the *nouveau roman* who focused more on form than on content and adds two important characteristics that are integral to a study of fragmented novels of this period: an attempt to destroy the traditional novelistic form and an insistence on readers' complicity in the narrative process (107, 109).[2] In his 1975 essay surveying the broad spectrum of new Mexican novelists, Luis Leal employs the same dichotomy, citing a concern with stylistic elements as the most important feature of *escritura* authors and attributing a cultural focus to the *Onda* group (Leal, "Nuevos novelistas mexicanos," 92), which echoes Glantz's summation: "Onda como crítica social y 'escritura' como creación verbal" [*Onda* as social criticism and "*escritura*" as verbal creation] (Glantz, *Repeticiones*, 113). The choice of such broad categories, however, invites warranted concern about the definition of the two groups and the determination of their membership, for an essential feature of the *Onda* writers is their inventiveness with language. Symptomatic of this confusion is the fact that José Agustín, considered a founding father of *Onda* fiction (although he was only nineteen when his first novel, *La tumba*, was published), claims an inability to define the term and frustration that it was ever coined (Teichmann 60).[3] Characteristics of *Onda* fiction will be discussed in the next chapter.

Within the novels falling under the rubric of *escritura*, fragmentation stands out as a common structural component. Indeed, the novels selected for this discussion—Juan José Arreola's *La feria* (1963), Salvador Elizondo's *Farabeuf o la crónica de un instante* (1965), and José Emilio Pacheco's *Morirás lejos* (1967, revised edition 1977)—represent the perfection of fragmented structure integrated with sociohistorical issues. They offer a much more sophisticated treatment than the earlier experimental vanguard fiction, marking the attainment of maximum aesthetic achievement and mastery of segmented form. All three have compactly woven components that variously mesh and clash until assembled into a coherent whole by readers. Each assumes competent readers, already versed in unconventional narrative strategies and well armed in the mental acuity necessary in order to come to terms with a fragmented, nonlinear, apparently incoherent text. In none of the three will one find overt instructions as to the process of unification. The clues are there, but they are more subtle, concealed within the narrative and only to be discerned through an analysis of discourse as well as content. In sum, all three treatments demonstrate that fragmentation as a discursive strategy, regardless of the difference of subject matter, relates to the elaboration of a profound reader aesthetic.[4]

For novels that have so much in common, however, *La feria, Farabeuf,* and *Morirás lejos* are very unique. Stylistic and thematic differences will be revealed in individual analyses, but a more encompassing distinction sets them apart even from a most superficial consideration. In *La feria*, Arreola successfully combines fundamentally Mexican themes and concerns in a most sophisticated treatment of fragmentation, joining regionalism and a new stylistics, as did Rulfo. In contrast, Elizondo's *Farabeuf* demonstrates a more abstract and universal outlook, linked in conception and execution with the *nouveau roman* in its insistence on readers' contemplation of the text as text. J. Ann Duncan has called Elizondo "the most uncompromisingly experimental of contemporary Mexican writers" (18). Although analogous in many ways to Elizondo's literary praxis, Pacheco's *Morirás lejos* firmly establishes a historical dimension focused on the persecution of the Jews, thus expanding the readers' role to include both narrative and moral commitment instead of a more narrowly defined, purely aesthetic experience.

### Juan José Arreola, *La feria* (The Fair)

Juan José Arreola's *La feria* (1963) is a unique blending of regionalism and universality, to the detriment of neither. Its regionalism is most evident in the content: an array of Mexican characters particular to Arreola's native Ciudad Guzmán, formerly Zapotlán el Grande; language replete with *mexicanismos* so crucial to the text that the translator for the English edition could not bring himself to mutilate the novel by translating certain of them (Upton vii); references to rural life that, although not specific to Mexico in theme (concern for the land, emerging sexuality, local literary groups), in treatment become the quintessence of Jalisco. *La feria*'s universality, on the other hand, can be traced directly to form, for its creative use of fragmentation links Arreola not only to Yáñez and Rulfo, but also to international authors who, through innovative narrative strategies, force their readers into an awareness of the need to work actively with the given text.

Any examination of *La feria* must take into consideration its fragmentation and the relationship of that narrative strategy to reader response. In *La feria*, diegetic and discursive elements consistently point toward a designated process for an active reader's role. Throughout the novel, whether reflected in actions, images, or language, one perceives a movement from the individual to the collective, from the microcosmic unit to the whole, thus drawing readers' attention to the process of unification. As a consequence of the repetition of this technique, one becomes aware of the dramatization of a possible cohesiveness attainable by responding to the author's inducing readers to work with the fragments to forge a whole, to construct and/or complete the novel(s) potentially there. To reinforce this notion, Arreola offers his readers a negative example of potential response. He includes as a model of a reader-in-the-text one who remains distanced from what he should be trying to understand. At the same time, this character voices the contrast between an active and passive reading of circumstance, hence of narrative. Although the active reading not only takes more effort but also reveals a more painful reality, it is, finally, the more satisfactory and fulfilling. It offers a complete experience that provides multiple levels of significance for readers.

By its fragmentation, *La feria* calls attention to its status as a nonwhole. Yet through elements of story, the text offers its readers an example of a role that will fulfill the novel's potential through their active involvement with the segments. The fragments cry out for unification. Indeed, one might say that in Arreola's novel, on various levels, story represents the dramatization of the desire of its discourse.

John Upton calls *La feria* "a gallery of voices" (vii), a complimentary phrase as used by the translator, yet also the source of initial disorientation for readers. In this novel a vast array of characters speak out in an ample spectrum of discourses.[5] Generally the narration is in the first person, although there are exceptions. Readers are exposed to, among others, an Indian *tlayacanque* who comments on the natives' claim to the land; a shoemaker who decides to try his luck at farming; a preadolescent experiencing sexual feelings and confessing all; a ladies' man flaunting sexual prowess; a few prostitutes and their madam; a poetess who sells cosmetics as a complement to her erotic verse; assorted shopkeepers; a budding poet recording his efforts to court a young girl; and San José, the patron saint of Zapotlán. One meets the rich and the poor, the educated and the ignorant, the experienced sexually obsessed and the innocent sexually obsessed. Characters either speak out themselves or are spoken about; rarely do they speak to each other. Some voices appear with frequency, others surface but once; some are identified, others are left anonymous. Frequently readers must make their own identification through the content of the speech: references to the narrator's profession; certain peculiar characteristics traceable to one personage; an indication of reciprocity in a relationship about which readers have been informed from the other point of view; reiteration of language or theme. Complicating matters even further is the inclusion of recorded voices from historical documents, newspapers, even the Bible. Readers' initial reaction is very likely to be that the fragments have been thrown together haphazardly (Chávarri 419).

Arreola divides his text into 288 fragments, a self-referential strategy flaunting nonlinearity, a lack of respect for traditional norms of narrative continuity. He further calls attention to this truncated discourse by inserting a variety of vignettes, one for each space between fragments. Some of the drawings relate to the preceding segment (194/125–126; 195/126–128),[6] some to what follows (5/9–10; 15/14), and others have no clear linkage to surrounding fragments. The segments vary in length from a minimum of one line (116/71; 184/117; 286/181) to a maximum of three-and-a-half pages (135/83–86).

Contiguous fragments at times demonstrate the use of perspectivism, that is, different points of view in relation to the same occurrence. Frequently, however, contiguity yields nothing more than spatial concurrence, as the segments seem totally unrelated. In addition, one finds sections dating from colonial times, the *Reforma,* and the revolution interpolated into those of the "present," the latter not identified by a year but clearly established as a linear movement from the spring sowing to the autumn harvest and October fair, as reinforced by the farmer's notes and the young poet's diary.

Certain linear coherence within an apparently otherwise unordered discourse, in fact, soon lessens the reader's initial disorientation. As with *Pedro Páramo,* readers are drawn to recognizable linking through story. Arreola has identified five linear episodes: the farmer's sequences, the fight for land, the Ateneo meetings, the boy's confessions, and the poet's saga (Carballo, *Diecinueve protagonistas,* 405). To this should be added the Licenciado's funeral, important not only for its linear development but also for its bringing together of story, discourse, and reader's role, as shall be demonstrated.

Arreola confesses to having had the intention of writing a novel in the traditional manner or, in his words, "puro y extendido, esto es, continuo" [pure and extended, that is, continuous] (Carballo, *Diecinueve protagonistas,* 404). Soon, however, he found himself disillusioned with what he had written; it lacked the rhythm he desired. Recognizing the quality of some shorter sections and relating them to his earlier works consisting of brief pieces led Arreola to an approach that would use fragments to capture his impressions and reactions to his surroundings (Carballo, *Diecinueve protagonistas*, 404). Arreola mixed creative sections based on experiences in Ciudad Guzmán with the aforementioned written excerpts from actual documents plus biographical information requested from some of his fellow citizens and incorporated almost verbatim (Carballo, *Diecinueve protagonistas*, 405). The sections are all brief and evocative in some way of life in Zapotlán, with special emphasis on language.

In an interview with Gustavo Sainz, Arreola in a sense justifies his selected discourse by contrasting the twentieth-century author with his nineteenth-century counterpart. As paraphrased by Yulan Washburn, "Arreola says that the twentieth-century writer's mind is simply not the same as that of the earlier writers who developed so many of the techniques that have come to be associated with the novel. The interior of the mind and memory are not made up of long discourses" (118). Washburn goes on to compare Arreola's fragmented discourse to the sensorial impressions one would experience in a stroll through an actual fair: "they would encounter people they did not know and would never get to know; they would hear passing scraps of conversation, exclamations, and tones of voice; they would see faces at one point and reencounter them at another, never knowing their names" (118–119). Arreola's analogy of the same process is even more provocative, as he makes a comparison between his novel and "un archipiélago de pequeños islotes que al fin y al cabo suponían bajo la superficie de los hechos narrados una masa continental. Esto es, la novela probable de la cual sólo he querido dar, finalmente, una serie de puntos o de situaciones agudas" [an archipelago of small islands that finally assume a continental mass under the surface of narrated events. That is, the probable novel of which I have only wanted to give a series of high points or crucial episodes] (Carballo, *Diecinueve protagonistas*, 404–405).[7]

Without mentioning it explicitly, Arreola has touched upon the readers' role, for to reach the "continental mass," the probable novel, requires movement, activity. It is important to note that the author does not impose strict limits on his readers; the outcome is "the probable novel," not a rigidly defined construct. Arreola does, however, incorporate through story and discourse a suggestion of what type of activity or movement on the part of readers will initiate the process, beginning with a subtle indication of grouping in the fragments related to the Licenciado's funeral.

Although manifesting multiple narrative voices, segments sixty-four through eighty-three (41–50) all relate to one occurrence: the death and burial of the usurer. Until this point in the novel, the voices, although possibly speaking about the same theme (land, for example), did not reach out to each other in communication but, instead, spoke in isolation. Speakers were as disconnected as fragments. Here, however, one finds for ten pages communication among characters as well as cohesiveness among fragments, since each successive segment yields more information. As readers combine the multiple perspectives to form a more ample vision, they begin to understand the inadequacy of a single point of view, such as that generally used in nineteenth-century fiction. Characters group together, either to bury the Licenciado or to gossip about him; fragments are united into a cohesive whole; finally, readers have illustrated before them tangible evidence that combining certain parts can produce a unit. This piece of story reflects both discourse and readers' participation, making readers aware of the attempts at grouping they have already made in response to the initial incoherence of the fragmented text. The Licenciado's funeral is, in effect, a dramatization of readers' activity and confirmation of the positive results attainable through involvement with the text.

Significantly, there are other pieces of story subsequent to the Licenciado's funeral that reinforce the notion of grouping, of going from the individual to the collective. Those who owe money to the deceased speak of forming a debtors' association; some with literary leanings decide to form the Ateneo for cultural exchanges. Gradually, following the story-induced impetus, readers move beyond the more superficial level of grouping individual stories (all the confessional scenes; the farmer's notes) to a more profound stratum of artistic composition where other aspects of Arreola's masterfully controlled unity are waiting to be discovered.

Once readers allow themselves to move in and among the fragments, they are more likely to notice that the movement from the individual to the collective is reflected throughout the novel, giving it a cohesiveness that could not be appreciated from a more distanced view. In this sense, the readers' role can be seen in contrast to the inadequate vision of the whole presented early in the novel dramatized by the priest's ascending a nearby hill to view Zapotlán:

> Veía el valle como lo vio la primera vez Fray Juan de Padilla, sólo por encima: "Pero yo, Señor, lo veo por debajo. ¡Qué iniquidad, Dios mío, qué iniquidad! Un río de estulticia me ha entrado por las orejas, in-

cesante como las aguas que bajan de las Peñas en las crecidas de julio y agosto. Aguas limpias que la gente ensucia con la basura de sus culpas . . . Pero desde aquí, desde arriba, qué pueblo tan bonito, dormido a la orilla de su valle redondo, como una fábrica de adobes, de tejas y ladrillos. (14/14)

[He saw the valley as Fray Juan de Padilla saw it for the first time: only from above.

"But I Lord, see it from below. What iniquity! My God, what iniquity! A river of folly has poured into my ears, as incessant as the waters that come down from Las Peñas in the freshets of July and August. The clean waters that people pollute with the offal of their guilt . . . But from here, from above, what a pretty town it is, sleeping at the edge of its rounded valley like a fairy-tale village of adobes, bricks, and roof tiles!][8]

It is true that the priest's vision unites Zapotlán spatially and serves as a temporal unifier, joining the priest and Fray Juan de Padilla. The priest's own words, however, indicate the inadequacy of such a distanced vision. From afar, one can appreciate the picturesque quality of the sleepy town. But such a vision is a distortion of reality as the priest knows it; reality, for him, involves the souls of the people, and to know the people, one must be among them and interact with them.

The priest is, in effect, a dramatization of the reader-in-the-text. Contrasting his two visions, one passive from above, the other active and involved, one perceives a direct parallel with the readers' role. Readers of *La feria* cannot remain distanced from its fragments without sacrificing the dynamism of the novel. They must move mentally among the segments relating the pieces of discourse, characters, and images.

Readers who undertake such involvement should appreciate the unity of *La feria*. As a specific example, movement from the individual to the collective transcends fragments to yield a cohesiveness indicative of Arreola's controlled artistic vision, both of the novel and of the suggested readers' role. The following are some of the more important indicators of collectivity emphasizing imagery and language: instead of two hundred candles costing one peso apiece, don Fidencio is asked to construct one massive candle at the price of two hundred pesos (171/109); because of inclement weather, the private funeral oration will instead be published in the newspaper for all to read (83/49); the farm laborers join the majordomo in tossing their hats to the ground, where the individual units fall into the shape of a cross (151/96); even sexual peccadillos are spatially unified in the infamous *Zona de Tolerancia* (Tolerance Zone). Through language Arreola reinforces readers' awareness of unification, as he has a character comment on the new arrangement: "Más vale tener un lugar de a tiro echado a la perdición, que no todas esas lacras desparramadas por el cuerpo de Zapotlán" [It's better to have one area totally devoted to sin than all those blemishes spread out over the body of Zapotlán] (118/72).

Wording once again emphasizes movement from the individual to the collective with regard to the confessional scenes. At first the young boy confesses, on an individual basis, to having had thoughts about sex. Quickly readers are brought to associate the words, "Me acuso Padre" [I confess, Father], with the boy's part and thus should be well prepared for the collective confession after the earthquake that begins "Me acuso Padre de Todo" [I confess to Everything, Father] (135/83). The rest of the fragment, the longest of the novel, details a chaotic series of confessed sins that pulls together the townspeople to such an extent that the priests decide a single *Ego te absolvo* will suffice (136/86).[9] Circularity within the mass confession reinforces its unified status: it begins and ends with "Me acuso Padre de que me robé una peseta" (I confess, Father, that I stole a peseta). Even more impetus to consider the unity of the confession section is provided by the infrequency of periods to provide closure. Generally, individual voiced confessions are joined by commas, with occasional suspension points or exclamation marks. Mauricio Ostria notes the paradoxical nature of fragmentation's producing unity, precisely in the lengthy confession: "La fragmentación ha llegado, pues, a su máxima expresión. Sin embargo, mágicamente, los fragmentos narrativos se han unido indisolublemente hasta dar origen a un nuevo ser: el ser del pueblo" [Fragmentation has reached, then, its maximum expression. Nevertheless, magically, the narrated fragments have united indissolubly to the point of creating a new being: the essence of the town] (207).

Finally, language alone is capable of fostering a sense of collectivity. A reference within the text to "la gran familia mexicana" [the great Mexican family] (198/130) during the annual celebration of independence may not seem unusual enough to call readers' attention, but the beginning of the novel clearly presents a plurality: "Somos más o menos treinta mil. Unos dicen que más, otros que menos. Somos treinta mil desde siempre" [There are about thirty thousand of us. Some say more, some say less. We have always been thirty thousand] (1/7). In its privileged position, the first word of *La feria* is a signifier of collectivity: *Somos* (We are). Significantly, Arreola has stated: "El pasaje que condensa el espíritu del libro es el primero" [the fragment that condenses the spirit of the novel is the first] (Carballo, *Diecinueve protagonistas*, 406).

With such an emphasis on the movement from the individual to the collective with people, with objects, and with fragments, it comes as no surprise that there is also unity in theme. Chávarri gives particular mention to death, which he considers a classic theme for Mexican novelists (422–243). Death is not the most pervasive thematic unifier, however; it does not unite enough of the characters. By far the most thorough and persuasive treatment of theme in *La feria* is that of Luis Leal ("*La feria* de Juan José Arreola"), who clearly demonstrates that the thematic unifier for individuals, collectives, and institutions is *el fracaso* (failure), which allows Arreola movement from the comic to a more serious critique of sociopolitical circumstances.

The examples of failure of an individual are so numerous as to prohibit a full accounting; the following is a sampling that makes manifest Arreola's range of sardonic humor and genuine feeling for Zapotlán's inhabitants. The king fails in his efforts to protect the Indians; so does the priest, as he is recalled to Guadalajara because of his pro-Indian sympathies. The Licenciado is so in love with his money that he never marries. Don Salva spends considerable time thinking about girls, but when he finally makes a decision to propose to Chayo it is too late. Urbano, the bellringer, has a way of ringing thirteen instead of twelve, and Sahuaripa, the snaketamer, dies from the bite of a hognose immediately after assuring the public that the serpent is nonvenomous. The shoemaker-turned-farmer, since he has two parcels of land, decides to divide similarly his approach to farming: he plants one field in anticipation of the rain and the other after the rainy season starts. Both plots fail. Another note taker also fails: the young poet finally gives up on both his girl and his diary. Concha de Fierro considers herself a failure because she cannot lose her virginity. Because she *has* lost hers, Chayo fails as a daughter and, certainly, as a prospective virgin for the fair's parade float.

The fact that Concha de Fierro eventually is penetrated leads one to consider the exceptions to the rule. Interestingly, the individuals who succeed do so in sexual matters. In addition to Concha and her partner, Pedro

Corrales, one must consider the cases of María la Metraca and Alejandrina. The madam makes her fortune by buying property in the Zona de Tolerancia and using it advantageously. The poetess is also financially successful, though hardly on the artistic merits of her verse. Despite the clear pattern of exceptions, Arreola does not overtly moralize one way or another; any conclusions are left for his readers.

The theme of failure, however, pervades. Within the matrix of collectives, the church, with the exception of the priest, fails in its bias against the Indians. Furthermore, those governments that attempt more equity in terms of land distribution fail also. Although the Reformist government of the nineteenth century succeeded in confiscating church property, the lands were quickly snatched up by a privileged few. The Mexican Revolution certainly gave the Indians no relief, and its insufficiency can be felt throughout the implied or stated social criticism of *La feria*, denouncing the social conditions of the country and interrogating the failures of the revolution (de la Selva, Review, 253).

The best example of a failure for a collective is the misbegotten Ateneo. Its distinguished first guest, Palinuro, insists on toasting with a glass of cognac each of the literary enthusiasts, one glass apiece for eighteen members. As a result, the poet falls asleep before he is able to read from his works (167/105–106). At the second reunion, the speaker manages to deliver his address all too well: "La traición y los traidores en Zapotlán el Grande, durante las guerras de Conquista, de Independencia y de Reforma" [Treachery and Traitors in Zapotlán El Grande during the Wars of the Conquest, of Independence, and of the Reform] (174/110–112). Fortunately, most of the members manage to leave the premises during a blackout before having to suffer through the account of a plotted assassination attempt by some of Zapotlán's citizens against the national hero, Benito Juárez.

Leal links these multiple failures with what he considers the critical motif of the novel, the fair itself, into which all the characters have been integrated, as if in a mosaic ("*La feria*," 47). The novel culminates in the fair, and it, too, is a failure. Vandals spill kerosene about the bases of the fireworks display and then quickly ignite them. Here, however, the final narrative voice combines audience (reader) response with the (by now) predictability of another failure: "En vez de arder parte por parte y en el orden previsto por don Atilano, ya se imaginarán lo que pasó. El estallido fue general y completo, como el de un polvorín" [You can imagine what happened to the *castillo*. Instead of going off section by section, in the order Don

Atilano had planned, it exploded all at once, like a powder magazine] (288/ 182). The passage is also strikingly evocative of a reading of *La feria*. It is hard to read this novel, fragment by fragment, without having one's mind actively attempt to relate the parts.

Arreola moves readers beyond the fragments through grouping, through imagery, through themes that transcend the segmented discourse. As Sara Poot Herrera argues, the spaces between fragments afford readers time to reconsider what they have read by imposing a pause in their linear reading (185). Readers combine and contrast the multiple narrative voices, for to whom are these voices speaking if not to them? There seems to be little consensus among characters, and even less communication. Readers are called upon to unite these limited, isolated visions (fragments), joining the characters' efforts, opinions, emotions, and failures to form a fuller vision of Zapotlán past and present. There is a reality beyond these fragments, alluded to in an epigraph in modern Provençal from *Calendau* by Frédéric Mistral that evokes the ultimate reality as the soul of one's country, here used in the Spanish sense of *patria chica* (little country), evoking one's more local roots. Even more crucial in relationship to *La feria*, however, is the revelation of soul through words and deeds. From each narrative voice readers are directly exposed to a perspective of life in Zapotlán. There is no intervention, no extraneous person to color the readers' interpretation. To be sure, no one voice, no one character is capable of a true vision of the whole. The only character who attempts to conceive a whole from a singular perspective forms a distorted vision from afar. Not even the author can capture the total reality of Zapotlán through narrative description. Arreola must evoke that reality through fragmentation, through pieces of life as represented by words and deeds, and allow readers to construct their version of Zapotlán. The totality of these constructions might approach the real.

Lenica Puyhol has written of *La feria* that it cannot be told to someone else, that it must be read (Puyhol 386). The work is to be experienced. Readers must move in and among the fragments to sense a whole. There really is no need to make a chronological ordering of all events. To do so is tantamount to mutilating the text, as Jean-Paul Sartre has clearly demonstrated with his comments on Faulkner's *The Sound and the Fury*, in which he argues that readers who attempt to reformulate the story elements in nineteenth-century terms soon realize they are telling a different story and that the author had no choice but to relate his narrative exactly as he did (70).

Nor could the author of *La feria* change discourse without doing irreparable damage to his conception. Arreola has spoken with some frequency of his work as a manifestation of poetry in prose (*Confrontaciones,* 33). His readers must therefore be able to receive the work in the same spirit. Readers who remain passive, waiting to be told a full story, will either give up or dismiss *La feria* as a bad novel. But this is to refuse the experience promoted by a very evocative text, to ignore the poetic stimuli of this prose. Arreola's appreciation of the poetic nature of his work is apparent when he speaks about language:

> . . . ese lenguaje al que aspiro y al que me he acercado alguna vez, el lenguaje absoluto, el lenguaje puro que da un rendimiento mayor que el lenguaje frondoso, porque es fértil, porque es puro tronco y lleva en sí el designio de las ramas. Este lenguaje es de una desnudez potente, la desnudez poderosa del árbol sin hojas. . . . Tal vez mi obra sea escasa, pero es escasa porque constantemente la estoy podando. Prefiero los gérmenes a los desarrollos voluminosos, agotados por su propio exceso verbal. . . . El árbol que desarrolla todas sus hojas, hasta la última, es un árbol agotado, un árbol donde la savia está vencida por su propia plenitud. (Carballo, *Diecinueve protagonistas,* 391)

> [. . . that language to which I aspire and that I have come close to on occasion, absolute language, pure language that yields so much more than luxuriant language, because it is fertile, because it is pure trunk and it carries inside itself the design of its branches. This language possesses a potent nudity, the powerful nudity of a tree without leaves. . . . Perhaps I haven't written much, but that is so because I'm always pruning my work. I prefer the seeds to the voluminous, fully developed product, choked by its own verbal excess. . . . The tree that develops all of its leaves, to the last one, is a spent tree, a tree in which the sap is vanquished by its own abundance.]

Arreola's work is suggestion, evocation, and the fragmented structure of *La feria* serves his stated purpose well. Instead of burying readers in excessive verbiage, trying to relay everything about life in Zapotlán, he shows enough respect to allow them to supply the leaves for the tree in an individualized arrangement of a whole. Arreola achieves a shaping of reader response in an unobtrusive way, letting diegetic and discursive elements function within the text in such a manner as to dramatize for readers a potential process for unification without an overtly intervening authorial presence. Readers of *La feria* are indeed privileged: respected for their competence, allowed their artistic freedom, and privy to the experience of Zapotlán, through a joint creation.

## Salvador Elizondo, *Farabeuf o la crónica de un instante* (Farabeuf or the Chronicle of an Instant)

Salvador Elizondo's *Farabeuf* (1965) is a fragmented, nonlinear, seemingly incoherent novel that repeatedly confounds its readers by calling attention to its lack of conformity with narrative conventions of plot, character, and verisimilitude. By presenting itself as a problematic novel, *Farabeuf* forces its active readers into an awareness of the transformation of text as vehicle for or producer of story, to the text as aesthetic object. In other words, readers are brought to focus on the practice of writing, what Stephen Heath calls the "self-presentation as *text*" (22). In contrast to *Pedro Páramo*, *El libro vacío*, and *La feria*, however, Elizondo's novel is devoid of national thematics, closer in spirit to the vanguard writers who experimented in art for art's sake.

In his study of the French New Novel, Heath examines precisely the changing status of the text as a basis for defining the difference between the *nouveau roman* and what he, after Alain Robbe-Grillet, calls the "Balzacian" novel. Heath argues that the Balzacian novel represents the self-effacement of text: in its service to story, to the creation of the narrative illusion, the text is so comforting, so natural as to be potentially overlooked (21). In contrast, the *nouveau roman* represents those novels of the twentieth century that focus on discourse rather than on story.

*Farabeuf* can be viewed as a work about the shift from story to discourse, a novel about a historic moment in narrative tradition. In his novel Elizondo memorializes through textual strategies the movement away from nineteenth-century ideology of representation associated with the Balzacian novel to the twentieth-century vision that probes and challenges preconceived notions of narrativity. *Farabeuf* self-consciously presents itself as a problematic novel and, at the same time, offers readers a transition to aesthetic appreciation by altering their focus from text as a producer of story to text as text.

*Farabeuf* has proved a difficult novel, one that raises questions about narrative practice and prompts critics to comment on their own experience in reading. Indeed, those who write about this novel tend to include a few words or phrases to describe reader response; for the most part, the descriptions involve emotions. For George McMurray, readers react with "bewilderment and horror" ("Salvador Elizondo's *Farabeuf*," 601); Octavio Paz speaks of "angustia" (*El signo y el garabato,* 202); and Walter Langford says that readers are left "limp, bewildered and upset" (194). The feelings of horror are due in large part to the revulsion toward what few instances of realistic representation can be discerned. The other emotive responses result from a sense of disorientation before a text that fails to conform to narrative norms, the most basic of which is story.

What confronts readers is not a story but a series of descriptions of elements that might become part of a possible story or many possible stories. Manuel Durán notes, "La novela yace rota, en pedazos, ante nuestra presencia; a nosotros toca reconstruirla, y cada lector formará con estos fragmentos la novela que quiera—o que pueda—, con las consecuencias, soluciones y desenlace que tal solución le permita formular" [The novel lies broken, in pieces, before us; it is up to us to reconstruct it, and each reader will form with these fragments the novel that she or he wants—or that he or she can—with the consequences, solutions, and denouement that such a choice yields] (163). In fact, it could be said that in *Farabeuf* Elizondo eschews story completely, offering instead a series of scenes and descriptions that are repeated throughout the novel. The principal scenes are three:

1.  A beach scene: From the reiterations of this sequence and the cumulative detail gathered from each, one can proffer the following possibilities of action: two characters, a man and a woman, take a walk along a beach during which they encounter a child building a sand castle, a woman dressed in black, and a starfish, which the female apparently throws into the sea. At one point, the woman moves ahead. While trying to reach her, the man realizes that she has become *la otra* (the Other). Subsequently, they meet at a beach house and make love.

2.  A torture scene: There are many references throughout the text to a photograph showing a person being dismembered as part of the Chinese ritual torture, *Leng Tch'é.* Readers are brought through a crescendo of explicitness, culminating in a seven-page fragment into which

is inserted an actual photographic reproduction of such an incident. It is suggested that this picture serves as an aphrodisiac for the couple because of the look of ecstasy on the victim's face.

3. An apartment in Paris: A female character and Dr. Farabeuf apparently reunite in Paris, she having phoned asking him to come to 3, rue de l'Odéon. In the multiple evocations of this most perplexing scene, the following items and incidents can be discerned: Dr. Farabeuf crossing a street; Dr. Farabeuf climbing a stairway; a woman tracing an enigmatic figure on a window pane; a woman letting drop three coins; a woman consulting a Ouija board; a woman's foot striking a table; Dr. Farabeuf's bag of instruments; a mirror; a reproduction of Titian's *Sacred and Profane Love*; a marble-top table; velvet curtains; a pair of windows; a phonograph.

The minimal plot makes story itself problematic, which in turn leads readers to awareness that they are involved in the construction and maintenance of narrative illusion, that they are implicated in maneuvering the fragments of the text. If there is to be a story, then readers must supply it, and that is a hard task indeed, due to the ambiguity of Elizondo's givens. Increasing the difficulty is the enigmatic presence of unidentified narrative consciousness(es). One struggles continually to determine the sex of the narrator(s), to link the voice from one fragment with that or with those from another, to ascertain the number of characters involved. At times the text suggests three or more: "ella—la otra— . . . nos mira a los dos" [she—the other one—looks at the two of us] (82); "Dos de nosotros, un hombre y una mujer" [Two of us, a man and a woman] (105). By the same token, there are indications that the characters can be reduced to two, with hints at one female protagonist with a multiple personality: "Es preciso señalar el hecho que la persona que atravesó aquella estancia para dirigirse a la ventana y que se detuvo antes de llegar al alféizar produjo en su trayecto dos fenómenos sensibles, uno de orden auditivo y otro de orden táctil. El primero fue un ruido producido por el efecto de que al correr hacia la ventana mi pie golpeó la base de hierro . . ." [It is necessary to point out that the person who crossed that room toward the window and who stopped before reaching the splay produced two sensory phenomena in the process, one auditory and the other tactile. The first was a noise produced when my foot hit the iron base as I ran toward the window] (105).[10]

One surmises from the repeated use of self-conscious statements having to do with narrativity and with reader response that Elizondo seems well aware of the effect his confusing text might have on readers. Sometimes, the self-conscious remarks parallel potential reader response, as when, after enough textual ambiguities to confuse anyone, a narrative voice directs readers to a reordering of "events" into a traditional linear pattern: "Para poder resolver el complicado *rebus* que plantea el caso, es preciso, ante todo, ordenar los hechos cronológicamente, desposeerlos de su significado emotivo, hacer, inclusive, antes de ese ordenamiento en el tiempo, un inventario pormenorizado de ellos, independientemente del orden en el que tuvieron lugar en el tiempo" [In order to be able to solve the complicated *rebus* presented here, it is necessary, first of all, to order the events chronologically, to get rid of their emotive meaning, and to make, even before that temporal ordering, a detailed inventory of them, independently of the order in which they took place in time] (57, italics in original). This is very likely what many readers have been doing. Responding to conditioned habits rooted in conventional narrativity, they have been trying to isolate things and actions and then to piece them into a linear narration. Rather than aiding readers, Elizondo's words seem to mock their efforts.

Elizondo also reminds readers at frequent intervals of the text's refusal to fix explicit, stable meaning. He does so by flaunting the word *significado* (meaning), or a variation, in descriptions of both objects and people,[11] indicating the importance of their significance, but refusing to name it or to provide clues for its discovery. Supplementing this technique is phrasing that inculcates indecipherability: "una escena inexplicable" [an inexplicable scene] (15), "un hecho incomprensible o tal vez terriblemente claro" [an incomprehensible deed, or perhaps terribly clear] (16). Finally, there is Titian's *Sacred and Profane Love,* described repeatedly as an incomprehensible allegory: "una alegoría equívoca" [a mistaken allegory] (96); "una alegoría cuyo significado . . . nos es totalmente ajeno" [an allegory whose meaning . . . is completely obscure to us] (38); "el título ambiguo de aquella pintura bellísima e incomprensible" [the ambiguous title of that beautiful and incomprehensible painting] (63).

Readers are led to question what, if anything, is concrete in *Farabeuf,* and a close examination of the text suggests that the answer is very little. What Elizondo gives, he subsequently takes away; he teases his readers with apparent certainties only to sabotage these with doubts. The beginning of the novel establishes the paradigm of manifesting a certainty, then subverting it, a strategy for which Pierre Michaëlis provides a provocative

description: "estos elementos estructuran y desestructuran simultánea-
mente el impulso de la escritura" [these elements structure and destructure
simultaneously the narrative impulse] (66), as in the following passage:

> ¿Recuerdas . . . ? Es un hecho indudable que precisamente en el mo-
> mento en que Farabeuf cruzó el umbral de la puerta, ella, sentada al
> fondo del pasillo agitó las tres monedas en el hueco de sus manos
> entrelazadas y luego las dejó caer sobre la mesa. Las monedas no
> tocaron la superficie de la mesa en el mismo momento y produjeron
> un leve tintineo, un pequeño ruido metálico, apenas perceptible, que
> pudo haberse prestado a muchas confusiones. De hecho, ni siquiera
> es posible precisar la naturaleza concreta de ese acto. (9)

> [Do you remember . . . ? It is an incontrovertible fact that precisely
> at the moment that Dr. Farabeuf crossed the threshold, she, seated at
> the end of the hallway, shook the three coins in her hands and then
> let them fall on the table. The coins didn't hit the table at the same
> time and produced a slight tinkling sound, a tiny metallic noise,
> barely perceptible, that could have lent itself to many confusions.
> Actually, it's not even possible to assure the concrete reality of that
> happening.]

Readers are forced into an awareness of subversions of certainties, many of
which are effected very quickly: "rozando con tu mano mi mano (tal vez)"
[brushing my hand with yours (perhaps)] (114); "El nombre fue lo que ella
dijo . . . tal vez" [The name was what she said . . . perhaps] (10). Occasionally Elizondo ends a fragment with a statement of certainty, its location
adding emphasis to its message, only to contradict it in the contiguous segment: "Tú sabes que todo lo que yo digo es absolutamente cierto, ¿no es
así? [You know that everything I say is absolutely true, don't you?] (39;
Chapter 2, fragment 10); "Tal vez" [Perhaps] (beginning of fragment 11).

There are also a number of flaunted certainties, gratuitous certainties,
for which no subversion is necessary, as the following example illustrates:
"Es un hecho perfectamente concreto, por ejemplo, que: ' . . . Una vez al
mes, en día fijo, un hombre concurría a casa de su amante y le cortaba los
rizos que le caían sobre la frente. Esto le provocaba el más intenso goce.
Posteriormente no le exigía ninguna otra cosa a la mujer' " [It is a perfectly
concrete fact that " . . . Once a month, on an arranged day, a man would

go to his lover's house and cut the curls that fell on her forehead. This made him intensely happy. After that, he didn't ask her for anything else] (122). This passage constitutes an entire fragment and has little perceptible relationship with the rest of the novel. There is no need to sabotage it as a potential piece of "story" for *Farabeuf*. Upon a closer examination, however, one finds that there is, in fact, a subversion in this fragment, one brought about by discourse alone. This "perfectly concrete" action is nothing other than a story. Readers can tell this from the placement on the page; the passage is indented, set apart from the rest of the segment. Because of the difference in treatment, readers are brought to focus on discourse and to sense the discrepancy between fact and fictional construct. The novel flaunts its status as denier of story, in the traditional sense, by calling attention to what might have been an interior duplication of fiction, had the fuller text told a story.

Eventually, even the small snatches of activity readers have been able to discern from the three basic scenes are called into question. From the beach scene, the starfish is subverted as an illusion: "una estrella de mar putrefacta que habías imaginado recoger durante un paseo por la playa" [a putrified starfish that you imagined picking up during a walk on the beach] (121). Readers must immediately interrogate the existence of the whole scene as reality, as a lie, as a dream: "¿Cómo era posible todo esto si nunca habíamos salido de aquel cuarto y aquel cuarto pertenecía a una casa y esa casa estaba situada en una calle, conocida y precisable, de una ciudad de tierra adentro?" [How was all this possible if we had never left that room and that room was in a house and that house was on a known and identifiable street in a city far from the coast?] (121)

The cumulative effect is to question the text as text. Although there is a more superficial ontological questioning of character in *Farabeuf*, based on the female protagonist's pondering her identity, there remains to be considered the ontological questioning of the text. The characters' sense of being is constantly interrogated, "¿Quién soy?" (Who am I?) appearing frequently, furthered by multiple suggestions of our own status as not real but imagined or reflected beings: we are (are we?) a memory, our own or someone else's; a lie; a reflection in a mirror; a filmic image; characters in a novel; the materialization of another's desire (84, 91, 93, 121). The use of the first-person plural serves to expand the ontological questioning to include readers.

But now readers also question the text's existence. Beyond the obvious point that there is no story, one begins to doubt the credibility of any of the action heretofore perceived. Reinforcing readers' doubts as to the fictional verisimilitude of the occurrences described is the repeated use of the conditional and the pluperfect subjunctive, verb moods variously defined in Spanish grammars as forms of the imagination or tenses of the "have not happened." [12] Complicating matters even further is the fact that there actually existed a Dr. Farabeuf who was indeed the author of a medical text on surgical procedures (Rees 42–43; Elizondo, "Autobiografía," 44–45). Readers are confronted by a text containing a photograph, which their conditioning must have them accept as real, and supposedly detailing the actions of a Dr. Farabeuf, who is a historical figure. Reality blends with fiction, and it is increasingly difficult to have faith in either one. Elizondo reinforces this notion in his comments on the concept of horror in *Farabeuf:* "Es un efecto dramático. Y tiene un carácter artificial por el hecho de que está sucediendo un poco 'de mentira.' Todo lo que está pasando en *Farabeuf,* sobre todo en el último capítulo, que es como una representación dramática, es totalmente artificial" [It is a dramatic effect. And it has an artificial nature because it is a bit of a "lie." Everything that happens in *Farabeuf,* especially in the last chapter, which is like a dramatic presentation, is totally artificial] (Ruffinelli, "Salvador Elizondo," 39).

Obviously, the text will not yield meaning in the traditional sense, will not identify its narrators, and will not provide clear clues for unification. The answer must lie elsewhere. Another consideration of the enigmatic allegory ties in the notion of reader response with the ontological questioning of character and, more importantly, of text. *Allegory* has been defined thus: "When the events of a narrative obviously and continually refer to another simultaneous structure of events or ideas, whether historical events, moral or philosophical ideas, or natural phenomena" (*Princeton*). One must then question the status of an allegory that cannot be carried to its more profound meaning. If the concept of visual allegory presupposes viewer response, is an allegory an allegory, then, if no one can decipher it? Titian's painting is as difficult to comprehend as *Farabeuf* itself, thus attaining the status of a self-referential artifice that calls attention to its parity with the whole of Elizondo's work. Self-conscious statements in the novel respond to this ontological questioning of allegory by bringing readers to focus on the allegory as construct and on the text as text.

Elizondo suggests a solution by directing readers to process, not product. At issue in *Farabeuf* is a reorientation of the readers' approach to the text, a challenge to examine the novel as a self-conscious display of textual composition. The metanarrative discourse of *Farabeuf* directs readers not toward some ultimate meaning but to the actual process involved in working with a text, expanding upon the work begun in the previous decade by Rulfo and Vicens. In this novel, that process is one of unification through scenes and images, with readers as unifiers.

The following passage from the novel comments on the enigmatic allegory: "el significado trascendental de la alegoría debe buscarse más bien en los cánones geométricos y matemáticos que rigen la composición *interiormente*" [the transcendental significance of the allegory would be better sought in the geometric and mathematical patterns that govern the composition *interiorly*] (89, emphasis in original). Paralleling this inducement for a viewer to move beyond the surface ornamentation of the allegory to its artistic composition are statements within *Farabeuf* calling for active readers. The comments are blended within the text, in the sense that they ostensibly pertain to the narrating consciousness's efforts to establish identity through memory. The self-consciousness of the passages, however, leads directly to readers:

> Muchas veces pienso que no he pasado nada por alto, absolutamente nada, pero hay resquicios en esta trama en los que se esconde esa esencia que todo lo vuelve así: indefinido e incomprensible. (69)

> [Many times I think that I've overlooked nothing, absolutely nothing, but there are crevices in this plot in which is hidden that essence that makes everything like that: indefinite and incomprehensible.]

> Es preciso hacer un esfuerzo. Debes tratar de recordarlo todo, desde el principio. El más mínimo incidente puede tener una importancia capital. El indicio más insignificante puede llevarnos al descubrimiento de un hecho fundamental. Es preciso que hagas un inventario pormenorizado, exhaustivo, de todos los objetos, de todas las sensaciones, de todas las emociones que han concurrido a esto que tal vez es un sueño. (101)

> [It is necessary to make an effort. You should try to remember everything, right from the beginning. The tiniest incident could be of utmost importance. The most insignificant point is capable of bringing us to the discovery of a fundamental fact. It is necessary that you

make a detailed, exhaustive inventory of all the objects, of all the sensations, of all the emotions that have assembled here in what is perhaps a dream].

As readers try to implement the text's directions for an active reading, they must reach an impasse, if they are still tied to conventional practices. The allusion to crevices in the plot, seemingly a reference to fragmentation as a discursive reflection of ellipses in story, would appear to indicate that the readers' task is to fill in the gaps to complete the novel. But in *Farabeuf* there is no story to finish. Readers toil to (re)construct scenes and objects, and their rewards are: a nurse, Dr. Farabeuf climbing the stairs, a painting, a table, a fly. All these are or become objects equal in their (un)importance.

Yet it is precisely the emphasis upon tableaux rather than action or story that provides the transition to aesthetic appreciation. One then returns to the above-cited passage that seemed to ridicule readers steeped in narrative conventions no longer appropriate to this chaotic text. In the very first line, Elizondo dangles the interpretive key right before his readers' eyes, before launching them on a futile linear ordering of the suggested events. By choosing the term "rebus," Elizondo sends his readers a double message: on the one hand, he suggests a diachronic ordering and, on the other, a synchronic consideration. The pertinent clue is *rebus* accentuated by its appearance in italics: "a riddle made up wholly or in part of pictures or symbols" (*Webster's Third, Unabridged*).

While denying a complete story, the text *has* provided its readers with scenes, images, and symbols. Paradoxically both representational and enigmatic, the three scenes, Titian's painting, and the inserted photograph serve as self-referential signifiers that bring *Farabeuf*'s readers to awareness of the need to unify the text themselves by working with the given images. The result is a self-consciousness of purpose on the readers' part. Any meaning is in the readers, and it will be achieved only through their exertion. Significantly, upon a reconsideration of the text, one can see that the very first fragment of the novel evokes the same impetus toward a reader-created unity: "¿No alude este hecho a la dualidad antagónica del mundo que expresan las líneas continuas y las líneas rotas, los *yang* y los *yin* que se combinan de sesenta y cuatro modos diferentes para darnos el significado de un instante? Todo ello, desde luego no hace sino aumentar la confusión, pero tú tienes que hacer un esfuerzo y recordar ese momento en el que cabe, por así decirlo, el significado de toda su vida" [Doesn't this fact allude to the antagonistic duality of the world expressed in the continuous and broken lines, the yang and yin that combine in sixty-four different ways to give us the meaning of an instant in time? All that, naturally, does nothing but augment the confusion, but you have to make an effort and remember that moment into which fits, as one way of putting it, the meaning of your whole life] (10). From the beginning, Elizondo has suggested a feeling of oneness through his reference to yin and yang. In *El arco y la lira,* Octavio Paz explains that the ancient Chinese viewed the universe as a cyclic combination of two rhythms, yin and yang, rhythms based on *images* (59). There are two ways of envisioning yin and yang. One is as lines, divided (yin) or undivided (yang) (*I Ching* 421). The other is as a circle depicting the resolution of opposites—as a unit, a whole. In addition to the cosmic opposites of sun/ moon and light/shade, yin and yang unite masculine and feminine, as shown in the following definition of yin: "The feminine and negative principle (as of passivity, depth, darkness and cold, and wetness) in nature that according to traditional Chinese cosmology combines with its opposite yang to produce all that comes to be" (*Webster's Third*).

A careful consideration of *Farabeuf* shows that these two Chinese rhythms, presented on the first page, herald a most unified novel that awaits an active reader. In particular, forceful inducements toward unification are found among images that not only reflect each other but also become equations. At the core of this analysis and of the novel is the photograph of a human being undergoing dissection. In the source for the picture, *Les Larmes d'Eros,* Georges Bataille describes *Leng Tch'é* as "découpage en morceau," [cutting into pieces] (234), a provocative metaphor for this fragmented text. Keeping in mind the definition of the verb "to dissect," one senses more clearly the relationship among the text, the readers, and this photograph: (1) to cut apart piece by piece; to separate into parts, as a body for purposes of study; to anatomize; (2) to examine or analyze closely" (*Webster's New*). The vehicle, although nauseating, is most appropriate, as it draws the readers' attention to a fragmented text that demands closer examination. Once again, readers sense a self-referential aspect to discourse.

The *form* of the victim tied to the post is just one of many representations whose essence can be depicted most graphically by the ideogram for the Chinese numeral six (*Farabeuf* 150). Immediately after the appearance of this "sign" (it is labeled a sign in the text), the narrative voice calls attention to its parity with the victim's positioning and with a starfish. Recognizing this sameness, Margo Glantz extends the equation to include the hexogram of the *I Ching* ("*Farabeuf*," 34). Although the ideogram has five protrusions, not six, the expansion of the equation to six has already been prepared by meticulous analysis of the photograph that shows, as in a geometrical proof, that there are, in fact, six executioners placed symmetrically about the victim (144). To the numeral and the ritualistic symmetry one could then add the enigmatic *clatro*, evidently a Chinese divinatory piece consisting of spheres within spheres: six to be exact, each containing six orifices (*Farabeuf* 156; Rees 33).

Unification through images becomes even more pervasive as one considers the physical appearance of the victim. The figure is first referred to as masculine. Then there are hints that it is a woman (145). Whether viewed as a previously emasculated male or as a woman whose breasts have been removed as part of ritual dismemberment, the final figure is hermaphroditic and returns readers to yin and yang, to unity: "Ese hombre parece estar absorto por un goce supremo, como el de la contemplación de un dios pánico. Las sensaciones forman en torno a él un círculo que siempre, donde termina, empieza, por eso hay un punto en el que el dolor y el placer se confunden" [That man seems to be absorbed by a supreme pleasure, like that of one contemplating a panic god. Sensations form about him a circle that always, as it ends, begins; therefore there is a point at which pain and pleasure become confused] (145).

Such emphasis on yin and yang would suggest a oneness of character. Careful examination of the text reveals exactly that. Personality and profession fluctuate until one senses a reduction of character to two: one masculine and one feminine. Again, the very beginning of the novel germinates the conceptualization of gender rather than individual: "Es un hombre—el hombre—que desciende apresuradamente de un pequeño automóvil deportivo de color rojo" [It is a man—the man—who descends in a hurry from a small red sports car] (13); "Ahora has venido en busca del recuerdo de la Enfermera—la mujer—siempre vestida de blanco" [Now you've come in search of the memory of the Nurse—the woman—always dressed in white] (15). Characters reduce to Masculine and Feminine, and the hermaphrodite joins them in oneness.

Elizondo has presented readers with a series of images and potential signifiers that relate among themselves in internal cohesiveness but do not reach out to readers as signs. The "signs" in *Farabeuf* refuse to yield meaning in a conventional way. This is not to say, however, that active readers will not try to impose meaning, to see objects as symbols. McMurray identifies Farabeuf's surgical knives and the *dedos afilados* (sharpened fingers) of his stiff rubber gloves as phallic symbols, the hall door as a representation of the line between life and death, and the dead starfish as a prophecy of death. Signifiers that for him do not reveal a signified are dismissed as antisymbols. Yet his description is evocative of their structural function: "Other objects merely provide compositional effect or atmosphere and appear deliberately inserted as anti-symbols" ("Salvador Elizondo's *Farabeuf*," 598).

Some objects refuse to yield meaning; others evoke multiple signifieds. In *Farabeuf* one sign leads to another that, in turn, reflects a third, *ad infinitum* building a totally unified whole: "Todos estos signos confluyen en el ideograma *liú*, que es muerte que es una tortura que es rito erótico que es sacrificio religioso que es descabellada tentativa por cristianizar a China que es experiencia médica de un ilustre profesor de cirugía que es tortura que es una ceremonia erótica que es el paseo de una pareja por la playa durante el cual una mujer encuentra una estrella de mar que es el suplicio *Leng T'che* [*sic*] que es la crucifixión que es el ideograma *liú*" [All these signs conflate in the ideogram *liú*, that is death that is torture that is erotic rite that is religious sacrifice that is a crazy attempt to Christianize China that is medical experience of an illustrious professor of surgery that is torture that is an erotic ceremony that is a couple's walk on the beach during which a woman finds a starfish that is the sacrifice *Leng Tch'é* that is the crucifixion that is the ideogram *liú*] (Paz, *El signo y el garabato*, 204). All is one in a giant equation of equivalencies that eventually returns to the starting point.

The reality of *Farabeuf* is thus an aesthetic reality. For, in contrast to the elusive content, what attains concreteness is the notion of evocation in narrative incorporated masterfully into an intricate structure. Elizondo, in effect, moves readers away from reality: one need not consider *Farabeuf* either an expression of enigmatic reality or an enigmatic expression of reality. With this text, there is no necessity to relate the content to an outside verisimilar construct. Here, the emphasis falls on the text as text.

The interrogative *¿recuerdas?* that begins and ends the novel, seemingly a reflection of a character's pondering of identity through memory, does, in fact, evoke a memory, but it is the memory of realistic representation in the arts—in painting, in photography, and in the novel. The crisis in the readers' identity with relation to the text is represented by the blending of East and West, of yin and yang with traditional narrative possibilities. Literary conventions are indeed arbitrary, but the relativism that was masked by the Balzacian novel is now flaunted, and readers must adapt in some way.

Elizondo effects a change in the readers' focus from content to form by making the content so impenetrable that readers must grasp whatever patterns, images, and repetitions they can and work with them. *Farabeuf* is all vehicle and no tenor—unless readers provide it. Its content does not tell a story but does yield the machinations of artistic composition. *Farabeuf*'s fragmented structure belies its true aesthetic achievement. It is a most compact and controlled narrative whose parts all point toward unity. It is a celebration of oneness: in the novel, in the universe, in the collective consciousness.

## José Emilio Pacheco, *Morirás lejos* (You Will Die in a Distant Land)

In *Morirás lejos* (1967/1977), José Emilio Pacheco engages his readers within a double contextual framework, both aesthetic and moral. His use of fragmentation, evocation as opposed to full description, and intertextual references pushes readers into an active participation in the creative process. In contrast to Elizondo's largely hermetic writing, however, Pacheco includes a more humanistic plane, forcing readers to confront the ethical implications of historical knowledge. His strategy is to use the text as a simulacrum of larger issues in which the process of reading is seen as a historicized act, thereby defining the text as the site of encounter between history and fiction. By interweaving a fictionalized present with a factual past, he dramatizes the necessity of bringing historical consciousness to the reading experience.

Pacheco's fragmented structure in *Morirás lejos* serves both to emphasize the centrality of history as a concern for contemporary readership and to make readers interrogate the relationship among the segments. With a few exceptions (98–99; 124; 143–147),[13] the fragments of *Morirás lejos* are divided among seven major sections, each of which, when initially introduced, bears a title and a sign. Subsequent appearances of each are marked by title alone. The signs are ancient symbols, thus reiterating the timelessness of the subject matter. *Salónica* represents the "present" of the text, suggesting, rather than describing in detail, the antagonistic relationship between *eme* (the word for the letter M), perhaps a Nazi SS member–*cum*–butcher responsible for the torture and death of thousands, and *Alguien* (Someone), possibly a survivor of the concentration camps, who is waiting to exact revenge. The use of adverbials here is essential, as readers are offered a number of identities for each. Reduced in time and space, the scenario of this "encounter" is confined to a few minutes, late on a Wednesday afternoon in 1966,[14] as *eme*, peering through the blinds from a room in his sister's house in Mexico City, contemplates the figure of *Alguien* seated on a park bench below, reading the want-ads section of a Mexican newspaper, *El Universal*. The sign for *Salónica* is a combined form of two figures representing man, thus suggesting a physical struggle, which is interpreted as "men quarrel and fight" (Koch 10). Despite the evocation of violence, however, both *eme* and *Alguien* are stubbornly passive, one contemplating and the other reading. Any activity or confrontation is mental or apocryphal.

The fragments constituting *Diáspora* are further segmented into fifty paragraphs of approximately the same size, each preceded by a Roman numeral. The numbering system is, of course, very appropriate, as *Diáspora* relates the siege and destruction of Jerusalem by the Romans as told by one Flavio Josefo, later revealed to be a traitor and collaborationist (66). The narration is detached, replete with specific references to proper and place names and details that strengthen one's perception of verisimilitude in the recounting. *Diáspora*'s sign is hermaphroditic, both solar and lunar (Jiménez de Báez, Morán, and Negrín 251), and represents both the planet Mercury (Koch 52) and Wednesday, "dies mercurii" (Koch 59). Ivette Jiménez de Báez et al.[15] further associate the sign with Hermes and Woden, the German god of war (216).

Paralleling *Diáspora* on multiple levels is *Grossaktion*, whose sign immediately evokes the Nazi swastika but can also be recognized as a *crux gammata*, a cross composed of four Greek gammas, or as a *crux dissimulata*, a disguised cross used during the persecution of the early Christians (Koch 18). Pacheco links *Diáspora* and *Grossaktion* through thematics and, very particularly, through specific elements of content,[16] thus establishing a cyclical pattern first hinted at when it was earlier revealed that the temple in Jerusalem was destroyed by the Romans on the same month and day as it had been by the Babylonians. In *Grossaktion* it is the Nazis who persecute the Jews, culminating in the siege and destruction of the Warsaw ghetto. The horrors evoked in *Diáspora* are here exponentially increased.

*Totenbuch* (The Book of the Dead) focuses directly on *eme*, his sadism, his unspeakable experiments and torture systems. One reaches a point of reacting physically, as what seemed to be the culmination of inhumanity in *Grossaktion* is surpassed by far. Even norms of narration heretofore experimented with are at times all but abandoned as inadequate to express the subject matter. The sign for *Totenbuch* means "very poisonous, deadly" (Koch 64), although Jiménez de Báez relates it also to another hermaphroditic sign consisting of a horizontal element (passive and feminine) and a vertical one (active and masculine) (251).

The perceived intensification of evil as demonstrated from *Diáspora* to *Totenbuch* is reiterated in *Götterdämmerung* (Twilight of the Gods), as the focus moves from *eme* to Adolf Hitler. The title is taken from Wagner's "Ring of the Nibelung" cycle, specifically the last of the four music dramas (1874). In Pacheco's version, however, Siegfried's funeral pyre is reduced to a grotesque evocation of Hitler's body contorted by flames. This biography concentrates on two moments: conception and expiration. *Götterdämmerung*'s sign represents vinegar (Koch 70), an element whose odor permeates the park in which *Alguien* sits.

The penultimate section, *Desenlace* (Denouement),[17] relates and subsequently negates a scenario of action, as six men of varied nationalities advance upon *eme*'s house for the capture. The sign accompanying this portion of the text suggests a possible outcome; as an inversion of the figure representing man, it is interpreted as "the man dies" (Koch 10). Finally, there is a segment illustrated by an hourglass (Koch 83), which reinforces the suggestion made in *Desenlace* that, although the described action did not take place, its realization is inevitable. Entitled *Apéndice: Otros de los posibles desenlaces* (Appendix: Some Other Possible Endings), it details six possibilities, most of which involve the death or punishment of *eme*.[18]

Obviously, the structure of *Morirás lejos* is complex, recalling in a sense that of D. W. Griffith's film *Intolerance* (1916), an early cinematic attempt to conceptualize the reworking of history as a problem of narrative. Griffith depicts simultaneously four stories that are temporally distinct but linked thematically, as the work's subtitle would indicate: "Love's Struggle throughout the Ages" (Huff 1). Although Griffith's thematics seem trivial in comparison to Pacheco's, it should be noted that each story demonstrates that it is hatred and intolerance that inhibit love and charity (Huff 1), and there is ample violence in the film. A major discursive difference between the two representations is that in *Intolerance* the four parallel stories are "interwoven with a relentlessly increasing pace as the film progresses" (Huff iii). In *Morirás lejos, Salónica* alternates with *Diáspora* through *Götterdämmerung* each in turn; there is no interaction with the last two sections and none among the other four. Significantly, it is the section representing the fictional present that alternates with those of the historical (as opposed to fictional) past, connoting the pervasive influence of history on the understanding of all current occurrences.

The action of the text's "present" is provocatively minimal. With good reason, comparisons have been suggested with Alain Robbe-Grillet's *La Jalousie* (1957), a classic example of the *nouveau roman*. In addition to the obvious sameness in a character's looking through blinds, Jiménez de Báez indicates similarities in theme and content with special emphasis on the notion of seeing or being seen (265). Although many elements of *Salónica* exemplify the tenets of the *nouveau roman*, one must recall, as Saalmann argues, that the *nouveaux romanciers* eschewed overt sociopolitical commitment (91). Pacheco's treatment of the minimalist plot does serve to remind readers of what art-for-art's-sake can effect. By means of interweaving *Salónica* with the other sections, however, Pacheco also calls readers' attention even more powerfully to a different function that art can—some would say *should*—perform: not only reflect humanistic issues, but actively promote change.

The fact that the only apparently concrete action of that brief present involves the opening of blinds and the reading of a newspaper cannot be recognized by readers until further into the novel. Yet Pacheco flaunts this information in the opening passage: "Con los dedos anular e índice entreabre la persiana metálica: en el parque donde hay un pozo cubierto por una torre de mampostería, el mismo hombre de ayer está sentado en la misma banca leyendo la misma sección, "El aviso oportuno," del mismo periódico: *El Universal*" [With his ring and index fingers he opens the metal Venetian blinds a fraction. In the park, where there is a well covered by a masonwork tower, the same man who was there yesterday is sitting on the same bench reading the same section, the want ads, of the same newspaper: *El Universal*] (11). In its privileged position, this first sentence of the text would seem to mock those looking for a stable story line within a fictional present, but it is only upon a second reading that one can appreciate the full impact of the words. Perhaps Pacheco is indicating from the start that the present is not the intended focus here at all. What should be of concern are the circumstances leading up to this moment and, even more significantly, the possibilities of the future. The repetition of the adjective *mismo* (same) serves both to suggest an immediate past of similar (lack of) activity and to establish early in the novel one's perception of reiteration through time.

Given the restrictions of time and plot elements, the major portion of *Salónica* is devoted to various hypotheses regarding the possibilities of meaning, the identity of *Alguien*, and, in a self-conscious examination, the veracity of what has been presented. The possibilities of *Alguien's* identity are contained within subsections of *Salónica* marked by letters of the alphabet. Suggestions are proffered that *Alguien* is a displaced middle-aged worker, a sexual delinquent, a father in search of his lost son, a lover, a man seeking to recapture the past, a private detective, a frustrated playwright, or a writer. Behind all these choices, however, there is a sense of constancy in *Alguien's* identity as a survivor of a concentration camp who has come to Mexico City in order to pursue *eme*. Once readers have become accustomed to the text's practice of producing various scenarios in order to explain *Alguien's* presence in the park, a change is effected. Section [f], set apart spatially from the preceding material and concluding a section of *Salónica*, consists of a single sentence. This discursive difference gives even more impact to its message: "Es una alucinación: no hay nadie en el parque" [It is an hallucination: there is no one in the park] (28). Subsequently, denial of previously established information, despite how minimal a sketch readers had received, becomes commonplace: there are really no benches in the park; *eme* died long ago; it actually is not *eme* after all; the house was destroyed in 1959.

Significantly, it is only the present that is called into question. There would seem to be as many denials as presentations of possibilities with regard to the physical situation of *Alguien* and *eme* and their relationship. The present is ephemeral, lacking verisimilitude, an exercise in imagination, all of which stands in stark contrast with the sections with which *Salónica* interweaves. Counteracting the "Holocaust-as-lie" fabrication of the postwar period, Pacheco forces readers to confront the harsh realities of the persecution of the Jews, with excruciating detail, making history much more substantial than the contemporary moment.

Echoing the contrast in treatment between the past and the present is the effect of their juxtaposition within the text. Perhaps the most powerful example of the interaction of discourses that inevitably affects readers occurs at the end of the *Grossaktion* section. After the narration of unspeakable cruelty, *Grossaktion* concludes with a message from Jürgen Stroop to

Himmler displayed graphically in a self-referential manner; each word is given its own line, in descending fashion: "el antiguo barrio judío de Varsovia dejó de existir El número de judíos ejecutados o detenidos asciende a 56 065 [*sic*]" [the former Jewish Quarter of Warsaw is no more The total number of Jews executed or caught rises to 56,065] (69–70).[19] After such a sobering statement, the beginning of the contiguous *Salónica* fragment seems particularly innocuous: "[x] O tal vez la casa no existe: Alguien está efectivamente sentado en el parque desierto con olor a vinagre—pero frente a un terreno baldío donde hubo una casa demolida hace quince años y luego un edificio que se incendió por explosión de gas" [Or perhaps the house does not exist: Someone is indeed seated in the deserted park that smells of vinegar—but he is facing a wasteland, where a house once stood. The house was demolished 15 years ago, and was later replaced by a building that caught fire in a gas explosion] (70). It would be difficult for readers not to notice and thus to react to this blatant contrast in content and simultaneously have their attention called to form.

The relationship of content to form in *Morirás lejos* is particularly crucial, even controversial for some. For years survivors of the concentration camps, representatives of Jewish groups, and literary critics, among others, have debated the suitability of conventional literary forms to express the reality of the Holocaust.[20] There are those who feel very strongly that treating the Holocaust in fictional terms trivializes the subject (Pfefferkorn 88). Others argue for new forms that would be more appropriate to represent the dehumanization and horror (Pfefferkorn 89). Pacheco's approach is to emphasize the Holocaust among other examples of persecution of the Jews that reflect a brutal reality, including examples of actual documents or simulations of same to contribute to their verisimilitude, yet to interweave this with an ephemeral fiction. Paradoxically, what binds the sections together is his use of an innovative fragmented discourse and, within the segments, a very poetic form, leading one critic to comment that *Morirás lejos* reflects "literature not as mimesis but as experiment, evocation, suggestion, and, above all, provocation" (Saalmann 99).

Pacheco's control and artistic sensibilities are particularly evident in the novel's form. He uses spacing, punctuation, and rhetorical techniques normally associated with poetry. At times there are very specific borrowings, as in his use of anaphora (23–24, 131–132, 147) and enjambment (76, 137, 141). A clear sense of flow and an augmented emotive response are effected by the author's use of extended series of words, most frequently of nouns and adjectives, but occasionally of verbs, as in the following example:[21] "El eco de las montañas circundantes multiplicó el fragor de quienes morían, mataban, huían, luchaban, destruían, saqueaban" [The echo from the surrounding mountains magnified the din of those who killed and were killed, those who fled, fought, wrecked and pillaged] (38). Note the rhythmic quality achieved by the alteration of imperfect endings. Other series take the form of lists and are represented as such. A listing of eme's "accomplishments" (133), now incorporated into the prose, was more spatially graphic in the first edition (113).[22]

Form is also called to the readers' attention by Pacheco's use of changes in discourse, usually with relation to heightened emotion (Duncan 54; Jiménez de Báez 255). Quite early in the novel there are instances of the joining of paragraphs with the effect of a forward momentum (18, 19), but as examples of violence and gruesome detail increase, there are more and more instances of paragraphs without closure. Generally, they end in a semicolon, and the subsequent paragraph begins with a lowercase letter, reaching on occasion one long sentence of some two or three pages (30–32; 86–88; 131–132). In other fragments, Pacheco omits punctuation all together, finally abandoning conventional discourse, perhaps as a consequence of the nature of the subject matter. Normal writing simply is not able to express it (76–80; 81–82; 91–94).

Pacheco's choice of spacing is equally effective. Although in general he uses expanded spacing between sections, frequently he employs double spacing between paragraphs, making them stand apart as if he were framing the content. A particularly striking example is appropriately found in Totenbuch, the section containing the most horrendous details of eme's butchery: "y no sabemos siquiera la mitad de cuanto ocurrió en los campos de exterminio" [and we do not even know the half of what happened in the extermination camps] (80). Under the same heading, another framed sentence, added in the 1977 edition, provides a brief but powerful image: "Muertos de sed los niños de brazos lamían el sudor en el rostro de sus madres" [Dying of thirst, babes in arms would lick the sweat off their mothers' faces] (88).

In all of these examples it is both form and content that insist upon readers' attention, calling for them to become involved with the text and with the issue.[23] For, in contrast to the passivity embodied in both eme and Alguien in the novel's "present," Pacheco's readers must be actively involved not only with the process of writing, but also with the historic responsibility in which we all finally must participate (Jiménez de Báez 211). Reaching out to them, Pacheco incorporates into the text clear references to readers, either as addressees or as actual readers-in-the-text.[24] Mention is made of *usted* (18, 106, 132) or *tú* (156–157) by one of the narrators, ostensibly to an interlocutor, but with clear linkage to readers. Of even more importance is his inclusion of readers' responses within the narrative, as if the readers were in direct communication with the narrator(s). Jiménez de Báez sees this as the reader as narrator and identifies the readers by nationality (217–219). The intrusions reveal optimum interest, moreover, when analyzed for their function.[25] Numerous responses comment on the narrator's methods of telling: *"Eso ya lo sabemos. Continúe"* [*We know that already. Go on*] (58); "No filosofe, no poetice" [Do not philosophize. Do not poeticize] (116). After one particularly brutal section of *Totenbuch*, the reaction is visceral: "Ya es bastante. Por favor calle o cambie de tema" [That's enough. Keep quiet or change the subject] (94). Of maximum importance, however, are the interruptions that exemplify for readers a questioning of the narration in terms of the value or meaning of a specific element. The most sustained and illuminating example (119–121) centers on a reproduction of a painting by Pieter Brueghel, *The Tower of Babel* (1563). In the dialogue, the reader-in-the-text begins by questioning why the painting is there but subsequently probes deeper, asking about the *function* of the work and, finally, participating in the analysis of its meaning. Thus this role model for readers moves from mere curiosity to full engagement with the narrative process.

Significantly, the painting emerges as a visual representation of the synchronization of time as presented in the novel. Within the text, it is associated with the well topped by a tower found in the park where *Alguien* sits (26, 120), thus connecting with *Salónica*. Its linkage with both *Grossaktion* and *Totenbuch* is multiple: it might represent the concentration camps, where prisoners were of various nationalities, hence spoke different languages (119); perhaps it is a metaphor of the German empire, with Aryans at the top (119); it resembles the ruins of the Reichstag in 1945 (120). Reference to *Diáspora* is clear when it is compared to the Roman Colosseum (120), considered to be a correct architectural analogy by various art critics (Klein and Klein 75; Seidel and Marijnissen 190). Thus, echoing the pervasive persecution of the Jews, the painting reiterates the historical trajectory in *Morirás lejos*, including a brief reference to the Babylonians, for Babel meant Babylon (Klein and Klein 75), and Brueghel's painting can be traced to Herodotus's description of the ziggurat, or sacred tower, of Babylon (Klein and Klein 77).

In addition to this imagistic, thematic, and metaphoric linkage, Pacheco offers a theoretic connection with the novel's present. First there is reference to the author-as-witness issue: "¿Con qué derecho se atreve a pintar algo que jamás observó?" [How can he dare to paint something he has never seen?] (121). This is followed by a clear verbalization of the sameness: "¿quién contempla *La Torre de Babel? ¿Quién nos cuenta la historia del acoso de eme?*" [who is looking at *The Tower of Babel?* Who is telling us the story of the relentless pursuit of em?] (121).

Finally, the painting relates to the novel as a whole. Joel Hancock notes that each of the major sections of *Morirás lejos* "has a distinct character and its own special style" ("Documentation," 103). Thus the work resembles the Tower of Babel in its different languages. Duncan also makes reference to a "collage of different styles" (56). What needs to be recognized, however, is that the tower is not merely an image in the text but constitutes an image *of* the text: the Tower of Babel can be conceptualized as a whole made up of individual parts, just as the fragments of *Morirás lejos* interact to form a unit. In this way, Pacheco's employment of the Brueghel painting corresponds with Rulfo's privileging of the final image, *un montón de piedras,* in *Pedro Páramo.*

Obviously, the connections are multiple, as are the possible meanings. Despite the flaunted opportunity to choose among the significances, however, there remains a sense of unity, of wholeness. In much the same way, there is a pattern inherent in *Morirás lejos,* established early in *Salónica* and sustained consistently, that emphasizes choices while, paradoxically, reducing difference through equations. That is to say, readers are encouraged to participate in the narrative process by means of making a choice regarding a character's identity, for example, yet at the same time there are multiple instances of conflation into sameness that would make choice within the fictional present futile.

The notion of choice is apparent from the beginning, as noted in the possibilities of identities for *Alguien.* Yet the reduction to sameness is equally present, although not as easily perceived. Toward the end of [b], in which *Alguien* is depicted as a sexual delinquent, the narrator equates the identities contained in [a] and [b]: "Actor nato, *vive* a su criatura, *es* el obrero" [A born actor, he lives his own creation, he *is* the worker] (19; emphasis in the original). The equation is both extended and clarified at the end of [d] with the special placement of the last words standing out, calling readers' attention to the expansion to infinity of *Alguien*'s identity:

> o en el mejor de los casos será tema del hombre que acecha tras las persianas y le adjudica hipótesis que lo hacen ser a un tiempo víctima del progreso, corruptor de menores, padre sin hijo, amante desdeñado
> y las siguientes. (25)

> [or in the best of cases, this is all the obsession of the man who spies from behind the blinds and who imagines that he is all of the hypotheses at once: a victim of progress, a corruptor of minors, a childless father, a spurned lover
> and subsequent ones.]

The text is replete with opportunities for readers to participate through choice. In addition to *Alguien*'s identity, one can consider that of *eme* (123). Readers are offered a series of possibilities regarding where *eme* served as a Gestapo officer (116–117) and which concentration camp he directed (83). Certain choices are made more explicit by the insertion of a series of the word *o* (or), most conspicuously with regard to the possible scenarios of *eme*'s death (155). There are even choices to be found within the footnotes (27). One can select the most personally satisfying meaning for the name *eme* (131–132) or the cause of *eme*'s old head wound (144). Ultimately, readers are offered the opportunity of selecting the novel's denouement.

Yet, analogous to the equations introduced to conflate *Alguien*'s possible identities, Pacheco employs within the text, in contrapuntal fashion, a series of equivalencies that argue for a status of sameness. Although stating that the supposed Supermen and their victims are equal in death may seem obvious (127), Pacheco is even more specific. In the course of his experiments, *eme* notes that people of various nationalities, including the occasional Aryan, are finally equal to the Jews in their response to the tortures inflicted (79). In the description of Hitler's death (142), it is revealed that the epitome of *Übermenschentum* (Superman; a standard expression in Nazi racist propaganda) burns at the same temperature as that of his victims (*jüdischen untermenschentum* or "Jewish sub-humanness" [84]). A further identification is made between Hitler's death and that of the worms that *eme* used to torture and then smash. In a footnote readers learn that the worms when flattened secreted a "líquido amarillo purulento" [yellow, purulent liquid] (15). The special location of this information should be sufficient to enable readers to recognize the equation when informed that Hitler's burning body gave off the same fluid, but Pacheco explicitly mentions the sameness to make sure (143).

Such an emphasis on the absence of difference is reflected in the characters themselves. Margo Glantz argues that the characters "se desdibujan y acaban convirtiéndose en símbolos múltiples con lo que se colectivizan" [deconstruct and wind up turning into multiple symbols, thus collectivizing themselves] ("*Morirás lejos,*" 186). Many have commented on the notion of *Alguien* as Everyman (Hancock, "Perfecting a Text," 17; Jiménez de Báez 221, 224). Hancock speaks specifically of *Alguien* as an "Allegorical someone" ("Documentation," 102), and numerous references are made within the text to *Alguien*'s status as representative of all the victims of the Holocaust, which would be consistent with the variety of professions preferred for him. If one accepts the label of Everyman for *Alguien*, however, one must do the same for *eme*.[26] An immediate dichotomy surfaces with *Alguien* as victim, *eme* as victimizer; *Alguien* representing good, and *eme* a symbol of evil. Pacheco reinforces the notion of *eme* as a more universal evil in a number of ways. Among the choices of the meaning of the name *eme*, there is at least one that transcends the immediate Nazi connection: "eme, la letra que cada uno lleva impresa en las manos" [em, the letter that is imprinted on the palms of our hands] (131),[27] evidently a reference to the creases that occur naturally in one's palms. This particular list of possible significances is revealing in other ways as well. The collection of words, all beginning with the letter *m*, spans a number of languages, thus reinforcing a more universal character and returning readers to the Tower of Babel.

Furthermore, within the multiple connotations of evil associated with the name *eme* there are a number of intertextual references, the most intriguing of which is a Fritz Lang film, *M* (1931): "eme, para recordar a Fritz Lang y a una película que usted, él y yo vimos en la Alemania de 1932: *M, el vampiro de Düsseldorf,* retrato de un criminal que muy pronto, con el ascenso de Hitler al poder, de monstruo se convertiría en paradigma. Además, no lo olvide, eme pasó sus años de juventud en Düsseldorf" [em, to remind us of Fritz Lang and a film that you, he and I saw in Germany in

1932: *M, the Vampire of Düsseldorf*, portrait of a criminal who, very quickly, with Hitler's rise to power, would be transformed from a monster into a paradigm. Furthermore, do not forget that em spent his youth in Düsseldorf] (132). The title in Spanish can be somewhat misleading, for the vampirism in Lang's film is metaphoric, not literal.[28] *M* tells the story of a serial killer of children, Franz Becker (Peter Lorre), supposedly based on the actual crimes of one Peter Kürten, who was called by some "The Vampire of Düsseldorf" (Jensen 93).[29]

The parallelisms between the film and *Morirás lejos* are compelling. Both use innovative discursive techniques, *M* being recognized for its expressionism and use of intercutting in order to show two concurrent actions (Jensen 102). Becker whistles Grieg's "In the Hall of the Mountain King" (Eisner 122) as his sexual/murderous instincts increase, while *eme* is partial to Wagner (Pacheco 103). When one of the community of beggars who had joined the underworld characters in pursuit of the child killer marks Becker's overcoat so that he will be easy to identify, he does so by writing with chalk the letter *M* in the palm of his hand, then pressing it onto Becker's back. According to Lotte Eisner, "Lang again and again reverts to the idea that 'Any one of us might turn a murderer in certain circumstances' " (112),[30] which finds an echo in Pacheco's comment "Nada, repito: nada puede expresar lo que fueron los campos. Olvídelo si no quiere despreciarse al saber de lo que usted, yo y todos somos capaces" [Nothing, I repeat: nothing can express what those camps were. Forget it if you don't want to despise yourself when you realize what you and I and all of us are capable of] (95). There is even a discursive linkage in that Becker loses control during his self-defense at the mock trial held by the underworld: "At this point his defense becomes disjointed, almost stream-of-consciousness. His words suggest images rather than sentences. His voice does not complete his thoughts, but our imagination does" (Armour 101).

In addition, there is striking similarity in the inversion of the roles persecutor/persecuted and in the notion of a doppelgänger (Eisner 113). Becker, the stalker of little girls, is finally hunted down himself. In a similar manner, there is a reversal in the roles of *eme* and *Alguien* whereby the victim becomes the victimizer and vice versa. Of even greater significance is the suggestion of a reduction to oneness. Eisner mentions Lang's long-standing desire to make a film dealing with the problem of the Jekyll-and-Hyde double nature of man (113), a notion reinforced in Paul Jensen's analysis: "But the greatest threat to him [Becker] comes from the underworld of his own mind, and the other part of his personality that lurks there waiting to destroy the everyday Franz Becker. This part consists of the emotional desires generally held in check by logic and reason" (98). A portion of Becker's dialogue in his defense speech reveals the same sense of duality within identity: "I am always forced to move along the streets, and always someone is behind me. It is I. I sometimes feel I am myself behind me, and yet I cannot escape" (Kracauer 221).

Lilvia Soto rightly argues that *Alguien* and *eme* constitute a similar duality: "el personaje es el hombre en su sentido más genérico . . . Alguien en la banca y eme tras la persiana constituyen las dos dimensiones de la dualidad del hombre" [the character is man in his most generic sense . . . *Alguien* on the bench and *eme* behind the blinds constitute the two dimensions of man's duality] (368). She further notes the inclusion of the reader in the questioning of identity (368). For, behind the given choices of identity for both *eme* and *Alguien*, there lies the suggestion of choice for oneself. If *Alguien* is an Everyman and *eme* is an Everyman, then there is good and evil in everyone, as Pacheco indicates in the text of *Salónica:* "eme y un hombre sentado—uno es culpable, el otro inocente; los dos culpables; ambos inocentes" [em and a seated man—one is guilty, the other innocent; both guilty; both innocent] (81). If there is to be an end to the repetitive cycle of persecution, it is up to those in the present to actively confront the issue, to choose to accept our mutual responsibility. By paralleling aesthetic choice with moral choice, Pacheco moves readers beyond complicity with the text to a much more significant historical complicity, revitalizing the message by expanding the notion of persecution to the historical present: Vietnam, Korea (Jiménez de Báez 292, n. 40; Glantz, "Morirás lejos," 190), and Mexico as well (Pacheco 64).

Ultimately, there is a conflation of history and fiction, as noted by Duncan: "The boundaries between history and fiction are therefore confused . . . with the consequent fusion of both" (52). Paralleling the intertextualities among novels, plays, and films, an example is offered of the postmodern in a global intertextuality in which all nations respond to and reflect each other and all people share responsibility. In this (hi)story, we are the protagonists and thus must make the ultimate choices, in a sense choosing the denouement of history as we are privileged to do in the novel. After all, as many of Pacheco's primary intertextual artistic examples are German, he demonstrates that the same country that produced aesthetic successes was also capable of yielding Nazi atrocities. It is a matter of personal choice.

Analogous to the largely ideologically framed *desenlaces* suggested for the novel's fictional present, one notes an evocation of hope within images and signs at the end of *Morirás lejos*. Jiménez de Báez argues that, because one of the antagonists leaves the park at the end of the novel, it is possible to break out of the persecutor/persecuted relationship (211). There is also a positive significance in the death in flames of Hitler, not only as the destruction of evil per se but also in its intertextual relation with Wagner's *Götterdämmerung:* Twilight of the Gods. In Wagner's opera the deaths of Siegfried and Brünhilde, combined with the flaming funeral pyre, symbolize "the birth of new hope as the 'redemption through love' motif soars upward in the strings to close the cycle with a benediction" (Headington, Westbrook, and Barfoot 187). Evidently there was no closure to the Nazi era with Hitler's death, for there were clear signs of antisemitism in Mexico as well as in other countries even as Pacheco wrote his novel (Saalmann 90). With the depicted expiration of Hitler and the suggested punishment of *eme*, however, Pacheco promotes the end of an era: the twilight, not of gods, although they might have been seen as false gods by some, but of a period of evil combined with a passivity on the part of others who might have been instrumental in interdicting the Nazi momentum. It would seem to be no coincidence that the time of day on that Wednesday in 1966 is twilight.

The notion of rebirth, of the promise of a new era, is also captured in the last sign of the text, that accompanying *Apéndice: Otros de los posibles desenlaces* (152). The hourglass symbol has a double significance: it is at once temporal and thematic. Temporally, it marks the inevitable reappearance of inhumanity unless action is taken to effect change. Thematically, it can be conceptualized as the resolution of opposites (Jiménez de Báez 251), of male and female (Koch 3–4), of good and evil, thus evoking a sense of peace through togetherness and representing a fellowship of man, in the sense of species rather than gender.

Pacheco's sense of man is a post-Holocaust man, as noted by Saalmann (98), and, as such, is charged with making sure that there is no further repetition of such horrors. By equating readers with both *Alguien* and *eme*, with both victim and victimizer, and by drawing them into the text through engaging narrative strategies, Pacheco pushes readers into an active role on a double plane and charts a course beyond a merely aesthetic notion of readership by (re)introducing the issues of history and morality. The passivity embodied by the two enigmatic protagonists in the novel's present must be replaced by an act of choice, both within the fiction and beyond it, as an example of co-creation of the text and as a confrontation with historic responsibility.

# CHAPTER 7

# *LA ONDA*

In her 1969 essay on young Mexican writers, "Narrativa joven de México," Margo Glantz specifies the following characteristics of *Onda* fiction, a literary movement initiated in the mid-1960s by José Agustín (*La tumba*, 1964; *De perfil*, 1966) and Gustavo Sainz (*Gazapo*, 1965): the authors are involved in a fundamental break with tradition, on both a linguistic and a moral level; their chosen language allows them to mock themselves as well as the reified society in which they live; they display an "importamadrista" attitude, that is to say, a complete disdain for societal norms and values; the works reflect a preference for projecting atmosphere rather than developing characters or story lines; the authors incorporate sexual thematics with a naturalness new to Mexican fiction; and there is a marked influence from other media, especially rock music (Glantz, *Repeticiones*, 79–81).[1] Two years later, in "Onda y escritura en México," she develops her characterization around the notion of self-contemplation, self-marginalization, and a reconsideration of language now shown to be a means both of isolating the individual from the disparaged adult world and of drawing the individual into a collective solidarity with peers (Glantz, *Repeticiones*, 91–98).

In *La novela mexicana contemporánea (1960–1980)*, M. Isela Chiu-Olivares groups the characteristics of the *Onda* texts into four main categories: language, the attitude of the narrator, themes, and narrative strategies. Within language, she specifies the incorporation of slang used by Mexican adolescents, neologisms, word play, humor, and the inclusion of foreign tongues, especially English. In terms of attitude and thematics, she is in basic agreement with Glantz but stresses drugs as a focus as well as sexual relations and music. As for narrative technique, the only specified commonality is the use of recording and communication technologies such as tape recorders and phones as a form of narration, although she adds that these writers were quite innovative in their discursive strategies (14–16). Subsequent to this discussion, Chiu-Olivares appends two points of importance: the privileging of the city as locus for the novels (16) and the temporal emphasis on the present rather than a historically contextualized presentation (19). Her analyses highlight the groundbreaking works of Agustín and Sainz with brief mention of three other writers associated with the movement: Parménides García Saldaña (*Pasto verde*, 1968), Orlando Ortiz (*En caso de duda*, 1968), and Margarita Dalton (*Larga sinfonía en D y había una vez . . .*, 1968).[2]

It must be stressed that few if any of the novels associated with the *Onda* contain all the characteristics cited above. The presence of drugs, as just one example, although strong in García Saldaña's *Pasto verde* (a slang term for marijuana) and Dalton's *Larga sinfonía en D* (note the code for LSD), plays little part in Sainz's *Gazapo*. At best one could say that there is a degree of commonality and overlapping in the novels grouped within the rubric of the *Onda*. Actually, many writers hastened to disassociate themselves from the term, in part because some felt it connoted works somewhat frivolous in theme and form and transitory in duration, in part because the authors felt that the word was inadequate to encompass the true variety and richness of the works so designated.[3] In fact, the following analyses will reveal aspects of narration that are clearly linked with *escritura* writing.

Be that as it may, there are certain common features among the three novels that constitute the birth of what would be termed the *Onda: La tumba, De perfil,* and *Gazapo*. As Agustín concedes, he and Sainz both began writing at an early age and introduced Mexican youth as central figures in their literature: "Nosotros escribimos sobre la juventud desde la juventud. Empleamos un lenguaje diferente, una mentalidad distinta, una sensibilidad enteramente distinta" [We wrote about youth while we were a part of it. We used a different language, a distinct mentality, and an entirely distinct sensibility] (Teichmann 61). The three novels present visions of adolescence of a young male in rebellion against his parents' generation and in search of his own identity. His rebelliousness is echoed within discourse largely through language, specifically the slang used both as a marker of difference used to shut out the adult world and as a badge of defiance employed to solidify camaraderie with one's peers. It is reflected as well in the various forms of experimentation employed by these authors. There are, moreover, two specific discursive characteristics common to the novels (and to a number of others within the rubric) that have yet to be mentioned:

the use of first-person narration and of fragmentation, both of which can be related to the notion of marginalization.[4]

Rosario Castellanos has argued that the marginalization experienced by the adolescents in novels such as *Gazapo* is not imposed from without but rather is the result of a conscious decision that results in the youths' being able to explore their identity (183). This pairs well with Chiu-Olivares's assertion that the young people defy the establishment in an attempt to assert their individuality at the same time that they experience internal conflict and insecurity (51). The significance of the first-person narration stems from the shifting from the margin to the center, in literary terms, of Mexican youth.[5] Although living a marginalized existence, adolescents now attain the status of protagonists. Authors like Agustín and Sainz literally give voice to figures who previously were at best minor characters if present at all.[6] By pairing that first-person narration with fragmentation, the authors allow the metaphoric possibilities of the latter technique to convey to readers a sense of disconnectedness suggestive both of internal doubts and fears and of being removed from the surrounding adult world.

Thus the original novels of the *Onda* reveal yet another source for fragmented discourse that continues the established pattern of pairing the aesthetic and the social: a metaphoric statement of the alienation of youth, the creation of a counterculture that finds affinity in a literary style that rebels against previous conventions of linearity.[7] The emphasis is on adolescents, their search for identity, and their chosen marginalization from an older generation mired in antiquated ways and perverted ideals, the embodiment of Fuentes's new bourgeoisie. *Onda* writers accent their break with the past by privileging the present in their narrations, in clear contrast with the writings of Rulfo and Fuentes, in which the weight of Mexican history is omnipresent. At the same time they carry on the creative use of discourse as initiated by Azuela early in the century that brings readers to focus on the storytelling process. Although Inke Müller's comment on the contrast between generations refers to the social, there are aesthetic implications as well, for the statement could just as easily describe the *Onda* writer's creative discourse that stands in opposition to a nineteenth-century style perceived as stodgy: "La inflexibilidad, el conformismo, y la hipocresía del mundo de los adultos contrasta con el dinamismo y la curiosidad, el inconformismo y la inocencia de los adolescentes [the inflexibility, the conformity, and the hypocrisy of the adult world contrast with the dynamism and curiosity, the lack of conformity, and the innocence of the adolescents] (68).

I have chosen for analysis Sainz's *Gazapo* and Agustín's *De perfil* in order to explore the rebellion in theme and form of what is known as classic *Onda* fiction. The third selection, Héctor Manjarrez's *Lapsus* (1971), serves as an indicator of the movement's fluidity and influence on later novels. For *Onda* fiction in the mid-1960s, with its emphasis on youth, in a sense parallels *Al filo del agua* in that it immediately precedes or is on the edge of another storm, the student massacre at Tlatelolco on October 2, 1968. The harsh realities of 1968 leave their mark on subsequent novelists, and Manjarrez proves adept at blending elements of *Onda* writing not only with the more cerebral engagement of readers associated with *escritura* writers but also with a more serious attitude toward social and political issues.

### Gustavo Sainz, *Gazapo*[8]

Gustavo Sainz's *Gazapo* (1965)[9] focuses on a group of adolescents in Mexico City who, tellingly, use *stories* as a means of exploring their identity and establishing their worth in the eyes of their peers. The youths engage in fabricating or embellishing on their sexual exploits and skirmishes with rivals, thus adopting the roles of storytellers, with regard to their own experiences, and audience (readers) to the narrations of others. In an effort to savor the details of the exaggerated accounts and, consequently, to be able to consider them again and again in a form of self-analysis, the characters record fictionalized experiences in both written (letters, diaries) and oral (tape recordings) renderings.

Sainz centers his narration on Menelao, age undefined but probably in his late teens,[10] and his relationship with a young girl named Gisela. Menelao narrates his encounters with Gisela, his efforts to achieve sexual intimacy, and the interfering presence of parents and other relatives. Additional accounts are presented, similar in sexual focus and even more invented, for his friends Mauricio and Vulbo and their adventures with Bikina and Nácar, respectively. The remaining peers serve as audience to the tales.

Representing the older generation are the parents of Menelao and Gisela and the latter's two aunts. Long divorced, Menelao's father has since married a woman aptly named Madhastra (a slight variation of the Spanish word for stepmother), who, according to Menelao, is the dominant figure of the pair. Menelao has little contact with his mother, although he is staying in her apartment while she is in Cuernavaca. Gisela's father, a taxi driver, is at home only on Sundays and is generally inebriated. Her aunts, both extremely religious, albeit of different denominations, are very rigid with her. Clearly relations are strained between generations. The elders ignore the presence of Menelao and his friends on more than one occasion. Menelao's father voices his disapproval of Gisela, and it is only in a dream that Menelao finds harmony between the two.

Given this sense of alienation, it is not surprising that among the youths there is a need not only to voice but also to dramatize their rebellion. Activities range from pasting captions from the comics' "Little Lulu" on a depiction of the Last Supper (118–119) to planning a robbery of Menelao's father's apartment in order to salvage Menelao's possessions after he is banned from the house. Despite the adolescent pranks, however, *Gazapo* is not so much about delinquency as it is about a search for identity. The youths, both male and female, are trying different poses, gestures, and identities in an effort to sort out the changing inner self that remains a puzzle both to peers and to older relatives as well as to themselves.

The characters' sense of estrangement, their marginalization from the adult society, is reflected in multiple ways in the structure of *Gazapo*. James Brown argues that the novel contains not chapters but scenes and segments of scenes (238), and Lanin Gyurko relates the fragmentation of the novel to the incompleteness of the adolescents' lives: "Instead of complete scenes there are embryonic chapters, outlines of dialogues and confrontations, or mere isolated images" ("Reality and Fantasy," 131). In the original Joaquín Mortiz edition, ten units of material are set off graphically, thus suggesting a more traditional chapter division, but they are not numbered. Instead, the first full line of each unit is presented completely in uppercase letters. All but one of these "chapters" are subdivided into fragments set off by a blank space, for a total of thirty-two.[11] In the Aguilar, León y Cal edition, the ten divisions again have no title or number but are marked by a collection of stars, circles, and an exclamation mark that, in conjunction with the first line of capital letters, connotes heightened emotion. A reduced number of representative markings are on all left-hand pages in lieu of page numbers, along with the novel's title written thus: gaZApo. In both editions there is an appended afterword referring to some photographs, and in some of the Joaquín Mortiz reprints, there are, in fact, images of a young girl suggesting a likeness of Gisela.[12]

As Sainz describes the temporal structure of the novel, the action is situated on a Monday. From this point, Menelao recalls incidents from the previous three days, retelling what he has experienced as well as fantasizing or elaborating upon the details. In addition, he projects into the future the following two days, imagining hypothetical encounters with Gisela and with the other youths (Rodríguez Monegal 5). Expanding upon this division, Gyurko describes a two-part structure, the first part consisting of real time, in which Menelao reconstructs events of the recent past, and the second involving potential or oneiric time, in which he creates or authors a future for himself ("Reality and Fantasy," 128).

The recountings, whether real or imaginary, are presented in a variety of ways: anecdotes within conversations as recorded on a tape player, selections from diaries, and letters. The multiplicity of format recalls Arreola's *La feria*, but in contrast to the perspectivism inherent in the earlier text, in *Gazapo* all is filtered through Menelao's consciousness. In addition, Arreola's work reflects constants throughout the centuries, whereas Sainz focuses on the immediate present.

That present, however, is difficult to grasp chronologically. The events retold are in haphazard order, just as memory and fantasy generally fail to follow linear paths.[13] The ambiguities that result from the embellished tales and the difficulty in distinguishing fantasy from reality further cloud readers' perceptions, leading to a feeling of disorientation. In this sense, *Gazapo* has much in common with Elizondo's *Farabeuf*, published in the same year. Both texts offer choices; actions are suggested and then discounted. More significantly, there is a reduction to oneness inherent in *Gazapo* similar to that in *Farabeuf* that makes Menelao the conduit for the expression of all adolescent turmoil and confusion. Sainz affirms the youth's representational status in an interview with Emir Rodríguez Monegal: "casi todos hablan igual, los influyen las mismas cosas, y hasta es probable que demuestre así que es él mismo todos los personajes" [almost all of them speak the same way, the same things influence them, and it is even possible that he himself is all the characters] (6). Contributing to this sense of oneness are the visual stimuli in the Joaquín Mortiz editions. The front cover suggests a painting by Georges Seurat in its series of dots in white, black, and grey. One can barely perceive the head and upper chest of a youthful figure, sex unclear. Of the appended eight photographs, one is the same as that suggested on the front cover design. All seem to be of the same young woman, thus leading one to assume it is Gisela, although in some poses the figure is decidedly androgynous. Thus there is a clear conflation to oneness similar to that seen in both *Farabeuf* and *Morirás lejos*.

Indeed, with *Gazapo* Sainz joins Elizondo and Pacheco in breaking with traditional norms, and thus his novel shares many characteristics with texts known as *escritura*. Its multiple ambiguities have been commented upon by a number of critics, among them Gyurko: "Chronological time, physical space, and continuity of character and episode are replaced by simultaneity, protean space, and arbitrary, multiple identities" ("Reality and Fantasy," 129). In addition, within the narration, there are frequent examples of changes in discourse that call readers' attention to the writing process. Sainz includes a poem-*cum*-supplication that depicts Menelao's appeal for prayer on his behalf from assorted people and places (91). On occasion Menelao's thoughts run together, as in the stream-of-consciousness sample that immediately follows the poem (91–92) and his impressionistic viewing of his grandmother's body (72).

For a novel that breaks with conventional narrative practice, however, there are numerous examples of suspense privileged at the end of "chapters," as if flaunting the text's refusal to provide closure to a more traditional reading. At the end of the fifth unit of fragments, Gisela's father overhears a conversation regarding his daughter's supposed intimacy with Menelao. Similarly, at the close of section 7, a confrontation between Menelao and Gisela's father seems imminent. Both endings surely pique readers' interest. As in "lo de Damián y Micaela" from *Al filo del agua*, however, readers never receive the desired stories.

Thus *Gazapo* displays certain elements associated with narrative practice centered on story but nestles them within a slippery narrative replete with ambiguities, disorienting time jumps, and multiple conflations of reality and fantasy. It is as if the text suffered from an analogous crisis of identity as seen in the characters. For, although Sainz has written a novel that reflects the tradition-breaking strategies associated with *escritura*, his content, albeit elusive, is clearly rooted in contemporary issues. *Gazapo's* thematics are very specific to Mexico City in the early 1960s, and an essential part of that reality involves youth counterculture and the search for identity.

The adolescents depicted in *Gazapo* lack a clearly defined personality, a solid sense of self. As Federica Domínguez Colavita argues, because of this absence, they engage in the invention of character or the substitution of a pose (190). They study each other's words and gestures as well as borrow those of other cultures. Menelao repeats Vulbo's stories in an effort to learn from his speech patterns (89) and frequently studies his own gestures in the mirror (27). Indeed, mirrors figure prominently in the text as if a confirmation of a character's desired image, in particular serving as visual confirmation of Menelao's identity as a lover (Gyurko, "Reality and Fantasy," 127). Analogously, the tape recorder serves as an audio reflection of self, allowing the speaker to listen as if to another's discourse. In a manner consistent with teenagers' constantly viewing themselves, analyzing their appearance, Sainz has Menelao observe and listen, scrutinizing his life as told in story form.

Menelao's fluctuating sense of self is reflected also in the variations on his name as termed by the other characters: Melenas (12, 69, 97, 101, 104), Mentolado (14), Menelado (24, 60, 72), Nelao (40, 64), Melao (64), Melomeas (38, 46), and Melachupas (46, 78). It is not just Menelao, however, who experiences changes, but all the adolescents. Furthermore, the fluidity within identity is deeper than that signified by one's name. In essence, Menelao and his peers are caught between childhood and adulthood. They seek to participate as adults in matters involving sex, yet there are repeated incidents that reveal their immaturity. They snicker when someone passes gas, play a game similar to Checkers using condoms as the pieces (79), and place condoms on their eyes as if they were glasses (118). Although Gisela deceives her aunts and father, seeking time alone with her boyfriend, she demonstrates remarkable ignorance regarding matters both sexual and physically functional, asking Menelao to explain menstruation (58–59) and the meaning of the word *coitus* (25).

The combination of fragmentation, ambiguities of time and space, and disorienting changes in narration contributes to creating in readers a sense of confusion similar to that felt by the adolescents. Complicating matters further is the consistent need to interrogate the veracity of incidents related, for there is an increasing suggestion that fantasy predominates over reality. Sainz brings to the foreground the notion of exaggeration or fabrication in the title. As defined at the beginning of the text by two sources, both very erudite, *gazapo* can mean either a young rabbit (*conejito;* a term of endearment between Menelao and Gisela) or a big lie (6). Furthermore, although readers would find it difficult at the beginning of the novel to recognize the embellished tales for what they are, there are suggestions from the start that these actions are imagined. One notes particularly the use of words such as *probablemente* (probably) and *quizás* (perhaps), again in striking similarity to *Farabeuf.* In addition, Menelao offers alternative scenarios as readers progress through the segments; if a character did not say this, perhaps it was that. At times, a narration begins tentatively, as with the term *parece que* (it seems that), only to be followed by an authoritative statement of the same material (60). There are other occasions in which the inventions are quite clear, as with Vulbo's greatly exaggerated account of his encounter with Nácar and her mother (63).

Even recognizing that much of the material presented is a fictionalized account on Menelao's part, readers may still find it difficult to maintain a clear distinction between real events and desired fantasies. There are moments in which the retelling of previous experiences is so complete, so full of details regarding conversations, that one has the impression of being witness to the actual scene. Encounters are imagined with such concentration that they seem to be recountings of events rather than fantasies. Finally, there is the inclusion of photographs, which, as in *Farabeuf*, evokes from readers' conditioning a testament to veracity.

The ultimate deception is revealed at approximately the halfway point of the novel. There, a third-person narrator describes Menelao's latest recording, including a three-paragraph excerpt that closes the first fragment of the unit (61–62). This portion is, in fact, an exact duplication of the beginning of the novel. It is very likely that most readers, although conditioned by the text to question the youths' recounting of experience by the time they reach this point, have not called into question the beginning of the novel. Previous conditioning would have them accept the first pages as grounding material, as a stable introductory section, rather than what appears retrospectively to be one more retelling within Menelao's catalog of stories. Readers experience a need to reevaluate as seen in *Pedro Páramo*, although in this instance more analogous to that felt at the end of Gabriel García Márquez's *Cien años de soledad* when they realize that the novel they have been reading is actually authored by Melquíades. In this case, however, the flaunting of the fiction within the fiction occurs earlier, giving readers ample time not only to reconsider earlier sections but also to proceed with their reading from a less innocent point of view.

Appropriately, this section that makes readers aware of the narrative process constitutes a story, one of the many stories narrated in the novel from one perspective, yet also *the* story that, in turn, constitutes the novel when seen from the halfway point. The effect is dizzying when one considers that, upon reading pages 61–62, readers are sent back to the beginning, only to reach once more the same impasse. It almost seems natural, then, that the text, at best elusive and confusing in the beginning, becomes even more amorphous as one continues. In the last segments, Menelao's conjectures are quite explicit. Section 7 begins with "O MENELAO FRENTE A LA GRABADORA [OR MENELAO, FACING THE TAPE RECORDER] (73), an alternative scenario that will find echoes, increasing in frequency, as the novel draws to nonclosure. Menelao's options become the readers' also. Brief sketches of possibilities attain the status of a prose poem, with the word *o* (or) beginning each strophe as an example of anaphora (118).[14] The text ends with a more extended series of projections. There is a common base to the hypothetical scenes, as Menelao, Gisela, and Vulbo converse at a table in a restaurant. There are even elements of dialogue that repeat in the different versions.[15] The narration, however, appears to break loose from whatever control it might have once possessed. As Menelao imagines the various possibilities, his fictionalized account becomes reality both for him and his friends and for readers. The characters are so immersed in the story that it is as if they were actually doing the narrated actions. Menelao's narration of different versions of the same fiction places his friends *in* that situation, as the scenario changes at his whim, necessitating an occasional reminder that the three are still seated in the restaurant La Vaca Negra (134). Readers are presented with a selection of narrations similar to that dramatized in Akira Kurosawa's 1951 film *Rashomon,* only the variations are all from one source.

Both Gyurko ("Reality and Fantasy," 128) and Chiu-Olivares (37) make reference to Menelao as an author-in-the-text. Indeed, all the adolescent males are so given to fabrication and storytelling that they refer to themselves as "la pandilla de cuenta-anécdotas" [the gang of storytellers] (31). The activity is so common among the group that it merits comment when no stories are related at one party (87). Tales are told again and again, at times producing frustration in the listeners: "¡Hijos!—dice Vulbo. Lo cuentas a cada rato" ["Jesus!" says Vulbo. "You tell that one all the time"] (69). As principal storyteller, Menelao is critical of others' narrations, in one section referring to Vulbo's tedious dissertations about Nácar (97), yet he is also hard on himself, as he describes his "frases de una cursilería intolerable" [intolerably tacky sentences] (95).

Such an emphasis on *story,* established right from the beginning with the repetition of the verb *contar* (to tell a story),[16] raises the issue not only of authorship but of audience (implied readership) as well. As Domínguez Colavita argues, self-affirmation requires the approval of others (189). Even more significantly, however, the notion of plurality of response is emphasized, beginning with the multiple definitions of the title presented before the text commences. Sainz promotes difference in point of view in his description of the youths' meanderings: "Llegaron al final de la vecindad (o al principio, según se mire) [They arrived at the end of the neighborhood (or at the beginning, depending on how you look at it)] (17). Individual response of interpretation is signaled even more clearly in the following passage: "En eso llegó Gisela, y Menelao la saludó sorprendido (según Arnaldo), acostumbrado (según Balmori)" [Just then Gisela arrived, and Menelao greeted her in surprise (according to Arnaldo), in his usual fashion (according to Balmori)] (36).

The examples of readers-in-the-text are multiple. On occasion, the model is one of a perceptive, active reader, as when Mauricio analyzes Gisela's letter in which she details (much too precisely) Menelao's rival's family situation (100) or when Mauricio deduces correctly that Menelao's reference to a friend involved Vulbo (102). Tellingly, these consecutive illustrations are found in the penultimate unit of fragments, thus serving as indicators of the active readers' role necessitated by the last, enigmatic section in which Menelao offers so many choices. In other instances, characters voice enthusiasm regarding the desire to hear a story. There are frequent pieces of dialogue in which the command *Cuéntame* (Tell me) or a variation is repeated (36, 104, 113, 130). One example is particularly revealing, since it voices readers' interest in receiving the full story of the suggested encounter between Menelao and Gisela's father (104). The desired tale, however, is never revealed. Not all responses to the stories are favorable. In particular, Vulbo's elaborate tales about Nácar become tedious in their blatant falsehood and endless repetition, prompting Menelao to comment at one point, "Y ¿a mí qué me importa?" [And *what does that matter to me?*] (108, emphasis in the original). When poorly told or infinitely reiterated, even sexual exploits can become boring for teenagers, as indicated by Menelao's comment about Vulbo's "hormonal adventures" (109).

By creating a novel rooted in storytelling, Sainz flaunts his fiction as fiction, thus participating in the self-conscious narrative movement in conjunction with the *escritura* authors like Elizondo and Pacheco. In contrast to their universalist tendencies, however, *Gazapo* is clearly based in the reality of Mexico City in the 1960s. The very first paragraph situates the boys in Sanborns Lafragua right at Reforma, and the specificity of street names and monuments makes clear the centrality of urban life to their existence. Sainz's text is removed also from Pacheco's concern with historical issues; here, the youths' sense of history is largely limited to changes in street names. As epitomized in Menelao, their interests are in the recent past, as grist for storytelling; the present with its opportunities for sexual conquest; and the ephemeral future, envisioned in fanciful reveries. These lives are incomplete; it is therefore fitting that there should be no closure to *Gazapo*. The novel ends with multiple possibilities, conjectures regarding the future. Readers have been exposed to the characters' search for identity, but, in accordance with Sainz's youthful status when he composed the work, "No hay final. . . . Faltan otros encuentros" [There is no end. . . . There will be more episodes] (114).

### José Agustín, *De perfil* (In Profile)

José Agustín's[17] second novel, *De perfil* (1966) is analogous to *Gazapo* in many ways. In first-person narration, a sixteen-year-old Mexican exposes readers to his friendships, social activities, sexual fantasies, sexual initiation, and attitudes toward family and culture. Fundamental to the telling is his creative use of language. Agustín moves beyond Sainz, however, in his opening of the text to contemporary politics and the resulting byproduct of sociopolitical criticism.[18]

Agustín leaves his narrator unnamed, thus enabling him to embody the youth of the Mexican middle to upper-middle class.[19] He lives with his parents, Humberto and Violeta, and a younger brother (also anonymous) in comfortable housing. In the course of the present tense of the narration, the narrator details his involvement with a new acquaintance, Octavio; the narrator's friend, Ricardo, a troubled youth who constantly urges him to join him in running away; Queta Johnson, a singer he meets at a party who becomes his first sexual partner; his cousin Esteban, whose social rebellion is more aggressively defined than the narrator's; and a number of less prominent characters who, nevertheless, have important roles within the contextual social fabric of the novel: a homosexual record promoter, some lower-class youths, and a few politically involved university students. Given the brief three-day time span of the novel's present, the elements constituting "story" are sparse: a party at Queta's populated by musicians and teens, a party for family members in celebration of Esteban's twenty-first birthday, the narrator's sexual encounter with Queta, visits to his father's office, and a trip to the university to obtain his credentials for school. Interspersed with these activities are conversations, phone calls, and the narrator's analysis of his relationships, all punctuated with visits to the large rock in the garden of his home where the narrator seeks solitude and a chance to smoke.

Agustín divides his novel into eight "chapters," not numbered or titled, but designated by a wider space than that used for the fragmentation within these larger divisions. There are 122 segments within the eight sections, separated by a blank space and marked by the lack of indentation in the first paragraph. The longest fragment is unusually large compared to the others, a full eighteen pages (155–183), the shortest a mere line and a half (331). The novel appears to begin in linear fashion, with fragmentation apparently initially serving to allow the omission of unnecessary detail. Soon, however, one realizes that the narration begins on what will be seen to be day three of a three-day span, then reverts to the telling of the occurrences of this period. This narration of the present time is further fragmented by the interpolation of diary episodes, imagined scenarios, projections of what other characters might be doing, fantasies, and memories. Of the diary episodes, two are authored by others: Ricardo leaves his diary at the narrator's house and the latter takes advantage of the opportunity to read it; Esteban shares with the narrator his recorded adventures of escapades with his lower-class friends. The third diary is actually a datebook belonging to Humberto that the narrator steals. The dramatizations of episodes based on the datebook are a creation of the narrator's, as one surmises upon being presented with the actual entries (328). Humberto's words are brief, offering only the bare facts of his encounters and experiences. They serve, however, as an authenticating source of the youth's imagined scenarios. Among the narrator's personal fantasized sequences are sexual encounters with maids, a meeting with Queta's father, and the circumstances of the narrator's death. The more factual scenes that one assumes are memories include illnesses, a scene on the highway when the family car breaks down, and an incident from school that the narrator found particularly embarrassing.

Fragmentation thus allows for time jumps and changes in focus. It is also effective as a technique with which to frustrate readers. Beyond the uncertainty produced by the disorienting switches of focus, there are instances of the interdicting of segments at moments of heightened interest. The most obvious of these is the sex scene between the narrator and Queta that is interrupted by a fragment focusing on Humberto and Violeta. Although it may suggest a parallel in the coupling or constitute a reflection on what happens when passion passes, it also suspends the narration when readers are most likely wanting it to continue.

Interdiction is, in fact, an agent of fragmentation throughout the text. In many instances, there is a vertical line attached to the end of a broken-off sentence as a marker that the speaker has been interrupted. Within the first examples, Agustín includes a verbal explanation to complement the graphic symbol, thus educating readers as to its function (11). On a larger scale, fragments themselves are also interdicted. One segment ends with the word *Y* [And] (86). There are no markers to indicate either pause or closure. The subsequent fragment begins in lowercase, as if in continuation, but the impression is false, for the segment is a dream sequence that bears no clear relation to the previous section. Another fragment is cut off in the middle of a word with the now recognizable vertical line reinforcing the lack of continuation (109). Furthermore, the novel itself ends with the same signifier of interruption, thus connoting lack of closure and suggesting further developments that have been denied to readers. Paradoxically, the interdiction that severs the novel serves to open the ending to reader involvement as readers are prompted to speculate about what might have followed.

Critics have argued that readers have already enjoyed an intimate relationship with the novel, so the invited participation at the end is not considered unusual. Given the personal nature of the information imparted, the diaries and the narrator's candor in relating his thoughts and experiences, Chiu-Olivares notes the highly confidential nature of the narrator-reader relationship, arguing that readers become the narrator's confidant (48, 50). To this one could add the assumption of camaraderie rooted in the act of employing language typical of the *onderos* in Mexico, thus placing readers within that referential group (Carter and Schmidt 1). Such intimacy is supported by various statements that reach beyond the fiction to readers who are explicitly targeted as the narrator's peers. When he sits alone fantasizing about running away, the narrator adds, "Ya verás cuando quieras escaparte de casa" [You'll see when you want to run away] (259). The use of the familiar *tú* form reinforces the closeness. Subsequently, after a retelling of a scene of fighting and chaos involving university students, in a position of privilege at the end of a fragment, the narrator addresses a projected reader: "¿Observaste todo bien? Suave. Retenlo en la memoria, cuate. No lo olvides" [Did you observe carefully? Cool. Keep that image in your memory, my good buddy. Don't forget it] (293).[20] Even more significantly, having taken into account the numerous asides within parentheses that comment on how the story is being told, John Brushwood sees reader involvement extended to an awareness of the act of narrating ("Art and Trivia," 58). Readers, then, move from intimacy of detail and language to the narrative process itself.

Having focused on discourse, readers will note the flaunted repetition that occurs at the end of the seventh chapter (278).[21] Again in a privileged position, almost exact textual phrasing from the first fragment is repeated, signaling the temporal primacy of day three as the source of the narration. Chiu-Olivares notes the circular pattern thus created even though the narrative continues well beyond this point (Chiu-Olivares 43, 45). Acknowledging the same structure of a circle with an appended tail, Agustín subsequently likens the shape of the novel to a comet (Teichmann 46). This is not, however, the first repetition in the text. With minimal variation, some five lines are reiterated with reference to Ricardo's diary (95, 193), and the beginning of two separated fragments depict Esteban's entering a club despite not having proper identification (206, 216). There would appear to be an iterative pattern within the novel that suggests circularity, thus providing no closure. These false circularities finally culminate in the circularity that comes, appropriately, at the end of the novel. The last fragment dramatizes the narrator's birth, much like what Fuentes presented in *La muerte de Artemio Cruz*. Thus a circle is formed with the first fragment, which, in addition to providing the thematic roots of rebelliousness and attitudes toward sex, makes clear reference to the narrator's birth (7).

Agustín has affirmed his belief that form is tightly linked with content (Guerra-Cunningham et al. 34), and the multiple metaphoric implications arising from the novel's circularity illustrate his adeptness in putting into practice that principle. In contrast to the end of *La muerte de Artemio Cruz*, in which the commonplace of birth as new life and hope is subverted by readers' knowledge of Artemio's fate, the depiction of new life in *De perfil* in one sense does proffer a sense of opportunity. As Agustín states, "el personaje termina nuevamente naciendo a la vida [the character winds up being reborn to life] (Guerra-Cunningham et al. 33), and for the author this means that the narrator has endless possibilities open to him (Mier and Carbonell 61).

Given the insistence on circularity, however, readers might well question this optimistic interpretation. The notion of repetition could just as easily reflect the inevitability of the youth's continuing his parents' patterns of behavior and attitudes, just as his smoking and drinking constitute more of an apprenticeship to adult practice than a rebellion. In this sense, the cycles evoked in *De perfil* echo those dramatized by Fuentes in *La región más transparente*. Complementing this interpretation are comments on the conflicting attitudes experienced by the adolescents in *De perfil*. Brushwood has noted the contradictory coupling of nonconformism with a basic respect for conventionality ("Art and Trivia," 56), and Chiu-Olivares mentions the opposing forces that both push the youths toward an independent stance and tie them to society (51).

Upon examining the narrator's behavior, one senses a basic lack of self-definition. He imitates the actions and gestures of those around him, copying Octavio's manner of sitting in a chair (31), and adapting himself in chameleon fashion to the political leanings of the university students. Significantly, Agustín has likened the narrator to a sponge, absorbing what surrounds him (Teichmann 45). He has internalized society's poses and frequently adopts a learned gesture or manner that will be readily recognized by the culture that engendered this display: "mi mejor cara de mártir fanático" [my best fanatic martyr face] (254). In doing so, he appropriates his parents' behavior, for they, too, are acting out chosen roles. Humberto is especially enmeshed in the pose of modern parent and successful professional. His suits are always impeccably neat, and it is he who suggests that the children address their parents by their first names. Although she maintains a frigid distance from her children, Violeta also succumbs to society's demands, as when the narrator refers to her as the "abnegada-madre-que-cuida-al-hijo-agonizante" [self-denying-mother-who-takes-care-of-her-dying-son] (78). The hyphens serve to emphasize the clichéd quality of the behavior, as if all aspects of the pose were inextricably intertwined. Juan Bruce-Novoa argues that, in fact, in all of Agustín's works prior to 1969, the author "viewed his characters' antiestablishment attitudes and actions as essentially a pose" (41). Noting the superficial aspect of the character's rebelliousness, Bruce-Novoa concludes that the narrator will follow a path leading to a repetition of his parents' life (52). Inke Gunia agrees with a more pessimistic view of the ending, stating that there have been no indications that the youth has distanced himself ideologically from his parents (185).

This would fulfill the metaphoric aspects of the novel's insistence on circularity. The youth's ultimate ceding to society's systems is confirmed in the penultimate fragment of the text that serves as a partial résumé of the influences on the narrator's life. In rapid succession, he imagines scenes with many of the characters he has encountered in the three-day period, adding a fantasy involving Queta's father and segments of diary entries. From among this whirlwind of experiences, the preoccupation that endures centers on a course of studies at the university, an internalized obsession of occupation that stands for class, status, and the responsibility of adulthood, all rooted in bourgeois mythology: "¿qué diablos voy a estudiar?" [what the hell am I going to study?] (353).

The narrator's lack of commitment to social change prompts skepticism in Rosario Castellanos regarding the youths' sense of alienation. She too questions their sincerity, commenting that they never really interrogate their social circumstances or ponder remedies to perceived injustice (181). Finally, the adolescents are as acritical and apolitical as the upper-middle-class against which they supposedly rebel, the basic defects skewered by Onda writer Parménides García Saldaña (Poniatowska, ¡Ay vida, 178). Agustín, then, situates as the target of his criticism both conventional bourgeois demeanor and the behavior of his contemporaries, as Brushwood has maintained (La novela mexicana, 47). The critical focus on youth is perhaps best illustrated by the narrator's lack of political awareness. When caught with a friend in a police raid on one of the cafés cantantes (rock clubs), he personalizes the experience, not questioning the political realities of the situation, but wondering how this could have happened to him (148–152).[22]

Agustín places the majority of the novel's political material in the tail of his comet, dramatizing there the narrator's trip to the university and his exposure to the politicized students. By doing so, the author presents a stunningly timely analogy to the social restlessness preceding the Mexican Revolution, which was prefigured in popular lore by the appearance of Halley's Comet as presented in the last chapter of Al filo del agua.[23] Once again, form complements content, for, in addition to the novel's structure's evoking a parallel with the revolution, the university students' lack of organization and unity echoes the fragmentariness of the revolutionary efforts: "sucede que somos pocos y estamos desunidos. Dentro de nuestra federación hay como mil grupos y todos quieren imponer sus tácticas" [What happens is that there are just a few of us and we're not united. Within our federation there are about a thousand groups and every one of them wants to impose its own strategy] (316).[24]

More significantly, by drawing these parallels, Agustín brings to the foreground a society in need of change, and change is, as he has stated, the fundamental raison d'être of the *Onda* (Agustín, "Cuál es la onda," 12–13). Despite the imminence of more serious student unrest in Mexico, this call for revolution is more cultural than political. It is in this way, however, that Agustín links the literature of the *Onda* with the ramifications of the student movement that was to culminate in the tragic massacre at Tlatelolco on October 2, 1968. For the author, the events of 1968 are rooted in "Cambio en todos los órdenes, político, económico, social pero fundamentalmente . . . yo diría, cultural" [change in all the orders, political, economic, and social, but fundamentally . . . I would say, cultural] (Guerra-Cunningham et al. 26).

Other critics are in agreement that *Onda* literature prefigures the events of 1968 (Brushwood, *Narrative Innovation,* 62; Mier and Carbonell 64). This is certainly true in terms of the breaking of barriers, the liberation of language, and the introduction of once taboo subject matter like sex and homosexuality.[25] By the same token, Carlos Monsiváis argues persuasively that 1968 effectively severs the possibility of continuing to present youthful characters with humor and inoffensive rebellion (Ruffinelli, "Notas," 49). Support of one of these views need not preclude acceptance of the other. Agustín's depiction of politicized youth in contrast with the protagonist of *De perfil* both dramatizes the restlessness among university students and promotes change among the apathetic. Characters who are involved politically criticize the apolitical stance of the majority of students (296) and target the corruption prevalent within the top echelon of their own organization (304–305), leading John Kirk to find parallels between student and national politics ("En torno a *De perfil,"* 114). Agustín would seem to be making a call for adolescents such as the narrator to free themselves from their self-immersion. By satirizing their posturing, he provides the aperture to more serious considerations.

The events of 1968 touch off a profound change in Mexican letters. According to Schaffer, subsequent works are marked by a sense of pessimism, tragic themes that recall the violence of Tlatelolco, content rooted in identity crises, and references to the reality of government repression (225–226). Writers' interrogation of the individual and of the nation dramatize the reflective posture of the entire country that had been shocked into political awareness in 1968 and forced into a new preoccupation with social and national issues (Ruffinelli, "Notas," 48, 56). Much of the subsequent fiction and literary criticism, whether implicitly or explicitly, acknowledges the impact of 1968.[26] One should not assume, however, that the legacy of Tlatelolco is all negative. As Elena Poniatowska has argued, the events of '68 occasioned a cultural revolution of the kind to which Agustín alluded and an opening toward a new spirit of freedom that is still unfolding (*¡Ay vida*, 204, 208).

## Héctor Manjarrez, *Lapsus (Algunos actos fallidos)* [Lapsus (Some Failed Actions)]

In Héctor Manjarrez's *Lapsus (Algunos actos fallidos)* (1971), experimentation spills into excess. Like Agustín and Sainz, Manjarrez was very young, twenty-six, when the novel was published. He was only twenty-three when he began work on it, moreover, and the date of initial composition is significant: 1968.[27] The chaos that reigns in this novel can be seen as a blending of *Onda* and *escritura* characteristics, marked indelibly by the sociopolitical factors of Tlatelolco, Paris '68, and Vietnam. An echo of the *Onda* is to be found in both thematics (drugs, the rebellion of youth) and experimentation in language. Manjarrez's preoccupation with the narrative process and self-referentiality aligns him with Elizondo: challenging the assumed privilege of authorship, frequent comments to his reader (used in the text as singular and masculine), the presence of the author in the text, and a narration that is frequently incoherent. The influence of 1968 can be seen beyond the explicit references to the student movement in Paris, Chicago's Mayor Richard Daley, and the horrors of the war in Vietnam. In sharp contrast to Menelao's efforts to establish his identity in *Gazapo*, the characters here are not clothed in humorous tones, and the notion of self-examination is more reflective of ontology presented with more than a hint of schizophrenia, which Jiménez de Báez relates to the schizoid nature of the 1960s (180).

Although it is hard to refer to the contents of *Lapsus* as "story," it does begin with the presentation of characters. Two men, Huberto Haltter, aged 24, and Humberto Heggo, 39,[28] are in New York en route from Mexico City to Paris. The humor in their names, emphasized in an endnote, quickly demonstrates a reduction to oneness (alter ego), yet the men are dramatized as two throughout the text. Each is seeking exile in France, Huberto escaping from the hypocrisy of his parents and their bourgeois culture, Humberto choosing to free himself from his family and a conformist existence. The two become involved with an Algerian Air France stewardess named Céline and join her in Paris, engaging in a *mènage à trois* reminiscent of François Truffaut's 1961 film, "Jules et Jim."[29] A fourth prominent character is an unusual dramatization of an author-in-the-text with the suggestion that this is not allegorical or metaphoric, but Manjarrez himself. He too was on the plane to Paris and is soon depicted as a voyeur perched on the rooftop of a nearby building observing through binoculars the activities of the others. Here, the function of author or narrator as observer is literalized, inscribed within the narrative.

The two chapters devoted to these elements of story are difficult to follow. In addition to word games, sentence fragments, words fused together, and the joining of letters that suggests the concept of a word but means nothing (for example, "Jjjjj"), the text is replete with sections in English and French with no translation provided. Continuing a trajectory from Fuentes through Sainz and Agustín, the author either assumes a sophisticated reading public or chooses to flaunt the complexities of language and the frustration of being excluded by a foreign tongue. Complicating matters further is the slippery narration that jumps between first and third person, most of the time with no indication as to who is speaking. Since the novel began with third-person narration, readers seem to be confronted with a *mènage à quatre* when the narrator appears to be in bed with Céline also (43). The first-person narrator is at times masculine, at times feminine, as judged from the use of adjectives, yet just when readers might feel somewhat secure in determining gender or speaker's identity, another change takes place, without a new paragraph or other marker to explain the difference. Readers might well question whether Huberto or Humberto is the narrator after all, yet the narrator refers to both of them in the third person (41). Interestingly, there is a condensed version of this confusion presented as a grammar lesson shortly after a particularly difficult section: "Haltter está durmiendo, tú no estás durmiendo, ¿acaso estoy durmiendo yo?: am, are, is: sleeping" [Haltter is sleeping, you are not sleeping, perhaps I am sleeping?] (48; text is in English at the end).

Beyond this skeletal basis for story, the elements of content are elusive and suggestively atemporal. In one chapter Humberto is a reporter in Vietnam, relating in a letter to Céline the atrocities he must witness. In another he has the role of ruler on a tropical island. One chapter is narrated by an English dog, formerly a Mexican dog, with the suggestion that this is Huberto high on drugs. Indeed, much of the presumed content gives the impression of being a dream or the result of a good or bad drug trip.

Manjarrez divides the text into two parts, the first, quite lengthy, containing these disjunctive narrative pieces and the second, a mere twenty-three pages, that, despite beginning with a section on the twin offspring of Céline and the author, is really devoted to self-referential commentary on authorship and readership. There is a total of eleven chapters, some of which are segmented with a blank space as marker of separation. The full impact of a fragmented reading experience, however, stems from Manjarrez's use of endnotes, a full fifty-seven pages of them. In the manner of Julio Cortázar in *Rayuela*, Manjarrez forces readers to deal physically with the novel, as they are cued to fragment their reading experience by periodically abandoning the basic text to consult the forty-three endnotes. The notes range in length from one word to thirty-three pages. Many are narratives themselves, although there are sources given as well in a traditional format. One finds also bibliographies, discographies, and filmographies for a number of the chapters, again with a nod to the *Onda* interest in multimedia. Some endnotes are fragmented, and one carries a dedication, as is the practice for all the chapters in the basic narrative. The placement of the notes within the text is innovative also. On more than one occasion, there are two endnotes on the same word. One note interdicts a sentence completely (24), and another separates a noun from its adjective (33).

The longest endnote stands out as a story, which immediately invites contrast with the confusing narrative to which it is appended. In echo of the main text, it is divided into two parts and is fragmented. It departs from the other narrative, however, in that its narration, at least initially, appears to follow conventional norms, reminding readers of what the other "story" lacks. Narration is in third-person omniscience, and readers receive ample information on characters and their societal roots. Yet this apparently standard tale of a group of people on a cruise in the Pacific gets out of hand too, as readers are presented with a dream sequence in which an older man masturbates and another has liquid pouring out of his ear. In Part 2, the narration switches to first person, a detective presenting his analysis of events surrounding the death of one of the passengers. This narration, although ostensibly conventional, approaches the chaos of Part 1. Finally, any narration can lose its coherence. At the end of the endnote story the characters conflate, as the detective argues that one man is the synthesis of two others, two antitheses (276).

Although Schaffer contends that the narrations in the endnotes are unrelated to the main story (221), surely there are ample parallels in this example within conception and attention to the reading process. Just as the endnote's characters conflate to oneness, the multiple confusions regarding Huberto, Humberto, and the author ultimately suggest that they are all the same. Huberto, a student of architecture, and Humberto, an architect, are synchronic representations of one individual, and that individual is the author. The suggestion is that Humberto represents what the author fears he will become (*Lapsus* 215), although the older man's attempt to dispose of his bourgeois baggage has earned Manjarrez's expressed admiration (Teichmann 206–207).

As further indication of the focus on the reading process, the detective who solves the mystery directly addresses readers and offers them a dramatization of a reader's role. This reader-in-the-text reaches out to his peers in a self-referential manner analogous to the character in film who violates the visual illusion by looking directly at the camera. The endnote's Part 2's focus on the readers' analytic function is a direct parallel with Part 2 of the basic novel, in which the notions of authorship and readership are scrutinized.

Toward the end of the novel proper, the author is reviled for his hubris in thinking he can establish the rules simply because of his status as author. Readers are reminded that for too long authors have been considered untouchable, members of a privileged class (214). They are especially urged to revolt against the depiction of Huberto's death as being crushed by the wing of the Biblioteca Central (Central Library) dedicated to the Humanities (209, 212–213). Manjarrez's charge to readers is most direct and prompts them to consider discourse rather than content:

> Y el lector debe interrogar. Interrogarlo TODO. No aceptarlo verbatim. ¿Por qué esos símbolos? ¿Y no otros? ¿Por qué todo ese simbolismo? Es claro que no es un simbolismo hermético. Y el lector simplemente no debe aceptar que el autor diga que así son las cosas y ya. El lector debe interrogar, preguntarse lo que significa la novela, para sí mismo, para el lector, y para otros lectores. Preguntarse lo que es el autor, lo que autor y producto significan juntos. Y si no encuentra el significado de la novela, entonces quizá debe preguntarse no lo que es el mensaje sino lo que es el medio, oh Mc Luhan [*sic*], no lo que dice sino el vehículo en que viaja. (216–217, emphasis in original) [30]

> [And the reader should interrogate. Interrogate EVERYTHING. Not accept it verbatim. Why all these symbols? And not others? Why

all this symbolism? It is clear that it is not hermetic symbolism. And the reader simply should not let the author say that that's the way things are and that's it. The reader should interrogate, ask himself what the novel means, for himself, for the reader, and for other readers. Ask himself what the author is, what the author and the product signify together. And if he doesn't find the meaning of the novel, then perhaps he should ask himself not what is the message but what is the medium, oh McLuhan, not what it says but the vehicle in which it travels.]

Readers must keep in mind that here Manjarrez directly challenges himself. As author he appears in the text, marries a fellow character, and sires a pair of homosexual twins who become each other's lover. The crux of the consideration of authorship, however, becomes much more significant in these final chapters when Manjarrez, in an act of defiance, turns the table on himself. In a way he dramatizes his literary alter ego, who will not tolerate any hubris from his authorial self. Manjarrez demonstrates in his role as a character that content pales, indeed can seem frivolous, when considered in conjunction with these larger issues. As author, he depicts his action in the text as ludicrous, but, again as author, he allows himself to be denuded of pretense, thus exposing for readers the illusion of narrative authority that deserves to be penetrated.

As a final movement toward active reader participation in the narrative process, Manjarrez offers readers a questionnaire in which the following questions are posited: (1) Why was this novel or catalog published? (2) Who is the author? What is the author? (3) What is LAPSUS? Readers are encouraged to select up to three responses for each section from up to twenty-six possibilities, many humorous, others more provocative. Manjarrez then adds six possible interpretations for the age difference between Haltter and Heggo, including the option that there is no way of knowing (217–219).

Inserted within the questionnaire is a brief paragraph that refers to the crisis of contemporary prose fiction, of which *Lapsus* is, finally, an example (Schaffer 220). Indeed, Manjarrez seems to have taken experimentation to its limits, leading critics to analogous extremes in their responses. Although recognizing qualities in the novel that relate both to Agustín and to Fuentes, George R. McMurray describes it as "at times needlessly obscure" (Review, 117). For Juan Manuel Molina, the work is a series of beginnings that never reach closure (38), and José María Espinasa, although conceding to

*Lapsus* the status of novel, contends that it is illegible (143). On the other hand, José Joaquín Blanco argues that this text and Jorge Aguilar Mora's *Cadáver lleno de mundo* (1971) demonstrate that novels carrying the mark of *Onda* characteristics can also be extremely intelligent (*Crónica*, 98).

Although reflecting elements of *Onda* writing, *Lapsus* clearly cannot be equated with either of the other two novels analyzed here. Indeed, there are almost no subsequent novels that truly conform to the characteristics associated with the narratives that gave name to *Onda* fiction. Yet elements of *Onda* writing can be found in a large number of novels of the 1960s and 1970s and beyond. It is reasonable to conclude, then, that there *is* a legacy from these novels that broke with tradition and liberated thematics. Reinhard Teichmann sums up the lasting influence by stating that *Onda* fiction introduced colloquial language into mainstream fiction, giving impetus to such writers as Rafael Ramírez Heredia and Luis Zapata, and contributed toward freeing novelistic practice to pursue new themes and techniques (31).[31] Among the beneficiaries of this new openness are writers of gay and lesbian fiction and women authors who have greater opportunity to have their voices heard after the smashing of restrictive norms by *Onda* writers.

# CHAPTER 8

# WRITING FROM THE MARGINS

In Western Europe and in the United States, fragmentation appears to have peaked in the 1960s.[1] In Mexico, however, fragmentation becomes more of a norm than a deviation, becoming part of the canon. Some authors, such as Carlos Fuentes, in part join the international trend of returning to linear narrations with clearly established plots.[2] Other writers of outstanding fragmented texts from the 1950s and 1960s such as Elizondo, Pacheco, and Arreola largely abandon the novel for other genres, and Rulfo never again publishes a major work.[3] On the other hand, the majority of those who continue writing novels and authors who begin their careers in the 1970s and 1980s assume fragmentation as accepted convention, a practice that continues into the early 1990s. Agustín again turns to various degrees of segmentation both in shorter pieces and in novels (*Se está haciendo tarde* [1973], *La mirada en el centro* [1977], *Cerca del fuego* [1986]), although the fragmentation is not as pronounced as it was in his earlier fiction. In Sainz's novels, however, the disruption of linearity is flaunted consistently: *La princesa del Palacio de Hierro* (1974), *Compadre lobo* (1975), *Fantasmas aztecas* (1982), *Paseo en trapecio* (1985), and *Muchacho en llamas* (1987).[4]

Of the many authors making use of fragmentation as a mode of expression that joins the social and the aesthetic, two groups emerge whose voices have only recently been granted full expression in Mexican letters: the homosexual community and women.[5] For both, the disconnectedness of discourse serves as fundamental metaphor of a marginalized status within Mexican society. At the same time, however, these novels serve to demarginalize the very groups who historically have been deemed of lesser value or nonexistent. Just as the *Onda* writers moved Mexican youth from the periphery to the center, so these authors give voice to characters who have previously not been heard as clearly if at all.[6] This sexual demarginalization is a radical departure from Paz's notion of machismo as dramatized in Fuentes's novels, demonstrating that the "macho" paradigm is inadequate to represent all Mexicans and enunciating a sexual parallel to the falseness of the concept of equality of citizenry. The works discussed in this chapter follow the spirit of demarginalization that characterized *Onda* fiction by presenting new challenges to the illusion of a homogeneous national discourse, thus reflecting the need for a more inclusive society, one that would incorporate "minorities," whether truly reduced in number or simply constructed as inferior. Clearly, in post-1968 Mexico, more voices are absorbed into the literary fabric, thus offering different points of view on the national condition.

## Gay and Lesbian Fiction

The three gay and lesbian novels studied here, Luis Zapata's *El vampiro de la Colonia Roma* (1979; The Vampire of Colonia Roma) and *en jirones* (1985; *in shreds*)[7] and Rosamaría Roffiel's *Amora* (1989; *Love*),[8] are quite different in tone and focus. Although they represent three distinct presentations of homosexual life in fiction, each novel's fragmented form is tightly paired with content in a way that highlights a sense of marginalization. In *El vampiro*, Zapata gives new expression to the picaresque genre while incorporating its anticanonical stance (Torres-Rosado 178) and its critique of society.[9] The focus, however, is more inward than outward. That is to say, the protagonist, Adonis García, is more concerned with his personal status than with the ills of his surrounding culture. He thus shares an introspective nature with the narrator of *De perfil*, one of the many links between this work and the literature of the *Onda*. Adonis is presented as a man content with his sexual identity, although elements of story and discourse suggest a problematic existence. With *en jirones*, that inward vision is narrowed to the point of obsession. In his diary the protagonist records exclusively actions and feelings related to an affair he is having, so much so that personal information about family or employment is superfluous and all external factors disappear. Here, Zapata presents a raw, unflinching dramatization of both passion and violence between two men. Rosamaría Roffiel, on the other hand, in addition to offering a woman's point of view, fuses the personal with a sociopolitical perspective. In contrast with Adonis, Roffiel's protagonist presents a sharp critique of Mexico's inherently gender-biased society, making a broader statement because she is able to look beyond herself. Hers, finally, is the healthy sense of self-acceptance that Zapata seems to want for Adonis and yet has trouble presenting.

## Luis Zapata

Luis Zapata's *Las venturas, desventuras y sueños de Adonis García, el vampiro de la Colonia Roma* (1979; The Adventures, Misfortunes and Dreams of Adonis García, the Vampire of Colonia Roma), better known by its shortened title, *El vampiro de la Colonia Roma*, draws inspiration from the writers of the *Onda*, particularly Agustín and Sainz. In an interview with Reinhard Teichmann, Zapata acknowledges the influence, especially with respect to the incorporation of street language and the presence of a Mexican youth as the central figure (Teichmann 357, 371). In contrast to Sainz's mildly rebellious youths, however, Zapata's protagonist is a gay male hustler who works the streets of Mexico City and, in his personal life, goes through a series of relationships as well as anonymous sexual encounters. As David William Foster argues, "Zapata is an excellent example of the extension of the antiestablishment and countercultural principles of *onda* writing to include the unabashed treatment of homosexual identity" (Foster, *Gay and Lesbian Themes*, 37).

The form of the novel is structured on a series of seven tape recordings, apparently made for a person planning on writing a book, with the suggestion that this is Adonis's psychiatrist (Schaefer-Rodríguez 33). On a few occasions the listener asks questions or makes comments, although they are not included in the text. Readers are aware of these interruptions because Adonis responds to them (95, 115). Each tape recording begins with a one- to two-page dream sequence, enclosed within parentheses, followed by Adonis's recounting of episodes from his life from youth to the time he moves to Colonia Cuauhtémoc, an unspecified date prior to his present age of twenty-five. From a middle-class family, Adonis, orphaned at an early age, turns to prostitution at least in part because it offers autonomy and basic freedoms. Adonis relates his first sexual experiences, his life as a prostitute, his enduring relationships with lovers, his failed efforts to hold other kinds of employment, his bouts with drugs and alcohol, and his lack of concern for redemption. As stated by the author, Adonis is satisfied with his life, comfortable with his sexual identity (Teichmann 370). He views prostitution as his "business," at times speaking of neglecting the business when he is more involved in sex for pleasure and of modernizing the business when he buys a motorcycle.

Although the seven divisions of taped monologue offer the appearance of chapters, there is innovative use of fragmentation within this discourse. Zapata eschews punctuation almost completely: there are no commas nor periods, although he retains question marks, quotation marks, exclamation points, and an occasional dash. Blank spaces of varying lengths substitute for traditional punctuation, with a complete empty line of space, usually divided between two consecutive lines on the page, serving to mark a more obvious change of subject in lieu of paragraphs. In addition, Zapata refuses to use capital letters, giving no words privilege over others and leaving the impression that all phrasing blends together. The result is that each page appears to have multiple gaps or holes, resulting in a somewhat paradoxical point-counterpoint: a fluid prose in which the speaker seems to glide through topics without pause, countered by the feeling of a staccato rhythm produced by the breaks between phrases.

According to Zapata, the material presented in *El vampiro* is a mixture of fact and fiction. Having recorded the voice of a male prostitute, Zapata modified sections and added episodes, producing a narration with striking similarities to the picaresque novel (Teichmann 360). He then developed this aspect more fully, but with a decidedly twentieth-century urban ambience in an effort to "actualizar lo que podría ser la picaresca, o de contextualizarla concretamente en un ambiente urbano" [to bring the picaresque novel up to date, or to contextualize it concretely within an urban atmosphere] (Teichmann 360). In order to emphasize the picaresque quality of the novel, Zapata begins with an epigraph from *Lazarillo de Tormes*, not the original, but a second part attributed to H. de Luna. In a sense, this source suggests that *El vampiro* is Lazarillo "take two," totally updated and transferred to Mexico City. Furthermore, each taped section is preceded by an epigraph taken from a different Spanish or Mexican picaresque classic: *El Periquillo Sarniento*, the original *Lazarillo*, *La pícara Justina*, *Santa*, *Guzmán de Alfarache*, *La vida inútil de Pito Pérez*, and *Vida del Buscón don Pablos*. Significantly, the selection for the first tape is José Joaquín Fernández de Lizardi's *El Periquillo Sarniento*, the nineteenth-century Mexican picaresque novel (1816), which again suggests an updating of the genre. Zapata immediately brings to the foreground the notion of the picaresque but then infuses it with twentieth-century-in-your-face realism rooted in contemporary Mexican (sub)culture. As an example of a modernization of the genre, let us consider the episode of the blind man. Zapata moves readers from the crafty fellow who catches Lazarillo when he consumes more than his share of grapes to the lecherous blind man who fondles Adonis's lover in the bus only to be horrified and outraged when he discovers that his target is really a male (84–85). In this picaresque novel, the *amos* (masters) are a mixture of lovers and clients, as Adonis migrates from one mate to another or, on occasion, balances more than one at the same time.[10]

Following picaresque paradigms, Adonis is an orphan who has to fend for himself. He demonstrates the strength and self-sufficiency of the *pícaro*: "si yo no hacía nada por mí nadie en el mundo iba a hacerlo" [if i didn't do anything for myself nobody in the world was gonna do it] (101).[11] It is he who saves himself, not the clinicians or psychiatrists he visits. He eats more nutritious food, exercises, and quits drinking, referring to the change as a type of renaissance (200). He is offered as well the possibility of redemption, through the aegis of a client, but here too, Zapata turns away from classical picaresque offerings by rendering the question of redemption moot. In Alemán's *Guzmán*, it was possible for the *pícaro* to change his life, to be redeemed, a notion that Quevedo smashed in his *Buscón*, with a more cynical attitude toward cruel realities of life. In *El vampiro*, presented with a clear opportunity to change his life, Adonis rejects it, because he likes his life the way it is. He has the freedom to do what he wants, and he enjoys the sex. Significantly, the passage from *Guzmán* that serves as epigraph comes right after Adonis rebuffs his chance at redemption and embraces the life of the streets once more (129). Furthermore, the last tape, whose title again raises the question of redemption, carries as epigraph a portion of the *Buscón*, here intimating not so much that this is not a viable option for Adonis as the fact that he simply does not seek it.

The message from Adonis is that he is happy with his life: "me di cuenta de que ps no sé de que sí la estaba haciendo ¿no? de que sí la estoy haciendo de que en realidad hago lo que quiero y cuando quiero y eso ps creo que eso es la felicidad" [i realized that well i donno that i was really making it y'understand? that i really am with it that actually i do what i wanna do when i wanna do it and that's well i think that's happiness] (218). He feels neither guilt nor shame. Yet at the end of the novel, he fantasizes about escaping Earth, being kidnapped by gay Martians. Claudia Schaefer-Rodríguez argues that this is a manifestation of the conceptualization of self-liberation, of movement toward a utopian existence (37). There is a fine line, however, between moving toward and escaping from. Adonis's voiced satisfaction with his circumstances loses credibility, forcing a re-evaluation of his narrative.

From the beginning, Adonis's narration has proved troublesome. Within the first few lines of tape 1, he admits to a faulty memory (15), a condition confirmed consistently throughout the text, as he pauses to correct himself or to search for information. In addition, there are ample examples of his terminating a line of thought by confessing that he has exaggerated or by negating details of his story. Despite these revelations, or perhaps because of them, Adonis makes frequent queries of his interlocutor in order to ascertain if he has understood a point or, in a couple of instances, to seek approbation. Yet, as Adonis continues, his discourse becomes even more problematic. At one point his ramblings become quite incoherent regarding the order in which events occurred and what really happened (136, 148). There are a number of examples of fragmented sentences that are interdicted only to be replaced with another truncated thought. At times he slips into a digression and must ask where he was in his commentary. The inconstancy of Adonis's narration pairs well with the segmented discourse, especially when one recalls his problems with drugs and alcohol. The spaces between phrases seem most appropriate to capture his hazy thoughts, his fragmented thinking.

There is ample reason, moreover, to consider connotations of fragmentation beyond the spatial separation of words. The notion of a segmented status is privileged on the first page of the text, in the initial dream sequence. Adonis describes a ballroom containing a suspended globe consisting of pieces of mirror or metal that throw off little lights when the ball spins, suggesting a dazzling lifestyle, but, at the same time, a loss of control. Upon a second reading, it would appear that this dual interpretation, one positive and one negative, sets the tone for the entire work. Adonis claims to be at peace, making it in twentieth-century Mexico City, and yet, the fragmentation serves to highlight metaphorically both his marginalized status as a homosexual and his solitude. The employment of blank spaces evokes the disconnectedness of gays from the dominant culture. In a parallel with the point-counterpoint aspect of discourse, Adonis appears to glide through life with a good attitude, yet he is trapped. The use of monologue, although giving voice to a marginalized figure, connotes his solitary existence. For Adonis has raised the theme of solitude and abandonment, having played alone as a child (19) and having felt abandoned when his father died: "entonces sí me sentí ya totalmente solo abandonado a la vida" [now i really felt completely alone abandoned in life] (28). When he breaks up with his first lover, that sense of isolation is complete: "me daba cuenta de que siempre había estado solo de que siempre iba a estar solo" [like i realised [*sic*] that i'd always been alone that i was always gonna be alone] (101).

Complementing Adonis's statements regarding solitude are the series of enclosed spaces that he inhabits. When he describes living with relatives as a youth, he makes a point of saying that the space was cramped (29). Later, his liberated state is undermined by the series of hotel rooms and tiny apartments his economic state makes necessary. His awareness of space can be discerned in his comment regarding his lover's departure: "rené ya se había ido de la casa del cuarto" [now that rené had left our house our room] (107). The presumable freedom of the streets is countered by the enclosed steam baths and bathroom stalls used for anonymous sex. Significantly, the first dream sequence introduces the notion of abandonment and of isolation; it is entitled "y tú ¿qué vas a hacer cuando dios se muera?" [hey you watcha gonna do when god dies?] (11).

Consequently, although Zapata makes a point of introducing within Mexican letters a gay male who is unashamed of his sexual practices, Adonis's own words belie the light tone of the novel, revealing what Didier T. Jaén calls "un proceso de desilusión general" [a process of gradual disillusion] (26). Jaén is right to turn to Claudio Guillén's discussion of *Guzmán de Alfarache* for a compelling statement on the subtext of Adonis's illusion of independence: "This would be [*sic*] freedom, however, is thwarted by fact" (Guillén 100).

Zapata's later novel, *en jirones* (1985; *in shreds*), is a much darker vision of homosexual relationships. Zapata continues to employ a first-person narration, but he presents as protagonist a man completely enmeshed in an obsessive gay relationship that is tinged with violence from the beginning. Although there are a number of very explicit scenes of lovemaking that dramatize the full passion of homosexual desire,[12] Zapata imbues his text with images of death, nightmares, self-destructive actions, and violence toward others, resulting in a powerful but fundamentally negative representation of gay love.

The novel is structured as a series of entries made in a notebook that serves as a diary. The protagonist, Sebastián, begins writing upon his first encounter with A., the man who will become his lover and destroyer. In his narrations Sebastián details and then interprets the events leading up to their affair, the eroticism they share, A.'s conflict between his desire for Sebastián and his adherence to society's imposed norms, A.'s caving in to social conditioning by marrying and severing his ties with Sebastián, and their eventual reunion, marked at first by violence and then by tedium, leading Sebastián to abandon the relationship.

The fact that the characters are known only by the names Sebastián and A. is symptomatic of the lack of information provided for readers. The narrator's name is not revealed until some fifteen pages into the novel, and he is frustratingly elusive about revealing details about his circumstances. The "basic facts," which are casually scattered within the book and never detailed, are that he is temporarily located in an unnamed city some one to two hundred kilometers from Guadalajara, working at an unnamed Institute on a project that is never specified. Zapata has his character withhold the information in such a manner as to suggest a teasing mechanism directed at readers. There are repeated references to Sebastián's "trabajo" (work),[13] but no specifics as to its nature. At one point Sebastián records a conversation with a friend of A.'s, including his inquiry as to Sebastián's family and employment, but denying access to the response (74). Analogously, Sebastián offers little information about A., ostensibly because he too is ignorant of the facts: "prácticamente, ignoro todo sobre él" [I know almost nothing about him] (73). Consequently, readers are sucked into the obsessional focus on the relationship between Sebastián and A., since their vision is made as severely limited as the narrator's.

Sebastián's diary is devoted almost entirely to recording his encounters with A. and his interpretations of A.'s words and actions. Each entry is separated by a blank space from the contiguous segments for a total of 223 fragments. In Part 1, entitled *diario de un enamorado* (diary of a man in love), containing fifty-one sections, Sebastián labels certain fragments First Day, Second Day, and so on through Nineteenth Day, then abandons the practice after an episode of violent lovemaking. Part 2, called *en jirones*, contains more than three times the number of fragments than the first, even though the length of the two parts is about the same, with many examples of segments consisting of just a few words. The increase in frequency of Sebastián's entries, combined with the extreme brevity of some of them, serves to reflect his heightened emotional state, particularly in the portion in which he is separated from his lover and in the final sequencing leading to his departure. In addition, the spatial fragmentation metaphorically dramatizes his increasing separation from his surroundings, as he withdraws from social contact and focuses exclusively on his partner, augmenting the isolation of his already marginalized state.

Although the spatial separations are the most obvious use of fragmentation in the novel, there are other levels as well. Within some sections, at moments of great emotion or as markers of a passage of time, Zapata employs double spacing between paragraphs instead of the usual single line of separation.[14] He also includes examples of more experimental discourse rooted in fragmentation. In one section, Sebastián's phrases are separated by solid lines, as if there were gaps in his thinking or Zapata were inviting readers to extend the thought themselves (216–217). Other segments revert in part to the style employed in *El vampiro;* there are no capital letters or periods, just a series of sentence fragments separated by dashes (218, 224–226).

The most powerful use of fragmentation, however, is that of imagery, for it is here that Zapata conveys the overwhelming sense of violence inherent in the relationship between Sebastián and A. The conflation of fragmentation with violence is announced in the title of the novel, *in shreds,* which is then echoed within the text when Sebastián tears up A.'s shirts after the announcement of the impending marriage and destroys a bus ticket he has bought for a trip to Guadalajara in an effort to follow A. (157, 163). These examples, albeit violent, are directed at things, not people, although they are evocative of Sebastián's impending decayed physical and mental condition in response to the abandonment: he too will be in shreds. The destructive aspects of this obsessional relationship become much more potent when fragmentation is linked to the body. When A. admits his love for Sebastián, in order to prove his feelings, he smashes his fist against a mirror, dashing it to pieces and covering himself in blood (101–102). This is paralleled later on when Sebastián, in a frenzied state due to his separation from A., locks himself in the bathroom and slams his head against a mirror. Zapata comes full circle toward the end of the novel after A. attacks Sebastián on the street and then follows him home: "De pronto la mano de A. estrella el cristal de la ventana y la atraviesa; me agarra por la garganta" [Suddenly A.'s hand smashes the window pane and comes through; he grabs my throat] (258). Significantly, the verb *estrellar* (to dash to pieces, to smash) is used in all three instances, reinforcing the sameness.

Other references to or images of fragmentation rooted in violence abound. Sebastián hears the story of a gay man who is murdered by paid assassins at the bidding of his lover's wife. The man is "hecho picadillo" [made into mincemeat] (127), his body carved into pieces. Sebastián has a dream in which he must eat a severed hand, possibly his own, that is described as broken, perhaps torn to pieces (224). As a final example, Sebastián and A.'s lovemaking, which has been described with elements of violence from the beginning, using words such as "pain" and "unconscious violence" (103), reaches new levels of fury when A. returns to Sebastián after his marriage, unable to stay away and hating himself for it. Both engage in destructive passion: "sin que nos demos cuenta (debido a la progresiva tolerancia—e incluso disfrute—del dolor) en qué instante el cuerpo es mutilado y sus pedazos pasan a ser posesión del otro" [without our realizing (due to the progressive tolerance—even enjoyment—of pain) at what moment the body is mutilated and its pieces become the possession of the other] (237).

This notion of possession can be traced from the start of the relationship. The two engage in games of control from their first meeting. Before their initial sexual experience, Sebastián observes: "te voy a tener . . . hasta que tu voluntad sea la mía [I'm going to have you . . . until your will is mine] (33). Even more importantly, Part 1 ends with the italicized words "A. por fin me pertenece" [A. finally belongs to me] (140). A relationship rooted in antagonism and violence, combined with innumerable references to death and suicide, may well lead readers to expect the death of one or both men at the end of the novel. By means of a series of Sebastián's asides and metanarrative comments, Zapata has, in fact, raised levels of expectation regarding the status of the story and a potential denouement: "Si esta historia no tiene clímax . . . ¿sólo puede tener desenlace?—¿únicamente la muerte de A., o la mía sería un verdadero desenlace? ¿O ni eso: la historia continuaría, continuará?" [If this story has no climax . . . can it have only a denouement? Would only A.'s death or mine be a true denouement? Or not even that: the story would continue, will continue?] (265).

At the end of the novel, Zapata's use of fragmentation also plays a role in raising readers' expectations. In the final pages, the number of fragments increases, with the maximum of seven per page, given spatial limitations, reached near the end (273), giving the impression of a dramatized heartbeat or rapid breathing. At this point, however, instead of an explosion of violence, the words reduce to the iteration of a single phrase: "Viene. Cogemos" [He comes over. We fuck] (273–274). Subsequently, after an unusually large spatial break, there are two final fragments, of one paragraph each, that totally deflate the previous intensity, merely indicating Sebastián's decision to return to Mexico City and his sense of loss.

In retrospect, it can be seen that the last sentence of the passage above regarding story and denouement gave an indication that there would be no climactic ending, that the story would simply go on and on in endless repetition. Sebastián's words, however, have alerted readers to his perception that being condemned to repetition is the equivalent of being in Hell (194). Furthermore, there have been other signals that Sebastián's relationship with A. has indeed reached a point of circularity, of sameness: "Esto nunca va a terminar. Debo aceptar que la relación está condenada a la repetición" [This is never going to end. I should accept the fact that the relationship is condemned to repetition] (271). At the end there is nothing left, the two have been reduced to mechanical sex in sharp contrast to the earlier passages describing their passion. Unable to free himself from societal pressures, A. is incapable of an unfettered gay relationship, leaving their love, as Foster argues, "fragmented and made monstrous by social obstacles internalized by the individual" (*Gay and Lesbian Themes*, 42).

Rosamaría Roffiel

At one point in *Amora* (1989), purportedly the first lesbian novel published in Mexico (Foster, *Gay and Lesbian Themes*, 115), the narrator states: "En todo relato hay que seguir un hilo. Para escribirlo y para leerlo" [In every story it is necessary to follow a thread. In order to write it and in order to read it] (88). Indeed, there is a story to follow in Roffiel's novel, that of the journalist Guadalupe's relationship with Claudia (no last names are given). In an intimate style akin to diary entries, Lupe's first-person narration guides readers through her initial encounter with Claudia, initially perceived as an apparently straight *superburguesa*; the events leading up to their affair and those forecasting its dissolution; the support provided by her friends and co-workers; and, finally, the announcement of her reconciliation with Claudia. One could assert just as easily, however, that the thread running through *Amora* is the declaration of feminist and lesbian principles that serves as an education both within the text, for Claudia and the narrator's niece, Mercedes, and, beyond the text, for readers.

Guadalupe is a thirty-six-year-old writer associated with *fem*, a well-known feminist periodical published in Mexico City. The fact that Rosamaría Roffiel has a similar affiliation is merely one of the parallels between the two, as announced from the beginning of the volume. The novel is autobiographical, with most names changed, but based on actual people and events (Roffiel 5). As part of her feminist activism, Guadalupe is a volunteer for the Grupo de Ayuda a Personas Violadas (Group for Aid to Rape Victims). She is also the eponymous Amora, a nickname bestowed by Claudia that is, as Foster rightly describes, "a strategically important feminization of the masculine-defined concept of *amor*" (Foster, *Gay and Lesbian Themes*, 116).

Roffiel divides her text into thirty-two segments, averaging five pages in length, all but the first of which bear titles that relate to the subsequent content. A third of these sections contain further subdivisions, seven of which take the form of entries in a diary, amounting to twenty-five additional interior divisions. Curiously, the internal fragments are not evenly divided; instead there are three in segment four, ten scattered among segments fourteen through twenty, and then a second cluster of twelve in the four sections preceding the final piece. At times the fragmentation within sections serves to isolate dialogue from descriptive passages. In other examples, the blank spaces mark the passing of a period of time, whether a few hours or two weeks. The irregularity of placement, however, suggests the possibility of a further metaphoric function, perhaps reflective of a heightened emotional state.

Roffiel's choice of fragmentation is appropriate for the multitude of voices she incorporates into her novel. Guadalupe engages in dialogue with her friends and roommates, women both straight and lesbian, those tolerant of heterosexual unions and those who are consistently negative in their attitudes toward men to the point that Lupe accuses one of sexism in reverse. By including this variety of points of view, Roffiel is able to maintain a dynamic discourse on feminism, lesbianism, the concept of love, and the tribulations associated with being a resident of contemporary Mexico City. Acknowledging her success in interweaving this range of thematics, Foster praises Roffiel for the "skillful juxtaposition of narrative fragments that make up this testimonial of voices" (*Gay and Lesbian Themes*, 117).

It is, however, Lupe's voice that predominates and, as a consequence of her privileged positioning, her philosophy that prevails. She emerges in the role of educator, first with Claudia, who is ignorant of nonconformist behaviors, having absorbed society's lessons quite thoroughly. This is, in fact, a frequent theme in Lupe's discussions: cultural conditioning, the burdensome weight that everyone assimilates initially and the target of feminism's revisionist ideology. Lupe's philosophy begins with the inner being: "Vivir de acuerdo a lo que piensas, no permitir que alguna parte de tu yo esté negada, darle a todo tu ser la posibilidad de desarrollarse" [live in accordance with what you think, don't allow any part of your self to be denied, give your entire being the possibility of developing] (75).

A sense of personal value is also part of what Lupe wishes to impart to her niece, Mercedes, but she also takes advantage of the opportunity to enlighten Mercedes and her friend, Verónica, both twelve, when they ask questions about lesbians: "las lesbianas son mujeres comunes y silvestres, de todos los colores, edades, nacionalidades y profesiones que simplemente aman a otras mujeres en lugar de amar a los hombres" [lesbians are common and natural women, of all colors, ages, nationalities, and professions who simply love other women instead of loving men] (101). Verónica, having already absorbed society's prejudices, is appalled, but Mercedes, clearly showing a more open nature, proves more accepting.

In a sense, Claudia and the young girls function as readers-in-the-text, as they respond to Lupe's discourse on her philosophy of life and ways of loving. Although Verónica is resistant, both Claudia and Mercedes demonstrate not only understanding but also personal growth in response to their dialogue with Lupe. Perhaps Roffiel is searching for a similar reaction from readers, for her text is replete with information and interpretive commentary directed in part to other characters but with a clear trajectory beyond the text as well. In one example, a defense of lesbianism, she includes readers within her audience, addressing them as *ustedes* (you) within a section in which she also has Lupe adapt a Shylockian discourse: "en realidad también somos personas . . . nacemos, crecemos, nos reproducimos y morimos . . . igualito que el resto de la raza humana; nos gustan los helados y los tacos" [in reality we too are people . . . we are born, we grow, we reproduce and we die . . . just like the rest of the human race; we like ice cream and tacos] (33).

Not all of Lupe's commentary remains in the abstract. There is a gritty reality reflected in these pages as well. Readers are privy to a description with explicit detail of a particularly horrendous rape, as related by one of the counselors from the Group. There are also constant reminders of the dysfunctional system of justice in Mexico, in which the laws consistently favor men. Numerous cases are cited in which rapists are able to pay a mere fine or bribe a judge in order to escape punishment. Readers are instructed on Mexican law, in which rape is the only crime for which the victim must prove her status as victim, and on Mexican justice, which Lupe perceives as an oxymoron, a system that provides no security for women, whether one is speaking of laws, the police, the bureaucratic apparatus, or judges (29).

The frequent mention of injustice in the courts and in the streets, from rapists eluding even verbal censure to the daily harassment women endure as they walk, provides a segue to a broader criticism leveled at the city and, by extension, the nation: "Cada caminata por el DF me confirma mi teoría de que la Tierra es un planeta de castigo, y que nacer mujer y vivir en esta ciudad es una de las últimas pruebas que debe pasar un ser humano para llegar a elevadísimos planos del espíritu [Every walk in the DF (Federal District) confirms to me my theory that the Earth is a planet of punishment, and that to be born a woman and to live in this city is one of the ultimate tests a human being must pass in order to attain the most elevated spiritual planes] (81).

Despite being doubly marginalized, as a woman and as a lesbian, and despite having to endure the economic crisis, the urban road systems, the *machista* attitudes, and everything else endemic to Mexico of the 1980s, Lupe's spirit continues. The overwhelming attitude that pervades is positive, in contrast to that of *en jirones* or even *El vampiro*. Adonis tried to laugh at it all, yet was always alone and in enclosed spaces. On a symbolic level, Lupe's bedroom is large, and she decorates it to suit her personality. Significantly, she can do so because she knows herself and accepts herself. For all her complaints, Lupe is surrounded at all times by her feminist and lesbian friends, always ready to pick up the pieces.

This "picking up the pieces" is not simply a casual clichéd reference, but yet another level of fragmentation incorporated within the novel. Victoria, a fellow worker in the Grupo, appears so frail that Lupe fears that another ruined relationship or the next rape crisis "la va a romper en trocitos" [will break her into little pieces] (15). Analogously, Lupe's friends, concerned by her thoughts of exposing herself to further heartbreak by returning to Claudia, predict that she will be "hecha trizas" [torn to bits] (156). Finally Claudia too suffers a segmented existence on a more continuing plane, for she feels that there are two women within her: one who responds instinctively to her desire for Lupe and another who suffers from culturally induced repression.

The feelings of solitude that one might expect from an atomized existence, however, are largely limited to Lupe's memories of childhood. In her youth Lupe felt isolated and different from all the others (31, 45); she lived a segmented existence. From her perspective as an adult, however, she appreciates the solace of friendship and solidarity, a fact that is announced from the beginning of the novel, in a sense setting the tone: "Me tengo a mí, y a mis amigas" [I have myself and my (female) friends] (10). The early placement stresses the importance of two of the main messages of the novel: there is unity in sisterhood, and one must learn to value one's self.

Lupe's journey from solitude to solidarity can be traced to two changes in her life. The first is learning to know herself and to be comfortable with who she is. The second is her embrace of feminism, which she defines as "un proyecto de vida que nos devuelve nuestro valor histórico" [a life project that returns to us our historical value] (75). As a realist, she knows that the effort, particularly in Mexico, will be difficult, with many setbacks to counter advances. It is the same attitude that she manifests at the end of the novel with regard to her reconciliation with Claudia. For in the final segment, story collapses. Readers are told that Claudia initiates a meeting by sending flowers and a letter. What in a more conventional novel would likely be a moment of heightened interest, given the development of the relationship, is passed over. The section begins with reductionist statements: "Pues sí, volví con Claudia. Lo de siempre: besos, abrazos, promesas [So yes, I went back to Claudia. The usual thing: kisses, hugs, promises] (159). The description of the reunion is then given a mere three paragraphs, before the narration turns to broader issues (the economic crisis, both in Mexico and in the rest of the world; the appearance of AIDS in the United States), followed by an update of Lupe's work situation and of her roommates. Somehow the diminution of story seems appropriate, for *Amora* delivers so much more than a love story. Roffiel has spent as much time, if not more, on expounding feminist ideology from various points of view and has presented a character engaged in issues rather than submerged in self.

The final note regarding Claudia is indicative of Lupe's recognition that nothing is forever: "Estoy dispuesta a disfrutarlo mientras dure. Después, seguramente vendrán otras sorpresas" [I'm prepared to enjoy it while it lasts. Afterwards, surely other surprises will come] (162). Roffiel appears to allude to a cyclical pattern, a rhythm in life, which finds parallel in the clustering of internal fragments within the basic thirty-two units of the novel. Perhaps these fragments serve as metaphor for the cyclical feelings of falling apart and healing, of feeling segmented and then being aided by the solidarity of one's friends.

## Recent Women's Fiction:
## A Feminine Voicing of National Malaise

Although employing a mixture of methods and focuses, a significant number of women authors offer central female characters and fragmented texts that touch aspects of the dysfunctional systems, whether social, political, familial, or interpersonal, that exist in the Mexico of the 1980s (with roots in its history). Until now the call for active response both within and beyond the text had largely been associated with works by male writers such as Yáñez, Rulfo, and Pacheco, but one must keep in mind that until recent years, not many women were able to be heard. The novels selected for this section represent various facets of the uses of fragmentation within a feminist consideration of the problems of identity for the individual and for the nation: Mónica de Neymet's *Las horas vivas* (1985; The Vibrant Hours), which depicts a bleak portrait of the isolation of women within the atomizing atmosphere of Mexico City; Carmen Boullosa's *Mejor desaparece* (1987; Better It Vanishes)[15] and *Antes* (1989; Before), focusing on dysfunctional family life and the cultural shaping of the female; and María Luisa Puga's *La forma del silencio* (1987; The Form of Silence), full of angry diatribes against the government, presenting a female's version of the national malaise, every bit as critical as Fuentes's works. Significantly, all three of these writers look to Mexico's past, with a particular emphasis on the early 1960s, a time of middle-class utopia when the idea of Modern Mexico actually seemed possible. That notion, however, was shattered by the oil bust and economic crisis of the 1980s. Writing with historical perspective, these women reread the past, highlighting the debilitating conditions that existed in that earlier period but were ignored, and dramatize a middle-class consciousness so splintered that intuitively it seeks to return to its origins to interrogate its identity.

### Mónica de Neymet

In *Las horas vivas* (1985), Mónica de Neymet employs fragmentation as a reflection of the marginalized status of women in Mexican society. By breaking her narration into fragments, she is able to present separated stories about a variety of women spread across social classes and occupations. Although distinct in personality and circumstances, the women share a sense of isolation both within society and from each other, thus echoing in their daily life the segmented status of the novel's discourse. Both maids and *patronas* suffer from solitude and mistreatment or misunderstanding by males, thus demonstrating that the marginalized positioning is rooted not in class but in gender. Gender is the leveler.

De Neymet sets her narration in Mexico City between January and September of 1961. The main characters of the novel are women who live in an apartment building at 710 Calzada de Tacubaya, a "caja de cristal" [glass box] (11) as described by Matilde, the protagonist and, as it is later suggested, the author of all the stories. The modern, five-story building has four apartments on each floor, twenty boxes within the bigger unit, twenty potential stories from which readers are privy to six. The general pattern of narration is to focus on one woman per segment, for within the novel's eight chapters there are ninety fragments, each set off by a blank space.

The principal narration is that of Matilde as told in the first person. An orphan, she lives a solitary but comfortable existence, receiving periodic payments from her parents' estate. At twenty-five, she is writing a masters thesis that consists in part of translating letters written by a Spanish nun during a pilgrimage to holy sites sometime around 4 A.D. Ill equipped to cope with even the most basic social relationships, Matilde spends most of her time immersed in her books at her apartment or in the library.

The fragments devoted to Matilde's neighbors are told in the third person, an omniscient voice that provides access to inner thoughts, fears, and sufferings. There are five women residents featured:

1. Laura: A forty-year-old professional woman struggling to make her second marriage work. Her husband, Mario, thirteen years younger than she, is progressively more restless in their relationship. Laura's preoccupations regarding her appearance and the financial strain of caring for the two children from her first marriage appear to augment the distance between herself and her husband.

2. Sandra: A young prostitute who is hired by lawyers and government bureaucrats to provide companionship at parties. Her basic concern is to maintain her body, the instrument of her trade. Sandra's growing insecurity alienates her boyfriend, resulting in her attempted suicide.

3. Griselda: Another prostitute, but of a lower class. Griselda is willing to spend a few hours with anyone she can engage on the street. Her incestuous relationship with an older brother very likely contributed to her lack of self-worth.

4. Yolanda: A woman who left home to escape the whims of a despotic father only to become trapped in a marriage to Fernando, who regards her with either indifference or scorn. She looks upon her pregnancy as the catalyst to improve the relationship. When her male child is born, however, she soon realizes that her suffering is generational, that all of the men with whom she has contact have the power to harm her.

5. Anastasia: An elderly woman who had to leave the teaching profession because of increasing bouts of incapacitating fears that have grown to paranoia. She is convinced that the sinfulness surrounding her in the apartment building bodes ill for all.

In addition to Matilde and her neighbors, there are two other women who exert a significant influence in the novel. Matilde devotes a lot of thought to Egeria, the nun whose letters she is translating from Latin to Spanish. Although Egeria is to be envied for her freedom to travel to holy places, one notes references to her gullibility in believing everything she is told. She thus functions as the antithesis of secluded Matilde, yet she cannot be accepted as a true positive female role model. Finally, there is la niña quemada (the burnt child), a teenager named Chayo, aka María del Rosario, who lives in the neighborhood. Chayo was injured as a baby when her mother left her alone at night. The candle used to ease her fears (and to honor the Virgin of Guadalupe) blew over, thus setting fire to the room. Her face is badly disfigured, causing horror to all who see her. Chayo bears her scars externally, in contrast to the other women of Las horas vivas, who are damaged spiritually.[16]

There are few men featured in the novel; only two have active participatory roles. Julio, Sandra's boyfriend and an acquaintance of Matilde's, is quick to criticize the latter for her seclusion and her avoidance of reality yet rapid, too, in abandoning Sandra after her suicide attempt. The only sympathetic male character is Antonio, Matilde's former classmate at the university and a potential suitor, who has suffered a memory loss due to circumstances that are never made clear. He is the only man who is afforded his own fragments (159–160, 176–180, 197–198), the only one privileged to share the female-dominated narration. Significantly, the male selected is one whose slate is clean; he is no longer encumbered by the socially codified prejudices of the patriarchal system. At his stage of recovery, he is trying to master the vocabulary of household items.

The alternation of first-person and third-person omniscience suggests the lack of a strong authorial voice. Each cedes to the other, as if in response to the apparent need for multiple perspectives in order to comprehend the surrounding reality, to reconstitute a fractured image of life for women in Mexico City (Iglesias 67). De Neymet offers readers in segmented form pieces of fragmented lives that, when received as a whole, evoke the blunt impact of what constitutes reality for the female in Mexico. The overall picture is devastating: women are marginalized figures in youth as in old age, as housewives or as professionals, at all levels of the economic hierarchy.

Fundamental to de Neymet's presentation of the female's atomization is the notion of being seen; women are either objects as possessions (objects of the male gaze) or they are invisible, totally insignificant, barely discernible in the patriarchal society. It is not just men, however, who partake of these attitudes. Women not only have assimilated the visual dichotomy of (not) being seen but also seem to enjoy their status. As prostitutes, Sandra and Griselda are accustomed to being the object of men's attention. The latter wears revealing dresses (26), and the former experiences pleasure when men stare at her (119). In a repeated example of personification, the building's illuminated windows serve as eyes that view the women when they return at night (169, 192).

Matilde remarks that her servant, María, is transparent and attributes her invisibility to the fact that she is insignificant, docile, and submissive (27). Matilde comments also that another maid, Evelina, is doubly condemned: by her family (class) and by her gender (152). Upon describing Evelina, Matilde extends her views to encompass all women: "Además era mujer, y ser mujer es tener que ser, casi inevitablemente, como los otros quieren y exigen que se sea" [Besides, she was a woman, and being a woman means having to be, almost inevitably, just like the others want and demand that one be] (152).

For her part, Matilde appears to thrive on her condition of invisibility. She feels that she is a witness to the reality that surrounds her, not a participant. It is a sensation that began in childhood, looking through her bedroom window, feeling that she had no identity, no face for others to contemplate (25). Matilde's lack of identity, her invisibility, is emphasized in the text through discursive strategies. Readers first encounter the first-person narration with no direction or clarification as to the identity of the speaker other than that it is a female. Matilde is not named until shortly before the end of the first chapter (40). There is also a strong emphasis on imagery involving glass. Instead of serving as a symbol of reaching out or of constituting an aperture through which to attain freedom or knowledge, windows for Matilde are a protective covering behind which she can retain her invisibility (82). Analogously, her glasses function as a shield (189) or a protective mask that maintains a distance from the things that surround her (117). The only places in which she feels no need for such defensive covering are the safe, comfortable sites: her apartment and the library. The apartment itself is repeatedly referred to as a glass box (43, 46, 70, 117).

Whether invisible due to their insignificance or by design, whether the object of male desire or disdain, the women in *Las horas vivas* lead solitary existences, as evidenced by progressive alienation from spouses, increasing distance between inner feelings and superficial social roles, or simply a neurotic self-alienation, as in the case of Anastasia. This is augmented by a mutual mistrust among the women. There is no momentum among the neighbors to forge a unit, to share aspects of their lives. What brings them together is Matilde's narration. She is the medium through which the lives of other women are "illuminated."

Matilde is, in fact, the author of both her first-person narration and of the descriptions of the other women. Although this is by no means evident from the start, gradually readers are presented with textual clues that clarify her authorship. Matilde has already been established as both a translator and a "translatee." She transposes Egeria's letters and, in turn, requires a Julio or a María to interpret reality for her. She considers herself slow in not being aware of one maid's pregnancy and another's drinking problem. She cannot communicate well with the world around her and appears to inhibit communication among others as well: conversation stops as she passes by (107).

Yet it is Matilde who translates the experiences of her neighbors into the written word. It is she who renders their daily existence into a more enduring form so that their stories will be read and remembered. As readers are repeatedly told, Matilde finds more stability in her books than in the confusing, chaotic world that surrounds her (84, 100, 157). It seems natural, then, to attempt to control the exterior reality that she has viewed as a witness by making it concrete through writing: "Pero si yo escribiera, la mía sería la versión verdadera, con esa realidad que solamente las palabras, y precisamente las palabras escritas, dan a la vida" [But if I were to write, mine would be the true version, with that reality that only words, and precisely written words, give to life] (128). She proffers an analogy between characters in a novel and clouds. When one writes about clouds, one gives them form. Their having briefly attained a particular shape is thus recorded and subject to being relived in the imagination of future readers (203). Analogously, fictional characters, having been captured in prose, continue to live: "Los que están en los libros, los personajes, se conservan, viven, son vividos muchas veces, tantas como lectores los encuentran" [Those who are in books, the characters, are preserved, they live, they are experienced many times, as many times as there are readers who find them] (158). The objective would seem to be to concretize and valorize the reality of these Mexican women by capturing their experiences in fiction.

The external reality of Matilde's neighbors takes second place to their inner consciousness. Much more attention is given to personal relationships than to actual social or political occurrences. The most developed political reference is to the Cuban situation of the early 1960s, for some *gusanos* (Cuban exiles) attack the apartment building because there are Cuban diplomats living there. The Mexican reality is less specific, more diffuse, and therefore more persistent and oppressive. Reference is made to police violence and to ubiquitous bribe taking. One brief mention of the revolution is given in the context of Yolanda's complaint that politics in Mexico have little relation to her personal reality.

In a similar way, the allusions to Mexico City are more abstract or imagistic than fully developed. When precise names are supplied, they are devoid of picturesque descriptions. Sites are simply named: Sanborns (96), Reforma (189), the Zona Rosa (134), Pedregal (163), Avenida Chapultepec (189), Avenida Mazatlán (145). When speaking more metaphorically of the city, de Neymet recalls Azuela's bleak vision of *La luciérnaga*. For the newly arrived *campesinos*, "La ciudad que crece sin sentido los recibe de mala gana, madrastra, usurera; pero los va absorbiendo, se pierden en sus calles" [The city that grows aimlessly receives them begrudgingly, stepmother, usurer; but it then absorbs them, they get lost in its streets] (195).

Consequently, Matilde's narration focuses on the more intimate details of everyday reality. It makes sense, then, that the female residents are presented to readers on a first-name basis. At the same time, one notes from the narration that Matilde does not really know these women well at all, that much of the information about their circumstances comes from her maids. Indeed, there is ample evidence in the text that Matilde only imagines the relationships and incidents described: "La otra noche soñé que escribía una novela y para eso tenía que imaginar las vidas de los vecinos, solamente así podía conocerlos, imaginándolos y traduciendo lo que oía y veía a la palabra escrita" [The other night I dreamt that I was writing a novel and to do so I had to imagine the lives of the neighbors, only thus could I get to know them, imagining them and translating what I heard and saw to the written word] (203).[17]

Matilde is, evidently, writing a fiction. She speaks of purchasing notebooks that will be filled with her thoughts (220). The narration includes numerous self-referential observations on the writing process, in the style of Vicens's *El libro vacío*. Her comments refer to both form and content. In addition to questioning how to achieve her literary goals, she criticizes Egeria's narration, specifically for its avoidance of everyday-life detail: "Quiso escribir olvidando el mundo sucio, pecaminoso, florido, alegre, profano, múltiple; ignorando todo lo que no fueran los Santos Lugares y los hombres de Dios" [She tried to write avoiding the dirty, sinful, flowery, happy, profane, multiple world; ignoring all that wasn't a Holy Place or a man of God] (223).

The self-consciousness regarding the writing process becomes quite blatant toward the end: "Los golpes de los muebles verdes, brillantes, estorbosos, que entraban con dificultad por la puerta del departamento vecino me habían despertado esta mañana. Estas deben ser, sin duda, las primeras palabras. ¿Qué seguirá? No sé. Pondré atención a la realidad en adelante" [The banging of the green, lustrous, annoying furniture that was being carried with difficulty into the neighboring apartment had awakened me this morning. These should doubtless be the first words. What will follow? I don't know. I'll pay attention to reality from now on] (220). The sentence describing the furniture, with its emphasis on the mundane matters of apartment living, is indeed the first sentence of *Las horas vivas* (9).

Matilde's attempt to imagine the lives of her neighbors and to give them life in prose has both positive and negative effects. In her quest for intimacy, Matilde perhaps oversteps certain boundaries, identifying too closely with her subjects. Toward the end of the novel, the alternating first- and third-person narrations become slippery, as the first-person narrator appears to take over the consciousness of one of the neighbors (209, 215), or suddenly Matilde is described from an unidentified third-person omniscience (162). At the same time, one must consider that the fluctuating narrations combined with the technical strategy of fragmentation contribute to making *Las horas vivas* an example of what Antonio has defined as a signature characteristic of contemporary literature: one that puts readers in conflict. According to Antonio, one has to *live* literature directly (40).

The novel's fragmentation is crucial on both discursive and metaphoric levels. Clearly, the alternating focus allows for multiple perspectives. Although the characters do not interact beyond brief conversations, readers are able to relate all the stories, thus focusing on the plight of Mexican women in the 1960s. Matilde's concrete reality, consisting of books, an occasional glimpse from the window, and bits of gossip gleaned from the servants, combines with the piecemeal reality of the other characters to form a disturbing unit. All these women live a fragmented existence that is reflected in their psyche and even in the building in which they live. The apartment complex does have a glass door that, in an interior duplication, is reduced to fragments when hit by a drunk man (103). Parallel to its inhabitants' atomization, the building is described as an "isla de interiores complicados y desconocidos" [an island of complicated and unknown interiors] (192). In yet another reiteration of a segmented status, Laura, when feeling stronger, refers to a sense of wholeness in opposition to her former fragmented existence: "Era otra, se sintió segura, entera, sus pedazos reunidos otra vez bajo su voluntad" [She was different, she felt sure of herself, whole, her pieces reunited again through her own effort] (214). Laura's sense of renewal may seem anomalous in a novel so replete with descriptions of devastated women, but there are other examples of a positive outlook toward the end. Yolanda, too, finds a new determination, resolving to be firm and strong: "lucharé y saldremos adelante" [I will fight, and we will move on] (208). Furthermore, Matilde and Antonio are reunited in the novel's final pages in a somewhat surprising and inverisimilar denouement.

Readers have not been prepared for a happy ending. All signs have indicated that each new year brings nothing but more disillusion (39). Yolanda's generational suffering is paralleled by the maid's returning to her abusive, distrusting husband, her second pregnancy assuring a life of continued bondage. In addition, Anastasia's role as the representative of an older generation of women suggests that no improvement is to be expected. It would seem that the positive elements found at the novel's closing are part of Matilde's wishful thinking. As she writes her own happy ending with Antonio, she also provides for some of the other women.[18]

Whatever the motivation, readers are returned at the end of the novel to the notion of the function of fiction, in a final self-referential segment that helps to clarify the work's title. The last fragment of *Las horas vivas* again alludes to the power of literature to extend life by means of readers' reactions and interpretations. Speaking specifically of "hours," the last line of the novel states: "Pienso en un momento privilegiado, de encuentro, de dicha compartida que será vivido, ya en el recuerdo, ya por otros, una y otra vez" [I'm thinking about a privileged moment, of encounter, of shared joy that will be lived, in memory, by others, again and again] (228).

In contrast to the Spanish nun's writing, criticized for its avoidance of daily routine, *Las horas vivas* concentrates on the intimate reality of a broad spectrum of Mexican women. By emphasizing the female condition, de Neymet valorizes these women's lives, be they servants or professionals. Once committed to paper, the quotidian reality will endure in the minds of future readers who might choose not only to be sympathetic to the female's plight but also to work to effect change in Mexican society. For, even if Matilde has imagined the lives of her neighbors, she still does so by drawing upon existing conditions in Mexico. Antonio may be blessed with memory loss with regard to society's controlling, male-dominated cultural codes, but that exterior reality still exists and needs to be challenged. Since for Matilde windows do not provide a means of breaking out or moving toward a new freedom or sense of identity, then the window as aperture must be replaced by the text. In *Las horas vivas* the text is the vehicle that can lead toward an exit, for, as readers are repeatedly told, written words give reality to life.

### Carmen Boullosa

*Mejor desaparece* (1987) [19] is a novel about family, in the generic rather than the specific, and the atomized existence experienced by all members: children, father, and mother. The work's formal fragmentation parallels the isolation as manifested in the family members; multiple sections echo multiple points of view. Although narrators vary, each in her or his way (females predominate) remains isolated from others either through self-exclusion, forced separation, total indifference, or a combination of these.

Boullosa divides her narrative into four main sections preceded by a one-page "Explicación" (Explanation) that appears to do little to illuminate what follows, as it merely relates the arrival of a parent, sex unidentified, carrying something, also unidentified, to show the children. The structure of the first three parts is essentially the same: a series of fragments of one or two pages in length, each bearing a title and beginning on the right-hand page. The resultant blank pages on the reverse of briefer sections are filled with drawings of vases and flowers in largely nonrepresentational stylized form. Although difficult to interpret or penetrate, the sections seem to focus on the Ciarrosa family, but readers are hard-pressed to be precise as to who these people are. One is exposed to fleeting images of the family's life and may quickly conclude that very little if anything can be categorized as normal. The female children, all named for flowers (Orquídea, Margarita, Dalia, Magnolia, Azucena, Acacia), live a very strange existence, confined mostly to their house since the arrival of *eso* (that), never identified or characterized other than something rather revolting that one would not want to touch with one's hands. In some ways, readers might recall Julio Cortázar's short story "Casa tomada" (House under Siege), in which a brother and sister are driven from their house by a persistent but unidentified something—only in Boullosa's novel the father is the one who brought *eso* into the house, and, when the females are confined to one room, it is he who gives the orders. There is always a human presence to the oppression in Boullosa's narrative.

The Ciarrosa children are isolated both within their home and without. After their mother's death, their father takes special care with regard to their feeding, but in other respects he ignores their needs. Communication is so poor that a lawyer must serve as intermediary. Because the disconnectedness among fragments parallels that among family members, at times it is difficult to identify the narrators: although it seems clear that Dalia narrates Parts 1 and 2, Part 3 is less accessible. In one fragment, it would appear that Acacia narrates (73), yet she is referred to in the third person in the preceding segment (71). Cumulatively, however, Parts 1 through 3 present glimpses or brief sketches of an enigmatic yet clearly unhappy home situation. Among the more realistic possibilities of action, there are suggestions of a second marriage and a stepmother whom the children resent. Less plausible aspects of their existence include the extended presence of strangers who simply arrive one day and stay on, as papá treats them far better than he does his own children. There is also "el Caballero," (the Gentleman), whose relationship with the children is unclear, although he serves as a disciplinarian on at least one occasion. Confusing readers even further is the fact that there is no stable temporal referent. In some sections the narrator relates aspects of childhood, yet in others the children are grown and engaged in a profession.

Part 4 does little to clarify readers' confusion. Discursively distinct, it is separated into three basic sections, each related by a different narrator. In the first, "La fiesta" (The Party), a female narrator named Berta invites a group of siblings (the Ciarrosa children?) to her house, signing the invitation "mamá." After they have assembled, she confesses to the hoax, for their mother is dead. The next segment, "Sí, mejor desaparece" (Yes, it's better if you disappear),[20] is narrated by a woman who has chosen to enclose herself in a room where her needs are tended by servants. She speaks incessantly of some children making noise on the other side of the wall, one or more of whom might be hers. Evidently the hate she assumes they feel for her is reciprocal, as she considers some form of violence toward them, her husband, and even the house: "soy una flama devastando, comiendo, devorando lo que la rodea" [I'm a flame devastating, eating, devouring what surrounds it] (98). Alternatively, she might simply disappear, and an inner voice, repeating the novel's title, urges this solution. Finally, the closing section of Part 4 and of the novel, "No desaparece," (He [or she or it] Doesn't Disappear), relates, paradoxically, the physical disappearance of the only male narrator of the text, a father who shrinks into nothingness. Although his narration begins with an apparently trivial anecdote about being locked out of his house, the psychological and metaphoric levels of interpretation of this segment emphasize yet another failed relationship. This father is so removed emotionally from both his family and house that he has no consciousness of them until he is literally and figuratively locked out: "Mi casa, ¿la había visto alguna vez? No sabía dónde se tocaba para entrar, no sabía en qué cuarto dormía quién . . . No recordé el lugar de mi mujer, no pude recordar su nombre ni dónde estuvo en mi corazón, pero tampoco sus rasgos" [My house, had I ever seen it? I didn't know where you rang to enter, I didn't know who slept in what room . . . I didn't remember my wife's place, I couldn't remember her name or where she was in my heart, not even her features] (105; italics in original).

Although the father in "No desaparece" may or may not have any relation to the Ciarrosa family (the children here have different names: Lucía, Isabel, and Rosario), there is a consistency apparent in the thematics of failed relationships and an almost animalistic quality to the interaction that exists. The sameness is made clear discursively as well. The above-cited passage is part of a long block section in italics that returns readers to the opening "Explicación," as both are in italics and share repugnant images rooted in cruelty and vomit. In retrospect, readers can appreciate how the "Explicación," at first perceived as the antithesis of what its title might imply, does, in fact, serve as an establishing discourse, introducing both thematics and tone that will be carried through the full text of Mejor desaparece.

Of even greater significance is Boullosa's technique of addressing potential reader response in her establishing sequence. She includes within the text the embodiment of a passive response that stands in contrast to the role that readers must accept in order to appreciate fully the fragments that follow. The specific passage describes the children's reaction to their father's having brought *eso* home: *"revoloteamos alrededor de eso todos sus hijos, convertidos de súbito en mosquitas indecisas alrededor de él sin atrevernos a permanecer junto a eso para inspeccionarlo lo suficiente, sin saber que había llegado para quedarse a convivir con nosotros por un tiempo infinito. No nos atrevíamos a preguntar ¿qué es?, o ¿de qué está hecho?"* [All of us children gathered around "that," suddenly converted into hovering indecisive (female) mosquitoes without daring to stay close enough to inspect it carefully, without knowing that it had arrived to stay with us for an infinite period of time. We didn't dare to ask "What is it?" or "What's it made of?"] (7; italics in original)

In its privileged position, the first page of Boullosa's novel emphasizes a negative example of reception. Unlike the Ciarrosa children, readers of *Mejor desaparece* must ask questions in order to relate the parts of this segmented text. It is only through their active participation that the fragments will yield narrative and/or thematic coherence. In recognition of her readers and their implied role, Boullosa has the narrators address themselves directly to them on a number of occasions. The examples range from a simple formal command of the sort used by Vicens, "créanme" [Believe me] (85), to more detailed comments or acknowledgment of possible reactions on the readers' part. Dalia assumes that readers will question the children's staying in such a strained situation: "Se preguntará el lector por qué no escapamos" [The reader will probably ask why we didn't escape] (15). Berta involves readers in the matter of choice given the same circumstances: "¿Qué hubieran hecho ustedes?" [What would you have done?] (84). The female narrator of "Sí, mejor desaparece" is even more explicit in her inclusion of readers, as she voices her motivation in terms of the chosen discourse. Having repeated a description of the children in the adjacent room, she states: "Lo vuelvo a decir para que crean en mí: no fue un discurso retórico, es verdad" [I'm repeating it so you will believe in me: it was not rhetorical, it is true] (97). The most direct communication between narrator and reader, however, reflects reader response to a nontraditional narrative: "¡No se aburran! ¡No se duerman! . . . ¡No dejen de oírme! Créanme, les voy a contar algo terrible para que no abandonen el lento pasear de esta historia" [Don't get bored! Don't fall asleep! . . . Don't stop listening! Believe me, I'm going to tell you something terrible so that you don't abandon the slow pacing of this story] (96). After such a self-conscious statement, the following "confession" seems somewhat ludicrous, as the narrator tells of her sense of panic when tree branches strike a window.

This is hardly what one would have expected as the announced "something terrible." But it is, finally, consistent with Boullosa's choice of unconventional form and content. She fills her fragmented, nonlinear discourse with a collage of vignettes of atomized family life and intimate revelations of isolation that may or may not be interrelated. There are no guidelines for readers in terms of rendering coherent this complex text other than the call for active questioning. As Federico Patán indicates, the fragmented discourse complements diegesis: "a un núcleo social en desintegración corresponde una expresión desintegrada, aunque desintegrada siguiendo un orden artístico cuidadosamente trazado" [to a social nucleus in disintegration there corresponds a disintegrated expression, although disintegrated following a carefully traced artistic order] (*Los nuevos territorios*, 57).

As readers work with the segments, as they become involved with the text, they should eventually move beyond the search for a stable story. Despite Boullosa's having warned them of her unconventional narrative through the "Explicación" and the first section of Part 1 that focuses on *eso*, they might have initially succumbed to the temptation to understand the Ciarrosa family within more traditional narrative norms. Given the unrealistic elements, multiple narrators, and enigmatic qualities of the text, however, a more fruitful response is to abandon that futile exercise and respond to the novel on its own terms.

What emerges are negative visions or evocations of marginalized characters, failed relationships, and broken lines of communication. The Ciarrosa children do not know when their mother died or from what (25). The woman who complains about the children next door questions their lack of communication even in physical terms: "Entre ellos, ¿se tocan?" [Among themselves, do they touch each other?] (94). Finally, because of the prevalence of female narrators and characters, one comes to focus on the status of women. Their sense of marginalization goes beyond that of living within a phallocentric world. Clearly papá and the Caballero are empowered figures; it is they who determine the roles and pass judgment. But the male's attitude toward women is revealed in other ways as well. That all the female Ciarrosa children are named after flowers might seem to be just an idiosyncratic whim on the parents' part, yet early in the novel there is clear evidence that, from the father's perspective, the children are interchangeable. Women constitute a generic; there is no sense of individuation. When playing the board game "Turista" (Tourist), as Orquídea and Dalia leave their seats at their father's bidding to answer the door or to fetch some water, they are replaced by other females. Oblivious to the change, papá calls the new player by the missing person's name or limits himself to the impersonal *usted* or *niña* [you or (female) child] (13). When the house becomes overcrowded because of the presence of the strangers who linger on, all the women are confined to a distant darkened room (32). It becomes clear that this is the desired status of women from the male's point of view when Dalia has the audacity to show evidence of "a face." Whether metaphorically or literally, a doctor operates on her to remove any trace of her individualized appearance (51–52).

By writing about the status of females, however, Boullosa confronts the issue, challenges its legitimacy. Despite the negative imagery and the sense of selflessness experienced by these women, it is, finally, the *male* who disappears. *Mejor desaparece* fights tradition both in narrative terms and with regard to society's codified generic prejudices, as suggested by Bruce Swansey on the book's jacket: "*Mejor desaparece* no es una novela pulcra, edificada sobre las reglas ruinosas del realismo decimonónico, sino una máquina de guerra que aspira a crear su propio orden y legalidad, que lucha contra un lenguaje 'novelesco' petrificado, contra una verosimilitud solemne y contra la falsa conciencia moral y literaria" [*Mejor desaparece* is not a tidy novel, built upon the ruinous rules of nineteenth-century realism, but a war machine that aspires to create its own order and legality, that fights against a petrified 'novelistic' language, against a solemn verisimilitude, and against the phony moral and literary consciousness]. In contrast to the faceless, interchangeable women perceived by her male characters, Carmen Boullosa achieves an individualized statement that insists on active reader participation. She asserts a strong female presence for the committed readership of Mexican letters of the 1980s.

Boullosa's second novel, *Antes* (1989), again focuses on the notion of family, but from a much more personal perspective.[21] In first-person narration, a woman looks back to her childhood from birth to the onset of puberty, describing memories that hold a special significance for her and using the viewpoint of the child who lived the experiences. By giving voice to herself as a child, the narrator succeeds in sharing the exaggerations, distortions, and magical thinking associated with innocence, resulting in a type of expressionistic dramatization of youth. At the same time, the repeated references to an undetermined present time from whence the adult woman savors her nostalgic memories serve to remind readers that not only is this a representation of paradise lost for the individual, but it is also an implicit criticism of present-day Mexico.

The unnamed narrator gives as her year of birth 1954, the same year Boullosa was born, thus suggesting an element of autobiography (Brushwood rev. 119). As a child she lives with her two older sisters, her father, and Esther, a woman she alternately accepts and rejects as her mother. The children live a life of privilege in a clearly upper-class existence, with servants to take care of their every need. The incidents recounted focus on quotidian events in the house and at school, two places that constitute the world for her, as with most children. Although the narration begins with her birth, the woman's memories are largely concentrated in the years 1962–1964, dates that have no clear historical significance for her as a child other than to situate her progress in grade school. Children commonly identify with the school year, society's routing of their lives, rather than widen their perspective to a historical context. As viewed from within the past, then, the experiences are personalized rather than contextualized.

Boullosa divides her novel into sixteen chapters, all but one of which are further fragmented for a total of seventy-three segments. Interestingly, the first chapter has an inordinate number of sections in comparison to the others (twenty), as if the narrator had difficulty at the beginning organizing her thoughts, finding a focus with which to order her memories. Frequently the fragmentation serves as a divider between memories or as a marker of a passage of time. Because a number of segments stem directly from the previous section, however, readers are encouraged to consider metaphoric connotations of the fragmented text.

*Antes* can be viewed as the dramatization of a woman's trying to piece together or read her childhood with the goal of understanding herself. The narrator states at one point that her purpose is to convey to her listeners who she is (86). She addresses her audience (readers) quite consistently throughout the book, first in the familiar *tú* form, then as a plural. It is as if she were projecting or inventing readers as an authorization of her telling. She demonstrates concern about reader perception as well: "¿Para qué les cuento un sueño? Hago mal en dispersar el orden de mi narración" [Why am I telling you a dream? I shouldn't break the order of my narration] (72).

The desire to communicate is, however, obfuscated by the elusiveness of the content, although readers can certainly understand, even be charmed by the magical occurrences accepted by this child as a part of her life. She lays white stones around her bed at night to protect her from menacing noises as she sleeps; pen marks on her jacket turn into spiders; and a special closet converts a drawing of stones into the real thing. The more ominous incidents must also be viewed through the prism of childhood: after the kitchen scissors appear mysteriously under her pillow, she finds slaughtered the turtle destined for a special birthday soup. Everything seems bigger, scarier, more imposing.

The aggrandizement of childhood events culminates in the depiction of the onset of her menstrual cycle as death. Puberty does, in effect, mark the death of childhood, and this woman feels acutely the distance from that world, as seen when she observes some children playing: "Cierto, yo era como esos niños, yo era esos niños y aquí estoy, divorciada de su mundo para siempre. ¡Niños! ¡Yo era lo que ustedes son! [It's true, I was like those children, I was those children and here I am, divorced from their world forever. Children! I was what you are!] (11). Even as a child she had seen maturation as a threat, when her sisters closed her out upon reaching an age at which they could whisper about bras.

The novel's ending with her "death," coupled with the repeated reminders that this is being related from an adult's present time, albeit unspecified, raises questions regarding the status of the narrator at the moment of telling. Here again, the cues are amorphous. In one fragment that functions as an aside directed to readers, she states that she is alone and has come to be comfortable in her enclosed state (45). Elsewhere she includes ambiguous references to an unspecified "they" who came to get her (12, 88). Nothing concrete is offered regarding the woman's current circumstances. Nevertheless, along with frequent distancing comments that announce her separation from the events portrayed, there is introduced a certain cynicism that comes with age. One feels the presence of a woman of social conscience, a person who has come to comprehend the cultural shaping achieved by the schools, the church, and society in general, as well as the environmental damage caused by industrial development. In the more blatant examples, her commentary is direct. Her father's family forces him into a lucrative business reflecting "confianza en las capacidades de los hombres, ebrios de un nuevo renacimiento que envenenaría el aire, los ríos, los mares, los pulmones de los trabajadores de su industria y más pulmones" [confidence in men's capacity, drunk with thoughts of a new renaissance that would poison the air, the rivers, the seas, the lungs of their industry workers and other lungs] (55). She is critical also of her privileged class. When the children are encouraged to make a drawing illustrative of their school's motto, *serviam* (I shall serve), the narrator states "cuál lavar platos en mi casa habiendo una mujer cuyo trabajo era hacerlo y que no me hubiera permitido interrumpirla, cuál 'ayudar' a los niños de la *baranca* para los que nuestra sola presencia era una ofensa, cuál *serviam*, cuál 'servir' si entre nosotros nos encargábamos de que el país entero nos sirviera" [what kind of wash the dishes having a woman in my house whose job it was to do it and who wouldn't have let me interrupt her, what kind of "help" the lower-class kids for whom our mere presence was an offense, what kind of *serviam*, what kind of "serve others," if among ourselves we tried to ensure that the entire country would serve us] (63, emphasis in original).

Rather than level an explicit criticism against the church, Boullosa lets its influence make itself known through its tentacles. In addition to the Catholic school headed by Mother Michael and the church-sponsored exchange program in which the child participates, it turns out that some if not all the house servants are trained at a preparatory academy run by Opus Dei (57). The pervasiveness of the church's molding, however, is seen in a particularly illuminating section in which she allegorizes a school incident in religious terms. When older students grab her underpants in the school bathroom, her interpretation of the events converts the offenders into angels, her slip (miraculously burnt by holy water) into a stigma, and the underpants into her soul (43).[22]

The woman's retrospection, then, shows growth, demonstrates the value of the process of reconsidering one's past as a conduit to understanding. It is a continuing process though, one that has not yet yielded a vision of herself as a whole, a fact that is dramatized by the text's fragmented discourse. The vision is still piecemeal; there is more work to be done. The presentation of that process, however, is fundamentally positive in that it portrays an active response to the question of identity. Furthermore, the act of sharing such a personal examination of self through analysis of the past suggests an expansion that moves beyond textual boundaries. *Antes* presents a female figure looking back on her life, an uncommon perspective in Mexico's male-dominated literature and society.[23] Boullosa's inclusion of social and ecological criticism appears to constitute an invitation to extend the process to the search for comprehension of national identity by means of a reexamination of the past, perhaps now with a feminine sensibility as a new lens. The suggestion could well be that to understand Mexico one must look to the past with a nonphallocentric perspective.[24]

María Luisa Puga

María Luisa Puga's *La forma del silencio* (1987), although sharing an intimate atmosphere and nostalgia for childhood as seen in Boullosa's *Antes*, has a wider scope that addresses more directly the issue of the nation. Puga employs fragmentation as a device through which to include within her critique the crisis that exists in Mexico in the 1980s as manifested in the atomization of the individual, the urban and economic disintegration, and the political fraudulence that strangle Mexico in the present.[25] She insistently calls her readers' attention to the narrative process by means of self-referential comments on the ontology of narration and, even more provocatively, promotes the readers' active consideration of how ways of telling relate to a sense of Mexican identity. For, throughout the segments, there is a subtext of nationalism, albeit existentially queried rather than defined.[26]

Puga begins Part 1 of her novel with nine elements that constitute, as she says, a form of index (11; "a manera de índice") naming the essential premises on which the text is constructed: "La casa," "Acapulco," "La escuetez," "Juan," "Distrito Federal," "El país," "Yo," "La novela," and "La crisis" ("The house," "Acapulco," "Concision," "Juan," "Federal District," "The nation," "I," "The novel," and "The crisis"). Thus, from the start, the personal (yo and Juan) is meshed with the national (Acapulco, DF, and el país) as well as the self-referentially literary (la escuetez and la novela), all in a state of collapse because of "la crisis": "Se desestructuran las cosas: la pareja, la familia, la sociedad, el país" [Things are deconstructing: couples, families, society, the country] (25). The items presented are not described but rather evoked through references, memories, and allusions that will be clarified in part later in the text. Readers then confront a series of twenty-seven fragments that immediately establish a pattern of varied focus, alternating among Juan, the unnamed female narrator, the city (as a generic as well as specific references to Acapulco, Mexico City, and, within the latter, the Colonia San Rafael area), and language (both concrete, as in regional accents, and in the abstract). In apparent recognition that readers might well question the direction of the fragmented pieces of narrative, Puga closes this section with a segment devoted to a self-referential statement regarding the *story* she wants to tell: "Ni la de Juan ni la mía, sino otra. Una que yo no conozco y que es la que puede fracasar" [Not Juan's nor mine, but another. One that I'm not familiar with and one that can fail] (76). Having emphasized the elusive component, Puga then adds *story* as a tenth premise—"Lo que faltaba en el índice" [what was missing in the index] (77)—yet the content of this fragment yields no new focus on its stated subject (story), instead reverting to (one assumes) the narrator, as she recalls moments of rebellion in her youth. The lack of clarification or delineation of a story is appropriate, because the rest of the novel continues as begun: concluding the first part are fifty-nine fragments that resume the alternating focus presented to readers before the flaunting of the absence of coherent narrative content along traditional lines. Part 2 presents a parallel fifty-nine segments that draw to a close in the middle of a dialogue between the narrator and Juan, just as the novel began after the index. *La forma del silencio* both begins and ends *in medias res*.

The two main characters of this nonstory, the female narrator and Juan, sustain a dialogue in an ephemeral present, located temporally in the 1980s and spatially in a generic office building in Mexico City. They sit at a table across from each other discussing the novel in which she has invited him to take part. It should be noted, however, that toward the end of the text there is a strong suggestion that she imagines the exchanges (246). Despite the apparent parity of these conversations, the woman's point of view prevails, as it is she who sustains the narration of both her experiences and his in the form of selected memories of youth. The frequency of personal recollections notwithstanding, readers receive very little concrete information about these characters, not even the narrator's name. They must paste together an overview from the pieces provided in isolated episodes constituting in her case a type of nostalgia for childhood tinted with an adult's cynicism and, in the segments devoted to Juan, her attempt to comprehend his psychological profile. What is more, some of the frustratingly limited information readers are given about Juan is repeated (such as his leaving school because he knew more about the subject than the professor) as if Puga were flaunting her denial of a more complex character development within conventional norms.

Readers also lack information about the physical appearance of these characters. Much more attention is devoted to the description of Mexico City and Acapulco, the filth and uncontrolled expansion of the former, the Malinche complex of the latter, having sold out to the cultural colonizers (tourists) of the north, and the chameleonlike self-negation of both, as they define themselves in terms of European and "North-American" style and culture, reflected in architecture, cinema, the clothes they wear, even the foods they eat.[27]

There is a cohesiveness to be discerned from the mixture of the personal and the national, as they both form part of the pervasive crisis in Mexico in the 1980s, which is, finally, the focus of *La forma del silencio*. Puga's text, using as vehicle the two main characters, makes reference to recent Mexican history from the 1940s to the present, having first paired each decade with its signature association: the 1940s with World War II, the 1950s with plastic (plates and credit cards, shoddy material), the 1960s with love, the 1970s with death, and the 1980s as a period of crisis (25). Most of the time, there is little temporal specificity other than situating the occurrence within a decade. Only twice do dates truly stand out. The first is September 19, 1985, when the reality of Mexico's devastating earthquake penetrates the fiction. At the same time, it offers yet another possibility to allude to the crisis: even the government buildings fall: "estos gobiernos que tanto aseguran, que tanto prometen" [these governments who assure us so much, who promise so much] (131). The other temporally specific example, were it any other year, would have less impact. At the end of a fragment, set apart graphically in a short, one-sentence paragraph, one reads: "Corría el año de 1968" [1968 was swiftly passing] (238). Even without this privileged positioning, the year would signal a response from readers, as it immediately evokes the tragic occurrences at Tlatelolco.

Obviously, the crisis in Mexico has many echoes in the past. Continuing the emphasis from Azuela through Fuentes on cyclical patterns in history, the narrator makes reference to the progression through Aztec, Spanish, *criollo* (creole), and PRI tyrants (184). Tellingly, she states as well that her preoccupation is not so much with the crisis itself, for that has always afflicted the nation, but with the current way of dealing with it (113). This is a national issue, one that reverberates on many levels, and thus stands in contrast with the other items representative of previous decades: war, plastic, love, and death can be linked internationally, but the crisis of the 1980s, as depicted here, is *Mexico's*. Puga's diatribe finds targets in the city, in the government, in the "Northamericanization" of Mexico, and in language itself. The Federal District is no longer a place ideal for walking and viewing; instead, it requires self-defense (227). All are witness to corruption, impotence, and violence (127) and to a government that treats its citizens as children, telling them to be quiet, that everything will work out (173), in yet another example of the continuing cycles enunciated in *La región más transparente*. Acapulco is the most beautiful and the most destroyed little pearl of the Pacific, the largest brothel in Latin America (211). Government officials sack the country, while those in the middle class nestle in their very civilized Western habits and pretensions (238). Language is dysfunctional; people lose respect for words such as "responsibility" that have little meaning in such a jaded atmosphere (146). Noting the fragmented condition of the people, she suggests that one needs to "[d]esmantelar el lenguaje para que no divida, subdivida, clasifique y condicione: clases sociales, gobernantes, parientes, amigos" [dismantle language so that it might no longer divide, subdivide, classify, and condition: social classes, leaders, relatives, friends] (255).

Symptomatic of the crisis is the silence of the title, there used in the singular, but manifested in multiple ways within the novel. *La forma del silencio* is permeated with discussions of or references to silence, both peaceful (the night, the dawn, the rain, the sea) and malevolent (remaining quiet while an acknowledgedly corrupt government deceives the people). The silence of the conversation one has with oneself, upon realizing that others are not what they seem or claim to be, pairs with the silence among estranged family members, the muted relationship between father and son, or the distance between mismatched spouses. There is the silence connoted by a lack of sex education, the silence of traveling with strangers in *peseros*[28] or the metro, and, the most dangerous form, that of accepting the status quo with the result that irresponsibility goes unchecked.

Finally, silence reflects the atomization of individuals, which joins thematics and discourse in *La forma del silencio*. When absorbed in that noncommunicative state, people are effectively separated, alone. Yet solitude is also a consequence of living in such an immense city: "en este vasto y caótico universo que es el D.F., están solos" [in this vast and chaotic universe that is the D.F., they are alone] (74). One then senses a metaphoric use for the fragmentation in Puga's novel. The segmented status emphasizes the estrangement of the individual.

Within the novel Puga encourages the association of content (in this case, another aspect of the crisis) and form, specifically the use of fragmentation. She begins by relating the appearance of white tourists in the Mexican market as fissures or breaks in the overall picture and then, at a point of privilege at the end of a fragment, further likens them to the spaces in her narration, the blank spaces between segments (174). Subsequently, her tone becomes ominous, as she extends the analogy to what happens in chaotic Mexico, focusing her criticism on the constitution: "Porque se ha querido organizarlo con una constitución, y se ha querido reorganizarlo con enmiendas a esa constitución, y vivirlo con violaciones a la constitución, y salvarlo con denuncias de afrentas a la constitución" [Because they have tried to organize it with a constitution, and they have tried to reorganize it with amendments to that constitution, and to live it with violations against the constitution, and to save it with denouncements of affronts to the constitution] (174).

Other discursive elements echo the truncated existence evoked within the text, such as the frequent use of sentence fragments and the abrupt interruption of dialogue in conversations between the narrator and Juan. Enhancing this consistency are the cover designs. The front cover shows a series of squares marked off in black, twenty-five boxes, all but one of which contain drawings of what appear to be leaves (the bottom right box gives the name of the publisher). The leaves are roughly divided in half and colored with two of three hues: blue, green, and brown. Although green, of course, is a color for leaves in their prime, brown connotes the end of life, and blue is a cold, unnatural shade. It is possible to consider the two-tone leaves as a reflection of Mexico's *mestizo* population. This sense of blending, an integrated interpretation, however, is belied by the segmentation of the boxes, evoking the atomization of individuals within Mexican culture. Although forming a part of an apparent whole, each leaf is separated from the rest, just as the fragments of Puga's narrative stand apart, separated by blank spaces. An analogous depiction appears on the back cover.

Puga's segmented structure pairs well with her varied content. She is able to contrast male with female, evoke the sights and sounds of Acapulco and Mexico City, consider philosophically such abstractions as responsibility and nationalism, and level a series of sharp criticisms against those in power for their ineptitude and deceit. Her collage technique is echoed within the novel with reference to the singer Lola Beltrán's concert style. The narrator would like to write in the same manner: "entre canción y canción hace comentarios, preguntas o simplemente juega" [Between songs, she makes comments, asks questions, or simply has fun with her audience] (112). Portions of *La forma del silencio* are like songs in their lyric quality. This is especially true of the sections focused on the narrator's childhood and her vivid memories of visual, auditory, and olfactory stimuli.

There is a fluidity in the prose that suggests poetry, augmented by the author's recurrent use of anaphora.

Employing methods of narration that break with traditional norms, Puga also demonstrates textually an awareness that the unusual techniques will affect readers. Quite frequently within her commentary there are self-referential remarks about the ontology of the novel and about projected reader response. She emphasizes the nonchronological sequencing of segments, at times asking rhetorically why not tell a direct story (102), and yet also defending her choice by saying that logical sequencing loses importance when compared to the need to examine and understand better the human condition (84). The way of telling really can be flexible, as long as one's goals are met. She states that in her narrative there is no denouement because there is no plot, which, she acknowledges, might well be disconcerting for readers (139). Nevertheless, it is precisely this quality that provides movement and vitality in the work: "No hay trama y aunque resulte osado decirlo, tiene todas las tramas posibles. No parte ni llega, pero está siempre haciéndose" [There is no plot and, although it might seem bold to say it, it contains all possible plots. It neither begins nor ends, but it is always forming itself] (139). Puga thus suggests the multiple interpretations or pluralism of response possible with this type of narration.

Referring once again to more conventional fiction, Puga describes novels as an illusion to which readers might turn for escape or for consolation (231). By including in her narrative the brutal realities of Mexico in the 1980s, however, she succeeds in forcing readers to confront their present, thus thwarting their escapism. What they might have hoped to avoid by picking up a book looks back at them from its pages. *La forma del silencio* has characters, but it is not about them; it depicts Mexico City and Acapulco, but it is not an urban novel per se. As Puga queries, how can one narrate a city (183)? To narrativize the city is to stop it in time, which denies its dynamism. Her subject is the crisis, and the personal, political, urban, and literary aspects depicted are all part of the problem. Readers must respond to the layers presented and take a hard look at Mexico, the nation.

If *La forma del silencio* is a different kind of novel (166; "Novela de otro modo"), it is because Mexico is a different kind of country (166; "País de otro modo"). If Mexico is to have a national literature, then writers must abort their efforts to imitate the more recognized, if not revered, writing emanating from Europe and the United States. Puga is calling for a *Mexican* novel and, consequently, like Pacheco, urges readers toward a double commitment, here both narrative and sociopolitical. In the 1940s and 1950s, people did not refer to Third World underdevelopment (107); they did not exhibit consciousness of a national identity (108). Mexico in the 1980s is clearly in a time of crisis, however, and Puga, for one, is ready to have her voice heard.

Puga provides stimuli toward unification within the narrative both to promote activity on the readers' part with regard to relating her segmented fiction and to exact a similar response to Mexico's plight. Joining the fragments are the repetition of specific words (similar to Arreola's technique) and a common thematics in contiguous sections. Furthermore, a number of segments begin with words that connote continuity: "And" (83, 223), "Because" (222), and "But" (99). She makes specific reference, as well, to other forms of connectors or unifiers: the *periférico* that joins the neighborhoods of the Federal District (54) and the commonality in the people's attitude toward thieving politicians (75).

The source of strength of her sociopolitical argument comes also from a focus on unification, in this case of the people, *all* Mexicans, not just those in power, the pampered middle class, or the very poor considered in isolation. As Alfonso González argues, *La forma del silencio* demonstrates "a new consciousness, a new attitude toward power and authority" (38). Puga's promotion of a nationalist consciousness calls upon the recognition that one cannot invent a nation or a culture, that Mexico is not the country that the PRI has fabricated in its propaganda. One must be alert to actual circumstances. In response to her self-referential question asking the identity of the you, we, and they who appear in the novel (102), she answers: "Todo para decir que ese tú, nosotros, ellos, uno, yo, en fin, no son sino el concierto de voces asambleístas que todos llevamos dentro" [It's all in order to say that that you, we, they, one, I, finally are nothing but the concert of representative voices that we all carry inside ourselves] (104). The emphasis is on *we*, the group, the nation. Puga calls for the inclusion of all Mexicans and makes a case for the writer's opportunity, indeed responsibility, to promote a more active role among readers. As she has stated, "me pregunto si en esta crisis, quien escribe no podría ser el que vaya abriendo los huequitos para que la gente, ella, se pregunte cosas como: ¿qué es la nación? ¿qué es la pareja, ser mujer, ser hombre, la familia? ¿Quién es la madre? ¿Qué es el poder y por qué?" [I ask myself if in this crisis, the one who writes couldn't be the one to open little holes in order that the people, she,[29] could ask themselves things like: what is the nation? what is a couple, being a woman, being a man, the family? Who is the mother? What is power and why?] ("Escribir," 65). In an intriguing way, her reference to the opening of little holes or gaps falls back upon the discourse of *La forma del silencio,* suggesting that the spaces could signify a pause for thought, for interrogation. Another interpretation has been offered by Verónica Salceda, who argues that readers are invited to participate in the novel by filling in the historical gaps or spaces with which the author simply has had no experience (60).

A continuing sense of community is evident in the penultimate fragment of the text, in which Puga appears to yield to the emotion associated with the crisis she depicts. The entire segment is devoted to various aspects of the crisis, as though it were a résumé of the multiple devastations already introduced. The words "the crisis" begin four paragraphs in a final example of anaphora. Puga touches on the government, the bogus notion of nation heretofore accepted, language, and the need to focus on the people (255). Furthermore, the emphasis on the plural is manifested in the insistent use of "nosotros" (we). At the end of the fragment, Puga returns to the ultimate form of silence: "La última forma del silencio, pues, y por la crisis, sería la de la ausencia de atención a los modos, promesas y verborreas del poder. Una ausencia de la gente ante el poder. Un ir abriendo el espacio que nos separa, un ir dejando que ellos, los que gobiernan, sean ese país que dicen ser y que no tiene nada que ver con nosotros. Un irlos dejando solos" [The ultimate form of silence, then, because of the crisis, would be that of the lack of attention to the methods, promises, and verbosity of those in power. An absence of the people before power. An opening of the space that separates us, allowing them, those who govern, to be that country that they say they are and that has nothing to do with us. A leaving them alone] (256).

This impassioned outburst, however, is muted also, for the final fragment reverts to the dialogue between the narrator and Juan. He reiterates his distaste for that type of discourse (pontificating), resulting in her apologizing. Even more significantly, the final words of the text return readers to the "Northamericanization" of Mexico, as one offers the other a Halls cough drop.[30] Dialogue is interdicted when one sucks on a cough drop, connoting yet another silence beyond the end of the novel, unless readers have been prompted to continue the exchange of ideas and to challenge those in power.

# CONCLUSION

Other than occasional incursions into art for art's sake, notably in vanguard writing and Elizondo's *Farabeuf*, fragmented Mexican literature of the twentieth century has maintained a steady intertwining of the aesthetic and the social. From the novels of the revolution to recent fiction that seeks to demarginalize isolated groups and urges a reexamination of Mexico's political and social (de)formation, examples abound of texts that engage readers with both thematics and discourse, pulling them into their exposed construction, inviting them to work with the pieces, and provoking an attempt at rendering a nexus among parts. Within the purely aesthetic realm, fragmentation is effective in prompting active reader response, both in working with the text and in focusing on the narrative process and on internalized assumptions about fiction. Novels that reach out to readers on social issues, from Azuela through Fuentes and Puga, would suggest that they have an agenda involving reader activity as well.

Puga has stated that an author should strive to serve as a mirror, as a reflector of the world in which one lives ("Escribir," 63), which suggests a provocative comparison with the emphasis on mirrors, windows, and other reflectors in *La muerte de Artemio Cruz*. Cruz is the *aprovechado* (one who takes advantage), the man who fights in the revolution and then is instrumental in denying benefits to workers while adding to his coffers daily. Instead of contributing to his country, he takes for himself and winds up contaminating those around him in such a way that his family and business associates become a reflection of his values. He creates his own darkness. Cruz could thus be seen as a negative example of a "citizen-in-the-text," an echo of the reader-in-the-text who stands out as the embodiment of a dubious model, although the parallel is not complete when one focuses on the notion of passivity. In fact, in an interesting way, there is a fluctuation within the categories of active/passive as one shifts from a consideration of aesthetic structures to one of social implications. As readers, we should engage with the fragmented text, question its patterns and ellipses, move within and among the segments, and consider various levels of signification. Within the social context, the activity embodied by Cruz that enriches him at the expense of others reverts to Porfirian practice and thus is seen as part of a cyclical drain on hopes for a Mexican democracy. On the other hand, readers are prompted to be active mentally, questioning the official (hi)story, challenging the bogus unity presented first by Díaz, later by the "institutionalized" Revolutionary Party (PRI). Although these novels will not send readers into the streets, they are instrumental in keeping sociopolitical issues alive, thus challenging complacency, and discerning readers will be reminded of the disparate economic and social status of Mexico's citizenry as well as the marginalization of many of its inhabitants. One must remain mindful, however, that Puga and others address a limited audience: those who can read, those (increasingly fewer) who can afford to buy a book, and those who tolerate being reminded of the imbalance of power and basic rights within Mexican society.

The analyses here presented of novels written between 1915 to 1989 suggest certain cardinal features that serve to stabilize a category of work:

1. A fundamental movement away from the traditional notion of story: Fragmented novels that break with narrative norms flaunt their status as a nonwhole by laying bare the gaps in their structure. Many of these novels, however, go even further, denying the most basic tenet of conventional narrative, the notion of story (E. M. Forster 27). The supremacy of story cedes to a focus on, among others, language, ambience, poetic tropes, the narrative process itself, or sociopolitical critiques. In apparent recognition of readers' conditioning, some authors appear to manipulate the desire for story as a lure with which to make readers aware of their internalized expectations.

2. The city as locus of atomization: From Azuela through Puga, authors have privileged the depiction of the sprawling, venal, and atomizing city in anticipation of or as complement to how it has been depicted in socioeconomic essays of recent years (Danel and Ortiz). The women authors in Chapter 8 suggested that the idealized Mexico City of the 1960s was already tainted, and in *Casas de encantamiento* (1987;

Houses of Enchantment), Ignacio Solares moves another generation closer to the revolution, having his character return to the Mexico City of the 1940s: "en ese otro México, descubrimos el inicio de la pesadilla que hoy vivimos" [in that other Mexico we discover the beginning of the nightmare that we live today] (back cover). Solares joins others who have demonstrated that there were warning signs that were not heeded, and he, for one, appears to be of the school that espouses apocalyptic measures, an urban Götterdämmerung, if there is no staving off the demographic explosion, on the assumption that a rebirth will follow: "nuestra ciudad está en plena destrucción y en lugar de frenar el proceso hay que acelerarlo, llevarlo a sus últimas consecuencias" [our city is in full destruction, and instead of slowing down the process, it is necessary to accelerate it, to carry it to its ultimate consequences] (31).

3.  Open endings and circular structures that foster a reconsideration of the text: Readers are forcefully removed from a position of potential passivity as mere receivers of story. They are sent back to the beginning of the novel to reevaluate the already read, asked to provide closure when none is supplied, and invited to interrogate the text's systems.

4.  The inscription of authors-, narrators-, readers-, even "citizens"-in-the-text who present a model, whether positive or negative, of ways of dealing with a complex narrative or ways of being within a complex society.

5.  The dramatization of the responsibility of the individual to reassess the past, a revisionist effort or rereading of history from a nonphallocentric point of view: Beyond being encouraged to question aspects of narration or the assumption of authorial control, readers are presented with characters who look to the past with a critical eye, reassessing childhood and "institutionalized" national history as a means through which to achieve personal growth and perhaps to effect change.

6.  A focusing on readers, whether by addressing them directly or forcefully dislodging them from previous narrative assumptions: There is a directness in the novels of the twentieth century that goes far beyond the notion of a "dear reader" of earlier times. Many works are marked by an intimacy between narrator and readers, particularly from the *Onda* fiction to the present.

7. The presentation of stimuli pointing toward a coherence within narrative that suggests ways of unifying the fragments and the bringing to the foreground of unique moments of social coherence that provoke images of national unity, not a false unity decreed yet thwarted by government but a more realistic movement toward a society capable of accommodating difference.

The last point, a prodding toward a more stable construct to be forged with the building blocks (fragments) of the text or of society, needs to be examined carefully so as not to be considered a facile solution without substance. We have seen that the pluralism of these segmented texts does not yield a tightly defined, singular vision. Readers are invited into the novel as coparticipants, and are allowed the freedom to personalize their interpretations. Moving from the aesthetic to the social, one must allow for flexibility of the outcome as well. The notion of unity is not a simplistic call for total equality in Mexican society. There is, however, a widespread sense of urgency in both fiction and cultural criticism regarding the need for a joining of voices to counter hegemonic governmental practice. In a sense, in an age of corruption and dissolution, the fragmented novel vies with the essay as a genre of cultural criticism in an exploration for a widened readership through more direct communication. One notes ample examples within Mexican fiction of references to brief moments of harmony within Mexican history and calls for a more integrated society. In *La región más transparente*, the intellectual Manuel Zamacona explains to a cynical Federico Robles his vision of a more equitable society: "Lo que a mí me interesa es encontrar soluciones que correspondan a México, que permitan, por primera vez, una conciliación de nuestra sustancia cultural y humana y de nuestras formas jurídicas. Una verdadera integración de los miembros dispersos del ser de este país [What interests me is to find solutions which are suited to Mexico and will permit us for the first time to reconcile human and cultural being with lawful forms. A true integration of the scattered members of what this country is] (282). Later, Fuentes has Artemio Cruz reflect upon a collective embrace among the men of Sonora and Chihuahua during the revolution and issue a warning to the new elite that harmony among the poor could return to threaten them: "dirás a los demás que lo teman: teman la falsa tranquilidad que les legas, teman la concordia ficticia, la palabrería mágica, la codicia sancionada: teman esta injusticia que ni siquiera sabe que lo es" [you will tell the others to fear it: fear the false calm you bequeath them, fear the fictitious concord, the magical patter, the sanctioned greed, fear this injustice that doesn't even know what it is] (276). The historical range includes the time of the Aztecs, which Carmen Boullosa sees as a harmonious culture, described in *Llanto: Novelas imposibles* with a plant metaphor: "aquí conseguimos que las plantas del desierto y las de la humedad convivan a pocos pasos" [here we are successful in getting the desert plants and the tropical plants to live near each other] (32). A more recent reference can be found in Solares's *Casas de encantamiento*, in which a character laments after the 1985 earthquake: "esa solidaridad que de pronto unió y humanizó—¿por qué sólo entonces?—a esta ciudad tan injusta y adormecida" [that solidarity that suddenly united and humanized—why only then?—this city that is so unjust and asleep] (176).

In both *Llanto* and *Casas de encantamiento*, characters return to the past in part to better understand the identity of the nation. They are, in a sense, typical of recent trends in Mexican fiction toward, on the one hand, a nostalgic desire for the past (Brushwood, *La novela mexicana*) and, on the other, a critical view of the past or a revisionist depiction (García Núñez, Taylor). Just as readers need to rethink a novel in order to fully appreciate its vitality, so one must rethink Mexico's past in an effort to interrogate both personal and national formation. In Mexican fiction, fragmentation has been an indispensable technique with which to provoke both.

In his comparison of *La muerte de Artemio Cruz* and the film *Citizen Kane*, speaking specifically of Cruz's failure to achieve rebirth and self-transcendence, Lanin Gyurko extends Fuentes's vision from the individual to the collective, moving from one man's story to a macro level in which the history and future of the nation are intertwined: "Cruz's final and irrevocable incarceration in self, his inability to reconstitute the shattered remnants of both his moral and his physical self, constitutes Fuentes' warning to his countrymen about the extreme dangers to the national integrity and autonomy that could result from Mexico's failure to unify the fragments of the national self—its diverse social classes, the poverty and disease-stricken masses on the one side and its economic and social elite on the other, its Indian and its *criollo* identities, its pre-Columbian heritage and its commercial and technological present" ("*La muerte* and *Citizen Kane*," 66).

Fuentes's warning was for naught, for the inequalities contributing to a fragmented society in the late 1950s and early 1960s persist. Cultural analysts of the past decade speak of a "clase media pulverizada" [a pulverized middle class] (Reyes Govea 251) and a situation in 1987 in which 46 percent of the population lacked the most basic necessities of food, employment, health, and education while 1.24 percent constituted the extremely rich (Reyes Govea 247). Others focus on more abstract cultural issues, calling for an authentic cultural synthesis that goes beyond the racial *mestizaje* that has been there since the conquest (Basave Benítez 144). Finally, in his *Pensar nuestra cultura* (1991; To Think about Our Culture), Guillermo Bonfil Batalla argues that previous efforts to create a "unified" culture have been exclusionary and that what is needed is not a uniform national culture but a space that is constituted for the flourishing of diversity, in which there would be fluidity, movement among the differences rather than one subgroup's ceding to the ways of another (120, 122–123). Like fragments within a novel, the various subcultures would maintain a sense of identity within themselves and yet would have a place within the larger unit, here, the community, just as we saw in Rulfo's "montón de piedras."

I stated in the introduction that no writer composes from within a vacuum. That is certainly true in terms of literary influences. It takes on another meaning, however, when one considers the project of an author. The aesthetic considerations for a writer of creative fiction are obvious, but, for the majority of these authors, writing is rooted in social and political realities, and their fragmented texts reflect the society in which they live.

# NOTES

## Introduction

1. See Stanley E. Fish; Norman Holland, *The Dynamics of Literary Response* and *5 Readers Reading*; Wolfgang Iser, *The Implied Reader* and *The Act of Reading*; and Jonathan Culler. For an annotated bibliography of reader-response criticism arranged by category, see Inge Crosman.

## Chapter 1: Fragmentation

1. Mexicans now refer to "México A.C. y México D.C. (antes de Chiapas, después de Chiapas)" [before Chiapas, after Chiapas] (West 4; the initials here linked with Mexico are the same used in Spanish to designate B.C. and A.D. with reference to the birth of Christ). Among the numerous books and articles that examine the Zapatista movement, see Castañeda, Collier, Katzenberger, and La Botz.

2. Lomnitz-Adler refers here to Roger Bartra's argument (*La jaula*).

3. It is not surprising that fragmentation has been associated with both the modern and postmodern literary movements (Tytell 3; Martin 121; Smith 175).

4. The notion of linear development does not, of course, bar the narrator from pausing in the tale to develop a new character's description beginning from a point earlier than the narrative's "present." Although the actual telling may at times waver from a strictly linear rendition, the fact remains that the story consists of a well-established beginning, middle, and end.

5. See, for example, segments 4 and 5 of Part 2, Chapter 1.

6. As one example of an illusion-breaking strategy to be found in this otherwise traditional novel, see Part 4, Chapter 6, fragment 16, paragraph 1, in which one character's summation of another's peripeteia prompts the remark that surely that would make fine

material for a play or a novel. Galdós's wink at readers also extends to commenting on what was the best part of the story, a truly self-referential statement.

7. It should be noted, however, that in the "Tablero de dirección," in which the numerical sequence is listed, there is a powerful hint urging readers to free themselves even further and to combine the boxes however they like.

8. The description of *Composition No. 1* is based on Sharon Spencer's analysis in *Space, Time and Structure in the Modern Novel* (85–87, 209–212).

9. John C. Akers includes a discussion of the uses of fragmentation in "Fragmentation in the Chicano Novel" (132–133).

10. This term is used by Mikhail Bakhtin in *Problems of Dostoevsky's Poetics* (5).

11. M. Ian Adams relates fragmentation to a divided personality in the works of Juan Carlos Onetti (47, 55).

12. For a thorough treatment of the United States's cultural penetration in the 1960s in Mexico, see Parménides García Saldaña's *En la ruta de la onda*.

13. These examples are all from José Agustín's *De perfil*.

14. Enrique Yáñez de la Fuente concludes that if measures are taken to curb the demographic explosion, the population of Mexico City might be "held" to 25 million by the beginning of the century. If not, the total is likely to be 35 million (94). Aldo-José Altamirano reports a national increase of 70 percent per decade, with a strong acceleration in recent years (24).

### Chapter 2: The Initiators

1. In addition to Nellie Campobello's *Cartucho*, the following examples, as presented in *La novela de la revolución mexicana I* illustrate the use of fragmentation in the novels of the revolution. Martín Luis Guzmán's *El águila y la serpiente* (1928; The Eagle and the Serpent) is broken into two parts, each containing seven major sections that are further subdivided into from two to seven titled segments. Within these smaller sections, there is further fragmentation evidenced by a blank space occupied by a single asterisk. Guzmán's *La sombra del caudillo* (1929) also has subdivided major structural sections, here from three to seven in number. Although there is less fragmentation to be found among the smaller sections, it is called to the readers' attention by a gap on the page. José Vasconcelos's *Ulises Criollo* (1935) contains a total of 111 fragments, ranging in length from a minimum of two paragraphs to a maximum of ten pages.

2. Seymour Menton gives ample evidence of such negative response, citing passages from Manuel Pedro González, José Rojas Garcidueñas, and Luis Leal (1011, n. 3).

3. Portal describes the revised 1920 edition (Imprenta Razaster de México) as the model for succeeding versions. Citing the investigations of Professor Stanley L. Robe, she calls attention to an augmentation of some 5,400 words (66–67).

4. Translations of *Los de abajo* are by E. Munguía, Jr.

5. Although Menton perceives a triangular structural unity (1005; 1009–1010), he also refers to a circular route (1009).

6. The term *bola* is difficult to translate. It can be seen as a ball, with an inherent ability, once set in motion, of gaining momentum and losing control. Translators have also used more generalized terms like "the whole mess" or "fight."

7. It should be noted that Azuela prepares the way for Cervantes's descent by presenting his dubious motivation for joining the revolutionaries (23, 29).

8. This strange approximation of anaphora is paralleled by the series of "yo me robé" [I stole] that closes Part 2 (120), thus forming a frame to the second major segment, which, fittingly, focuses on barbarism.

9. Other references to narrations can be found on pages 71–72, 82, and 127.

10. Leal, *Mariano Azuela*, 57; E. Martínez 4. The technical and conceptual unity of these novels is evident from their being grouped in a special edition published by the Fondo de Cultura Económica (Ramos).

11. *Los de abajo* was not brought to full public attention until 1924.

12. Luis Leal notes some earlier activity among those who would become known as the *Contemporáneos* in the previous decade (1916–1918) ("Torres Bodet y los 'Contemporáneos,' " 291). A third group associated with the vanguard were the *agoristas*, who promoted social commitment as integral to the literary purview (Forster and Jackson 116).

13. For a discussion of this polemic within Mexican letters, see Brushwood (" 'Contemporáneos' and the Limits of Art," 128–132) and Schneider (*Ruptura y continuidad*, 159–189).

14. In *Idle Fictions: The Hispanic Vanguard Novel, 1926–1934*, Gustavo Pérez Firmat includes two others he considers essential within what he calls the "second movement of vanguard fiction—its transatlantic or American fiction" (20): José Martínez Sotomayor (*La rueca del aire*, 1930) and Eduardo Villaseñor (*Extasis*, 1928).

15. See, in particular, 19–25, 41, 48–49, 57–60.

16. This is termed "decharacterization" by Gustavo Pérez Firmat. See his Chapter 4, centered on the novels of Jaime Torres Bodet.

17. The inclusion of an asterisk makes the fragments easier to perceive. In the anthology of Torres Bodet's prose narrative, despite the fact that a new fragment is marked by a

paragraph with no indentation, a couple of separations are very easily missed. Furthermore, there is a discrepancy in the total number of fragments contained in *Proserpina rescatada*, with the original having one more than the later edition. Although in varying amounts, there is some degree of fragmentation in *Margarita de niebla, Proserpina rescatada, El retrato de míster Lehar, Estrella de día, Sombras,* and *Primero de enero.*

18. *La señorita Etcétera* had already been published in 1922 in *El Universal Ilustrado.*

19. As reprinted in Luis Mario Schneider's *El estridentismo*, the segments are one to two pages, but the pages are quite large.

20. Beth Miller suggests that Delfino's inability to truly capture or comprehend Proserpina's character is due more to his faults than to her ambiguous nature. As a doctor, he tries to analyze her scientifically, and her essence will not yield to such scrutiny (Miller 99–100). This would complement María José Bustos Fernández's assertion that the two constitute opposing versions of the "modern" condition, his being the practical, scientific, bourgeois approach and hers characterized as antibourgeois, apocalyptical, and irrational (19).

21. See, for example, 159, 179, 193, 201, 203, 204, and 207.

22. Pérez Firmat summarizes the attitude this way: "A one-hundred page narration, with wide margins and lots of metaphors, and with a female protagonist, cannot be the work of a man" (37).

23. Azuela has stated that la Malhora forgives the two, but the last passage could easily be interpreted as an act of vengeance.

24. E. Martínez argues that the techniques used in *La Malhora* are neither direct nor indirect interior monologue but constitute first-person monologue with flashbacks (29).

25. Levy argues for a more expanded interpretation of *luciérnaga* as a leitmotif of the novel and for a less flattering characterization of Conchita.

26. Wood mentions Azuela's call for reader participation specifically with regard to his use of time and space (193). See also E. Martínez (80–81, 86).

27. The Zócalo is Mexico City's main square.

## Chapter 3: Nationalist Literature

1. John Brushwood's comprehensive *Mexico in Its Novel* devotes a chapter to the years 1931 to 1946. Significantly, the chapter is called "The Mirror Image," connoting contemplation of self.

2. Many of the novels with a focus on the indigenous population have some degree of fragmentation, usually marked by a geometric arrangement of asterisks indicating a

change of scene or a pause, but occasionally by a blank space: Miguel Ángel Menéndez, *Nayar*, 1941; Miguel Lira, *Donde crecen los tepozanes*, 1947; Magdalena Mondragón, *Más allá existe la tierra*, 1947; Armando Chávez Camacho, *Cajeme, novela de indias*, 1948; Ramón Rubín, *El callado dolor de los tzotziles*, 1949; *El canto de la grilla*, 1952; *La bruma lo vuelve azul*, 1954; and *Cuando el Táguaro agoniza*, 1960.

3. Interestingly, John Akers has suggested that analogies in music rather than the visual arts (montage, mosaic, tapestry) be used to explicate strategies of fragmentation. *Al filo del agua* would seem to be a perfect example of his notion of an orchestrated work (131).

4. The English translation, by Anita Brenner, retains the Spanish title: *El indio* (New York: Frederick Ungar, 1961). Translations are from this edition.

5. Brenner leaves *gente de razón* (people of reason) in Spanish. In an added note she describes the term as used by whites and mestizos to distinguish themselves from the Indians (87).

6. In both the Colección Suma Veracruzana edition and the Botas illustrated edition (1937), the appended "Vocabulario" (Vocabulary) section is given the same treatment as if it were another chapter, making eight in Part 3.

7. This translation is my own.

8. The Botas edition contains photographs that accent dress and customs, including two depictions of the *volador* ritual.

9. See, among others, J. L. Martínez (30, 36), Fernández (307), Vázquez Amaral (247), Haddad (522), and Durand (333). It is important, however, to recall Mariano Azuela's early contribution to narrative experimentation in Mexican fiction in his innovative trilogy: *La Malhora* (1923), *El desquite* (1925) and *La luciérnaga* (1932).

10. Translations are by Ethel Brinton.

11. To facilitate location, references will be given first to chapter, then to the fragment. When direct passages are cited, a page number will be supplied and, when appropriate, both chapter and fragment numbers.

12. Dellapiane has an interesting discussion of a contrapuntal structure in *Al filo del agua*, although her focus is more on story than discourse (183). See also O'Neill ("El espacio en *Al filo del agua*," 239), Romano (70), and Bary (201).

13. Elaine Haddad cites Chapter 5 (523), while Rojas Garcidueñas argues for Chapter 8 (155). See also Brushwood ("La arquitectura," 103), who, although not actually defining the start of story, states that chapters 1 through 7 establish the thematics with which the novel is concerned.

14. This translation is my own.

15. The series of short translations up to this point in this paragraph are my own.

16. The presentation of Padre Islas's mental collapse is another example of this technique (341–344).

17. See also Merrell, who argues that both "Canicas" and "Victoria y Gabriel" best reflect what he considers an essential component of the text: the dialectical struggle between "sacred" and "profane," or between Divine Providence and free will (54–58).

18. The verb forms in Spanish are in the present tense, adding momentum and suspense.

19. Merrell adds another possibility of interpretation: the *bola* "can signify . . . the protoypical [*sic*] spherical object (marble) from the mechanistic secular view" (56), which fits into his discussion of a dialectical struggle.

20. Emphasis in original. The similarity in wording with the beginning of *Don Quijote* has, of course, been noted (Durand 335).

21. Dellapiane also notes the use of *interrogación retórica* [rhetorical interrogation] (202). For a textual example see (15;1).

22. For example, Haddad has identified frustration as a unifying theme (528), while Romano has chosen incommunication (62). The fact that Rojas Garcidueñas selects love and religion (162) and Durand an apocalyptic vision (333–334) as thematic unifiers suggests the notion of multiple possibilities of meaning stemming from a polysemic text.

23. Danny J. Anderson makes an interesting addition to the notion of individual characters as readers on a concrete level, demonstrating that the specific novels that the characters read are markers of their critical attitude toward or assimilation of society's values (50–59).

**Chapter 4: Addressing the Reading and Writing Process**

1. Aralia López González asserts that Vicens presents the first character in Mexican literature to show the clear effect of an anomic society, that is, one that is unstable, alienated, and disorganized ("Quebrantos, búsquedas y azares," 664).

2. At least one other novel from the 1950s should be mentioned for its narrative innovation: Carmen Rosenzweig's *1956*, which is characterized by spatial fragmentation, poetry mixed with prose, and a variety of technical experimentation.

3. In order to facilitate the location of references, two methods will be used, according to need: a fragment number or a page number.

4. Terry Peavler's *El texto en llamas* includes a discussion of the variations among editions (31–44).

5. See, for example, Luis Leal ("La estructura de *Pedro Páramo*," 46, 50). Carlos Blanco Aguinaga argues for two sections separated by a four-page "remanso" [backwater] (107). Samuel O'Neill agrees with Blanco Aguinaga's reasoning but calls the central section a "paralización transicional" [transitional immobilization] ("*Pedro Páramo*," 287).

6. The narrator is identified as Juan Preciado in fragment 25 (55).

7. The following are merely a few of the many examples: (a) It is mentioned in fragment 18 (44) that Toribio Aldrete was hanged. The contiguous fragment evidently tells of the murder, although it is only in segment 23 that one understands the motivation. (b) Susana's first mentioning of the name Florencio is ambiguous until readers later deduce that he was her first husband (128–129). (c) The strange presence of an unidentified woman in Donis's house is subsequently revealed to be his sister (70, 73).

8. There are numerous additional examples that come to reflect what appears to be an unusual number of words in *Pedro Páramo* that begin with the prefix *des* (Latin *dis:* from the idea of division, of the separation of a whole into parts). See 32, 96, 108, 117, 157.

9. See also Freeman's "La caída de gracia: Clave arquetípica de *Pedro Páramo*," in which he examines the episode of the incestuous couple as a key archetypal pattern.

10. Although speaking about a different medium, James Agee manages to capture the spirit of Rulfo's revolution in the following comment on the films of John Huston: "Most movies are made in the evident assumption that the audience is passive and wants to remain passive; every effort is made to do all the work—the seeing, the explaining, the understanding, even the feeling. Huston is one of the few movie artists who, without thinking twice about it, honors his audience. His pictures are not acts of seduction or of benign enslavement but of liberation, and they require, of anyone who enjoys them, the responsibilities of liberty. They continually open the eye and require it to move vigorously; and through the eye they awaken curiosity and intelligence. That, by any virile standard, is essential to good entertainment. It is unquestionably essential to good art" (Agee 329–330).

11. All references are to the first edition.

12. It should be noted that Vicens frequently wrote under a masculine pseudonym (Domenella 76) and spoke against the existence of masculine and feminine distinctions in narration (Saltz 81).

13. At one point José cites three paragraphs that he wrote in the second notebook but then adds that he rejected them (19–20).

14. Castillo et al. refer to the *Proceso de escritura* (the process of writing) in their semiotic analysis of *El libro vacío*.

15. Translations are by David Lauer (*The Empty Book,* Austin: University of Texas Press, 1992).

16. See, for example, 27–28 (in the translation, 11).

17. Castillo et al. list fourteen "microrrelatos" [ministories] (162–168).

### Chapter 5: Carlos Fuentes

1. Significantly, Yáñez's text is composed of a series of brief scenes that Karl Hölz calls a collage, adding that the author selected a structure that expresses the arbitrary and disordered movement of the city (68).

2. Although the year of publication is 1958, the "present" of the novel is 1951–1954. Furthermore, Richard Reeve demonstrates that portions of the text are taken from Fuentes's earlier stories and essays (37–39).

3. Translations are by Sam Hileman unless otherwise noted.

4. References are to the 4th edition, 1972 (9th printing, 1990).

5. See, among others, Zuluaga (90), Faris (17), Gómez Carro (111), Fernández Retamar (124), and Castro Arenas (46). Castro Arenas is quite specific in comparing *La región* to Rivera's mural in the Hotel del Prado in Mexico City.

6. See Zuluaga (82, 89). In an interview with Debra Castillo, Fuentes likens Ixca Cienfuegos to Lucifer, the only one able to serve as a guide in the night (158).

7. Wendy Faris makes the argument that Pola's rise is a fall and Robles's fall a rise (18).

8. This translation is my own.

9. Page numbers refer to the examples in *La región.*

10. In Spanish the key terms here are *no abrirse* and *no rajarse*—to not open oneself or let oneself be torn open.

11. This translation is my own, although Hileman's is close: "The city came apart" (Hileman 323).

12. See 122, 250, 315, and 329.

13. In his study of history and myth in Fuentes's works, Luis Leal argues: "Mexico City, as the modern version of ancient Tenochtitlán, is the center of the world" ("History and Myth," 7).

14. Zuluaga calls him the incarnation of the metropolis (85).

15. The association with the eagle and the serpent, of course, is based on the mythology of the founding of Mexico City.

16. See, among others, Zuluaga (84) and Faris (38).

17. Interestingly, José Emilio Pacheco notes the poetic quality of Fuentes's work in an early review ("La hora del lector," 19). In *Morirás lejos* (1967, revised 1977), Pacheco brings to fruition many of these techniques.

18. Some critics have argued for an ordered disorder in the arrangement, among them Sommers ("Individuo e historia," 148), Hammerly (211), and Dixon (93). Dixon aligns *Artemio Cruz* with baroque literature, specifically poetry, in which "apparently discordant and unbridled elements conform on close examination to a logical pattern" (93). See also Shaw, who presents an analysis of the ordering of episodes.

19. *La muerte de Artemio Cruz*, 1962; first edition in Letras Mexicanas, 1973. All citations are from this edition. Unless otherwise stated, translations are by Alfred Mac Adam.

20. The translation is mine. I disagree with Mac Adam here, for he attributes this to Catalina, saying "She didn't dare."

21. This translation is mine.

22. The fact that these join the *tú* and *él* sections reinforces the notion of twelve full cycles of *yo/tú/él* followed by two more, rather than an introductory *yo/tú* followed by twelve complete tripartite sections. Of course, it could also be considered a joiner of cycles within the latter interpretation. The lack of closure within the *tú* sections (they end in suspension points), however, tends to support the *yo/tú/él* construction. Lower sees a transitional connector between the *tú* and *él* sections in all twelve cycles (24).

23. One should recall that, in a diegetic flaw in *Citizen Kane*, no character is present to hear those last words.

24. Glaze makes brief mention of this process (119).

25. The lack of communication, of course, is not limited to Artemio's relationship with Catalina, nor is he the only character to exhibit this inhibition. Words are left unsaid between Lorenzo and Miguel, Artemio and Lunero, and Ludivinia and Pedro, relationships that should be intimate, as they represent, respectively, male comrades in the Spanish Civil War, boy and surrogate father, and mother with son. See Gyurko ("Self, Double, and Mask," 380–382).

26. Paz also uses the term *rajarse* (to split open), which is found in the same discussion in the novel: "déjeme morir sin que me raje" [let me die without spilling my guts] (197).

27. The translation is by Lysander Kemp.

28. This is generally translated as "son of a bitch," but there is a clear difference in meaning.

29. In addition, Lower argues that the *tú* sections have a mythic quality that makes both Artemio and the land symbolic (22).

30. See Sommers, who addresses the notion of cyclic history ("Individuo e historia," 150).

31. See Meyer-Minnemann for a thorough discussion of the fifty-two-year cycles and their relation to the novel ("*La muerte*," 90). In another article, Meyer-Minnemann delineates a miscalculation on Fuentes's part with regard to the exactness of the cycle in the novel ("Tiempo," 97–98). See also Shaw (140).

32. See Meyer-Minnemann, "*La muerte*," 94–95. See also Daniel de Guzmán, who addresses Fuentes's early political formation (65–68).

33. In the English translation, the four sections of *Agua quemada* are separated among a number of short prose pieces and not identified as the original material. The English translations of the four segments, in the order of the Spanish text, are: "Mother's Day," "These Were Palaces," "The Mandarin," and "The Son of Andrés Aparicio."

34. Translations are by Margaret Sayers Peden.

35. Andrés Aparicio complements a character from *La región más transparente*, Librado Ibarra, one of the few who actually try to implement the ideals promoted by the Mexican Revolution.

36. Obviously, the new rich have also targeted Pedregal, as is the case of Rodrigo Pola in *La región más transparente*, although his wife Pimpinela is from the old families.

37. The front cover varies among editions. This description applies to that of the first edition.

**Chapter 6: *Escritura***

1. See Spencer, whose analyses indicate a plenitude of fragmented novels in Europe in the sixties, specifically in France and Italy. In particular, Spencer examines Maurice Fourré's *Tete-de-Nègre* (1960), Michel Butor's *Mobile: Étude pour une représentation des Etats-Unis* (1962), Anaïs Nin's *Collages* (1964), Marc Saporta's *Composition No. 1* (1962), and Edoardo Sanguineti's *Capriccio italiano* (1963).

2. In her discussion Glantz makes reference to R. M. Albérès's *Métamorphoses de roman*, from which she offers the following translation: "esta tendencia se preocupa menos del

contenido de la novela que de su forma, de su escritura" [this tendency is less preoccupied with the content of the novel than with its form, its way of being written] (*Repeticiones*, 107). Glantz, however, appears to have made a mistake. This work was not by Albérès and not published in 1967. The author is Réné Marill and it was published in 1966.

3. Theda M. Herz points out that Juan José Arreola, whose *La feria* will be discussed as an example of *escritura* writing, also had a powerful influence on *Onda* writers and should not be limited to the former group (25).

4. Magda Graniela-Rodríguez adds as a characteristic of the *escritura* novels the inscription of an implied reader within the text (23). In recognition of the expanding readers' role in these novels, she refers also to the "Boom del lector" [the readers' Boom] (12).

5. Ostria reports forty identifiable voices (199).

6. To facilitate location, I have numbered the fragments and will give both the fragment and page numbers, in that order.

7. It is interesting that Arreola uses the same metaphor in *La feria* (155/100).

8. Translations are by John Upton, *The Fair* (Austin: University of Texas Press, 1977).

9. Sara Poot Herrera refers to the collectivization of the individuals in the confessional (163).

10. John Incledon argues for the reduction of characters to two: the author/narrator and his interlocutor, the reader (65, as cited in Graniela-Rodríguez 136–137).

11. The occurrences are too numerous to list completely, but the following should give some idea of frequency: "significativo" (105); "significación" (25, 170, 176); "significado" (13, 19, 29, 88, 89, 127, 132, 133, 136, 165, 166, 168, 173).

12. See, for example, pp. 17, 39, and 87.

13. Page numbers are from the revised 1977 edition unless otherwise stated.

14. Despite Pacheco's having removed other temporal markers in the second edition, one can gauge the year based on a reference to the house in which *eme* resides, repeatedly referred to as constructed in the year 1939, which Graniela-Rodríguez rightly associates with the German invasion of Poland. Toward the end of the novel, the narrator negates the existence of the house, saying it was destroyed fifteen years ago in 1951 (155). This would coincide with the dates given as the composition period of the first edition, March through December of 1966.

15. Future references in the text will read simply Jiménez de Báez.

16. For an extensive discussion of the parallelism between the two sections, see Cluff (29–31). Among the similarities are the specific temporal and psychological factors in-

volved in the siege and the method of determining the fate of prisoners with the simple movement of a thumb.

17. Translations are by Elizabeth Umlas, *You Will Die in a Distant Land* (North Miami: University of Miami, 1991).

18. Duncan (61) and Jiménez de Báez (212) argue that readers' choice of a *desenlace* is ideologically framed, as all possibilities include *eme*'s death or punishment, but there are exceptions, *desenlace 2*, for example.

19. In the text there is no period after "existir" nor in the numeral, which is consistent with the omission of punctuation in sections of heightened emotion in *Morirás lejos*. The effect of the graphic display is even more dramatic in the first edition, as it all falls on one page (58).

20. See Pfefferkorn, for example, for a discussion of the debate. In the following reference to this article, arguments are culled from other writers: T. W. Adorno and Alvin Rosenfeld. Pfefferkorn argues that the subject matter can, in fact, be treated in more conventional forms and gives various examples. See also Dorra (197).

21. Other series can be found on pages 14, 24, 69, 79, 86, 89, 91, 96, 99, 103, 116, 117, 133, 154, and 155.

22. There are further examples of lists displayed as such in the 1967 edition, for example on page 69. In general, the spacing is more experimental in the first edition. Regarding graphic form, see Dorra, who argues that *Morirás lejos* is a novel that must be *seen* (205).

23. Hancock ("Documentation," 104) discusses active reader participation, as do Saalman (95–96) and Jiménez de Báez (225), the latter two specifically with regard to the readers' being called upon to make a moral choice.

24. Graniela-Rodríguez individualizes reader activity: three by profession or function (as editor, as historian, and as critic) and two by nationality or ethnicity [a Jewish reader and a Mexican reader] (110–112).

25. Meléndez includes a discussion of the function of reader interventions (75–78).

26. See Ortega, who states that both men are many men ("Tres notas mexicanas," 670).

27. Interestingly, Pacheco has bridged the gender gap in the second edition, emphasizing the universalism even more. Previously the wording was "la letra que cada hombre lleva impresa en las manos" [the letter that is imprinted on the palms of man's hands] (112).

28. There was, in fact, another serial killer during the same period in Germany, a man named Haarmann, whose literal vampirism was depicted in a Rainer Werner Fassbinder film entitled *Zärtlichkeit der Wölfe* (1973) (Fischer, Hembus, and Sirk 84–86).

29. There is some ambiguity as to the base of the film in actual circumstances. Eisner states that $M$ is related neither to Kürten nor Haarmann (113).

30. Eisner gives no source for this direct quote from Lang.

### Chapter 7: *La Onda*

1. The authors Glantz selects are Juan Tovar, Gerardo de la Torre, Eugenio Chávez, Xorge del Campo, Elsa Cross, Eduardo Naval, Roberto Páramo, Manuel Farill, Juan Ortuño, René Avilés, and José Agustín (82–87). In "Onda y escritura en México," Glantz deletes many of these names and adds Héctor Manjarrez, Jorge Aguilar Mora, Parménides García Saldaña, Orlando Ortiz, and Juan Manuel Torres. The fluctuation in names is indicative of the disagreement among critics as to who should be included as *Onda* writers. The only three about whom there appears to be complete accord are Agustín, Sainz, and García Saldaña, who constitute Reinhard Teichmann's short list of those within the group (Teichmann 14).

2. Chiu-Olivares continues with an examination of Sainz and Agustín's later works and a discussion of Armando Ramírez, who is not really associated with the *Onda* but, according to Chiu-Olivares, shares certain characteristics with Sainz and Agustín. Ramírez is more appropriately grouped with the authors in Chapter 8 who join *Onda* writers in giving voice to those marginalized in Mexican society but are not part of the *Onda* set.

3. See Teichmann's interviews with José Agustín (60–65), René Avilés Fabila (85–86), and Federico Arana (184–185). In an interview Agustín has stated that *De perfil* does not belong to *la Onda* (Mier and Carbonell 62).

4. Interestingly, Glantz employs an image of fragmentation to refer to the identity crisis of the youths of the *Onda:* "el espejo que lo refleja se fragmenta antes de que su imagen se clarifique" [the mirror that reflects him breaks into fragments before his image can become clear] (*Repeticiones*, 91).

5. In "La naturaleza de la Onda," Carlos Monsiváis refers to movement from clandestinity to center stage with regard to Mexican youth in the social movement known as the *Onda* (227).

6. Inke Müller presents a résumé of the treatment of adolescents in earlier Mexican novels, concluding that as a literary theme adolescence had been only marginally addressed, either from a remote retrospective point or with characters who lacked authenticity (78–79).

7. Cynthia Steele adds that *Onda* writers also reject "the social realist aesthetic and solemnity characteristic of the Novel of the Mexican Revolution and the Muralist movement" (113).

8. In the English translation by Hardie St. Martin (New York: Farrar, Straus and Giroux, 1968), the title remains *Gazapo.*

9. As originally published by Joaquín Mortiz. Page references, however, are from the Aguilar, León and Cal edition of 1989, which is now more available. The translations are my own.

10. Inke Gunia estimates the ages of the youths as 14–18 (49).

11. Brown concludes that there are thirty-one fragments. It is important to note that there are discrepancies between the two editions. The 1989 text shows a new fragment on page 136 beginning with the words "Vulbo arranca" (Vulbo starts the car) that does not appear in the Joaquín Mortiz edition. Despite the fact that in the Aguilar, León y Cal edition the fragments are also marked by a lack of indentation in the beginning paragraph, there are still confusions most likely attributable to printing errors. On page 24, for example, there is no indentation, usually a marker of a new fragment, yet there is no blank space. The Mortiz edition places a break there.

12. According to Gunia, the photographs start with the second edition (75).

13. Brown gives a chronological ordering in his article (238–239). See also Gunia, 309–317.

14. As noted, Pacheco expands upon this experimentation in *Morirás lejos.*

15. See 130 and 133; 127 and 137; 131 and 137.

16. The first verb in the narrative is *contar,* to tell a story.

17. The author's full name is José Agustín Ramírez Gómez (Kirk, "Development of an *Ondero,*" 10), but he prefers to omit the surnames.

18. Steele argues that Agustín's works become increasingly political (19, 110). According to Monsiváis, the social movement called the *Onda* was apolitical from the start ("La naturaleza," 234).

19. The anonymity also occasions a number of evasions employed throughout the text to avoid naming the character, much as Rulfo did with the character Abundio. Early in the novel, when the narrator meets someone new, one reads: "Le dije mi nombre" [I told him my name] (24). Later he criticizes his friend, Ricardo, for referring to him in his diary as "X" (161, 339).

20. Stella Clark points out that by targeting this inclusive group, Agustín also denies access to those not familiar with the adolescent milieu and language (109).

21. There seems to be some discrepancy among editions, as Chiu-Olivares places the repetition on page 264 of the sixth edition (43).

22. *Cafés cantantes* had a brief existence in Mexico City between 1959 and 1965. According to Müller, they were raided by police and closed in response to a newspaper campaign against vice-ridden lairs (76).

23. See also Brenner (1943 edition, 18).

24. The parallel with *La muerte de Artemio Cruz* is strong here. See 184 and 194 in Fuentes's novel.

25. Both Agustín and Manjarrez include homosexual characters in their novels. In *De perfil* these include the record promoter and Toto, a member of the rock band. It is more than hinted that Octavio begins a relationship with the record promoter, and even the narrator's sexuality is called into question. In yet another repetition, he admits twice that he has never been greatly interested in sex (7, 133). When he attempts to have sex with Queta, he is at first impotent, prompting her to call him a *maricón* [queer] (144). In a fantasized sequence, the narrator saves Octavio from Toto and then kills Octavio and has violent sex with Queta on the youth's body (131–132). As a final note of ambiguity, while showering he imagines cutting his pubic hair until it resembles Queta's (256).

26. For a discussion of the literary response to Tlatelolco, see both Young and Gyurko ("Literary Response").

27. Manjarrez describes himself as a middle-class rebel, one of the first dropouts from education and everything else. He left Mexico for Europe at the age of 17, living in Yugoslavia, France, Turkey, and then England (Campbell v).

28. There is some discrepancy as to the age of the two figures. In an interview, Manjarrez refers to the younger as an 18-year-old and the other as being around 40 (Teichmann 206). Schaffer gives their ages as 28 and 43 (223). Coordinates from the text are somewhat ambiguous, as the initial temporal presentation is vague: "196 ." (*Lapsus* 11), but in Chapter 3 the date is listed as October 2, 1968. Significantly, this is the date of the Tlatelolco massacre, and it is the only specific date in the novel. Manjarrez, however, has given the time frame of the novel as 1967–1969 (Teichmann 206), and, within the text, the birth years of the men are listed as 1928 and 1943.

29. In fact, the men are referred to in the text at one point as Hubert et Humbert. This intertextual reference is merely one of many nexuses to sources both literary and cultural, cinematic and musical. Literary influences are clear from Julio Cortázar's *Rayuela*, Vladimir Nabokov's *Lolita*, William Burroughs's *Naked Lunch*, and Cabrera Infante's *Tres tristes tigres*. As well, Manjarrez demonstrates his awareness of contemporary cultural criticism and theory, with specific mention of Marshall McLuhan, Michel Foucault, and Jacques Lacan. Homage is paid to the musical greats of the time, including the standard *Onda* reverence for the Beatles, Mick Jagger, Bob Dylan, and Janis Joplin, as well as to Charlie "Bird" Parker.

30. The reference is clearly to Marshall McLuhan's *The Medium is the Massage*, an important book of cultural commentary from the sixties.

31. Indeed, technical innovation was so standard by this point that Manjarrez speaks of experimenting with realism in his 1987 novel, *Pasaban en silencio nuestros dioses* (Our Gods Passed by in Silence), since it was in such disuse (Teichmann 216).

### Chapter 8: Writing from the Margins

1. In *Space, Time and Structure in the Modern Novel*, Spencer indicates a plenitude of fragmented novels in France and Italy in the 1960s. In particular, she mentions Maurice Fourré's *Tête-de-Nègre* (1960), Michel Butor's *Mobile: Étude pour une représentation des Etats-Unis* (1962), Anaïs Nin's *Collages* (1964), Marc Saporta's *Composition No. 1* (1962), and Edoardo Sanguineti's *Capriccio italiano* (1963).

2. Fuentes continues into the 1970s with a fragmented structure in *Terra nostra* (1975) but subsequently with some novels appears to move away from segmentation and toward a more traditional presentation of story. *La cabeza de la hidra* (1978), although containing fifty segments within a larger four-part structure, has sections of fairly uniform length. In *Una familia lejana* (1980) and *Gringo viejo* (1985), Fuentes abandons fragmentation altogether. On the other hand, *Agua quemada* (1981), *Cristóbal Nonato* (1987), and *La campaña* (1990) are segmented.

3. Rulfo continues to be associated, however, with experimental narrative. The 1964 Rubén Gómez film, *La fórmula secreta* (The Secret Formula) is based on Rulfo's writing. Critics have described the film as a "poetic essay" (Paranaguá 246) and as a non-narrative piece (Noriega and Ricci 76). Chon Noriega and Steven Ricci summarize *La fórmula secreta* as a work that "uniquely synthesizes sound and images into a cinematic collage. It is an experimental examination of the cultural and economic effects of foreign influences on Mexican life. This montage format manipulates elements of Mexican society, fusing urban and rural, mythic and real. The film relies on metaphor and a macabre sense of humor as a means of questioning national identity, power structures, and religious beliefs" (76). Once again, fragmentation is instrumental in provoking thought about Mexicanness and about atomization as a product of transnational influences.

4. The following is a partial list of the many novels written during this period that contain some degree of fragmentation: 1970: *Nudo*, Sergio Galindo; 1971: *Cadáver lleno de mundo*, Jorge Aguilar Mora; *El gran solitario de palacio*, René Avilés Fabila; *Lapsus*, Héctor Manjarrez; *Con él, conmigo, con nosotros tres*, María Luisa Mendoza; 1973: *Las jiras*, Federico Arana; 1974: . . . *y te sacarán los ojos*, Salvador Mendiola; 1976: *Las rojas son las carreteras*, David Martín del Campo; 1977: *Las muertas*, Jorge Ibargüengoitia; 1978: *Las mil y una calorías, novela dietética*, Margo Glantz; 1979: *Violación en Polanco*, Armando Ramírez; *Si muero lejos de ti*, Jorge Aguilar Mora; *El vampiro de la Colonia Roma*, Luis Za-

pata; *Violeta-Perú*, Luis Arturo Ramos; 1980: *Muertes de aurora*, Gerardo de la Torre; *¿ABCDErio o ABeCeDamo?*, Daniel Leyva; *Casi en silencio*, Aline Pettersson; *Cuando el aire es azul*, María Luisa Puga; *Lampa vida*, Daniel Sada; 1981: *El sol que estás mirando*, Jesús Gardea; *Doscientas ballenas azules . . . y . . . cuatro caballos*, Margo Glantz; 1982: *Que la carne es hierba*, Marco Antonio Campos; *Octavio*, Jorge Arturo Ojeda; 1983: *La decadencia del dragón*, Héctor Aguilar Camín; *Las púberes canéforas*, José Joaquín Blanco; *Utopía gay*, José Rafael Calva; *El tornavoz*, Jesús Gardea; 1984: *Soñar la guerra*, Jesús Gardea; *Síndrome de naufragios*, Margo Glantz; *Una piñata llena de memoria*, Daniel Leyva; 1985: *Las horas vivas*, Mónica de Neymet; *Los músicos y el fuego*, Jesús Gardea; *Chin-Chin el teporocho*, Armando Ramírez; *Sóbol*, Jesús Gardea; *Arráncame la vida*, Angeles Mastretta; *Las líneas de la mano*, Hortensia Moreno; *Quinceañera*, Armando Ramírez; *Ahora que me acuerdo*, Agustín Ramos; *en jirones*, Luis Zapata; 1986: *Sombra ella misma*, Aline Pettersson; 1987: *Mejor desaparece*, Carmen Boullosa; *Isla de lobos*, David Martín del Campo; *La noche de San Barnabé*, Víctor Alfonso Maldonado; *La forma del silencio*, María Luisa Puga; *Casas de encantamiento*, Ignacio Solares; 1988: *La "Flor de Lis,"* Elena Poniatowska; *Este era un gato . . .* , Luis Arturo Ramos; 1989: *Antes*, Carmen Boullosa; *Semejanza del juego*, Daniel González Dueñas; *Amora*, Rosamaría Roffiel; *Madero, el otro*, Ignacio Solares; 1990: *Dos mujeres*, Sara Levi Calderón; *La señora Rodríguez y otros mundos*, Martha Cerda; *La campaña*, Carlos Fuentes; 1991: *Son vacas, somos puercos*, Carmen Boullosa; *En cuerpo y alma*, Mónica Mansour; *La muerte alquila un cuarto*, Gabriela Rábago Palafox; *Posesión*, Margo Su; 1992: *Llanto: Novelas imposibles*, Carmen Boullosa; *Amor propio*, Gonzalo Celorio; *La ventana hundida*, Jesús Gardea; *Dulcinea encantada*, Angelina Muñiz-Huberman; *Novia que te vea*, Rosa Nissán; *Los colores del principio*, Alicia Trueba; 1993: *La casa del ahorcado*, Luis Arturo Ramos; 1994: *Duerme*, Carmen Boullosa.

5. The surge in women's writing, particularly in the 1980s, has been referred to as the "boom femenino" (the feminine boom) although at times in a disparaging way according to López González ("Quebrantos," 659, n. 1). Elena Poniatowska uses the term *boomcito* [little boom] ("Ser un escritor," 19). This increase in women's writing is visible throughout Latin America (see, among others, Álvaro Salvador).

6. Among writers of gay fiction, there is a marked tendency to use first-person narration. The authors literally give voice to a formerly marginalized group, making them the center of the narration, as Torres-Rosado has noted in the case of *El vampiro de la Colonia Roma* (277). There is no mediation; the characters are allowed direct access to readers. In addition to the novels examined here, see Miguel Barbachano Ponce's *El diario de José Toledo* (1964), which according to David William Foster is Mexico's first novel with a homosexual theme ("Social Pact," 92), José Ceballos Maldonado's *Después de todo* (1969), Jorge Arturo Ojeda's *Octavio* (1982), and José Rafael Calva's *Utopía gay* (1983). With the exception of Ceballos's text, all are fragmented. A less consistent, yet fairly common conceit employed in these novels is the format of a diary, conveying a sense of intimacy between readers and narrator.

7. The first edition uses a lowercase *e* at the beginning of the first word, although subsequent editions use uppercase.

8. A feminization of the Spanish word for love.

9. Elena Poniatowska, of course, contributed an earlier fragmented picaresque revival deeply rooted in twentieth-century reality, *Hasta no verte Jesús mío* (1969), with a female protagonist, Jesusa Palancares.

10. Alicia Covarrubias restricts the role of *amo* to Adonis's lovers (185).

11. Translations are by E. A. Lacey.

12. Foster calls *en jirones* "by far the most sexually explicit gay novel published so far in Mexico, perhaps in Latin America" (*Gay and Lesbian Themes*, 37).

13. See pages 99, 107, 110, 125, and 134.

14. See, for example, 50, 139, 172-173, and 251.

15. This is the translation used by Steele (155). It should be noted, however, that the absence of a subject pronoun in Spanish leaves uncertainty. The subject could be "you," "he," or "she," as well as "it." Gabriella de Beer chooses *Better Disappear* (8).

16. Federico Patán sees the *niña quemada* as a symbol of the world that de Neymet examines (*Los nuevos territorios*, 96).

17. See also 127, 173.

18. Patán finds this final happiness extreme (*Los nuevos territorios*, 97).

19. The novel was actually written much earlier, in 1980 (Pfeiffer 43).

20. Again, one should be aware of other subject possibilities.

21. One must be careful, of course, not to attribute too much autobiographical emphasis to the novel. Boullosa insists that her characters are fictitious, although she also reports having devoured her childhood diaries in preparation for the writing project (Pfeiffer 40).

22. Boullosa describes her own formation thus: "me educaron en una familia católica, católica, católica, rígida, burguesa, ordenada, el colegio de monjas, y además de niñas muy ricas, sólo mujeres" [they educated me in a Catholic, Catholic, Catholic family, rigid, bourgeois, in perfect order, a nun's school with only rich little girls] (Pfeiffer 32).

23. Susan Wehling's article on Boullosa's play, *Cocinar hombres* (To Cook Men), confirms that memory, childhood, and the deconstruction of patriarchal mythology are recurring themes in her work (51-53).

24. Boullosa's subsequent books do turn to historical issues: *Son vacas, somos puercos* (1991; They Are Cows, We Are Pigs) and *Llanto: Novelas imposibles* (1992; Weeping: Im-

possible Novels). The latter novel, in fact, includes a confrontation among three present-day Mexican women and Motecuhzoma (Moctezuma), not only dramatizing the suggested feminine perspective of historical events but also confirming the criticism of Mexico in the 1990s.

25. In another context, Alfonso González, among others, identifies Mexico's "crisis" as economically based. Although this is indeed the term employed to refer to Mexico's financial troubles in 1982, Puga's vision is much more encompassing.

26. In an earlier novel, *Pánico o peligro* (1983; Panic or Danger), Puga dramatizes the search for identity by the individual. Her protagonist, Susana (no surname is provided), through writing, is able to question prevailing social discourse and to achieve a deeper level of consciousness (López González, "Nuevas formas," 5–6).

27. Puga uses the adjective "North-American" in the text to refer to the United States. It is a common misnomer in Mexico, yet here may, in fact, contribute to her characterization of Mexico's nonexistence as a culture. In Puga's narrative Mexicans voluntarily reject their culture in order to favor jeans, Coke, and Dairy Queen. Canada does not figure into the equation at all. For Puga, the Estados Unidos Mexicanos (Mexican United States) would appear to have more than one meaning, one as a national name, another as a country that cedes identity through appropriation of a different culture's practices.

28. Originally *peseros* were cabs that would provide a ride along Insurgentes or Reforma for one peso. Drivers would assume a maximum capacity of some four passengers and drive with one hand outside the vehicle indicating how many seats were available. One could then flag the car at any point, thus joining the strangers inside for the desired distance.

29. The translation is difficult here. In English, the word *people* has no gender and is used in the plural. The Spanish, with the emphasis on the feminine, is most provocative.

30. This "Northamericanization" has roots in England, where Halls are made.

# BIBLIOGRAPHY

Adams, M. Ian. *Three Authors of Alienation: Bombal, Onetti, Carpentier.* Austin: University of Texas Press, 1975.

Agee, James. *Agee on Film: Reviews and Comments by James Agee I.* New York: Grosset and Dunlap, 1969.

Aguilar Mora, Jorge. *Cadáver lleno de mundo.* Mexico City: Joaquín Mortiz, 1971.

Agustín, José. "Cuál es la onda." *Diálogos* 10.55 (Jan.–Feb. 1974): 11–13.

———. *De perfil.* Mexico City: Joaquín Mortiz, 1966. 2nd ed., 1967.

———. *La tumba.* Mexico City: Mester, 1964.

Akers, John C. "Fragmentation in the Chicano Novel: Literary Technique and Cultural Identity." *Revista Chicano-Riqueña* 13.3–4 (1985): 121–35.

Altamirano, Aldo-José. "La selva en el damero: la evolución del espacio urbano latinoamericano." In *La selva en el damero: Espacio literario y espacio urbano en América Latina.* Ed. Rosalba Campra. Pisa: Giardini, 1989. 17–25.

Anderson, Danny J. "Reading, Social Control, and the Mexican Soul in *Al filo del agua.*" *Mexican Studies/Estudios Mexicanos* 11.1 (Winter 1995): 45–73.

Arguedas, Ledda. "Ciudad de México: Entre el mito y la política." In *La selva en el damero: Espacio literario y espacio urbano en América Latina.* Ed. Rosalba Campra. Pisa: Giardini, 1989. 47–57.

Armour, Robert A. *Fritz Lang.* Boston: Twayne Publishers, 1978.

Arreola, Juan José. *Confrontaciones: Los narradores ante el público.* Mexico City: Joaquín Mortiz, 1966.

———. *La feria.* Mexico City: Joaquín Mortiz, 1963. 6th (rev.) ed., 1971.

Azuela, Mariano. *Los de abajo.* 1915. 3rd ed. Mexico City: Fondo de Cultura Económica, 1964.

———. *El desquite.* 1925. In *3 novelas de Mariano Azuela.* 6th ed. Mexico City: Fondo de Cultura Económica (Colección Popular), 1968.

———. *La luciérnaga.* 1932. In *3 novelas de Mariano Azuela.* 6th ed. Mexico City: Fondo de Cultura Económica (Colección Popular), 1968.

———. *La Malhora.* 1923. In *3 novelas de Mariano Azuela.* 6th ed. Mexico City: Fondo de Cultura Económica (Colección Popular), 1968.

———. "El novelista y su ambiente [II]." In *Azuela: Obras completas III.* Mexico City: Fondo de Cultura Económica, 1960.

———. *Obras completas I.* Mexico City: Fondo de Cultura Económica, 1958.

———. *The Underdogs.* Trans. Enrique Munguía. New York: Brentano's, 1929.

Bakhtin, Mikhail. *Problems of Dostoevsky's Poetics.* Trans. R. W. Rotsel. Ann Arbor: University of Michigan Press, 1973.

Barbachano Ponce, Miguel. *El diario de José Toledo.* Mexico City: n.p., 1964.

Barthes, Roland. *S/Z: An Essay.* Trans. Richard Miller. New York: Hill and Wang, 1974.

Bartra, Roger. *La jaula de la melancolía.* Mexico City: Grijalbo, 1987.

Bary, David. "Poesía y narración en cuatro novelas mexicanas." *Cuadernos Americanos* 234.1 (1981): 198–210.

Basave Benítez, Agustín. *México mestizo: Análisis del nacionalismo mexicano en torno a la mestizofilia de Andrés Molina Enríquez.* Mexico City: Fondo de Cultura Económica, 1992.

Bataille, Georges. *Les Larmes d'Eros.* Paris: Jean-Jacques Pauvert, 1971.

Beitchman, Philip. "The Fragmentary Word." *Sub-Stance* 12.2 [39] (1983): 58–74.

Blanco, José Joaquín. *Crónica de la literatura reciente en México (1950–1980).* Mexico City: Instituto Nacional de Antropología e Historia, 1982.

———. Introduction. *Adonis García: A Picaresque Novel.* San Francisco: Gay Sunshine Press, 1981.

Blanco Aguinaga, Carlos. "Realidad y estilo de Juan Rulfo." *Revista Mexicana de Literatura* 1.1 (1955): 59–86. Rpt. in *Nueva novela latinoamericana I.* Ed. J. Lafforgue. Buenos Aires: Paidós, 1969. 85–113.

Bonfil Batalla, Guillermo. *Pensar nuestra cultura.* Mexico City: Alianza, 1991.

Boullosa, Carmen. *Antes.* Mexico City, Vuelta, 1989.

———. *Llanto: Novelas imposibles.* Mexico City, Era, 1992.

———. *Mejor desaparece.* Mexico City: Océano, 1987.

———. *Son vacas, somos puercos.* Mexico City, Era, 1991.

Bowers, Fredson, ed., *Vladimir Nabokov: Lectures on Literature.* New York: Harcourt Brace Jovanovich, 1968.

Brenner, Anita. *The Wind That Swept Mexico: The History of the Mexican Revolution of 1910–1942.* 1943. Second paperback printing. Austin: University of Texas Press, 1989.

Brown, James. "*Gazapo:* Novela para armar." *Nueva Narrativa Hispanoamericana* 3.2 (Sept. 1973): 237–44.

Bruce-Novoa, Juan. "*La Onda* as Parody and Satire." In *José Agustín: Onda and Beyond.* Ed. June C. D. Carter and Donald L. Schmidt. Columbia: University of Missouri Press, 1986. 37–55.

Brushwood, John S. "La arquitectura de las novelas de Agustín Yáñez." In *Homenaje a Agustín Yáñez*. Ed. Helmy F. Giacoman. Madrid: A. G. Ibarra, 1973. 97–115.

———. "Art and Trivia: Narratives by José Agustín." In *José Agustín: Onda and Beyond*. Ed. June C. D. Carter and Donald L. Schmidt. Columbia: University of Missouri Press, 1986. 56–67.

———. "'Contemporáneos' and the Limits of Art." *Romance Notes* 5.2 (1964): 128–32.

———. *Mexico in Its Novel: A Nation's Search for Identity*. Austin: University of Texas Press, 1966.

———. *Narrative Innovation and Political Change in Mexico*. New York: Peter Lang, 1989.

———. *La novela mexicana (1967–1982)*. Mexico City: Grijalbo, 1984.

———. Rev. of *Antes* by Carmen Boullosa. *CHASQUI* 19.1 (May 1990): 118–119.

Burgos, Fernando. "*Proserpina rescatada*: Metáforas de una metamorfosis." In *De la crónica a la nueva narrativa mexicana: Coloquio sobre literatura mexicana*. Ed. Merlin H. Forster and Julio Ortega. Mexico City: Oasis, 1986. 139–149.

Bustos Fernández, María José. "Resistencia a la modernidad en *Proserpina rescatada* de Jaime Torres Bodet." *Hispanófila* 38.3 (May 1995): 17–29.

Cabrera Infante, Guillermo. *Tres tristes tigres*. 1965. 2nd ed. Barcelona: Seix Barral, 1968.

Calva, José Rafael. *Utopía gay*. Mexico City: Oasis, 1983.

Campbell, Federico. "Que todos volvamos a ser humanos." *Siempre* 884 (June 3, 1970): iv–viii.

Campobello, Nellie. *Cartucho: Relatos de la lucha en el norte de México*. Mexico City: Integrales, 1931. 2nd ed., Mexico City: EDIAPSA, 1940.

Carballo, Emmanuel. "Agustín Yáñez." In *Homenaje a Agustín Yáñez*. Ed. Helmy F. Giacoman. Madrid: A. G. Ibarra, 1973. 13–62.

———. *Diecinueve protagonistas de la literatura mexicana del siglo XX*. Mexico City: Empresas Editoriales, 1965.

Carter, June C. D., and Donald L. Schmidt. "Introduction." In *José Agustín: Onda and Beyond*. Ed. June C. D. Carter and Donald L. Schmidt. Columbia: University of Missouri Press, 1986. 1–8.

Cassedy, Steven Dennis. "The Novel of Fragmentation: Belyj, Rilke, and Proust." Diss. Princeton University, 1979.

Castañeda, Jorge G. *The Mexican Shock: Its Meaning for the U.S.* New York: The New Press, 1995.

Castellanos, Rosario. "La juventud: Un tema, una perspectiva, un estilo." *Espejo* 6 (1968): 51–61. Rpt. in *La crítica de la novela mexicana contemporánea*. Ed. Aurora M. Ocampo. Mexico City: UNAM. 1981. 175–190.

Castillo, Debra A. "Travails with Time: An Interview with Carlos Fuentes." *Review of Contemporary Fiction* 8.2 (Summer 1988): 153–165.

Castillo, Florencia, et al. "Sentido e interpretación en *El libro vacío*." *Semiosis: Seminario de Semiótica, Teoría, Análisis* 18 (Jan.–June 1987): 149–197.

Castro Arenas, Mario. "Carlos Fuentes: La revolución frustrada." *Revista Nacional de Cultura* 224 (April–May 1976): 44–60.

Ceballos Maldonado, José. *Después de todo*. Mexico City: Diógenes, 1969.

Chatman, Seymour. *Story and Discourse: Narrative Structure in Fiction and Film*. Ithaca: Cornell University Press, 1978.

Chávarri, Raúl. "Arreola en su varia invención." *Cuadernos Hispanoamericanos* 81 (1970): 418–425.

Chiu-Olivares, M. Isela. *La novela mexicana contemporánea (1960–1980)*. Madrid: Pliegos, 1990.

Clark, Stella T. "A Glossary of the Language of the Early Novels." In *José Agustín: Onda and Beyond*. Ed. June C. D. Carter and Donald L. Schmidt. Columbia: University of Missouri Press, 1986. 109–117.

Cluff, Russell M. "*Morirás lejos*: Mosaico intemporal de la crueldad humana." *CHASQUI: Revista de Literatura Latino americana* 8.2 (1979): 19–36.

Colina, José de la. "Notas sobre Juan Rulfo." *Casa de las Américas* (Havana) 4.26 (1964): 133–138. Rpt. in *Recopilación de textos sobre Juan Rulfo*. Ed. Antonio Benítez Rojo. Havana: Casa de las Américas, 1969. 47–56.

———. "Susana San Juan, el mito femenino en *Pedro Páramo*." *Universidad de México* 19.8 (1965): 19–21. Rpt. in *La narrativa de Juan Rulfo: Interpretaciones críticas*. Ed. Joseph Sommers. Mexico City: Sep/Setentas, 1974. 60–66.

Collier, George A. *Basta! Land and the Zapatista Rebellion in Chiapas*. Monroe, OR: Institute for Food and Development Policy, 1994.

Coronado, Juan. Introduction. *De la poesía a la prosa en el mismo viaje: Gilberto Owen*. Mexico City: Consejo Nacional para la Cultura y las Artes (Lecturas Mexicanas 27), 1990.

Cortázar, Julio. "Casa tomada." In his *Bestiario*. Buenos Aires: Sudamericana, 1951. 9–18.

———. *Rayuela*. Buenos Aires: Editorial Sudamericana, 1963.

Covarrubias, Alicia. "*El vampiro de la Colonia Roma*: La nueva picaresca y el reportaje ficticio." *Revista de Crítica Literaria Latinoamericana* 20.39 (1994): 183–197.

Crosman, Inge. "Annotated Bibliography of Audience-Oriented Criticism." In *The Reader in the Text: Essays on Audience and Interpretation*. Ed. Susan R. Suleiman and Inge Crosman. Princeton: Princeton University Press, 1980. 401–424.

Culler, Jonathan. *Structuralist Poetics: Structuralism, Linguistics and the Study of Literature*. Ithaca, N.Y.: Cornell University Press, 1975.

Dalton, Margarita. *Larga sinfonía en D y había una vez . . .* Mexico City: Diógenes, 1968.

Danel Janet, Fernando, and Federico Ortiz Quezada. *Patologías de la Ciudad de México*. Mexico City: Némesis, 1991.

Dauster, Frank. *Xavier Villaurrutia*. New York: Twayne, 1971.

de Beer, Gabriella. "Mexican Women Writers of Today." *Latin American Literature and Arts* 48 (Spring 1994): 6–9.

Dellapiane, Angela B. "Releyendo *Al filo del agua*." *Cuadernos Americanos* 201 (1975): 182–206.

Dixon, Paul B. "*La muerte de Artemio Cruz* and Baroque Correlative Poetry." *Hispanófila* 28.3 (1985): 93–102.

Domenella, Ana Rosa. "Josefina Vicens y *El libro vacío:* Sexo biográfico femenino y género masculino." In *Mujer y literatura mexicana y chicana: Culturas en contacto 2.* Ed. Aralia López González et al. Mexico City: El Colegio de México, 1990. 75–80.

Domínguez Colavita, Federica. "*Gazapo* de Gustavo Sainz: Tema y estructura." *Revista Interamericana* 10.2 (Summer 1980): 188–194.

Dorra, Raúl. "*Morirás lejos:* La ética en la escritura" In *José Emilio Pacheco ante la crítica.* Ed. Hugo J. Verani. Mexico City: Universidad Autónoma Metropolitana, 1987. 195–209.

Duncan, J. Ann. *Voices, Visions, and a New Reality: Mexican Fiction since 1970.* Pittsburgh: University of Pittsburgh Press, 1986.

Durán, Manuel. Rev. of *La región más transparente,* by Carlos Fuentes. *Revista Mexicana de Literatura* 1 (Jan.–May 1959): 78–81.

———. *Tríptico mexicano.* Mexico City: Sep/Setentas, 1973.

Durand, Frank. "The Apocalyptic Vision of *Al filo del agua.*" *Symposium* 25 (1971): 333–346.

Eisner, Lotte. *Fritz Lang.* London: Martin Secker and Warburg, 1976. Trans. Gertrud Mander. London: Oxford University Press, 1977.

Elizondo, Salvador. "Autobiografía." In *Nuevos escritores mexicanos del siglo XX presentados por sí mismos.* Ed. Emmanuel Carballo. Mexico City: Empresas Editoriales, 1966.

———. *Farabeuf o la crónica de un instante.* Mexico City: Joaquín Mortiz, 1965.

Escalante, Evodio. "La narrativa mexicana en la encrucijada de los ochenta." In his *La intervención literaria.* Alebrije, Mexico: Universidad Autónoma de Sinaloa, Universidad Autónoma de Zacatecas, 1988. 9–16.

Espinasa, José María. "El texto testigo de sí mismo." In his *Hacia el otro.* Mexico City: UNAM, 1990. 141–153.

Estrada, Ricardo. "Los indicios de *Pedro Páramo.*" *Universidad de San Carlos* (Guatemala) 45 (1965): 67–85. Rpt. in *Recopilación de textos sobre Juan Rulfo.* Ed. Antonio Benítez Rojo. Havana: Casa de las Américas, 1969. 110–132.

Faris, Wendy B. *Carlos Fuentes.* New York: Frederick Ungar, 1983.

Faulkner, William. *The Sound and the Fury.* 1931. London: Vantage, 1995.

Fernández, Magali. "Análisis comparativo de las obras de Agustín Yáñez y William Faulkner (especialmente de sus novelas *Al filo del agua* y *As I Lay Dying*)." In *Homenaje a Agustín Yáñez.* Ed. Helmy F. Giacoman. Madrid: A. G. Ibarra, 1973. 297–317.

Fernández Retamar, Roberto. "Carlos Fuentes y la otra novela de la Revolución Mexicana." *Casa de las Américas* 4.26 (Oct.–Nov. 1964): 123–128.

Fish, Stanley E. "Literature in the Reader: Affective Stylistics." In his *Self-Consuming Artifacts: The Experience of Seventeenth-Century Literature.* Berkeley: University of California Press, 1973. 383–427.

Fischer, Robert, Joe Hembus, and Vorwort Douglass Sirk. *Der Neue Deutsche Film 1960–1980.* Munich: Goldmann, 1981.

Fogelson, Robert. *The Fragmented Metropolis: Los Angeles 1850– 1930*. Cambridge, Mass.: Harvard University Press, 1967.

Forster, E. M. *Aspects of the Novel.* 1927. Harmondsworth: Penguin, 1990.

Forster, Merlin H. *Los contemporáneos 1920–1932: Perfil de un experimento vanguardista mexicano.* Mexico City: Ediciones de Andrea, 1964.

———. "La obra novelística de Jaime Torres Bodet." In *Ensayos contemporáneos sobre Jaime Torres Bodet.* Ed. Beth Miller. Mexico City: UNAM, 1976. 61–72.

———, and K. David Jackson. *Vanguardism in Latin American Literature: An Annotated Bibliographical Guide.* New York: Greenwood Press, 1990.

Foster, David William. *Gay and Lesbian Themes in Latin American Writing.* Austin: University of Texas Press, 1991.

———. "Social Pact and Lesbian Writing in Mexico." In *Literatura mexicana/Mexican Literature.* Ed. José Miguel Oviedo. Philadelphia: University of Pennsylvania, 1993. 92–103.

Freeman, George Ronald. "La caída de gracia: Clave arquetípica de *Pedro Páramo.*" Rpt. in *La narrativa de Juan Rulfo; Interpretaciones críticas.* Ed. Joseph Sommers. Mexico City: Sep/Setentas, 1974. 67–75.

———. *Paradise and Fall in Rulfo's* Pedro Páramo. Cuernavaca, Mexico City: CIDOC, 1970.

Frenk, Mariana. "*Pedro Páramo:* Novela moderna." *Universidad de México* 15.11 (1961): 18–21. Rpt. in *La narrativa de Juan Rulfo: Interpretaciones críticas.* Ed. Joseph Sommers. Mexico City: Sep/Setentas, 1974. 31–43.

Fuentes, Carlos. *Agua quemada.* Mexico City: Fondo de Cultura Económica, 1981.

———. *Burnt Water.* Trans. Margeret Sayers Peden. New York: Farrar, Straus, and Giroux, 1980.

———. *Cambio de piel.* Mexico City: Joaquín Mortiz, 1967.

———. *The Death of Artemio Cruz.* Trans. Alfred Mac Adam. New York: Farrar, Straus, and Giroux, 1991.

———. "Diálogo con Carlos Fuentes." In *Simposio Carlos Fuentes: Actas.* Ed. Isaac Jack Lévy and Juan Loveluck. Columbia: University of South Carolina, 1978. 215–229.

———. "Discurso inaugural." In *Simposio Carlos Fuentes: Actas.* Ed. Isaac Jack Lévy and Juan Loveluck. Columbia: University of South Carolina, 1978. 3–19.

———. *La muerte de Artemio Cruz.* Mexico City: Fondo de Cultura Económica, 1962.

———. "Pedro Páramo." In *La narrativa de Juan Rulfo: interpretaciones críticas.* Trans. Joseph Sommers. Mexico City: Sep/Setentas, 1974. 57–59.

———. *La región más transparente.* Mexico City: Fondo de Cultura Económica, 1958. Colección Popular 4th ed., 1990.

———. *Where the Air Is Clear.* Trans. Sam Hileman. New York: Ivan Obolensky, 1960.

Fuentes, Sylvia. "Carlos Fuentes: Estos fueron los palacios." In *Espejo de escritores.* Ed. Reina Roffé. Hanover, N.H.: Ediciones del Norte, 1985. 80–104.

Gamboa, Federico. *Santa.* 1903. Barcelona: E. Gómez de la Puente, 1910.

García Núñez, Fernando. "Anotaciones a la función de la historia en la novela mexicana contemporánea." *Bulletin Hispanique* 91.2 (July–Dec. 1989): 335–363.

García Saldaña, Parménides. *En la ruta de la onda*. Mexico City: Diógenes, 1974.

———. *Pasto verde*. Mexico City: Diógenes, 1968.

Glantz, Margo. "*Farabeuf*, escritura barroca y novela mexicana." *Barroco* 3 (1971): 29–37.

———. "*Morirás lejos:* literatura de incisión." In *José Emilio Pacheco ante la crítica*. Ed. Hugo J. Verani. Mexico City: Universidad Autónoma Metropolitana, 1987. 183–194.

———. "The Novel of the Mexican Revolution and the Shadow of the *Caudillo*." In *Bordering Difference: Culture and Ideology in 20th Century Mexico*. Ed. Kemy Oyarzun. Riverside: University of California Press, 1991. 96–108.

———. *Repeticiones*. Veracruz, Mexico: Universidad Veracruzana, 1979.

Glaze, Linda. "La distorsión temporal y las técnicas cinematográficas en *La muerte de Artemio Cruz*." *Hispamérica* 14.40 (April 1985): 115–120.

Gómez Carro, Carlos. "Carlos Fuentes, narrador (1954–1967)." In *En torno a la literatura mexicana*. Coord. Mata Oscar. Mexico City: Universidad Autónoma Metropolitana, 1989. 107–124.

González, Alfonso. *Euphoria and Crisis: Essays on the Contemporary Mexican Novel*. Fredericton, N.B., Canada: York Press, 1990.

González, Manuel Pedro. "Acotaciones a *La muerte de Artemio Cruz*." In *Coloquio sobre la novela hispanoamericana*. Ed. Ivan Schulman et al. Mexico City: Fondo de Cultura Económica, 1967. 89–100.

Graham, Jay. "Beyond Fragmentation: Toward a Theory of Imagination and the Tradition of Greatness in Fiction." *Forum* 26.3 (Summer 1985): 45–51.

Granados Roldán, Otto. "El nacionalismo mexicano: Una reflexión." *Universidad de México* 42.443 (Dec. 1987): 15–19.

Granlela-Rodriguez, Magda. *El papel del lector en la novela mexicana contemporánea: José Emilio Pacheco y Salvador Elizondo*. Potomac, Md.: Scripta Humanistica, 1991.

Guerra Cunningham, L., M. Paley Francescato, and Inma Minoves-Meyers. "José Agustín: Entrevista." *Hispamérica* 8.22 (1979): 23–40.

Guillén, Claudio. *Literature as System*. Princeton: Princeton University Press, 1971.

Gunia, Inke. *¿"Cuál es la Onda"? La literatura de la contracultura juvenil en el México de los años sesenta y setenta*. Frankfurt am Main: Vervuert, 1994.

Guzmán, Daniel de. *Carlos Fuentes*. New York: Twayne, 1972.

Guzmán, Martín Luis. *El águila y la serpiente*. 1928. Mexico City: Porrúa, 1991.

———. *La sombra del caudillo*. 1929. Mexico City: Porrúa, 1991.

Gyurko, Lanin. "Abortive Idealism and the Mask in Fuentes' *La región más transparente*." *Revue des Langues Vivantes* 42 (1976): 278–296.

———. "The Literary Response to *Nonoalco-Tlatelolco*." In *Contemporary Latin American Culture: Unity and Diversity*. Ed. Gail Guntermann. Tempe: Arizona State University, 1984. 45–78.

———. "*La muerte de Artemio Cruz* and *Citizen Kane*: A Comparative Analysis." In *Carlos*

*Fuentes: A Critical View*. Ed. Robert Brody and Charles Rossman. Austin: University of Texas Press, 1982. 64–94.

———. "Reality and Fantasy in *Gazapo*." *Revista de Estudios Hispánicos* 8.1 (1974): 117–146.

———. "Self, Double, and Mask in Fuentes' *La muerte de Artemio Cruz*." *Texas Studies in Literature and Language* 16.2 (1974): 363–384.

———. "Structure and Theme in Fuentes' *La muerte de Artemio Cruz*." *Symposium* 34 (Spring 1980): 29–41.

Haddad, Elaine. "The Structure of *Al filo del agua*." *Hispania* 47.3 (1964): 522–529.

Hammerly, Ethel. "Estructura y sentido en *La muerte de Artemio Cruz*." *Explicación de Textos Literarios* 4.2 (1975–76): 207–212.

Hancock, Joel. "Documentation, Conjecture, and Reader Participation in José Emilio Pacheco's *Morirás lejos*." *Selecta* 1 (1980): 102–105.

———. "Perfecting a Text: Authorial Revisions in José Emilio Pacheco's *Morirás lejos*." *CHASQUI: Revista de Literatura Latinoamericana* 14.2–3 (1985): 15–23.

Headington, Christopher, Roy Westbrook and Terry Barfoot. *Opera: A History*. London: The Bodley Head, 1987.

Heath, Stephen. *The Nouveau Roman: A Study in the Practice of Writing*. Philadelphia: Temple University Press, 1972.

Herz, Theda M. "Artistic Iconoclasm in Mexico: Countertexts of Arreola, Agustín, Avilés and Hiriart." *CHASQUI* 18.1 (May 1989): 17–25.

Holland, Norman. *The Dynamics of Literary Response*. New York: Oxford, 1968.

———. *5 Readers Reading*. New Haven: Yale University Press, 1975.

Hölz, Karl. "Visiones literarias de México: Desde el lugar privilegiado de una urbe ideal a la anarquía de la ciudad perdida." In *Grossstadtliteratur: la literatura de las grandes ciudades*. Ed. Ronald Daus. Frankfurt am Main: Vervuert, 1992. 47–74.

Huff, Theodore, with an introduction by Eileen Bowser. *Intolerance: The Film by D. W. Griffith: Shot-by-Shot Analysis*. New York: The Museum of Modern Art, 1966.

*The I Ching: The Book of Changes*. Trans. James Legge. New York: Dover, 1963.

Iglesias, Adela. Rev. of *Las horas vivas*, by Mónica de Neymet. *Plural* 18.205 (Oct. 1988): 67.

Iser, Wolfgang. *The Act of Reading: A Theory of Aesthetic Responses*. Baltimore: The Johns Hopkins University Press, 1978.

———. *The Implied Reader*. Baltimore: The Johns Hopkins University Press, 1974.

Jaén, Didier T. "La neopicaresca en México: Elena Poniatowska y Luis Zapata." *Tinta* 1.5 (1987): 23–29.

Janson, H. W. *History of Art*. Englewood Cliffs, N.J.: Prentice Hall, 1963.

Jensen, Paul M. *The Cinema of Fritz Lang*. New York: A. S. Barnes, 1969.

Jiménez de Báez, Ivette, Diana Morán, and Edith Negrín. *Ficción e historia: La narrativa de José Emilio Pacheco*. Mexico City: El Colegio de México, 1979.

Katzenberger, Elaine, ed., *First World, Ha Ha Ha!: The Zapatista Challenge*. San Francisco: City Lights Books, 1995.

Kirk, John M. "The Development of an *Ondero*." In *José Agustín: Onda and Beyond*. Ed. June C. D. Carter and Donald L. Schmidt. Columbia: University of Missouri Press, 1986. 9–23.

———. "En torno a *De perfil*, obra maestra de la nueva narrativa mexicana." In *Hispanic Studies in Honour of Frank Pierce*. Ed. John England. Sheffield, England: University of Sheffield, 1980. 111–122.

Klein, H., Arthur Klein, and Mina C. Klein. *Peter Bruegel the Elder: Artist of Abundance*. New York: Macmillan, 1968.

Koch, Rudolf. *The Book of Signs*. 1930. Rpt. New York: Dover, 1955.

Kracauer, Siegfried. *From Caligari to Hitler: A Psychological History of German Film*. Princeton: Princeton University Press, 1947.

La Botz, Dan. *Democracy in Mexico: Peasant Rebellion and Political Freedom*. Boston: South End Press, 1995.

Langford, Walter. *The Mexican Novel Comes of Age*. Notre Dame: University of Notre Dame Press, 1971.

Leal, Luis. "La estructura de *Pedro Páramo*." *Anuario de Letras* 4 (1964): 287–294. Rpt. in *La narrativa de Juan Rulfo: interpretaciones críticas*. Ed. Joseph Sommers. Mexico City: Sep/Setentas, 1974. 44–54.

———. "*La feria* de Juan José Arreola: Tema y estructura." *Nueva Narrativa Hispanoamericana* 1.1 (1971): 41–48.

———. "History and Myth in the Narrative of Carlos Fuentes." In *Carlos Fuentes: A Critical View*. Ed. Robert Brody and Charles Rossman. Austin: University of Texas Press, 1982. 3–17.

———. *Mariano Azuela: Vida y obra*. Mexico City: Ediciones de Andrea, 1961.

———. "Nuevos novelistas mexicanos." *El Urogallo* 35–36 (Sept.–Dec. 1975): 89–94. Rpt. in *La crítica de la novela mexicana contemporánea*. Ed. Aurora M. Ocampo. Mexico City: UNAM, 1981. 215–223.

———, ed. *Pedro Páramo*. By Juan Rulfo. New York: Appleton-Century-Crofts, 1970.

———. "Torres Bodet y los 'Contemporáneos.'" *Hispania* 40.3 (Sept. 1957): 290–296.

Levy, Kurt. "*La luciérnaga*: Title, Leitmotif, and Structural Unity." *Philological Quarterly* 51.1 (1972): 321–328.

Lomnitz-Adler, Claudio. *Exits from the Labyrinth: Culture and Ideology in the Mexican National Space*. Berkeley: University of California Press, 1992.

López González, Aralia. "Nuevas formas de ser mujer en la narrativa contemporánea de escritoras mexicanas." *Casa de las Américas* 183 (April–June 1991): 3–8.

———. "Quebrantos, búsquedas y azares de una pasión nacional (dos décadas de narrativa mexicana: 1970–1980)." *Revista Iberoamericana* 164–165 (July–Dec. 1993): 659–685.

López y Fuentes, Gregorio. *El indio*. 1935. Mexico City: Porrúa, 1986.

———. *El indio*. Trans. Anita Brenner. New York: Frederick Ungar, 1961.

Lower, Andrea. "La unidad narrativa en *La muerte de Artemio Cruz*." *Tinta* 1.3 (Dec. 1983): 19–26.

Magaña-Esquivel, Antonio. Prologue to *El indio*. 1935. Mexico City: Porrúa, 1972; 10th edition, 1986. ix–xxi.

Manjarrez, Héctor. *Lapsus (Algunos actos fallidos)*. Mexico City: Joaquín Mortiz, 1971.

———. *Pasaban en silencio nuestros dioses*. Mexico City: Era, 1987.

Marill, Réné. *Métamorphoses du roman*. Paris: Albin Michel, 1966.

Martin, Stephen-Paul. *Open Form and the Feminine Imagination: (The Politics of Reading in Twentieth-Century Innovative Writing)*. Washington, D.C.: Maisonneuve, 1988.

Martínez, Eliud. *The Art of Mariano Azuela: Modernism in* La Malhora, El desquite, La luciérnaga. Pittsburgh: Latin American Literary Review Press, 1980.

Martínez, José Luis. "La formación literaria de Agustín Yáñez y *Al filo del agua*." *Mester* 12.1–2 (May 1983): 26–40.

McLuhan, Marshall. *The Medium is the Massage*. New York: Random House, 1967.

McMurray, George R. Rev. of *Lapsus*, by Héctor Manjarrez. *Books Abroad* (Winter 1973): 117.

———. "Salvador Elizondo's *Farabeuf*." *Hispania* 50 (1967): 596–601.

Meléndez, Anthony Gabriel. *El discurso narrativo de José Emilio Pacheco*. Diss. University of New Mexico, 1984.

Menton, Seymour. "La estructura épica de *Los de abajo* y un prólogo especulativo." *Hispania* 50 (Dec. 1967): 1001–1011.

Merrell, Floyd. "Structure and Restructuration in *Al filo del agua*." *CHASQUI: Revista de Literatura Latinoamericana* 17.1 (May 1988): 51–60.

Meyer-Minnemann, Klaus. "*La muerte de Artemio Cruz*: Tiempo cíclico e historia del México moderno." In *Simposio Carlos Fuentes: Actas*. Ed. Isaac Jack Lévy and Juan Loveluck. Columbia: University of South Carolina, 1978. 87–98.

———. "Tiempo cíclico e historia en *La muerte de Artemio Cruz* de Carlos Fuentes." *Iberoromania* 7 (1978): 88–105.

Michaëlis, Pierre. "Escritura y realidad en *Farabeuf*." *Plural* 4 (Jan. 1975): 63–68.

Mier, Luis Javier, and Dolores Carbonell. *Periodismo interpretivo: Entrevistas con ocho escritores mexicanos*. Mexico City: Trillas, 1981.

Miller, Beth. "La desmitificación de la mujer en las obras de Jaime Torres Bodet en los años treinta." In her *Ensayos contemporáneos sobre Jaime Torres Bodet*. Mexico City: UNAM, 1976. 95–106.

Molina, Juan Manuel. "Respuesta al catálogo de Manjarrez." *Revista de la Universidad de México* 26.9 (May 1972): 38–39.

Monsiváis, Carlos. "México: ciudad del apocalipsis a plazos." In *Grossstadtliteratur: La literatura de las grandes ciudades*. Ed. Ronald Daus. Frankfurt am Main: Vervuert, 1992. 31–45.

———. "La naturaleza de la Onda." In his *Amor perdido*. 1977. Mexico City: Era, 1988. 225–262.

Monterde, Francisco. "La etapa de hermetismo en la obra del doctor Mariano Azuela." *Cuadernos Americanos* 3 (1952): 286–288.

————. Introduction. *Azuela: Obras completas I.* Mexico City: Fondo de Cultura Económica, 1958. vii–xxi.

Müller, Inke. "'Realismo estilo kódak': José Agustín (*La tumba* 1964/1966) y Gustavo Sainz (*Gazapo* 1965), iniciadores de la literatura de la cultura juvenil en el México de los años sesenta y setenta." *Iberoamericana* 16.2 (1992): 65–83.

Nabokov, Vladimir. *Lectures on Literature.* New York: Harcourt Brace Jovanovich, 1980.

Neymet, Mónica de. *Las horas vivas.* Mexico City: Grijalbo, 1985.

Noriega, Chon A., and Steven Ricci, eds. *The Mexican Film Project.* Los Angeles: UCLA Film and Television Archive, 1994.

*La novela de la revolución mexicana I.* Mexico City: Aguilar, 1960. 4th ed., 1963.

Ojeda, Jorge Arturo. *Octavio.* Mexico City: Premia, 1982.

Olivier, Florence. "La prosa a tientas o la tentación de la prosa." In *Los contemporáneos en el laberinto de la crítica.* Ed. Rafael Olea Franco and Anthony Stanton. Mexico City: El Colegio de México, 1994. 289–295.

O'Neill, Samuel J., Jr. "El espacio en *Al filo del agua.*" In *Homenaje a Agustín Yáñez.* Ed. Helmy F. Giacoman. Madrid: A. G. Ibarra, 1973. 235–250.

————. "*Pedro Páramo.*" In *Homenaje a Juan Rulfo.* Ed. Helmy F. Giacoman. Madrid: Eosgraf, 1974. 283–322.

Ortega, Julio. "La novela de Juan Rulfo: *Summa* de arquetipos." In his *La contemplación y la fiesta.* Caracas: Monte Ávila, 1969. Rpt. in *La narrativa de Juan Rulfo: Interpretaciones críticas.* Ed. Joseph Sommers. Mexico City: Sep/Setentas, 1974. 76–87.

————. "Tres notas mexicanas. 2: Relectura de *Morirás lejos.*" *Cuadernos Hispanoamericanos* 381 (March 1982): 669–672.

Ortiz, Orlando. *En caso de duda.* Mexico City: Diógenes, 1968.

Ostria, Mauricio. "Valor estructural del fragmento en *La feria,* de Juan José Arreola." *Estudios Filológicos* 6 (1970): 177–225.

Owen, Gilberto. *La llama fría.* Mexico City: Publicaciones Literarias Exclusivas de "El Universal Ilustrado," 1925.

————. *Novela como nube.* Mexico City: Ulises, 1928.

Pacheco, José Emilio. "La hora del lector: Dos opiniones sobre *La muerte de Artemio Cruz.*" *Revista de la Universidad de México* 16.12 (1962): 19–21.

————. *Morirás lejos.* Mexico City: Joaquín Mortiz, 1967. Revised 1977.

————. *You Will Die in a Distant Land.* Trans. Elizabeth Umlas. North Miami: University of Miami, 1991.

Paranaguá, Paulo Antonio, ed. *Mexican Cinema.* Trans. Ana M. López. London: British Film Institute, 1995.

Pasquel, Leonardo. Prologue. *El indio.* By Gregorio López y Fuentes. Mexico City: Suma Veracruzana, 1964. ix–xiv.

Patán, Federico. *Los nuevos territorios: Notas sobre la narrativa mexicana.* Mexico City: UNAM, 1992.

———. "Recent Mexican Fiction." In *The Novel in the Americas*. Ed. Raymond Leslie Williams. Niwot, Colo.: University Press of Colorado, 1992. 91–100.

Paz, Octavio. *El arco y la lira*. Mexico City: Fondo de Cultura Económica, 1967.

———. *El laberinto de la soledad*. 1950. Mexico City: Fondo de Cultura Económica, Colección Popular, 1976.

———. *The Labyrinth of Solitude*. Trans. Lysander Kemp. New York: Grove Press, 1961.

———. *El signo y el garabato*. Mexico City: Joaquín Mortiz, 1973.

Peavler, Terry J. *El texto en llamas: El arte narrativo de Juan Rulfo*. New York: Peter Lang, 1988.

Pérez Galdós, Benito. *Fortunata y Jacinta*. 1887. Madrid: Turner, 1993.

Pérez Firmat, Gustavo. *Idle Fictions: The Hispanic Vanguard Novel 1926–1934*. Durham, N.C.: Duke University Press, 1982.

Pfefferkorn, Eli. "Fractured Reality and Conventional Forms in Holocaust Literature." *Modern Language Studies* 16.1 (1986): 88–99.

Pfeiffer, Erna. *Entrevistas: Diez escritoras mexicanas desde bastidores*. Frankfurt am Main: Vervuert, 1992.

Poniatowska, Elena. *¡Ay vida, no me mereces!*. Mexico City: Joaquín Mortiz, 1985.

———. *Hasta no verte Jesús mío*. Mexico City: Era, 1969.

———. "Ser un escritor en México." In *Literatura mexicana/Mexican Literature*. Ed. José Miguel Oviedo. Philadelphia: University of Pennsylvania, 1993. 10–20.

Poot Herrera, Sara. *Un giro en espiral: El proyecto literario de Juan José Arreola*. Guadalajara: Universidad de Guadalajara, 1992.

Portal, Marta. Introduction. *Los de abajo*. By Mariano Azuela. Madrid: Cátedra, 1985. 11–72.

*Princeton Encyclopedia of Poetry and Poetics*. Ed. Alex Preminger. Princeton: Princeton University Press, 1965.

Puga, María Luisa. "Escribir: Un derecho a existir." In *Por la literatura! Mujeres y escritura en México*. Ed. Mariano Morales. Puebla, Mexico: Universidad Autónoma de Puebla, 1992. 62–65.

———. *La forma del silencio*. Mexico City: Siglo XXI, 1987.

———. *Pánico o peligro*. Mexico City: Siglo XXI, 1983.

Pupo-Walker, Enrique. "Rasgos del lenguaje y estructura de *Pedro Páramo*." *Papeles de Son Armadans* 170 (1970): 117–136.

Puyhol, Lenica. Rev. of *La feria*, by Juan José Arreola. *Revista Iberoamericana* 34 (1968): 385–386.

Ramírez Mattei, Aida Elsa. *La narrativa de Carlos Fuentes*. Río Piedras, P.R.: Editorial de la Universidad de Puerto Rico, 1983.

Ramos, Raymundo. Introduction. *3 novelas de Mariano Azuela*. 6th ed. Mexico City: Fondo de Cultura Económica (Colección Popular), 1968. 7–18.

Rees, Earl Larry. "The Prose Fiction of Salvador Elizondo." Diss. University of Southern California, 1976.

Reeve, Richard M. "The Making of *La región más transparente*: 1949–1974." In *Carlos Fuentes: A Critical View*. Ed. Robert Brody and Charles Rossman. Austin: University of Texas Press, 1982. 34–63.

Rehbein, Edna Aguirre. *Vanguardist Techniques in Mexican Prose Fiction 1923–1962*. Diss. University of Texas, Austin, 1988.

Reyes Govea, Juan. *El mestizo, la nación y el nacionalismo mexicano*. Chihuahua, Mexico: Talleres Gráficos del Gobierno del Estado, 1992.

Rivera-Rodas, Óscar. "El discurso narrativizado en Owen." In *Prosa hispánica de vanguardia*. Ed. Fernando Burgos. Madrid: Orígenes, 1986. 115–123.

Robbe-Grillet, Alain. *For a New Novel: Essays on Fiction*. Trans. Richard Howard. New York: Grove Press, 1965.

———. *La Jalousie*. Paris: Editions de Minuit, 1957.

Rodríguez Monegal, Emir. "Gustavo Sainz: La novela de los nuevos." *Mundo Nuevo* 22 (April 1968): 4–11.

Roffiel, Rosamaría. *Amora*. Mexico City: Planeta, 1989.

Rojas Garcidueñas, José. "*Al filo del agua*." *Anales del Instituto de Investigaciones Estéticas* 16 (1948): 14–24. Rpt. in *Homenaje a Agustín Yáñez*. Ed. Helmy F. Giacoman. Madrid: A. G. Ibarra, 1973. 151–166.

Romano, Eduardo. "Novela e ideología en Agustín Yáñez." In *Nueva novela latinoamericana I*. Ed. Jorge Lafforgue. Buenos Aires: Editorial Paidós, 1969. 55–84.

Rosenzweig, Carmen. *1956*. Mexico City: Ediciones de Andrea, 1958.

Ruffinelli, Jorge. "Notas sobre la novela en México (1975–1980)." *Cuadernos de Marcha* (segunda época) 3.14 (July–Aug. 1981): 47–59.

———. "Salvador Elizondo." *Hispamérica* 16 (1977): 33–47.

Rulfo, Juan. *Pedro Páramo*. 1955. Rev. ed. Mexico City: Fondo de Cultura Económica, 1981.

Ruy Sánchez, Alberto. "*Dama de corazones* de Xavier Villaurrutia." In his *Al filo de las hojas*. Mexico City: Plaza y Valdés, 1988. 83–86.

Saalmann, Deiter. "Holocaust Literature: José Emilio Pacheco's *Morirás lejos*." *Hispanófila* 28.2 [83] (1985): 89–105.

Sainz, Gustavo. *Gazapo*. 1965. Mexico City: Aguilar, León y Cal, 1989.

———. *Gazapo*. Trans. Hardie St. Martin. New York: Farrar, Straus and Giroux, 1968.

Salceda, Verónica. "La historia, dentro de la creación literaria de acuerdo a María Luisa Puga." *Dactylus* 10 (1990): 54–60.

Saltz, Joanne. "*El libro vacío*: Un relato de la escritura." In *Mujer y literatura mexicana y chicana: Culturas en contacto 2*. Ed. Aralia López González et al. Mexico City: El Colegio de México, 1990. 81–86.

Salvador, Álvaro. "El otro boom de la narrativa hispanoamericana: Los relatos escritos por mujeres en la década de los ochenta." *Revista de Crítica Literaria Latinoamericana* 21.41 (1995): 165–75.

Saporta, Marc. *Composition No. 1*. Paris: Seuil, 1962.

Sartre, Jean-Paul. *Situations I.* Paris: Libraire Gallimard, 1947.

Schaefer-Rodríguez, Claudia. "The Power of Subversive Imagination: Homosexual Utopian Discourse in Contemporary Mexican Literature." *Latin American Literary Review* 17.33 (Jan.–June 1989): 29–41.

Schaffer, Susan Carol. "Prose Fiction of the Onda Generation in Mexico." Diss. University of California, Los Angeles, 1981.

Schneider, Luis Mario. *El estridentismo: México, 1921–1927.* Mexico City: UNAM, 1985.

———. *Ruptura y continuidad: La literatura mexicana en polémica.* Mexico City: Fondo de Cultura Económica, 1975.

Seidel, Max, and Roger H. Marijnissen. *Bruegel.* New York: G. P. Putnam's Sons, 1971.

Selva, Mauricio de la. Rev. of *La feria,* by Juan José Arreola. *Cuadernos Americanos* 132 (1964): 249–253.

Shaw, Donald L. "Narrative Arrangement in *La muerte de Artemio Cruz.*" *Forum for Modern Language Studies* 15.2 (April 1979): 130–143.

Smith, Paul Julian. *The Body Hispanic: Gender and Sexuality in Spanish and Spanish American Literature.* New York: Oxford University Press, 1989.

Solana, Rafael. Prologue. *Jaime Torres Bodet Narrativa completa I.* Xochimilco, Mexico: Editorial Offset, 1985.

Solares, Ignacio. *Casas de encantamiento.* Mexico City: Plaza y Valdés, 1987.

Sommers, Joseph. *After the Storm.* Albuquerque: University of New Mexico Press, 1968.

———. "Individuo e historia: *La muerte de Artemio Cruz.*" In *La novela hispanoamericana actual.* Ed. Angel Flores and Raúl Silva Cáceres. New York: Las Américas, 1971. 145–155.

———. "Los muertos no tienen ni tiempo ni espacio (un diálogo con Juan Rulfo)." *Siempre* 1051 (15 August 1973): vi–vii. Rpt. in *La narrativa de Juan Rulfo: Interpretaciones críticas.* Ed. Joseph Sommers. Mexico City: Sep/Setentas, 1974. 17–22.

Soto, Lilvia. "El hombre-víctima de sus intuiciones arquetípicas." *Nueva Narrativa Hispanoamericana* 4 (Jan.–Sept. 1974): 367–370.

Spencer, Sharon. *Space, Time and Structure in the Modern Novel.* Chicago: Swallow Press, 1971.

Stavans, Ilan. "Mexico on the Brink of a Second Revolution." *The Boston Globe* 25 March 1994: 19.

Steele, Cynthia. *Politics, Gender, and the Mexican Novel, 1968–1988: Beyond the Pyramid.* Austin: University of Texas Press, 1992.

Taylor, Kathy. *The New Narrative of Mexico: Sub-Versions of History in Mexican Fiction.* Lewisburg, Pa.: Bucknell University Press, 1994.

Teichmann, Reinhard. *De la onda en adelante: Conversaciones con 21 novelistas mexicanos.* Mexico City: Posada, 1987.

Torres, Vicente Francisco. *Esta narrativa mexicana: Ensayos y entrevistas.* Mexico City: Leega, 1991.

Torres Bodet, Jaime. *La educación sentimental.* Madrid: Espasa Calpe: 1929.

———. *Estrella de día.* Madrid: Espasa Calpe, 1933.

———. *Margarita de niebla.* Mexico City: Cultura, 1927.

———. *Primero de enero.* Madrid: Ediciones Literatura, 1935.

———. *Proserpina rescatada.* 1931. Rpt. in his *Narrativa completa Vol. 1.* Xochimilco, Mexico: Editorial Offset, 1985.

Torres-Rosado, Santos. "Canon and Innovation in *Adonis García: A Picaresque Novel.*" *Monographic Review/Revista Monográfica* 7 (1991): 276–283.

Trejo Fuentes, Ignacio. "Dos décadas de narrativa mexicana." In *Perfiles: Ensayos sobre literatura mexicana reciente.* Ed. Federico Patán. Boulder, Colo.: Society of Spanish and Spanish American Studies, 1992. 101–111.

Tytell, John. "Epiphany in Chaos: Fragmentation in Modernism." In *Fragments: Incompletion and Discontinuity.* Ed. Lawrence D. Kritzman. New York: New York Literary Forum, 1981. 3–15.

Unruh, Vicky. *Latin American Vanguards: The Art of Contentious Encounters.* Berkeley: University of California Press, 1994.

Upton, John, trans. *The Fair.* By Juan José Arreola. Austin: University of Texas Press, 1977.

Vargas, Margarita. "Las novelas de los Contemporáneos como 'textos de goce.'" *Hispania* 69.2 (March 1986): 40–44.

Vasconcelos, José. *Ulises Criollo.* 1935. Mexico City: Jus, 1968.

Vázquez Amaral, José. "Técnica novelística de Agustín Yáñez." *Cuadernos Americanos* 17.2 (1958): 245–254.

Vela, Arqueles. *El Café de Nadie.* Jalapa, Veracruz: Horizonte, 1926. Rpt. in *El estridentismo: México, 1921–1927.* Ed. Luis Mario Schneider. Mexico City: UNAM, 1985. 217–250.

Vicens, Josefina. *The Empty Book.* Trans. David Lauer. Austin: University of Texas Press, 1992.

———. *El libro vacío.* Mexico City: Compañía General de Ediciones, 1958.

Villaurrutia, Xavier. *Dama de corazones.* Mexico City: Ulises, 1928.

Washburn, Yulan. *Juan José Arreola.* Boston: Twayne, 1983.

*Webster's New Twentieth Century Dictionary.*

*Webster's Third New International Dictionary.*

*Webster's Third New International Dictionary: Unabridged.*

Wehling, Susan. "*Cocinar hombres:* Radical Feminist Discourse." *Gestos* 8.16 (Nov. 1993): 51–62.

West, Allan. "México en sus escritores jóvenes." *El Nuevo Día, Revista Domingo* 7 August 1994: 4–8.

Wood, Cecil G. "Nuevas técnicas novelísticas en *La luciérnaga* de Mariano Azuela." *Revista Canadiense de Estudios Hispánicos* 1 (1977): 185–196.

Yáñez, Agustín. *The Edge of the Storm.* Trans. Ethel Brinton. Austin: University of Texas Press, 1963.

————. *Al filo del agua.* 1947. 19th ed. Mexico City: Porrúa, 1986.

————. *Ojerosa y pintada.* Mexico City: Joaquín Mortiz, 1959.

Yánez de la Fuente, Enrique. "Ciudad de México, 1990." In *Como una piedra que rueda: Reflexiones de nuestro espacio cultural.* Ed. Eduardo Langagne Ortega, Carlos Véjar Pérez-Rubio, and Carlos Ríos Garza. Mexico City: Gernika, 1990. 90–94.

Young, Dolly. "Mexican Literary Reactions to *Tlatelolco* 1968." *Latin American Research Review* 20.2 (1985): 71–85.

Zapata, Luis. *Adonis García: A Picaresque Novel.* Trans. E. A. Lacey. San Francisco: Gay Sunshine Press, 1981.

————. *en jirones.* Mexico City: Posada, 1985.

————. *El vampiro de la Colonia Roma.* Mexico City: Grijalbo, 1979.

Zuluaga O., Conrado. "*La región más transparente* o la técnica como el asunto central de la creación artística." *Razón y Fábula* 26 (July–Aug. 1971): 78–94.

# INDEX

Adolescence: in Agustín, 174–181; in early Mexican novels, 245 n.6; in *Onda* writings generally, 163–165; in Sainz, 166–174

Adorno, T. W., 244 n.20

Affective stylistics, xii

Agee, James, 239 n.10

*Agoristas*, 25 n.12

Aguilar Mora, Jorge, 186, 245 n.1

Agustín, José: circularity in, 177–179; as founder of *Onda*, 122, 124, 163, 245 n.1; full name of, 246 n.17; homosexual characters in, 247 n.25; influences on, 122; interdictions in, 175–176; narrator-reader relationship in, 176–177; narrator's lack of definition in, 178–179, 246 n.19; and readers, 176–177; significance of, 164; sociopolitical criticism in, 174, 179–181, 246 n.18; structure of *De perfil*, 175; Teichmann's interview with, 245 n.3; time jumps in, 175; writing after 1960s, 187; and Zapata, 189

—works: *Cerca del fuego*, 187; *De perfil* (In Profile), 15, 164, 165–166, 174–181, 188, 245 n.3, 247 n.25; *La mirada en el centro*, 187; *Se está haciendo tarde*, 187; *La tumba*, 124, 164

Akers, John, 10, 237 n.3

Albérès, R. M., 242–243 n.2

Alemán, Mateo, 191

Alienation. *See* Atomization of individual

Allegory, 139, 142, 143

Altamirano, Aldo-José, 234 n.14

Anderson, Danny J., 238 n.23

Apocalyptic vision, 11–12

Arana, Federico, 245 n.3

Arreola, Juan José: blending of national and universal in, 90; circularity in, 131; failure as theme in, 132–134; on fragmentation, 128; fragmentation techniques in, 124–125, 127–128; influences on, 122; international recognition of, 123; linear episodes in, 127; Mexican themes in, 14, 90, 125; multiple narrative voices in, 126–129, 134; on nineteenth- and twentieth-century authors, 128; and *Onda*, 243 n.3; perspectivism in, 127, 128–129, 168; poetic nature of work, 135; and reader-in-the-text, 126, 130; and readers, 125–126, 128–131, 135–136; themes of, 132–134; time jumps in, 127; unity and unification in, 125–126, 129–132; universality in, 125; writing after 1960s, 187

—work: *La feria* (The Fair), 32, 124–136, 168

Atomization of individual: in Boullosa, 210–215; in De Neymet, 202, 205–206, 209–210; in fragmented fiction generally, 15–17, 228–229; in Fuentes, 92, 97, 101, 102; in Puga, 222; in Roffiel, 200–201; in Vicens, 69, 83–84

Authorial voice: in Owen, 32–34; in Villaurrutia, 35; in Yáñez, 65–66

Author-in-the-text, 172, 182, 229

Avilés, René, 245 n.1

Avilés Fabila, René, 245 n.3

Azorín (pseudonym for José Martínez Ruiz), 27

Aztecs, 97–98, 99, 102

Azuela, Mariano: and *anticaciquismo*, 21; circularity in, 22, 41; criticisms of, 21, 42; and desire for critical attention, 25; European influences on, 12; and fragmentation as metaphor, 19–20; fragmentation techniques in, 41–42; and Fuentes, 112, 121; on innovation's effect on readers, 44–45; interior monologue and dialogue in, 42, 46, 47; Mexican Revolution in, 20–24; Mexican thematics in, 12, 14, 15, 20–24; and readers, 24, 41, 44–45, 48; rhetorical devices in, 47–48; significance of, 48; sociopolitical perspectives in, 46–47; spacing in, 22, 41; storytelling process in, 23–24, 165; third-person omniscient narration in, 46–47; trilogy of, 3, 12, 20, 25, 40–48, 235 n.10, 237 n.9; urban environment in, 17, 40–41, 46–48, 91
—works: *Los de abajo* (The Underdogs), xi, 12, 19, 20–24, 41, 42, 48, 91, 112, 235 n.11; *El desquite*, 3, 12, 20, 25, 42, 237 n.9; *La luciérnaga*, 3, 12, 15, 17, 19, 20, 25, 42–48, 91, 236 n.25, 237 n.9; *La Malhora*, 3, 12, 20, 25, 40–42, 236 n.23, 237 n.9

Balzacian novel, 136

Barbachano Ponce, Miguel, 249 n.6

Barthes, Roland, 78

Bataille, Georges, 145

Blanco, José Joaquín, 186

Blanco Aguinaga, Carlos, 239 n.5

Bodies, fragmentation of, 31, 36, 38, 104–105

Bonfil Batalla, Guillermo, 232

*Boomcito* (little boom), 249 n.5

"Boom del lector," 243 n.4

"Boom feminino," 249 n.5

"Boom" period, 92, 123

Boullosa, Carmen: autobiographical elements in, 250 nn.21–22; childhood in, 215–217; first-person narrative in, 215–216; gender roles and relations in, 214–215; historical issues in, 250–251 n.24; and readers, 212–214; sociopolitical perspective in, 217–219; structure in, 210–212, 216
—works: *Antes* (Before), 202, 215–219; *Cocinar hombre* (To Cook Men), 259 n.23; *Llanto: Novelas imposibles* (Weeping: Impossible Novels), 231, 250–251 n.24; *Mejor desaparece* (Better It Vanishes), 202, 210–215; *Son vacas, somos puercos* (They Are Cows, We Are Pigs), 250 n.24

Brown, James, 167, 246 n.11, 246 n.13

Brueghel, Pieter, 155

Brushwood, John, 49, 50, 63, 85, 177, 178, 236 n.1

Burgos, Fernando, 38

Burroughs, William, 247 n.29

Bustos Fernández, María José, 38, 236 n.20

Butor, Michel, 242 n.1, 248 n.1

Cabrera Infante, Guillermo, 5–6, 247 n.29

*Caciquismo*, 1
Calles, Plutarco Elías, 46
Calva, José Rafael, 249 n.6
Campo, Xorge del, 245 n.1
Campobello, Nellie, 12–13, 234 n.1
Cassedy, Steven, 16
Castaño, Rosa de, 49
Castellanos, Rosario, 14, 123, 165, 179
Castillo, Debra, 240 n.5
Castillo, Florencia, 239 n.14
Castro Arenas, Mario, 100, 240 n.5
Catholic Church, 218, 250 n.22
Ceballos Maldonado, José, 249 n.6
Cervantes, Miguel de, xvi, 4, 121
Chatman, Seymour, xvi
Chávez Camacho, Armando, 237 n.2
Chávez, Eugenio, 245 n.1
Chevalier, Maurice, 116
Chiapas New Year's rebellion (1994), 2–3
Chinese cosmology, 145–148
Chiu-Olivares, M. Isela, 163–164, 165, 172, 176, 177, 245 n.2, 246 n.21
Circularity: in Agustín, 177–179; in Arreola, 131; in Azuela, 22, 41; in fragmented novels generally, 229; in Fuentes, 99–100, 112–113, 177, 178; in Puga, 221–222; in Roffiel, 201; in Rulfo, 78–79; in Zapata, 197
Citizen-in-the-text, 227–228, 229
*Citizen Kane*, 108–109, 231, 241 n.23
Clark, Stella, 246 n.20
Class. *See* Social classes
Cluff, Russell M., 243–244 n.16
Cocteau, Jean, 36
Colina, José de la, 81
Collage technique, 223–224
*Contemporáneos*, 12–14, 20, 25–26, 33, 40, 235 n.12 *See also* Vanguard fiction
Cortázar, Julio, xiii, 6, 71, 183, 211, 247

*Costumbrismo*, 53
Covarrubias, Alicia, 250 n.10
Cross, Elsa, 245 n.1
Cuban Revolution, 114–115
Cubism, 31, 36
Culler, Jonathan, xii, xiii
Cyclical rhythms. *See* Circularity

Dalton, Margarita, 164
Dauster, Frank, 35, 36
de Beer, Gabriella, 250 n.15
Decharacterization, 27, 235 n.16
Dellapiane, Angela B., 237 n.12, 238 n.21
De Neymet, Mónica: characters in, 203–204; ending of *Las horas vivas*, 209–210; first-person and third-person narrative in, 203, 204–206, 208; imagery in, 205–206; invisibility of women in, 205–206; Mathilde's narration in, 206–208; sociopolitical perspective in, 207; women as objects in, 205, 206; writing process in, 206–208
— work: *Las horas vivas* (The Vibrant Hours), 15, 202–210
Diary format, 193–197, 198, 249 n.6
Díaz, Porfirio, 1–2, 17, 18, 92, 93, 99–100, 102, 228
Díaz de Castillo, Bernal, 19
Dickens, Charles, 116
Diegesis, definition of, xvi
Diegetic, definition of, xvi
Discourse, definition of, xvi
Divisionism, 121
Dixon, Paul B., 241 n.18
Domínguez Colavita, Federica, 169, 172
Dorra, Raúl, 244 n.22
Dos Passos, John, xi, 14, 54
Drugs, 163, 164, 182
Duncan, J. Ann, 125, 156, 160, 244 n.18
Durán, Manuel, 77, 95, 137

Eden, Anthony, 116
Eisner, Lotte, 159, 245 nn.29–30
Ejército Zapatista de Liberación (Zapatista National Liberation Army), 2–3
*El estridentismo*, 236 n.19
Elizondo, Salvador: allegory in, 139, 142, 143; critics' responses to, 137; images and potential signifiers in, 145–147; influences on, 122, 125; metanarrative discourse of *Farabeuf*, 143; ontological questioning in, 141–142; problematic and experimental nature of work, 125, 136–142, 147–148; and readers, 124, 137–144, 147–148; *rebus* in, 139, 144; scenes in *Farabeuf*, 137–138; subversions of certainties and flaunted certainties in, 139–141; unity and unification in, 124, 144–146; and vanguard fiction, 28, 136; writing after 1960s, 187
—work: *Farabeuf o la crónica de un instante* (Farabeuf or the Chronicle of an Instant), 14, 124–125, 136–148, 168, 227
*El Universal Ilustrado*, 236 n.18
Endnotes, 183–184
*Escritura:* and Arreola, 124–136; characteristics of, xiv, 122, 123–124, 243 n.4; and dissolution of fictional limits, 3; and Elizondo, 124–125, 136–148; fragmentation techniques in, 124–125; and Fuentes, 122; and *Onda*, 164; and Pacheco, 124–125, 148–162; and reader-in-the-text, 126, 243 n.4; and Sainz, 169, 173
Espinasa, José María, 185–186
Estrada, Ricardo, 80
*Estridentistas*, 12–14, 20, 25–26, 28, 40. *See also* Vanguard fiction
Eyewitness accounts, 61–62

Family, 210–219
Farill, Manuel, 245 n.1
Faris, Wendy, 240 n.6
Fassbinder, Rainer Werner, 244 n.28
Faulkner, William, xi, 14, 54, 134
Feminism: in Boullosa, 210–219, 250 n.23; in De Neymet, 202–210; and destabilization of patriarchy, 10–11; in Puga, 219–226; in Roffiel, 197–201
Fernández de Lizardi, José Joaquín, 190
Films. *See* specific titles
First-person narrative: in Boullosa, 215–216; in De Neymet, 203, 204–206, 208; in gay fiction generally, 249 n.6; in Manjarrez, 182; in *Onda* writings, 14, 165, 174; in Roffiel, 197; in vanguard fiction, 26; in Vicens, 86–87; in Zapata, 189–190, 192, 193
Fish, Stanley, xii
Fitzgerald, F. Scott, 116
Forster, Merlin H., 26–27, 30, 36–37
Foster, David William, 189, 197, 249 n.6, 250 n.12
Foucault, Michel, 247 n.29
Fourré, Maurice, 242 n.1, 248 n.1
Fragmentation: as accepted convention, 187; as agent of activism and change, 1, 3, 7, 9; and apocalyptic vision, 11–12; characteristics of, xv, 4–12, 228–232; and conflict between tradition and modernization, 15–18; definition of fragmented novel, xi–xii; and destabilization of patriarchy, 10–11; formatting and spacing with, 5–6, 22, 27, 41, 52, 154, 167, 175, 183, 190, 194–195, 222–223, 235–236 n.17, 236–237 n.2, 246 n.11; historical development of, in Mexican fiction, 12–18; hypothetical plot situation illustrating, 7–8; illustrations in novels,

36, 121–122, 168, 210, 246 n.12; and imagery, 79–81, 104–105, 146–147, 195–196, 205–206; integration of, with thematics, 46–48, 53–54, 81–82; length of fragments generally, 5; linearity subverted generally, 6–8; list of novels in 1970s and 1980s, 248–249 n.4; and marginalization generally, 10–11, 14, 15; and Mexican context generally, xi, 1–3, 12–18; in Mexican Revolution novels generally, 12–13, 19–24, 234 n.1; and multiple points of view, 7, 126–129, 134; music analogies for, 10, 237 n.3; in nineteenth-century fiction, 4–5; ordering of fragments generally, 6, 234 n.7; pacing and rhythm changes, 55, 63–64; and poetic elements, 9, 31, 34, 35, 36, 37, 118, 135, 153–154, 224, 241 n.18; purposes of, 1, 3; and radical juxtapositions, 7; and readers' active involvement, xiii, 4–5, 7–9, 11, 64–68, 71, 121, 125–126, 154–157, 161–162, 185, 227; as representation of contemporary world, 10; and split Mexico, 17–18; symbolic or metaphoric aspects of, 10–12; and time jumps or lapses, 7, 70, 74, 127, 168, 175; and urban milieu generally, 15–17, 238 n.1; in vanguard novels, 20, 25–40; in Western Europe and U.S., 187, 248 n.1. *See also* Readers; and specific authors

Freeman, George Ronald, 80, 81, 239 n.9

French New Novel, 136

Frenk, Mariana, 81

Fuentes, Carlos: and Azuela, 112, 121; blending of national and universal in, 90; change and stasis in, 100–102; characters in, 93–96; circularity and cycles in, 99–100, 112–113, 177,

178; and citizen-in-the-text, 227–228; compared with Vicens, 83; cover design of *Agua quemada,* 118; criticisms of, 101–102; and Cuban Revolution, 114–115; and *escritura,* 122; on fragmentation, xvii; fusion of national and international in, 14, 92; gender roles and gender relations in, 97, 104, 105–106, 110–111; illustrations for works, 118, 121–122; imagery in, 104–105; indigenous past in, 97–100; international recognition of, 123; intratextuality in, 109–110; and intrusion of one established narrative discourse into another, 109–110; lack of communication among characters in, 106, 241 n.25; Mexican characteristics in, 14, 92, 97–100, 106, 110; and Mexican Revolution, 92, 101, 103–107, 111–115, 242 n.35; narration in *Agua quemada,* 118–119; poetic quality in, 118, 241 nn.17–18; progressions in, 118–119; and pronouns beginning fragments, 103–104, 241 n.22; and reader-in-the-text, 110; and readers, 108–110, 121–122; reiteration of language in, 108–109; sentence fragments and segments of conversations in, 107–108; significance of, 91–92, 122; social classes in, 94–95, 100–101; sociopolitical perspective in, 94–95, 110, 119–121; themes of, 92–93; unity and unification in, 80, 95–99, 104, 105, 109–111, 113–115, 117–118; urban milieu in, 91–95, 115–116, 119, 240 n.13; writing in 1970s and 1980s, 187, 248 n.2

—works: *Agua quemada* (Burnt Water), 92, 115–122, 242 n.33, 248 n.2; *La cabeza de la hidra,* 248 n.2; *Cambio de piel* (A Change of Skin), 48, 122; *La campaña*, 248 n.2; *Cristóbal Nonato*, 248 n.2; *Gringo viejo*, 248 n.2; *La muerte de Artemio Cruz* (The Death of Artemio Cruz), 14, 15, 48, 92, 102–115, 117, 122, 177, 227–228, 230–231, 231, 241 n.18, 247 n.24; *La región más transparente* (Where the Air Is Clear), 13–14, 15, 17, 48, 83, 91, 92–102, 106, 115–116, 117, 119, 122, 178, 230, 242 nn.35–36; *Terra nostra*, 121; *Una familia lejana*, 248 n.2

Fuentes, Sylvia, 121

Galdós, Benito Pérez, 4, 233–234 n.6
Gamboa, Federico, 2
García Saldaña, Parménides, 164, 179, 245 n.1
Gay and lesbian fiction: diary in, 193–197, 198, 249 n.6; first-person narrative in, 189–190, 192, 193, 197, 249 n.6; and *Onda*, 188; by Roffiel, 188–189, 197–201; by Zapata, 188, 189–197
Gender roles and relations: in Boullosa, 214–215; in Fuentes, 97, 104, 105–106, 110–111; in Roffiel, 188–189, 197–201; in Vicens, 83–84, 86–87
Gide, André, 14, 31
Giraudoux, Jean, 26
Glantz, Margo, 13, 123–124, 146, 158, 163, 242–243 n.2, 245 n.1, 245 n.4
Glaze, Linda, 241 n.24
Gómez, Rubén, 248 n.3
González, Alfonso, 251 n.25
González, Manuel Pedro, 234 n.2
Graham, Jay, 10
Graniela-Rodríguez, Magda, 243 n.4, 243 n.14, 244 n.24
Griffith, D. W., 150–151
Guadalupe de Anda, José, 49

Guerrero, Jesús R., 49
Guillén, Claudio, 193
Gunia, Inke, 246 n.10, 246 n.12
Guzmán, Daniel de, 242 n.32
Guzmán, Martín Luis, 234 n.1
Gyurko, Lanin: on Fuentes, 94, 100, 101, 104, 108, 111, 113, 114, 231; on Sainz, 167, 168, 172

Haarmann, 244 n.28, 245 n.29
Haddad, Elaine, 63, 237 n.13, 238 n.22
Hancock, Joel, 156, 244 n.23
Heath, Stephen, 136
Herz, Theda M., 243 n.3
Hitler, Adolf, 150, 157–158, 159, 161
Holland, Norman, xii
Holocaust: controversies about fiction on, 153; in Pacheco's fiction, 148–162
Hölz, Karl, 240 n.1
Homosexuality: in Agustín, 247 n.25; in Manjarrez, 247 n.25; in Roffiel, 188–189; in Zapata, 188, 189–197
Huston, John, 239 n.10
Huxley, Aldous, 54

*I Ching*, 146
Illustrations in fragmented novels, 36, 121–122, 168, 210, 246 n.12
Imagery: in De Neymet, 205–206; in Elizondo, 146–147; of fragmentation, 79–80; in Fuentes, 104–105; in Rulfo, 79–81; in Zapata, 195–196
Incledon, John, 243 n.10
Indians, 49, 50, 51–54, 102
*Indigenista* literature, 51
Indigenous past, in Fuentes, 97–100
Interdictions: in Agustín, 175–176; definition of, xvi; in Puga, 223; in Rulfo, 75–76; in Yáñez, 59–64
Interior dialogue, 42, 46, 47

Interior monologue, 34, 41, 42, 46, 47, 50, 54, 70
Intertextuality: in Manjarrez, 247–248 nn.29–30; in Pacheco, 158–161
Intolerance, 150–151
Intratextuality, in Fuentes, 109–110
Iser, Wolfgang, xii–xiii
Isolation. See Atomization of individual

Jackson, K. David, 26–27
Jaén, Didier T., 193
Jensen, Paul, 159–160
Jiménez de Báez, Ivette, 149, 150, 151, 155, 161, 181, 244 n.18, 244 n.23
Joyce, James, xi, 14, 54
Jules et Jim, 182

Kurosawa, Akira, 172
Kürten, Peter, 159, 245 n.29

Lacan, Jacques, 247 n.29
La fórmula secreta (The Secret Formula), 248 n.3
Lang, Fritz, 158–159
Langford, Walter, 137
La Onda: adolescence as theme of, 164–166; characteristics of, xiv, 14, 17, 122, 123–124, 163–166, 180, 245 n.7, 246 n.18; and escritura, 164; first-person narrative in writings, 14, 165, 174; founders of, 122, 124, 163; and gay and lesbian fiction, 188, 189; as influence on other writings, 186, 188, 189; influences on, 15, 122, 243 n.3; and music, 163, 247 n.29; writers within group, 245 n.1
Leal, Luis: on Arreola, 132, 133; on Azuela, 12, 21, 22, 41, 42, 46, 234 n.2; on Contemporáneos, 235 n.12; on escritura authors, 124; on Fuentes, 240 n.13; on Onda group, 124; on

Rulfo, 75, 80, 81, 239 n.5
Lector cómplice, xiii
Lector hembra, xiii
Lesbian and gay fiction: diary in, 193–197, 198, 249 n.6; first-person narrative in, 189–190, 192, 193, 197, 249 n.6; and Onda, 188; by Roffiel, 188–189, 197–201; by Zapata, 188, 189–197
Lira, Miguel, 237 n.2
Lomnitz-Adler, Claudio, 2
López González, Aralia, 238 n.1, 249 n.5
López y Fuentes, Gregorio, 20, 49–54
Los Angeles, 16
Lower, Andrea, 242 n.29

M, the Vampire of Düsseldorf, 158–160, 245 n.29
Machismo, 83–84, 86–87, 97, 110, 188
McLuhan, Marshall, 247–248 nn.29–30
McMurray, George, 137, 147, 185
Madero, Francisco, 18
Magaña-Esquivel, Antonio, 13, 50
Magdaleno, Mauricio, 49
Major, Clarence, 10–11
Manjarrez, Héctor: critics on, 185–186; endnotes in, 183–184; and experimenting with realism, 248 n.31; homosexual characters in, 247 n.25; identified as Onda writer, 245 n.1; intertextual references in, 247–248 nn.29–30; as middle-class rebel, 247 n.27; questionnaire in Lapsus, 185; and reader-in-the-text, 184; and readers, 183–186; urban environment in, 17
—works: Lapsus (Algunos actos fallidos) [Lapsus (Some Failed Actions)], 166, 181–186, 247 nn.28–29; Pasaban en silencio nuestros dioses (Our Gods Passed by in Silence), 248 n.31

Marginalization: in Boullosa, 210–219; in De Neymet, 202–210; in fragmented novels generally, 10–11, 14, 15; in gay and lesbian fiction, 188–201, 249 n.6; in *Onda* writings, 164, 167; in Puga, 219–226; in Roffiel, 188–189, 197–201; in Vicens, 83–84, 89; women's fiction, 202–226; in Zapata, 188, 189–197

Marill, Réné, 243 n.2

Martin, Stephen-Paul, 10

Martínez, Eliud, 48, 236 n.24

Martínez Sotomayor, José, 235 n.14

Meléndez, Anthony Gabriel, 244 n.25

Menéndez, Miguel Ángel, 49, 237 n.2

Menton, Seymour, 21, 234 n.2, 234 n.5

Merrell, Floyd, 63, 238 n.17, 238 n.19

Metanarrative commentary, 32–34, 85, 143

Mexican characteristics: in Fuentes, 97–100, 106; Paz on, 83, 84, 97–98, 106, 110–111; in Vicens, 83–84, 86–87. *See also* Nationalist literature

Mexican fiction: historical development of fragmentation in, 12–18. *See also* Fragmentation; Nationalist literature; and specific authors

Mexican Revolution: in Agustín, 179; in Azuela, 20–24; in Fuentes, 92, 101, 103–107, 111–115, 120–121, 242 n.35; historical event, 2, 12–13, 17; in novels generally, 12–13, 234 n.1; in Yáñez, 56, 63–64, 67

Mexico: Chiapas New Year's rebellion in, 2–3; criticisms of, in Fuentes, 119–121; criticisms of, in Puga, 219–226; current apocalyptic conditions in, 11–12; current fragmentation of, 2–3, 15, 17–18, 101–102; Díaz administration in, 1–2, 17, 18, 92, 93, 99–100,

102, 228; earthquake in, 18, 221; economic crisis of 1980s, 202, 220–222, 231–232, 251 n.25; growth of Mexico City, 15–17, 93, 234 n.14; Guerrero massacre of workers in, 2; indigenous past of, 97–99; international influences on, 15, 120, 251 n.27; justice system in, 199–200; Madero's assassination in, 18; and NAFTA, 3, 18, 102; oligarchy in, 100; Olympics of 1968 in, 18; rape in, 199–200; Salinas administration in, 18, 102; social classes in, 16, 94–95, 101; Tlatelolco student massacre in, 18, 102, 166, 180–181, 247 n.28. *See also* Mexico City

Mexico City: in Azuela's trilogy, 40–41, 46–48; Café Europa in, 28; *cafés cantantes* in, 179, 247 n.22; colonias in, 17; in De Neymet, 202, 203, 207; in Fuentes, 91–95, 115–116, 119, 240 n.13; growth of, 15–17, 93, 234 n.14; mythology of founding of, 241 n.15; in Puga, 219–221; in Roffiel, 15, 198; in Sainz, 166, 173–174; in Solares, 229; in Zapata, 189

Meyer-Minnemann, Klaus, 113, 242 n.32

Michaëlis, Pierre, 139–140

Miller, Beth, 236 n.20

Mistral, Frédéric, 134

Molina, Juan Manuel, 185

Mondragón, Magdalena, 49, 237 n.2

Monsiváis, Carlos, 2, 16, 17, 180, 245 n.5, 246 n.18

Monterde, Francisco, 45

Müller, Inke, 245 n.6, 247 n.22

Muralism, 51, 52, 94–95, 240 n.5

Music, 163, 223–224, 237, 247 n.29

Nabokov, Vladimir, xiii, 78, 247

NAFTA, 3, 18, 102

Narrator-in-the-text, 32–34, 38, 39–40, 57, 65–66, 70, 229

Nationalism, and Díaz administration, 1

Nationalist literature: by López y Fuentes, 51–54; by Yáñez, 54–68; characteristics of, 13; Indians in, 49, 50, 51–54; and *indigenista* literature, 51; and social consciousness, 49–50. *See also* Mexican characteristics

Naval, Eduardo, 245 n.1

New Year's rebellion (1994), Chiapas, 2–3

Nin, Anaïs, 242 n.1, 248 n.1

Noriega, Chon, 248 n.3

*Nouveau roman*, 123–124, 125, 136, 151

Ojeda, Jorge Arturo, 249 n.6

Olivier, Florence, 29

O'Neill, Samuel, 79, 239 n.5

Ortega, Julio, 79, 80, 244 n.26

Ortiz, Orlando, 164, 245 n.1

Ortuño, Juan, 245 n.1

Owen, Gilberto: cubist influences on, 31; first-person authorial voice of, 33–35; fragmentation techniques in, 31–32; poetic elements in, 13, 31, 34; and readers, 33–35; reiteration of language in, 32; unity in, 32

—works: *La llama fría*, 26; *Novela como nube* (Novel Like a Cloud), 20, 26, 29–34

Pacheco, José Emilio: *Alguien's* identity in *Morirás lejos*, 156–160, 161; and Brueghel's painting, 155–156; changes in discourse in, 154; choice in, 156–157, 160–162; compared with Puga, 225; equivalencies in, 157–160; historical dimension in, 125, 148–151, 160–162; hope and rebirth at end of *Morirás lejos*, 161–162; influences on,

122; intertextual references in, 158–161; juxtaposition of past and present in, 152–153; poetic elements in, 153–154; on poetic quality in Fuentes, 241 n.17; "present" in *Morirás lejos*, 151–152; punctuation in, 154; and readers, 124, 154–157, 160–162, 244 nn.23–25; and readers-in-the-text, 155; relationship of content to form in, 153–155; spacing in, 154; structure of *Morirás lejos*, 148–151, 156; and vanguard fiction, 28; writing after 1960s, 187

—work: *Morirás lejos* (You Will Die in a Distant Land), 124–125, 148–162, 241 n.17, 246 n.15

Pacing changes, 55, 63–64

Páramo, Roberto, 245 n.1

Patán, Federico, xii, xvii, 214, 250 n.16, 250 n.18

Paz, Octavio: on Chinese cosmology, 145, 147; on Elizondo, 137; international recognition of, 123; on machismo, 97, 188; on Mexican character, 83, 84, 97–98, 106, 110–111, 115–116, 188, 241 n.26; on poetry and fragmented novels, 9

Peavler, Terry, 238 n.4

Pérez Firmat, Gustavo, 26, 40, 235 n.14, 235 n.16, 236 n.22

Perspectivism, 127, 128–129, 168

Pfefferkorn, Eli, 244 n.20

Phenomenological strategy, xii, xiii

Picaresque genre, 188, 190–191, 250 n.9

Picasso, Pablo, 31, 36, 39

Poetic elements, 9, 31, 34–37, 118, 135, 153–154, 224, 241 n.18

Pointillism, 121

Poniatowska, Elena, 16, 181, 249 n.5, 250 n.9

Portal, Marta, 21, 235 n.3

Porter, Cole, 116

Poot Herrera, Sara, 134, 243n.9

Poverty, 1–2, 15–16, 17, 49, 101

Prostitutes, 2, 15, 28–29, 41, 46, 189–190, 203

Proust, Marcel, 26, 36

Psychoanalytical approach, xii

Puga, María Luisa: on author as mirror, 227; characters in, 220–221; circularity in, 221–222; collage technique of, 223–224; interdictions in, 223; lyrical quality of, 223–224; and readers, 224–225, 228; silence in, 222; sociopolitical perspective in, 15, 202, 219–226, 251n.25, 251n.27; spacing in, 222–223; structure in, 219–220; unification in, 225–226; urban milieu in, 15, 219–221

—works: *La forma del silencio* (The Form of Silence), 15, 202, 219–226; *Pánico o peligro* (Panic or Danger), 251n.26

Pupo-Walker, Enrique, 80, 81

Puyhol, Lenica, 134

Quevedo, Francisco de, *Buscón*, 191

Ramírez, Armando, 17, 245n.2

Ramírez Heredia, Rafael, 186

Ramos, Raymundo, 41

Rape, 199–200

*Rashoman*, 172

Reader-in-the-text: in Arreola, 126, 130; and *escritura*, 126, 243n.4; in fragmented novels generally, 229; in Fuentes, 110; in Manjarrez, 184; in Pacheco, 155; in Roffiel, 199; in Rulfo, 69, 70–71, 76–78; in Sainz, 173; in Torres Bodet, 39; in Vicens, 88–89; in Yáñez, 66–67

Reader-response criticism, xii–xiii

Readers: active involvement of, xiii, 4–

5, 7–9, 11, 64–68, 71, 121, 125–126, 154–157, 161–162, 185, 227; and Agustín, 176–177; and Arreola, 125–126, 128–131, 135–136; and Azuela, 24, 41, 44–45, 48; and Boullosa, 212–214; and Cortázar, xiii; and Elizondo, 124, 137–144, 147–148; and fragmented novels generally, xiii, 7–9, 11, 229; and Fuentes, 108–110, 121–122; and Manjarrez, 183–186; and narrator-in-the-text, 32–34, 38, 39–40, 57, 65–66; and Owen's first-person authorial voice, 33–35; and Pacheco, 124, 154–157, 160–162, 244nn.23–25; passive role of, xiii, 11, 58, 66, 73, 126, 135; and Puga, 224–225, 228; rereading and reevaluation of text by, 77–80, 171; and Roffiel, 199; and Rulfo, 69, 70–81; and Sainz, 171, 172–173; and Torres Bodet, 39–40; and Vicens, 69, 87–90; and Yáñez, 54–55, 57–68, 70

Reading process, in Rulfo, 70–81

*Rebus*, 139, 144

Reevaluation and rereading by readers, 77–80, 171

Reeve, Richard, 240n.2

Rehbein, Edna Aguirre, 27, 30, 32

Reiteration of language, 32, 75, 108–109

Rereading and reevaluation by readers, 77–80, 171

Rereading of history, 229, 231

Reverdy, Pierre, 39

Reyes, Alfonso, 115

Ricci, Steven, 248n.3

Rivera, Diego, 50, 52, 94–95, 240n.5

Robbe-Grillet, Alain, 84–85, 136, 151

Robe, Stanley L., 235n.3

Rodríguez Monegal, Emir, 168

Roffiel, Rosamaría: circularity in, 201; first-person narrative in, 197; and readers, 199; and readers-in-the-text, 199;

sociopolitical perspective of, 188–189, 199–200, 201; solitude and isolation in, 200–201
—work: *Amora* (Love), xi, 15, 188–189, 197–201
Rojas Garcidueñas, José, 63, 234 n.2, 237 n.13, 238 n.22
Romano, Eduardo, 65, 238 n.22
Rosenfeld, Alvin, 244 n.20
Rosenzweig, Carmen, *1956*, 238 n.2
Rubín, Ramón, 237 n.2
Rulfo, Juan: after 1960s, 187, 248 n.3; circularity in, 78–79; compared with other authors, 33, 67, 69, 70, 232; fragmentation techniques in, 69–70; fusion of national and international in, 14; imagery in, 79–81; interdictions in, 75–76; international recognition of, 123; italicized commentary in, 73; and joining of act of reading and allegory of reading, 70–81; narrator in, 73–77, 246 n.19; and reader-in-the-text, 69, 70–71, 76–78; and readers, 69, 70–81, 89–90; reevaluation and rereading of, by readers, 77–80; reiteration in, 75; rural milieu in, 69; textual strategies of, 71–78; time jumps and nebulous nature of time in, 70, 74; unity and thematic unifiers in, 80–81; and vanguard fiction, 28; and voice without name and body, 73–75
—work: *Pedro Páramo*, 13, 48, 69–81, 127
Ruy Sánchez, Alberto, 36

Saalmann, Deiter, 151, 161, 244 n.23
Sainz, Gustavo: and author-in-the-text, 172; characters' fluctuating sense of self in, 169–170; and *escritura*, 169, 173; fantasy versus reality in, 168, 170–172; formatting of scenes and segments of scenes, 167, 246 n.11; as founder of *Onda*, 163; influences on, 122; interview with Arreola, 128; present time in *Gazapo*, 167–168, 174; and reader-in-the-text, 173; and readers, 171, 172–173; and rereading by readers, 171; significance of, 164; storytelling process in, 166, 171–174; time jumps in, 168; visual stimuli in *Gazapo*, 168, 246 n.12; writing after 1960s, 187; and Zapata, 189
—works: *Compadre lobo*, 187; *Fantasmas aztecas*, 187; *Gazapo*, 15, 164, 165–174; *Muchacho en llamas*, 187; *Paseo en trapecio*, 187; *La princesa del Palacio de Hierro*, 187
Salceda, Verónica, 226
Salinas de Gotari, Carlos, 18, 102
Sanguineti, Edoardo, 242 n.1, 248 n.1
Saporta, Marc, 6, 242 n.1, 248 n.1
Sartre, Jean-Paul, 134
Schaefer-Rodríguez, Claudia, 191
Schaffer, Susan Carol, 180, 183
Schneider, Luis Mario, 28, 236 n.19
Schubert, Franz, 116–117
Seurat, Georges, 121, 168
Shaw, Donald L., 113, 241 n.18
Social classes: in Fuentes, 94–95, 100–101; in Mexico City, 16, 94–95
Solares, Ignacio, 228–229, 231
Sommers, Joseph, 69, 72–73, 242 n.30
Soto, Lilvia, 160
Spacing and formatting: in Agustín, 175; in Azuela, 22, 41; in fragmented fiction generally, 5–6; in López y Fuentes, 52; in Manjarrez, 183; in novels focusing on indigenous population, 236–237 n.2; in Pacheco, 154; in Puga, 222–223; in Sainz, 167, 246 n.11; in Torres Bodet, 235–236 n.17; in vanguard fiction, 27; in Zapata, 190, 194–195
Spencer, Sharon, 6, 242 n.1, 248 n.1

Steele, Cynthia, 245 n.7, 246 n.18, 250 n.15
Story, definition of, xv–xvi
Storyteller-in-the-text, 56–58, 60–61, 66–67
Storytelling process: in Azuela, 23–24, 165; in Sainz, 166, 171–174; in Yáñez, 56–59, 66–67
Stravinsky, Igor, 39
Stream-of-consciousness techniques, 32, 169
Structuralism, xii
Student massacre at Plaza de Tlatelolco, 18, 102, 166, 180–181
Swansey, Bruce, 215

Teichmann, Reinhard, 189, 245 n.1, 245 n.3
Third-person narration, 46–47, 52–53, 203, 204–205, 208
Time jumps or lapses, 7, 70, 74, 127, 168, 175
Titian, 139, 142
Tlatelolco student massacre, 18, 102, 166, 180–181, 247 n.28
TLC. See NAFTA
Torre, Gerardo de la, 245 n.1
Torres, Juan Manuel, 245 n.1
Torres Bodet, Jaime: asterisks marking fragments in, 27, 235–236 n.17; fragmentation techniques in, 36–37; and narrator-in-the-text, 38, 39–40; poetic quality in, 36, 37; and reader-in-the-text, 39; and readers, 39–40; references to art and artists in, 38–39
—works: Estrella de día, 26; La educación sentimental, 26; Margarita de niebla, 26; Proserpina rescatada (Proserpina Rescued), 20, 26, 36–40, 236 n.17, 236 n.20
Torres-Rosado, Santos, 249 n.6

Tovar, Juan, 245 n.1
Tratado de Libre Comercio. See NAFTA
Truffaut, François, 182

Unity and unification: in Arreola, 125–126, 129–132; in Elizondo, 124, 144–146; in fragmented novels generally, 230–231; in Fuentes, 80, 95–99, 104, 105, 109–111, 113–115, 117–118; in Owen, 32; in Puga, 225–226; in Rulfo, 80–81; in Vicens, 87–89
Unruh, Vicky, 26, 27
Upton, John, 126
Urban milieu: and atomization of individual, 15–17, 69, 83–84, 92, 97, 101, 102, 200–201, 202, 205–206, 209, 210–215, 222, 228–229; in Azuela, 17, 40–41, 46–48, 91; in fragmented novels generally, 15–17; in Fuentes, 91–95, 115–116, 119, 240 n.13; in Vicens, 69, 238 n.1; in Yáñez, 92, 240 n.1. See also Mexico City

Vampirism, 158–160, 244 n.28
Vanguard fiction: artistic influences on, 26; characteristics of, 26–27; criticisms of, 14, 25–26, 33, 40; description of, 13, 20, 25–28; and Elizondo, 28, 136; by Owen, 29–34; second movement of, 235 n.14; by Torres Bodet, 36–40; by Vela, 28–29; by Villaurrutia, 34–36
Vasconcelos, José, 234 n.1
Vela, Arqueles, 13, 20, 26, 28–29, 236 n.18
Vicens, Josefina: cohesiveness to fragments in, 87–89; compared with other authors, 33, 67, 69, 83, 213; first-person narrative in, 86–87; gender roles in, 83–84, 86–87; isolation in, 69, 83–

84; marginalization in, 83–84, 89; on masculine and feminine distinctions in narration, 239 n.12; masculine pseudonym of, 239 n.12; narrator/writer in, 81–82, 86–87, 89; and reader-in-the-text, 88–89; and readers, 69, 87–90; thematic use of fragmentation by, 81–82; unity and unifying devices in, 87–89; writing process in, 81–90, 208
—work: *El libro vacío* (The Empty Book), 13, 69, 81–90, 208
Villa, Pancho, 120
Villaseñor, Eduardo, 235 n.14
Villaurrutia, Xavier, 13, 20, 26, 34–36

Wagner, Richard, 150, 161
Washburn, Yulan, 128
Wehling, Susan, 250 n.23
Welles, Orson, 108–109
Women's bodies, fragmentation of, 31, 36, 38
Women's fiction: "boom feminino," 249 n.5; by Boullosa, 210–219; by De Neymet, 202–210; by Puga, 219–226; by Roffiel, 188–189, 197–201; by Vicens, 81–90
Wood, Cecil G., 236 n.26
Writer/narrator, 81–90
Writing process: in De Neymet, 206–208; in Vicens, 81–90, 208

Yáñez, Agustín: compared with other authors, 40, 67, 69, 70; contributions of, 54–55, 69; criticisms of, 63; eyewitness accounts in, 61–62; fragmentation techniques in, 54–55; influences on, 54; integrative strategy in, 62–63; interdictions in, 59–64; interior monologue in, 54; Mexican Revolution in,

56, 63–64, 67; and narrator-in-text, 57, 65–66, 70; pacing changes in, 55, 63–64; and reader-in-the-text, 66–67; and readers, 54–55, 57–68, 70; and storyteller-in-the-text, 56–58, 60–61, 66–67; storytelling process in, 56–61, 66–67; unification impetuses in, 66–68; urban milieu in, 92, 240 n.1
—works: *Al filo del agua* (The Edge of the Storm), 14, 20, 31, 39, 48, 50, 54–68, 70, 166, 169, 179, 237 n3; *Ojerosa y pintada*, 92, 240 n.1
Yáñez de la Fuente, Enrique, 234 n.14
Yin and yang, 145–146, 148
Youth counterculture. *See* Adolescence

Zapata, Emiliano, 2
Zapata, Luis: circularity in, 197; denouement in *en jirones*, 196–197; diary in, 193–197; first-person narration in, 189–190, 192, 193; imagery of fragmentation in, 195–196; Mexico City in, 17; mixture of fact and fiction in, 190–191; *Onda's* influence on, 186, 189; and picaresque genre, 188, 190–191; possession in, 196; punctuation lacking in, 190; solitude and abandonment in, 192–193; spacing of fragments in, 190, 194–195; taped monologue in, 189–190
—works: *en jirones* (in shreds), 188, 193–197, 200; *El vampiro de la Colonia Roma* (The Vampire of Colonia Roma), 15, 188, 189–193, 195, 200
Zapatista National Liberation Army, 2–3
*Zärtlichkeit der Wölfe*, 244 n.28
Zuluaga O., Conrado, 95, 101–102, 240 n.14